REFRAMING
& REFORM

REFRAMING & REFORM

Perspectives on Organization, Leadership, and School Change

ROBERT V. CARLSON
University of Vermont

Longman *Publishers USA*

Reframing & Reform: Perspectives on Organization, Leadership, and School Change

Longman, 10 Bank Street, White Plains, N.Y. 10606

Associated companies:
Longman Group Ltd., London
Longman Cheshire Pty., Melbourne
Longman Paul Pty., Auckland
Copp Clark Longman Ltd., Toronto

Acquisitions editor: Virginia L. Blanford
Associate editor: Mary Travis Lester
Assistant editor: Chris Konnari
Production editor: Linda W. Witzling
Cover design: Anne Pompeo
Text art: Fine Line Inc.
Production supervisor: Richard Bretan
Compositor: BookMasters

Library of Congress Cataloging-in-Publication Data

Carlson, Robert V.
    Reframing & Reform : perspectives on organization, leadership,
and school change / by Robert V. Carlson.
        p.   cm.
    Includes bibliographical references and index.
    ISBN 0-8013-1106-3
    1. School management and organization—United States.
2. Educational leadership—United States.   3. Educational change—
United States.   4. Organizational behavior—United States.
I. Title.
LB2805.C268   1996
371.2'00973—dc20

                                                95-11579
                                                CIP

1 2 3 4 5 6 7 8 9 10-CRS-99989796 5

Contents

Preface

American education is suffering from a crisis of perception. Each day, it seems, we are confronted with a litany of articles and news reports suggesting that something is wrong with our schools. Indeed, a recent Gallup Poll (Elam, Rose, & Gallup, 1994) of public opinion reveals that only 22 percent of those polled would award an A or B grade to public schools nationally, and nearly 50 percent would give only a grade of C. By contrast, however, this same poll reveals that 70 percent of parents would give an A or B grade to the schools attended by their oldest child. Such contradictory perceptions have spawned an opportunity for critics to feed public skepticism and self-doubt by impugning the reputation of American education and advocating their own particular brand of medicine to cure its ills. As a result, many educators, policy-makers, and parents are confused by multiple claims and reports that do not reflect their own day-to-day experiences. We are aware that the educational house is not in total order, but neither is it in total disarray. How we sort through these mixed messages and come to understand better the inner workings of schools as organizations is no doubt one of the greatest challenges for both present and prospective educational leaders.

The goal of *Reframing & Reform* is to encourage "frame experiments" (Schon, 1983) based on a variety of perspectives on organizations and leadership. The literature reviewed in this text offers views on the need and potential for developing the ability to reframe our experiences. Metaphors are seen as stimuli for forming new insights and perspectives on organizations, leadership, and school reform. In addition, through specific and typical organizational cases, the potency of alternative views is demonstrated. As two recognized experts on organizations and leadership, Bolman and Deal (1991), state, "Leaders fail when they take too narrow a view of the context in which they are working. Unless they can think flexibly about organizations and see

xi

them from multiple angles, they will be unable to deal with the full range of issues that they will inevitably encounter" (p. 450).

Educational organizations are facing difficult and challenging times. Efforts at the national level offer specific strategies for the perceived problems of our schools. Reports (e.g., *America 2000* [U.S. Department of Education, 1991] and *Educating America, State Strategies for Achieving the National Education Goals* [Task Force on Education, 1990]) and legislation (e.g., Goals 2000: Educate America Act) at the national level illustrate that the expectations for schools and their leaders continue to grow. Demands for the best educational systems are pressing in on our educational administrators and other leaders. This text explores reframing strategies and their potential for addressing the many forces for change. Also, a portion of the text reviews three major educational reform movements and demonstrates the power of linking reframing to school reform.

To aid in developing new "angles," *Reframing & Reform* employs several approaches. First, a fuller exploration of paradigms (worldviews) and their influence on how we view our social world and educational practices helps to establish a theoretical base for exploring alternative modes of thinking about educational organizations and leadership. These theories connect well to concepts of requisite variety, postmodernism, and the reflective practitioner. Reflection and diversifying our ways of knowing enable more meaningful leadership within an organizational context (see chapter 1, Prologue).

Following the prologue, the text is divided into four sections, each providing a variety of perspectives: on organizations (section 1), leadership (section 2), school reform (section 3), and the future (section 4). The introductions to sections 1, 2, and 3 provide historical overviews, chapter highlights, and case studies.

In section 1, Organizational Perspectives, an organizational case, *A House Divided*, describes a moderate-sized K-12 school district facing internal conflict and tension over styles of leadership; school system issues of student discipline, cultural diversity, feminism, and anti-Semitism; and the role of teachers, students, and parents in the administration of the school system. As a typical American K-12 school system, this system vividly reveals organizational stresses that can exist in many educational organizations but are often hidden from our view. The case contains organizational conditions that contribute to confusion and conflict and illustrates the explanatory power of the metaphors and related concepts presented in each chapter in section 1. This analysis establishes a process for looking at educational organizations in light of a variety of metaphors in other sections of the text.

The chapters in section 1 address organizations using the metaphors of culture, politics, theater, and brains. These metaphors provide ways to stimulate images, reflect on contemporary views on organizations, and demonstrate the potential of different paradigms. Each chapter provides a conclusion followed by a reexamination of the case study, discussion questions, and suggested activities. At the end of each section is a synthesis or summary of the major concepts presented.

Section 2, Leadership Perspectives, provides a vantage point on styles of leadership within an organizational context. Following a brief review of past theories on leadership, section 2 presents chapters on leadership as a transformational process, a dialectical process, and a democratic process. These leadership metaphors blend with the metaphors of organizations discussed in section 1. The section on leadership perspectives presents contemporary theories and research on leadership processes appropriate to an organizational context.

To explore the utility of the leadership concepts discussed in section 2, a case, *The Telephone Stopped Ringing,* presents the dynamics of change in a K–6 elementary school. The school in this case experiences a significant turnaround in solving some major problems and provides an excellent context for illustrating the leadership concepts of section 2. Section 2 concludes with a synthesis of major leadership concepts.

Section 3, School Reform Perspectives, summarizes three major schema or metaphors for solving the perceived problems of our schools. Following a brief review of past efforts at school reform, section 3 reports on contemporary strategies of school choice, school restructuring, and school-based management. Each offers a particular approach that has some unique elements having implications for school organization redesign and new styles of leadership. To help in examining these school reforms, a case study, *Hope Springs Eternal,* provides a portrayal of a secondary (7–12) union high school experiencing an effort at restructuring.

Section 4, Perspectives on the Future, reframes school reform and examines global trends and emerging theories potentially relevant to school organizations and their leadership. Chapter 12, Linking Reframing to School Reform Strategies, provides an opportunity to reflect on school reform strategies from the perspective of different metaphors of organization and leadership. Chapter 12 demonstrates the insights derived from a reframing process.

The closing chapter, Trends and Implications, is, as the words imply, a rounding out of the content of the text. This chapter reinforces the need to appreciate that ideas and ways of thinking about organizations and leadership, in general and in schools, are not static but are evolving. The text brings us to the present but would fall short if we did not try to speculate about the future. Heraclitus, a Greek philosopher, once observed that you cannot step twice into the same river, for the water is continually flowing on. In the same way, our paradigms, frames, lenses, and related metaphors are continually being replaced. Chapter 13 acknowledges the implications of constant flux for schools and for future leaders by exploring theories of chaos, organizational cycles, and feminism. This chapter highlights societal trends in motion and changes that are on the horizon. It attempts to foreshadow what these future trends portend for educational organizations and their leaders.

Reframing & Reform initiates a process of reflection on ways of seeing and understanding organizations, leadership, and school reform. These reflections should lead to insights that encourage personal change in how we come to know our educational systems and how we can draw upon our creativity and artistry to address major problems in the future.

ACKNOWLEDGMENTS

Obviously an undertaking such as the writing of a book of this magnitude requires the inspiration, encouragement, and support of a number of persons. The original idea and early thinking for this text emerged from thoughtful discussions with Naomi Silverman, a former editor at Longman. I would also like to acknowledge Longman editors Virginia Blanford and Mary Travis Lester, whose assistance in moving this project forward was greatly appreciated. Also two research assistants, Carolyn Carter and Karrin Wilks, helped with early literature searches that proved very helpful in getting the project started. It seems most appropriate to acknowledge the helpful feedback from the reviewers of various drafts of the manuscript.

> Janet Alleman, Michigan State University
> Robert Arnold, Illinois State University
> Gerald Bailey, Kansas State University
> Mason Bunker, University of Massachusetts
> Stanley Carpenter, Texas A&M University
> David Erlandson, Texas A&M University
> Tom Glass, Northern Illinois University
> Jim Henderson, Duquesne University
> Frank Merlo, Montclair State College
> Michael Richardson, Clemson University
> Edith Rusch, University of Toledo
> Martin Schoppmeyer, University of Arkansas
> Ulysses Spiva, Old Dominion University
> Carl Steinhoff, University of Nevada, Las Vegas
> Kathy Whitaker, University of Northern Colorado

Their support and critical comments proved most valuable in focusing the content and in influencing the organization of the text.

This book seeks to provide greater understanding of what it means to work and lead in an organizational context. And clearly, without such a diversity of opinions, attitudes, and beliefs, organizations would be dull and uninteresting places. The pursuit of a greater appreciation and recognition of our humanity was a major trail marker in the development and completion of *Reframing & Reform*.

DEDICATION

I wish to dedicate this book to my father, James A. Carlson, whose death in his eighty-sixth year and just prior to the completion of the final manuscript proved a powerful reminder of the rhythms of life and death that are outside our control. And to my wife, whom I affectionately call "DJ" and whose patience and support proved invaluable as the research and writing seemed to have no end.

REFERENCES

Bolman, L. G., & Deal, T. E. (1991). *Reframing organizations: Artistry, choice, and leadership.* San Francisco: Jossey-Bass.

Elam, S. M., Rose, L. C., & Gallup, A. M. (September, 1994). The 26th annual Phi Delta Kappa/Gallup poll of the public's attitudes toward the public schools. *Phi Delta Kappan, 76*(1), 41-56.

Schon, Donald A. (1983). *The reflective practitioner: How professionals think in action.* New York: Basic Books.

Task Force on Education. (1990). *Educating America, state strategies for achieving the national education goals: A report of the task force on education.* Washington, D.C.: National Governor's Association.

U.S. Department of Education. (1991). *America 2000: An education strategy sourcebook.* Washington, D.C.

REFRAMING
& REFORM

chapter **1**

Prologue

Art comes in many shapes, colors, and forms. Often it is maligned and misunderstood. Yet these labors of creativity without question add richness to our daily lives. It is difficult to imagine a world in which art in some form did not exist. The cave paintings of our earth's early inhabitants bear witness to the intrinsic need to reflect and replicate our daily existence. Forms of art have come a long way from these early drawings and find expression in a whole array of media. In spite of the ubiquitous nature of art, we seldom think of art as a metaphor or model for guiding our efforts as educational leaders.

Successful artists, whose ideas and creations stir our intellect and emotions, display qualities that hold promise for dealing with the major issues facing our schools in the present and into the future. To succeed as an artist requires many attributes, including intelligence, creativity, commitment, and hard work—qualities that any school would greatly benefit from but that often are absent.

This text is based in large part on the premise that there is more artistry than science to creating and sustaining healthy and successful schools. At the same time, however, good artists do not necessarily reject science or state-of-the-art technology in the practice of their art. It is the creative blend of art and science that helps us understand the complex dynamics involved in educational organizations and their leadership.

Jean Cocteau, a French poet, novelist, dramatist, essayist, film writer, and director, when asked his definition of art, offered: "For some people, art was a complicated way of saying very simple things. For us [artists], it is a simple way of saying very complicated things" (Tynan, 1989, p. 26). Leaders, as artists, appreciate this paradox and strive to find simple ways to help us see the complexities of organizational experiences with a freshness that comes from a new image.

This text was written in the spirit that Rimsky-Korsakov, a Russian composer, brought to his musical composition *Scheherazade*. From the thousand-year-old fairy tales known collectively as the *Thousand Nights and a Night*, including the adventures of Sinbad the Sailor, Rimsky-Korsakov took those fragments which most piqued his talent for orchestration and helped create aural images. About his composition he said, "In composing *Scheherazade* I meant these hints [aural images] to direct but slightly the hearer's fancy on the path which my own fancy had traveled, and to leave more minute and particular conceptions to the will and mood of each listener" (*Program Notes*, 1994, p. 5). It is hoped that the sights and sounds projected in *Reframing & Reform* catch your fancy and allow you to create your own composition.

Artistry involves for us too a way of thinking and seeing things differently and making connections between seemingly unrelated matters. There is an artist in all of us waiting to burst forth; it may take only a particular idea, metaphor, image, or experience to allow us to trust our instincts and appreciate our creative capabilities. Artists remind us of this potential and, in their works, challenge us to venture forth and attempt to see the world a bit differently.

Art, however, is not an excuse to be naive. There is little doubt that our educational institutions are becoming more complex. They are facing uncertainty due in part to unstable financial conditions, enrollment fluctuations, personnel turnover, and demographic shifts. In spite of these difficult conditions, schools continue to be called on to solve many of society's ills and to provide programs that meet a wide range of needs. The expanded role of schools knows no bounds. In Anyplace, U.S.A. (*The Expanding Role*, 1981), the fictitious school offers curricula and programs in the following areas:

- sex education
- gender equity education
- racial integration
- human relations education
- international education
- citizen education
- environmental education
- energy education
- drug abuse, health, and safety education
- consumerism and basic education
- marriage and family education
- basic skills
- marketable skills
- job search skills
- music, art, and gifted education
- handicapped programs

A result of these inordinate demands on our educational systems has been the creation of organizations characterized by fragmentation and specialization. Until the

1950s, our elementary and secondary schools operated primarily on a self-contained classroom model. Under this model, elementary school students spent most of their school day with one teacher. At the secondary level, it was common for students to be limited to the basic subjects of social studies, English, mathematics, and science and some electives (e.g., foreign language). A small number of specialists were employed as guidance counselors and assistant principals often in charge of discipline.

Most organizational charts of today's school systems include an array of specialists and special programs. In addition to the traditional administrative posts of superintendent and principal, administrators for the gifted, handicapped, disadvantaged, curriculum development, staff development, content area coordination, and grade level coordination are common. Also, specialists in such areas as substance abuse, psychological services, and social work complement and support this array of personnel. The coordination of services and programs has become exceedingly difficult, not least because they require considerable time to provide timely and accurate information. The challenges facing our educational organizations now and in the future will no doubt grow in complexity due in part to an increase in a diversity of internal and external demands. These conditions will require greater artistry, if you will, on the part of our educational leaders.

In this chapter we will explore the implications of these trends. First we will visit the concept of requisite variety and its importance to school organizations. Second, we need to understand the various paradigms or worldviews that are presently influencing our thoughts about how schools should be organized and led. Third, we place these paradigms within an intellectual revolution of postmodern thinking. And finally, we will examine how being a reflective practitioner will help advance our paradigms.

REQUISITE VARIETY

The twin challenges of complexity and uncertainty facing educational organizations require, of these organizations and their leaders, a greater capacity to understand and act. Requisite variety, a concept borrowed from General Systems Theory (Ashby,1956; Bertalanfy, 1968; and Flood & Carson, 1988), provides insight on the needs of social systems to remain viable and to survive.[1] As Flood and Carson explain, "Variety is a 'measure' of the possible distinguishable states of a system, of which control can be obtained only if the variety of the controller is greater than, or equal to, the signal or system to be controlled—this is the law of requisite variety" (p. 13).

Weick (1985) uses the analogy of photographic film to explain requisite variety. To capture the detail of a subject, a fine-grained film works best. A poorer quality or coarser grained film will not capture the level of detail that a higher quality of film allows. Such is the case in being successful in operating organizations that face unpre-

---

[1] General Systems Theory (GST) was first promulgated by Bertalanfy (1968) as an attempt to integrate many disciplines and to develop a science of holism. Although GST has been subjected to many interpretations and applications, some general principles prevail, including the notions of interdependence, input-process-output-feedback, mutual causality, adaptation and equilibrium, and hierarchy. For a more recent treatment of GST, see Flood and Carson (1988), and for an application in education, see Banathy (1988).

dictable and complex conditions. These organizations and their leaders need a greater repertoire of insights (a fine-grained film) in order to understand their complexity. Goldberg (1989) states it well when he comments, "Maintaining a diversity of response options is one of the ways that we can adapt better to uncertain and widely varying futures" (p. 42).

Without a requisite variety of persons and their ideas and belief systems, there is a danger of seeing problems and solutions from a limited point of view. The existence of requisite variety in our organizations allows for breaking with past assumptions and dominant paradigms that no longer serve the purposes of the organization and result in a poor match with new, emerging conditions.

INFLUENCE OF PARADIGMS

Knowing and understanding are not simple processes. Our culture and its prevailing paradigms influence our capacity to generate "response options." Bruner (1990) explores the influence of culture on our construction of meaning by suggesting the notion of "folk psychology." He explains that "folk psychology, though it changes, does not get displaced by scientific paradigms. For it deals with the nature, causes, and consequences of those intentional states—beliefs, desires, intentions, commitments—that most scientific psychology dismisses in its effort to explain human action from a point of view that is outside human subjectivity, formulated in Thomas Nagel's deft phase as a 'view from nowhere'" (p.14).

Putting it more succinctly, Bruner defines folk or cultural psychology "as a systems by which people organize their experience in, knowledge about, and transactions with the social world" (p. 35). For better or worse, we depend on our social context for meaning. As a consequence, we do not fully appreciate the degree to which this context affects our vision. This is the case when it comes to understanding our educational organizations and how to lead them.

For example, the concept of organization is from the Greek *organon*, meaning a tool or instrument. This metaphor has served Western culture's industrial movement in the design and operation of both private and public institutions, including schools. Organizations and machines became synonymous, resulting in a stress on efficiency. Callahan, in *Education and the Cult of Efficiency* (1962), reveals how school organizations have tried to emphasize efficiency, associated with uniform work procedures and standardization. Cubberly, as cited in Owens (1987), observed in 1916 that schools were "factories in which the raw materials are shaped and fashioned into products to meet the various demands of life" (p. 9).

The impact of the machine metaphor on educational organizations and how people perceive schools should operate is greater than we realized. For example, an examination of how schools typically organize, particularly at the secondary and post-secondary levels, reflects an assembly-line mentality. Our schools divide into many units, including grade levels, departments, and special services. Students follow time schedules, arriving at and departing from subject areas at precisely defined times often prompted by bells. Teachers often use top-down teaching methods that force-feed information and skills. The curriculum is linear and sequential, and subjects are separated from one another. The simplicity and perceived clarity of the machine orientation is seen as appropriate and comforting.

Not only has the machine metaphor affected how educational institutions organize, but it has influenced the leadership role of educational administrators. If schools are expected to operate efficiently, then those in charge are expected to provide close supervision and control. Frederick Taylor (1911) epitomized the desire for ultimate control through the principles of scientific management. He stressed the importance of managers personally setting overall directions and ensuring workers' compliance. Taylor used time-and-motion studies for standardizing work that resulted in making the worker an appendage to the machine.

Taylor's thinking and elements of scientific management are observable in schools. We can see traces of time-and-motion studies in present-day research of students' time on task, student behavioral modification, and effective teaching models. Also, we can often observe educational administrators locked in struggles for power and control in their organizations. These administrators defend this quest as legitimate and an appropriate use of authority. Ironically, as administrators stress the implementation of "one best way," they are often met with resistance. This resistance triggers more reliance on authority and power to gain compliance, which in turn is met with greater resistance. Soon an us-and-them polarization emerges and, of course, in the process efficiency is dealt a fatal blow.

Vestiges of the machine worldview continue to hold sway and serve as a dominant paradigm for educational organizations. We need to ask ourselves, as our society moves into the information age and becomes more service oriented, whether the machine metaphor provides for adequate insight for the design and management of organizations in a complex, pluralistic, and uncertain environment. As Morgan (1986) states, "The mechanization approach to organization tends to limit rather than mobilize the development of human capacities, molding human beings to fit the requirement of mechanical organization rather than building the organization around the strengths and potentials" (p. 38). Part of the effect of the mechanization view is to lock people into a paradigm that does not fit very well with a changing, dynamic environment.

A brief review of three dominant paradigms may enable us to more fully appreciate the influence of our culture on educational organizations and how we perceive them. We must keep in mind that paradigms carry considerable weight in our reasoning process. As Lincoln (1985) expresses it,

> A paradigm is much more than a model or pattern; it is a view of the world—
> a *Weltanschauung*—that reflects our most basic beliefs and assumptions
> about the human condition, whether or not there is any such thing as "sin,"
> what is real, what is true, what is beautiful, and what is the nature of things.
> (p. 29)

Although paradigms are plentiful (some say as much as zucchini in the summer), the major paradigms of positivism, interpretism, and criticism are sufficient to offer contrasting worldviews.

Positivism

Positivism, possibly the most dominant of the three paradigms, traces back to the scientific revolution in the late 1400s. Copernicus's and Kepler's establishment of the heliocentric model of the solar system and Galileo's development of mechanics initiated a new form of scientific thinking. Francis Bacon's advocacy of induction from collected facts, Descartes's insistence upon deductive chains of reasoning, and Newton's employment of scientific rationalism added to the discussions of the method of science. According to Checkland (1981), the scientific revolution replaced medieval science and has continued up to the early 1900s. John Stuart Mill enunciated his list of assumptions of the positivistic position as follows:

> that science's aim is the discovery of general laws that serve for explanation and prediction; that concepts can be defined by direct reference to empirical categories—"objects in the concrete"; that there is a uniformity of nature in time and space; that the laws of nature can be inductively derived from data; and that large samples suppress idiosyncracies and reveal "general causes." (quoted in Guba, 1985, p. 81)

As Mill's list of assumptions suggests, positivism is characterized by

- a value-free orientation to the object of investigation
- a certain logic that should apply in discovering new "laws"
- a process of reductionism in isolating causal relationships

The spin-off effect of the positivistic paradigm can be seen in the domination of organizational theory by theories of bureaucracy (Weber, 1947) and in hard systems thinking, particularly from a systems engineering perspective (Checkland, 1981). These theories stress functionalism, rationality, and an objective social world that is controllable.

Further, positivism and related organizational theories sustain the machine metaphor. According to Morgan, (1986), many of our modern organizations try to operate with clockwork precision: "People are frequently expected to arrive at work at a given time, perform a predetermined set of activities, rest at appointed hours, then resume their tasks until work is over" (p. 22). The machine metaphor places greater stress on management control that emphasizes the division of work, centralization of authority, discipline, and a chain of command.

Interpretism

In Hegel's dialectic, positivism is the thesis and interpretism (aka naturalism) is the antithesis. The emergence of interpretism evolves out of the difficulties of transferring the successful research methods of the natural sciences (e.g., physics, chemistry, biology) to the social sciences (e.g., anthropology, psychology, social psychology, sociology, political science, and economics). Checkland (1981) observes:

This concern with questions *about* rather than *in* the disciplines of social science is an indication not that social science attracts dilettantes, but rather that exceptionally difficult problems arise when the methods developed for investigating the natural world which exists outside of ourselves are applied to the social phenomena of which we are a part. (p. 67)

The laws of objectivity and logic begin to break down under circumstances in which a person may have a vested interest and/or preconceptions.

According to Guba (1985), the problem of value conflicts in social systems is not the only concern raised by positivistic thinking. He challenges the axioms associated with positivism, including in his list of challenges "counterindications" against

- naive realism (a single, tangible reality "out there" is unrealistic)
- subject-object dualism (observer influence is unavoidable)
- generalizability (interdependence of time and context precludes this)
- causality (causal loops limit single or one-way causes)
- value independence (scientists are human too)

The limitations of the positivistic paradigm have become increasingly evident as the problems of our social systems become aggravated by conditions of complexity, uncertainty, instability, and value conflicts—a situation that, according to Checkland (1981), is a portrayal of human or "soft systems."

Interpretism, which is Guba's naturalistic paradigm, contains the following basic assumptions:

- there are multiple constructed realities;
- there are mutual influences between the observer and the object of inquiry;
- there is value in discovering differences as well as similarities;
- there are multiple and plausible related reasons for observed actions; and
- there are multiple value influences on research, including choice of the problem, choice of the design and methodology, values present in the context or object of the study, and value congruence among these value orientations. (pp. 85–86)

As Guba argues, interpretism operates from a different and contrasting set of assumptions. These assumptions have important implications for how we view organizations. The major theory of organizations born from interpretism is *sociopolitical systems theory*, which recognizes the influence of the individual on organizational purposes and processes. Further, this theory tries to explain the motivation of employees, how persons affiliate with formal and informal groups, what underlies problems and conflicts, and what contributes to cultural norms. This theory also recognizes the existence of context and its influence on the organization.

Likert (1967) offers a System 4 model for organizations that builds a sense of personal worth and importance and captures the potential of sociopolitical systems theory. His model stresses three basic concepts: (1) the principle of supportive relationships, (2) group decision making, and (3) high-performance work norms. Likert's stress on greater levels of participation by a spectrum of persons in the organization is in sharp contrast to Weber's (1947) notions of bureaucracy and top-down management.

We also should note that the *human relations movement* in management theory and training is reflective of interpretism. Human relations theory places greater emphasis on employee satisfaction and the importance of employee support of organizational goals. The theory suggests that the more employees feel appreciated and have opportunity to share their ideas, the more productive they will become. In spite of the criticism (Etzioni, 1964) that human relations theory is somewhat naive and unrealistic in politically charged circumstances, this thinking continues to have relevance for less charged situations.

The interpretism paradigm and sociopolitical systems theory have also spawned their share of organizational metaphors. These metaphors reflect the assumptions associated with interpretism and include viewing organizations as organisms, as political systems, and as cultures. Each of these metaphors conjures up images of varying degrees of flexibility, unpredictability, and adaptation. If leaders are to meet the challenge facing today's complex organizations, they should consider reframing based on assumptions different from those heretofore based on positivism.

Criticism

More recently the paradigm of criticism has gained some recognition. According to Hlynka and Belland (1991),

> the critical paradigm is neither quantitative nor qualitative. It does not follow any traditional statistical or experimental methodology derived from the behavioral sciences, nor is it based on anthropological participant observation or sociological data-gathering models. Rather, this third paradigm focuses on criticism in the sense of art and literary criticism models within the humanities. (p. 6)

Critical theory, as part of Hlynka and Belland's grab bag of different viewpoints on the paradigm of criticism, offers us an additional vantage point in knowing and understanding our human experience. Critical theory provides the opportunity to go beyond traditional scientific inquiry and draws upon the humanities to deal with aspects of our lives that are subtle, aesthetic, and incidental in nature. To study social phenomena, the concepts of *social construction, deconstruction, connoisseurship,* and *semiotics* play a significant role.[2] Some common features of these views include

---

[2] These are complex concepts requiring more space for a fuller explanation. To put it simply, our knowledge is a result of *social construction,* which is a process of creating meaning by filtering perceptions through our social and physical reality. *Deconstruction* displaces conventional wisdom of what is right and reorders values by seeing the acceptable as unacceptable and vice versa. *Connoisseurship* draws heavily upon experience and expertise to discriminate subtle differences that the novice may not see. *Semiotics* is the study of signs or codes and sign systems and their meaning.

- putting confidence in a critic's thinking and experience rather than in the method used
- focusing on what is produced rather than on the intentions of the producer
- making the critique public and open to examination and debate
- viewing the critique as an initial effort at understanding rather than as conclusive

It is through this type of exchange that we come to know the complexities and contradictions in evaluating human experiences. As most of us can appreciate, the art of criticism in judging a highly symbolic theatrical performance or an abstract work of art parallels the problem of interpreting organizational rhetoric and events.

Often these critiques can be very challenging and quite revealing. They offer an opportunity to discover our own biases and preferred ways of viewing our world that often prevent appreciating other interpretations. As Taylor and Swartz (1991) remind us,

> Knowledge is not value neutral. . . . The emerging view holds that knowledge is created, but it is not created equal; that is to say knowledge is no longer assumed to have universal status. Knowledge is the result of a way of knowing and is marked as such. Knowing and knowledge are inextricably bound up together. (p. 51)

Foster (1986) offers a slightly different view of critical theory:

> Critical theory, then, questions the framework of the way we organize our lives or the way our lives are normally taken for granted and seen as natural outgrowths of the historical process. A critical theory locates human relationships in structural variables, particularly those of *class* and *power*, without, however, compromising the possibility for change. Thus, critical theory examines sources of *social domination* and *repression*, but with the caveat that since we ultimately make our worlds, we can ultimately change them. Finally, a critical theory is committed to values; its critique is largely oriented toward how created social structures impede the attainment of such values as *democracy* and *freedom*. (p. 72, emphasis added)

Foster suggests the need to examine some basic moral and ethical issues of society. He calls for a critique of present management theory and practices and their role in the perpetuation of class differences, social domination, and associated inequities.

Foster draws upon critical theory as a base for examining administration and the nature of our educational organizations. However, he recognizes that this contradicts the assumptions that administration is the handmaiden to an organization's status quo and maintains a strong allegiance to efficiency. The emphasis on efficiency, however, was born in the positivistic tradition and needs further consideration from the perspective of the criticism paradigm. Foster sees critical theory aiding both in the search for meaning and as social criticism.

Critical theory's contribution to organizational and leadership theory is still to be determined. However, two examples come to mind. First, dialectical leadership (Foster, 1986; and Matejko, 1986), explored in chapter 7 of this text, has features that relate to the underlying assumptions of critical theory. The second example is in the notion of the reflective practitioner (Argyris, 1982; Argyris & Schon 1974; and Schon, 1983), with relevance to bridging one's reframing experiences and initiating action based on these reflections.

There are, however, some organizational metaphors that begin to raise consciousness about organizational behaviors within the general framework of the criticism paradigm and associated critical theory. Examples include organizations as brains, theater, and instruments of domination. Each of these metaphors provides the potential to see current conditions in organizations from an entirely different perspective. These new perspectives bring to the surface issues of equity, freedom of choice, and domination. The consequence of this type of critique may be decisions based on authority of knowledge rather than authority by power.

Limited application of critical theory to school organizations contributes in part to many issues being unattended. One of the most controversial issues at the micro or school-site level, for example, involves grouping students for instruction, commonly referred to as tracking (Oakes, 1985). At the macro or policy level is the issue of funding education and the inequities of financial support between school systems. There is also the additional issue of empowerment and the degree to which members (e.g., teachers and students) of educational systems are allowed to provide their own interpretations of what they see and feel. It is often the case that these voices are preempted by authority figures who attempt to speak on their behalf. The results of these issues are extensive political debates that often generate more heat than light. The paradigm of criticism and associated critical theory offer an opportunity to use the methods of critique and consciousness raising to gain insight into deeply entrenched, long-standing social issues.

Table 1.1 provides a summary of the three paradigms and related features. This summary contrasts the paradigms, theories, and respective methods. It also demarcates the roots of different ideas and how they can subtly affect our worldviews of educational organizations and their leadership.

POSTMODERNISM

The shift in paradigms is probably best dramatized by a movement often referred to as postmodernism. Postmodern thinking has considerable implication for how we come to know and understand organizations. Burrell and Hearn (1989) explore what they refer to as contested visions of organization. In their view, the study of organizations from a modernist perspective has been too dependent on the concern for rationality, strongly guided by a science that emphasizes data from surveys, experimentation, and unity of method and by the desire to determine how organizations are to be understood and improved. They wish to move away from an attempt to understand organizations as a form of production toward a postmodern position of examining how an

TABLE 1.1 Paradigms and related features

Paradigm	Key Concepts	Methodological Approach	Organizational Theory	Organizational Metaphors	Management Theory	Management Strategies
Positivism	Value free Logic Functionalism Reductionism Objectivity Causality Quantitative analysis	Empiricism	Bureaucracy General systems	Machine Structure	Classical management Scientific management	MBO[a] PPBS[b] Rational planning
Interpretism	Value conflict Holism Subjectivity Mutual causality Qualitative analysis	Naturalistic inquiry	Sociopolitical systems	Organism Culture Politics	Human relations	Participation Negotiation Interactive planning
Criticism	Connoisseurship Semiotic Dualism Paradox Social construction	Critique	Dialectical	Domination Theater Brain	Reflective practice	Praxis Dissent Consciousness raising

[a]MBO = Management by objectives
[b]PPBS = Program-planning and budgeting systems

organization is produced and reproduced. The postmodernist perspective places greater emphasis on lived and deconstructed experience, stresses methodological pluralism built upon a cooperative network, and develops sources of data from art, literature and anecdote, and action research. Postmodernism is congruent with this text's theme of artistry in the use of theories of organization and leadership and builds on what Burrell and Hearn call "mosaic thinking."

Gergen (1993) explores three arguments for shifting away from romantic and modernist discourses to the postmodernism paradigm. First, to the modernist, language is a tool for logical representation of the real, whereas the postmodernist favors other sources of representation, including description and explanation. As Gergen puts it, since "what we call 'the real' is governed by the ideology of the caller, attempts to inform society of what is 'actually the case' must be regarded with suspicion" (p. 213).

Second, the postmodernist stresses sense-making, which requires joint action through coordinated participation of two or more persons. This stresses "the social basis of appropriate, just, or 'correct' description" of reality and "is congenial with feminist and critical school analysis of ideological bias, as well as postmodern literary theory" (Gergen, 1993, p. 214).

The third argument stresses the need for self-reflexivity, or critical suspicion of our suppositions, another theme of postmodernism. To control our tendency to define our own truth, the postmodernist looks to the practice of action research in which subjects are allowed to speak for themselves and control their own voices. Gergen suggests that rather than be founders of "the last word," "we should perhaps view ourselves as balloon craftsmen—setting aloft vehicles for public amusement" (p. 216).

Postmodernism challenges assumptions about how knowledge is constructed and how we come to "know" organizational life and/or leadership. Understanding is not brought about by searching for strict cause-and-effect relationships, but rather through the casting of a wide net capturing multiple impressions and descriptions that provide a rich picture of the dynamics present in any social-political-cultural context. The lines that separate organizations and their environments become blurred and enable to us to appreciate the total system of influences.

REFRAMING REALITY

New paradigms and postmodern thinking provide impetus and an intellectual base for looking at organizations and their leaders from new and different perspectives. Bolman and Deal (1984, 1991) discuss the importance of using new "frames" and "lenses," and Morgan (1986, 1993) speaks of "imaginization" and metaphors as ways to think about organizations. According to these authors, administrative leaders who are able to generate new viewpoints can potentially develop new insights in coping with the endless array of concerns and issues facing most educational organizations.

Bolman and Deal (1991) comment in their most recent book on reframing, "Too often they [leaders and managers] bring too few ideas to the challenges that they face. They live in psychic prisons because they cannot look at old problems in a new light and attack old challenges with different and more powerful tools—they cannot *re-*

frame" (p. 4). These authors developed four frames and multiple lenses for reframing. The structural, human resource, political, and symbolic frames provide a leader or manager with a means for developing different views of organizational situations. The process of reframing (rotating through and using *all four* frames) permits seeing a situation differently. As Bolman and Deal (1991) express it, "The ability to reframe experience enriches and broadens a leader's repertoire and serves as a powerful antidote to self-entrapment" (p. 4).

Morgan (1986, 1993) approaches the same concern for narrowness and over-reliance on habits of the mind by suggesting the power of "imaginization" and the use of metaphors: "My overall approach has been to foster a kind of critical thinking that encourages us to understand and grasp the multiple meanings of situations and to confront and manage contradiction and paradox, rather than to pretend that they do not exist. I have chosen to do this through metaphor, which I believe is central to the way we organize and understand our world" (1986, p. 339).

Through a variety of metaphors (e.g., machines, organisms, cultures, political systems, psychic prisons), Morgan encourages us to imagine different possibilities for various challenges facing members of an organization. He states, "The way of seeing itself transforms our understanding of the nature of the phenomenon" (p. 340). The process of "imaginization" not only encourages reframing, as suggested by Bolman and Deal, but also encourages viewing organizations through a wider range or variety of metaphors.

Whether we use the four frames of Bolman and Deal or Morgan's variety of interesting and challenging metaphors, we need to acknowledge our worldviews, psychic traps, and just old habits of thinking. There is a certain security in "old thinking": It is less than ideal but gets us through the day and we more or less know what to expect. In addition, our colleagues "know" us in a certain way, and new forms of expression or ideas may not be in keeping with their perception of how we should behave. Thus, as we try to experiment with alternative views and behaviors, there seem to be more forces—both intrapersonal and interpersonal—reinforcing the status quo. Reflecting and changing our thinking (and subsequent behavior) is not as simple as it appears. Reflecting and changing our notions about school organizations, leadership, and reform is even more complex.

REFLECTIVE PRACTITIONER

The existence of a rich and complex culture places a greater burden on our social institutions and on those persons who wish to lead them. As the earlier discussion of paradigms illustrates, our knowledge base is expanding and is linked in part to a wider range of alternative worldviews. We are also coming to realize the degree to which we construct our own meaning, particularly in a social context. The challenge before us who wish to be effective leaders of educational organizations is to develop approaches for eliciting and processing these new insights. Reframing and "imaginization" can help us to see new possibilities but leave us with the challenge of how to put these ideas into practice.

Argyris (1982) and Argyris and Schon (1974) have been pioneers in developing insights concerning the gap between espoused theory and theory-in-use. Their research documents the crisis in professionalism and the difficulty professional practitioners have in understanding and articulating their personal theories of practice. They found that there is a tendency to espouse idealistic notions of how we should perform our duties as professional practitioners; yet a gap often exists between our ideals and our actions. This gap between what we say and what we do contributes to the public's lack of confidence in the professions.

To understand how we create and maintain our theories-in-use, Argyris and Schon suggest single-loop and double-loop learning. Single-loop learning, which reinforces old thinking habits, includes such behaviors as

- needing to be in control
- sticking with our perception of what needs to be accomplished
- being self-protective
- being rational and minimizing emotionality
- attempting to minimize choice or risk taking

On the other hand, double-loop learning, which can encourage new forms of thinking, includes a different set of behaviors, such as

- sharing control
- minimizing defensiveness
- increasing opportunities for free and informed choice
- monitoring the implementation of ideas

Monitoring and getting feedback on performance are central to learning from one's errors and miscalculations and are critical to double-loop learning.

Schon (1983) developed a theory of reflection-in-action that helps to explain how we may come to know our theories-in-use. He explains, "Our knowing is ordinarily tacit, implicit in our patterns of action and in our feel for the stuff with which we are dealing. It seems right to say that our knowing is *in* our action" (p. 49). And if we do not know the message contained in our action, then seeking feedback should aid in closing the gap between a desired mode of behavior and an actual mode of behavior. Schon links reflection to reframing:

> When he [the professional practitioner] finds himself stuck in a problematic situation which he cannot readily convert to a manageable problem, he may construct a new way of setting the problem—a new frame which, in what I shall call a "frame experiment," he tries to impose on the situation. (p. 63)

Thus Argyris and Schon, through their notion of the reflective practitioner, provide a way for us to understand our performance better and to discover new options in a complex and uncertain environment. Also, they provide a way to close the gap between what we believe and what we do.

SUMMARY

In this chapter we have explored the concept of schools as complex organizations, the need for and the value of requisite variety, the subtle but significant influence of paradigms or worldviews on our thinking, the perspective of postmodernism, and the relevance of becoming a reflective practitioner. These concepts serve as a backdrop and a context for taking a closer look at a variety of metaphors for organizations, leadership, and school reform. Admittedly there are many influences on our capacity to understand our circumstances and to pursue alternative behaviors. The subsequent sections and chapters will provide a rich conceptual base for increasing our understanding of organizations and leadership. The exploration of alternative ways of knowing should help us to appreciate the degree to which we construct our realities and, in turn, have the power to revisit and revise them for the benefit of our youthful charges and colleagues. It is a challenge worthy of consideration as we explore the artistry of linking theories of organizations and leadership to school reform.

DISCUSSION QUESTIONS

1. How good is the fit between artistry and our performance as educators, especially as leaders?
2. When you reflect on your educational organization's daily operations, to what degree do you see evidence of the influence of the positivistic paradigm and the machine metaphor? Why do you think this influence has or has not been considerable?
3. When you think of your organization, what metaphors come to mind? Why these? What underlies these metaphors and what do they imply for you and other members of your organization?
4. How do you react to postmodernism? Does it have relevance for developing a better understanding of ourselves and our organizations? Why or why not?
5. Is the notion of a "reflective practitioner" viable? Why or why not?

SUGGESTED ACTIVITIES

1. Reflect with a trusted colleague and explore examples of espoused theories and theories-in-use in your organization. What conclusions do you draw from this analysis? Are Argyris and Schon right in suggesting that we may have a credibility problem because of noticeable gaps? Why or why not?
2. If activity 1 does not work for you, then try this. As you know, schools sometimes seem to be operating from values and beliefs that are different from official public pronouncements. These values and beliefs are often implicitly understood but not often talked about. Describe for your organization the actual, functional values and beliefs that are important. How do these contrast with the rhetoric provided to the public? Is there a difference? Why or why not?
3. As we have discussed in this chapter, metaphors often serve as shorthand for complex ideas. We know that teachers and parents sometimes describe schools as "circuses" or "oases" and students sometimes describe them as "prisons." These metaphors often have a way of telling it as it is and cutting through idealistic statements. With your organization in mind, identify

a metaphor that best describes it. Why did you select this metaphor? If you were to think of an ideal metaphor for your organization, what would it be? Why?

4. Meeting in triads, share with your classmates the results of activity 3. Discuss your different and similar metaphors. What differences, if any, do you observe between ideal and actual metaphors? Why are there differences? What are the implications of your metaphors for school change and leadership?

5. Repeat activity 3 for your principal and/or superintendent. What metaphors would best describe his or her behavior? Again, do you have an ideal metaphor? Is there a difference? Why or why not?

6. If you want to be brave, ask some colleagues in your organization what their metaphors might be. How do these compare with yours? What are the implications of these exercises for reframing our understandings of and reforming our organizations?

REFERENCES

Argyris, C. (1982). *Reasoning, learning, and action.* San Francisco: Jossey-Bass.

Argyris, C., & Schon, D. A. (1974). *Theory in practice.* San Francisco: Jossey-Bass.

Ashby, W. R. (1956). *An introduction to cybernetics.* London: Chapman and Hall.

Banathy, B. H. (1988). Systems inquiry in education. *Systems Practice, 1*(2), 193–212.

Bertalanfy, L. von (1968). *General systems theory.* New York: Braziller.

Bolman, L. G., & Deal, T. E. (1984). Modern approaches to understanding and managing organizations. San Francisco: Jossey-Bass.

Bolman, L. G., & Deal, T. E. (1991). *Reframing organizations: Artistry, choice, and leadership.* San Francisco: Jossey-Bass.

Bruner, J. (1990). *Acts of meaning.* Cambridge, MA: Harvard University Press.

Burrell, G., & Hearn, J. (1989). The sexuality of organization. In J. Hearn, D. L. Sheppard, P. Tancred-Sheriff, & G. Burrell (Eds.), *The sexuality of organization* (pp. 1–28). Newbury Park, CA: Sage.

Callahan, R. (1962). *Education and the cult of efficiency.* Chicago: University of Chicago Press.

Checkland, P. B. (1981). *Systems thinking, systems practice.* Chichester, England: Wiley.

Etzioni, A. (1964). *Modern organizations.* Englewood Cliffs, NJ: Prentice-Hall.

The expanding role of the schools in Anyplace, USA. *Journal of Teacher Education* (July-August, 1981), *32*(4), 5–6.

Flood, R. L., & Carson, E. R. (1988). *Dealing with complexity.* New York: Plenum.

Foster, W. (1986). *Paradigms and promises.* Buffalo, NY: Prometheus Books.

Gergen, K. J. (1993). Organization theory in the postmodern era. In M. Reed & M. Hughes (Eds.), *Rethinking organization* (pp. 207–26). Newbury Park, CA: Sage.

Goldberg, M. A. (1989). *On systemic balance.* New York: Praeger.

Guba, E. G. (1985). The context of emergent paradigm research. In Y. S. Lincoln (Ed.), *Organizational theory and inquiry* (pp. 79–105). Beverly Hills, CA: Sage.

Hlynka, D., & Belland, J. C. (Eds.). (1991). *Paradigms regained.* Englewood Cliffs, NJ: Educational Technology Publications.

Likert, R. (1967). *The human organization.* New York: McGraw-Hill.

Lincoln, Y. S. (1985). Introduction. In Y. S. Lincoln (Ed.), *Organizational theory and inquiry* (pp. 29–42). Beverly Hills, CA: Sage.

Matejko, A. J. (1986). *In search of new organizational paradigms.* New York: Praeger.

Morgan, G. (1986). *Images of organization.* Beverly Hills, CA: Sage.

Morgan, G. (1993). *Imaginization*. Newbury Park, CA: Sage.

Oakes, J. (1985). *Keeping track: How schools structure inequality*. New Haven: Yale University Press.

Owens, R. G. (1987). *Organizational behavior in education* (3rd ed.). Englewood Cliffs, NJ: Prentice-Hall.

Program notes. (May, 1994). Burlington, VT: Vermont Symphony Orchestra.

Schon, D. A. (1983). *The reflective practitioner: How professionals think in action*. New York: Basic Books.

Taylor, F. W. (1911). *Principles of scientific management*. New York: Harper & Row.

Taylor, W. D., & Swartz, J. D. (1991). Whose knowledge? In D. Hlynka & J. C. Belland (Eds.), *Paradigms regained* (pp. 51–64). Englewood Cliffs, NJ: Educational Technology Publications.

Tynan, K. (1989). *Profiles*. London: Nick Hern Books.

Weber, M. (1947). *The theory of social and economic organization*. London: Oxford University Press.

Weick, K. E. (1985). Sources of order in underorganized systems: Themes in recent organizational theory. In Y. S. Lincoln (Ed.), *Organizational theory and inquiry* (pp. 106–36). Beverly Hills, CA: Sage.

Organizational Perspectives

$\mathbf{I}$n setting the stage for examining different present-day perspectives on organizations, a brief review of past thinking on organizations seems in order. Following a brief history of organizational theory, we will overview the four chapters in section 1. To aid in explaining the various theories and concepts introduced in the chapters on organizations as culture, politics, theater, and brains, the case *A House Divided* is presented. This case of a K–12 school district is revisited in each chapter, permitting an opportunity to reframe and explore alternatives.

HISTORY OF ORGANIZATIONAL THEORY

The history of organizational theory basically divides into four eras: (1) 1900–1930, classical organizational theory; (2) 1930–1950, the human relations movement; (3) 1950–1975, the organizational behavior movement; (4) 1975–present, the socio-cultural period. Although these dates are somewhat arbitrary, they do provide a convenient way of marking a point in time when ideas on ways to view organizations shifted. Although these movements were primarily anchored in studies of private, for-profit organizations, educational organizations reflect similar patterns. Also, as we examine these alternative theoretical orientations, we can observe their influence in our present-day organizations.

Classical Organizational Theory

The emergence of organizational theory during the industrialization of the United States is more than coincidental. As managers and owners of companies had to deal with challenges such as limited capital and tough competition, scientific methods of inquiry provided needed answers. In addition, the influence of the positivistic paradigm on organizational thinking was probably greatest during this period. Thus was born *The Principles of Scientific Management* (Taylor, 1911). In this era, the metaphor of the machine held sway: Organizations were seen as machines and people were viewed as appendages to these machines. Efficiency (lower cost per unit of production) was the Holy Grail, and careful monitoring and documenting (time-and-motion studies) of worker behavior were the means to attaining lower costs.

The following description provides some insight to the level of detail for which Taylor and his followers were known:

> In the late 1890s, at Bethlehem, Taylor studied the yard labor gang. He found that each man in the gang furnished his own shovel and that they were of various sizes. Sometimes the laborers shoveled coal, sometimes iron ore, ashes, etc. The result was that the weight per shovelful varied considerably, depending on the material lifted. By experiment he found that the most work was done when about 21.5 pounds were moved per shovelful. He had the company buy a stock of shovels of various sizes. No matter what the material to be shoveled, the appropriate size shovel could be furnished to the workers. Large shovels were used for ashes, small shovels for iron ore, etc. In that way, the load could always approximate 21.5 pounds. As a result, the work done per worker increased and costs were reduced. (Moore, 1953, pp. 11-12)

There were some side benefits to all this precision. According to Drucker (1968) one of the effects of Taylorism was the improvement of productivity, which resulted in higher pay for unskilled labor. On the negative side, however, many problems emerged from the application of scientific management principles, not the least of which was worker alienation. As management attempted to maximize its controls in order to increase efficiency, workers found their work highly segmented by being subdivided into small, limited, and routine tasks. According to Owens (1987) the growth of industrial and other large organizations led to a great deal of friction between individuals and these impersonal giants:

> The years before World War I were punctuated by frequent outbursts of this conflict, such as labor unrest, revolution, and the rise of Communism. In this setting, a German sociologist, Max Weber, produced some of the most useful, durable, and brilliant work on an administrative system; it seemed promising at that time and has since proved indispensable: *bureaucracy.* (p. 7)

In many circles *bureaucracy* is a pejorative word. It conjures up images of impersonalization, red tape, delays, inertia, and resistance to change. There is a general feeling that the only persons who seem to benefit from bureaucracies are those who are in their employ serving their own needs rather than the needs of their clients. All of us have had the experience of trying to straighten out problems like incorrect billings, lost orders, wrongly delivered merchandise, surly clerks, and more. On the other hand, for reasons that are not always clear, we continue to rely on many of Weber's concepts, which include

- division of labor
- hierarchy of authority
- specified regulations
- specified work procedures
- minimal personal relations
- rewards based on technical competence

On the surface these bureaucratic principles make sense. They also illustrate how conditioned our thinking has been by the positivistic paradigm and the machine metaphor. These principles seem appropriate for conditions that require predictable results. On the other hand, many social systems, such as schools, are highly unpredictable and require greater flexibility in meeting the needs of those within and without the organization. In any regard, the strong emphasis on efficiency and impersonal relations in the large bureaucracies of the early 1900s sowed the seeds for the human relations movement.

Human Relations Movement

Maybe it was serendipity or inevitability that Mayo (1933) and his fellow researchers discovered the so-called Hawthorne effect and gave birth to the human relations movement. There are many definitions of this concept, but in effect it attempts to explain how one's behavior is influenced by being a part of a change process. The Hawthorne effect is not due to specific changes but rather is attributed to feeling a part of the change process itself. This insight grew out of Mayo and his colleagues' puzzlement with their research findings from experiments conducted at Western Electric's Hawthorne plant near Chicago. A part of the study was designed to determine the relationship of illumination levels and worker productivity. What puzzled the researchers was that it did not seem to matter whether the illumination levels were raised or lowered, production continued to climb. What was concluded, and why this research was so important to the human relations movement, is the importance of paying attention to worker needs. Apparently, these workers at the Hawthorne plant appreciated the attention paid them and the opportunity to interact more freely with their fellow workers. This research implies that designing for efficiency is not as crucial to productivity as recognizing the social conditions in the workplace.

What stemmed from this research and other studies was an appreciation of the influence of the informal work group or clique. It was recognized that these social groups were capable of controlling worker behavior and productivity in very subtle ways. A logical conclusion of these observations was the need to better train management to work more effectively with the social needs of workers. Training managers in group dynamics and small group behavior came into vogue. For example, managers were trained to recognize the varying roles individuals play within small work groups involved in planning and decision making. Greater stress was placed on democratic procedures, worker involvement, concerns for worker motivation, and an understanding of the interdependence of leaders and followers. Greater attention was given to morale, group cohesiveness, collaboration, and informal group dynamics.

We can see the influence of the human relations movement on educational organizations. Many staff development programs focus on group dynamics and interpersonal relations among school personnel. Much of this is based on the premise that the more teachers and staff feel a part of a school team, the greater is the likelihood of their support for needed changes. Retreats of administrative personnel often focus on relationships between administrators and the need to provide greater support for one another. In the minds of many, however, the emphasis on human relations overlooked the need for organizations to achieve results. Thus, the stage was set for another major movement in organizational theory.

Organizational Behavior Movement

Whereas bureaucratic theory appeared to stress organizations over people and human relations theory tended to stress people over organizations, the organizational behavior movement attempted to fuse these two perspectives. The organizational behavior movement focused on the dualism of the individual and the organization. Books written in this era reflected a concerted effort to view organizations differently from the past: Examples include *Personality and Organization* (Argyris, 1958), *Intergroup Relations and Leadership* (Sherif, 1962), *The Human Organization* (Likert, 1967), *The Human Side of the Enterprise* (McGregor, 1960), and *Management by Participation* (Marrow, Bowers, & Seashore, 1967). Owens (1987) defines the new approach: " 'Organizational behavior' is a narrower, more precise term that falls under the broader, more general meaning of human relations. Organizational behavior is a discipline that seeks to describe, understand, and predict human behavior in the environment of formal organizations" (pp. 18–19).

The organizational behavior movement opened the opportunity for behavioral scientists to study organizations and management problems. Although strongly anchored in the paradigm of positivism, a new management science was born. Attention was and still is directed at examining contextual factors, both internal and external, that are social, political, economic, and technological in nature. These new studies continue to provide managers with insight on decision making, organizational communications, conflict management, and change. The greatest weakness of the behavioral approach has been a begrudging acknowledgment of the paradigms of interpretism and criticism. As a consequence, the overdependence on positivistic thinking and related research methodologies has limited the scope and breadth of organizational behavior research and theories.

Sociocultural Movement

The sociocultural movement of the present is an amalgam of the behavioral approach and methodologies anchored in the paradigms of interpretism and criticism. That is to say, there is a greater appreciation for the intangible, the phenomena difficult to measure that influence the lives of people in organizations. A prime example of this is a strong interest in organizational culture, some aspects of which may be understood by survey research methodology so common to positivistic thinking. Something as subtle as culture, however, may be better understood through methodology associated with qualitative sociology, anthropology, history, and philosophy. Case studies and ethnographic studies provide a rich description of organizational conditions that explain more fully the natural influences on all members of an organization.

In addition to developing an appreciation for the multiple realities surrounding organizations, current sociocultural theories are less prescriptive and more descriptive in nature. Eisner (1991) emphasizes the importance of methodological pluralism and organizational holism when trying to understand educational organizations. In his support of the paradigm of criticism he states: "*Criticism* suffers from its association with negativism. Unfortunately many people think of negative commentary when they hear or read the word *criticism*. But this too is not a necessary or intended meaning. Criticism of art, music, literature, poetry, or social affairs does not impose an obligation to make derogatory comments. Criticism can be laudatory. It aims to illuminate a situation or object so that it can be seen or appreciated. We appreciate virtues as well as vices." (p. 7).

The sociocultural movement is still in process. A greater recognition, however, is being given to the potential power of the paradigms of interpretism and criticism in understanding social organizations and individual behavior. We also need to recognize that the influences of and vestiges from the eras of classical organizational theory, the human relations movement, and organizational behavior theory still exist. We may be moving into a fifth era that will attempt to synthesize the best of past theories and practices, one in which there is recognition of the role an observer's frame plays in defining an organization's "reality." Only time will tell. In the meantime, we have an opportunity to draw on the best of the past and to forge new organizational arrangements that fit best with the present and the future.

CHAPTER HIGHLIGHTS

In the chapters that follow in section 1, we examine four major perspectives or metaphors of organizational theory. Before offering an overview of each chapter, two important reminders are in order. First, the importance of metaphor:

> Metaphor is often just regarded as a device for embellishing discourse, but its significance is much greater than this. For the use of metaphor implies *a way of thinking* and *a way of seeing* that pervade how we understand our world generally. (Morgan, 1986, p. 12)

Second: the notion of diagnostic reading or being a diagnostician. As Bolman and Deal (1984) write, "A manager is a diagnostician who uses theories, or frames, to focus on certain things while ignoring others" (p. 21). Morgan (1986) states that diagnostic reading "is diagnostic not in the medical sense of attempting to identify diseases (or, in the case of organizations, problems) but in the old Greek sense of attempting to discern the character of the situation" (p. 328).

Using these ideas as a backdrop, a more detailed orientation to the chapters follows.

Chapter 2: Organizations from a Cultural Perspective

This chapter explores in some depth the current interest in thinking of organizations as having a *culture* and/or *subcultures*. As with any phenomenon, culture can mean different things to different people. Chapter 2 will explore some of these different points of view as well as key concepts associated with organizational culture. We will examine rituals, ceremonies, heroes and heroines, stories, and symbols and their role in informing members of an organization's important value systems. We know these values have origins. Thus, some attention is given to their derivation both historically and environmentally. The chapter will explore the implications of culture for managing an organization or creating a new culture and the moral implications of both strategies. Chapter 2 also suggests ways administrators may discover the nature of their organization's culture and the implications of viewing an organization from the metaphor of culture.

Chapter 3: Organizations from a Political Perspective

Politics and culture are but a short step from one another. In chapter 3, we will focus primarily on how organizations look when viewed through the lens of political systems. Belief systems that undergird organizational cultures have their influence on how politics are played out in an organization. In addition, there are other influences; these include access to resources, levels of trust, degrees of cooperation and competition, special interests, and how conflicts get resolved. A discussion of politics is not complete without some attention given to concepts of power and persuasion. A portion of this chapter is devoted to how administrators can better understand and manage politics in their organization. As one person said, "Thank God for politicians." To those who view politics as something negative and to be avoided, this note of appreciation may come as some surprise. Chapter 3 intends to offer a balanced view and some encouragement at being more understanding of organizations as political.

Chapter 4: Organizations from a Theatrical Perspective

The cynic's view of schools as politics likens school to a zoo that closes on the weekend. A less jaundiced view is to see organizations as theater. In chapter 4 we will examine the metaphor of theater and how dramaturgical concepts can explain how and why organizations behave as they do. Phrases like *performance, stage set-*

ting, costume, acting, role, script, rehearsal, and "the show must go on" are common to our everyday vocabulary. Yet, within an organizational context, they take on different meanings and help us appreciate that what we see is not always the complete picture. Organizations can be deceptive, and people in them act out different roles depending on what they think the script suggests. When looking through the lens of theater, subtle behaviors may become more apparent and transparent. A portion of chapter 4 addresses how to study one's organization using dramaturgical concepts and how to direct the show also known as *organization.*

Chapter 5: Organizations from a Brain Perspective

The brain has been compared to a computer, a control center, and a deep, dark cave hiding many secrets. In considering it as a metaphor for organizations, we will examine characteristics of the brain that are both mysterious and potentially exciting. Part of the mystery is our capacity to learn, to remember, to be creative, to be intuitive, and unfortunately to be addictive. We are often struck with wonderment at the reasoning and controlling capacities of our brains. When we look at an organization with these concepts in mind we come to appreciate its capacity to function in similar ways. Again we will explore how an administrator may use these concepts to understand and manage many dynamics associated with organizational life.

Summary

The summary at the end of section 1 provides a synthesis of the four chapters. Through probing questions we will revisit the four perspectives explored in each of the chapters; a metaframework will present the big picture and distinguishing features of the four metaphors. This exercise will show how these metaphors can be appreciated both holistically and individually.

CASE: *A HOUSE DIVIDED*

Introduction

To aid in understanding the various concepts suggested by the four organizational metaphors and to appreciate their practical value in explaining organizational situations, the case of a K–12 school district follows.

The Mountain View School District case was chosen because it offers a picture of what can result when a well-meaning and qualified administrator encounters a set of conditions, some of her own making and some not, that starts on a note of optimism and quickly deteriorates into a crisis and ultimate failure. The case illustrates how an organization with the best of intentions can lose sight of its ideals and almost lose control. Many lessons can be drawn from this case, and the metaphors of culture, politics, theater, and brain should light the way. (The case is based on actual events, but the context has been changed in order to protect the identity of those persons involved.)

MOUNTAIN VIEW SCHOOL DISTRICT

Mountain View School District (MVSD), as the name suggests, enjoys an idyllic location with a panorama of mountains and valleys. Unfortunately, this pastoral image belies the fissures and pressures that exist beneath the surface. MVSD is a moderate-sized school district with an enrollment of approximately 4,000 students distributed in five elementary schools, two middle schools, and a high school with an adjoining vocational school. Its community has many light industries, recreational support businesses, a medical center, and several small vocational and academic higher education institutions. Because of tourism and related recreational opportunities afforded by the area, the Mountain View community is very vulnerable to economic swings, and its ability to support public programs, including its schools, waxes and wanes with these economic cycles. Also, because of its geographic location and natural beauty, there has been a significant influx of persons seeking the "good life" and competing for limited and low-paying job opportunities. There are also sizable minority and low-income populations in Mountain View (approximately 20 percent of its 40,000 people); the minorities include African Americans, Southeast Asians, and Native Americans.

The MVSD has a central administration made up of the superintendent, associate superintendent for curriculum and instruction, personnel director, special education coordinator, and business manager. In addition, there are building principals at each of the schools, associate principals at the middle and high schools, and a vocational education director. There are a number of department chairs (e.g., math, science, English, social studies, foreign language, and technical courses) overseeing curriculum development and instruction from the middle school level through the high school. Also, there are project leaders assigned to special education services, Chapter I, early childhood education, and community service, to name a few. Overall there are 300-plus professional staff members and 45 support staff and teacher aides.

During the late 1960s and early 1970s MVSD was led by a superintendent whose style was laissez-faire. As our country shifted to a more conservative stance, as exemplified by the Reagan presidency, so did the administration of this school district. It recruited a conservative leader whose style was more authoritarian. During his administration he managed to address declining enrollment problems by closing a school and relocating students to several other schools in the district. He reduced the plethora of high school offerings, placing more emphasis on career education and preparation of students for work and less on foreign languages, humanities, and the arts. Acceptance of the dominant control of this superintendent was begrudging, although a general desire to open up the decision-making process and to take a harder look at quality issues began to emerge. When a new superintendent was recruited early in 1990, however, the calm exterior of the school district seemed to change.

A recognized scholar and researcher in educational administration with limited administrative experience received appointment as the superintendent of schools of Mountain View School District. At a previous administrative position, as associate superintendent for instruction, she developed a reputation as a soft-spoken administrator who pushed excellence in teaching, high academic standards, and cultural diversity. Besides her administrative experience, she had a doctorate in educational administration and taught at a leading state university. Her scholarly endeavors included 3 books, 2 edited books, and 25 articles. She brought vision, credibility, and enthusiasm to her new position. She seemed to be a perfect fit for a district that needed to take a hard look at the quality of its curriculum and instruction and how well it was serving its low-income and minority populations. She quickly captured the imagination and attention of those in attendance at the public meeting called to honor her appointment. At this meeting, the superintendent was asked to give a speech concerning her vision for MVSD. Her speech included quotes from Milton and Emily Dickinson and a sprinkling of puns and humor. She talked about making Mountain View "preeminent among the moderate-sized school districts of this state." She seemed very much in tune with the school excellence movement.

In spite of all this optimism, however, she offered her resignation less than six months after her appointment. She perceived a lack of support from central office administrators, building principals, and the board of education. She felt her decisions regarding the replacement of key administrative personnel, especially the associate superintendent for instruction, and her demands for greater emphasis on excellence in academics and cultural diversity were causing a rift in the community. Her resignation was accepted by the board of education chairperson. Suddenly the problems of the MVSD were open to public scrutiny.

This sudden and dramatic act raised a storm of protests. A sizable number of students, parents, teachers, and support staff members confronted the board of education chairperson, who agreed to conduct a public meeting to explain the superintendent's resignation. He attempted to quiet the protesters by suggesting the need to look ahead and indicated his willingness to appoint the high school principal as interim superintendent. Nearly 50 percent of the teachers signed a petition for reinstatement of the superintendent. Two days later MVSD's superintendent withdrew her resignation, claiming it had been forced. She subsequently filed a lawsuit in state court charging sexism and demanding reinstatement.

The state court judge ruled in favor of reinstatement. The judge felt that the board chairperson's testimony lacked credibility and that he based his opinions on secondhand and thirdhand complaints. On the other hand, the judge wrote that the testimony of the superintendent was clear and consistent. The school board reluctantly concurred with the judge's decision, and the superintendent returned to her position amid turmoil in the district.

A local newspaper covering her return ran a photograph of her being hugged by a member of the custodial staff as she left the courthouse. This picture symbolized the deep feelings for the superintendent of some MVSD employees, including the district's support staff, who felt they were being recognized for the first time for their contribution to the schools.

There is little doubt, however, that the superintendent's reputation for integrity had suffered during this period of litigation and staff unrest. Several central office administrators, including the associate superintendent, resigned or expressed grave doubts about the superintendent's ability to lead and her proposed policies for student discipline, school security, and cultural diversity. Others questioned her vision of excellence and proposed changes for a school district that served a sizable low-income population.

The school district was still under the cloud of allegations of sexism, and the state commissioner of education requested formation of a committee to investigate these charges. Students and teachers who were silent up to this point began to voice their opposition to the superintendent. They too began to question her leadership style and vision for the school district. The superintendent, however, expressed confidence that with the help of her supporters she could rebuild relationships in the community and in the school district. She told a colleague that *insurmountable* was not in her vocabulary.

The ad hoc committee that investigated charges of sexism in the MVSD the following fall found more than they had bargained for. After conducting interviews with 85 people, they realized that the problems of this school district transcended gender-related issues: They found a school system rife with conflict. The issues were many and quite complex, including (1) a discrepancy between the rhetoric desiring freer exchange of views and the climate of mistrust and intimidation, (2) the inappropriate match between proposals for academic excellence and the nature of the student population, (3) the seemingly arbitrary methods used by the administration to impose change, (4) the resignations forced with insensitivity and lack of appreciation for past contributions to the school district, and (5) the lack of consensus over what kind of system MVSD was and should become. The committee reported, "Sexism is a part of [the] conflict, but the conflict reaches beyond and confuses the issues of sexism. The committee is concerned that the climate of conflict and factionalism does not support diversity, works against constructive discussion of gender-related issues, and has the potential to contribute to the attrition of teachers and administrators, especially women." The committee was also concerned about staff members' fear of reprisal and reluctance to testify. The superintendent was urged "to reduce conflict and tension and to build mutual trust and respect."

At a celebration of Martin Luther King Day, the superintendent announced a four-year, multi-tiered "Plan for Cultural Change in the Mountain View School District." The plan, divided into eight "thrusts," indicated the extensive use of outside consultants and leading experts to address matters of communication, gender issues, and future planning. A special districtwide committee of students, teachers, and parents was appointed, and members attended a two-day training session to learn to be "Ambassadors of Cultural Change" for the school district.

The superintendent's plan drew mixed reviews. Some complimented her for bringing the issues of communication, gender, and the need for future planning more into the open and pushing for needed changes. Others felt the plan was too idealistic and relied too much on outside experts. One aspect of her plan that drew some criticism was Thrust IV, calling for the establishment of a Mountain View School District Brain Trust that would include, among others, the superintendent and her husband. In providing a rationale for the brain trust, the superintendent wrote in her proposal that it "is helping me to take the excellence model of the man who discovered quality, W. Edwards Deming, who is largely responsible for the Japanese industrial success story, combine it synergistically with the collaborative educational model, and produce a new way of educating that will serve industry and education." Some in the community questioned whether the "excellence" plan and attention to cultural diversity would be too much for a school district striving to achieve such basic goals as ensuring basic competencies for all students. The president of the teachers' association reacted to the brain trust proposal by observing that "It looks good on paper" but did not address the more pressing social problems of student discipline at the high school. She cited a recent example of how the high school students did not support diversity, when a candlelight vigil held during a Mideast teach-in nearly ended in violence: "They [students] were going to beat a kid up because they thought he was going to burn a flag. Those things just happen around here. People don't listen to each other."

In April, in reaction to a number of changes in MVSD policies initiated by the superintendent and her newly appointed associate superintendent for curriculum and instruction, a no-confidence petition was circulated by the teachers. Reportedly they got over 700 signatures of teachers, parents, and even high school students calling for the ouster of the superintendent and the associate superintendent.

The associate superintendent was known to be highly critical of teacher and student behavior, including teacher's lack of professionalism in dealing with incidents of harassment directed at minority and female students. She had proposed a cultural diversity policy mandating that all classroom teachers provide multicultural and gender-relations content and instruction in their subject areas at the middle and high school levels. Needless to say, there was a negative and, in some cases, angry reaction to this mandate, further dividing teachers and students along lines of income, ethnicity, and race. As one teacher described the situation, "I've seen crap here that really scares me—confrontations, abuse, harassment. I was threatened that I'd be beaten up for my views on cultural diversity. It's ridiculous. On the other hand, the associate superintendent has burned a lot of people, including me, and has a very aggressive style. She goes right for the jugular." The associate superintendent herself had been a target of harassment and anti-Semitic acts. She had found a piece of paper slipped under her office door that had a swastika with "Jew" written on it.

Strict policies on student discipline and school building security had many students, their parents, and members of the community complaining. One student said, "Free and open access to the school's facilities once helped bring the community together. There used to be a really tight community in Mountain View School District when I got here." The student discipline and school building security policies resulted in greater divisions, particularly between white and African American students. Minority students claimed that they were being blamed for altercations during and after school and were otherwise being treated unfairly.

June graduation at the high school was held under tight security after telephone threats were made to both the superintendent and associate superintendent. Everyone was relieved when MVSD came together, if only temporarily, to celebrate graduation without incident.

Approximately two years after her appointment, the superintendent of MVSD tendered her resignation for the second time, citing rampant anti-Semitism and hatred of women as the reasons. She said, "Over the last month I had found myself battling against moral disgust at some of the things that had gone on, notably anti-Semitism, and I did not want my leadership to come out of that sort of environment."

Thus came to a close one leader's experience, after seeing her vision of excellence ground under by resistance, animosity, and threatened violence. In reflecting upon her experience she stated, "I don't know if education in general is facing a number of problems and part of it is a backlash at the gains that have been made by minorities and women. This is not new to Mountain View School District. It is a legacy all minorities are facing." Her resignation was effective June 30.

With this case study as a backdrop, the following chapters on organizations as culture, politics, theater, and brains offer an opportunity to reframe the problems of Mountain View School District and explore larger implications for reframing and reform.

REFERENCES

Argyris, C. (1958). *Personality and organization.* New York: Harper & Row.

Bolman, L. G., & Deal, T. E. (1984). *Modern approaches to understanding and managing organizations.* San Francisco: Jossey-Bass.

Drucker, P. (1968). *Age of discontinuity.* New York: Harper & Row.

Eisner, E. W. (1991). *The enlightened eye.* New York: Macmillan.

Likert, R. (1967). *The human organization.* New York: McGraw-Hill.

Marrow, A. J., Bowers, D. G., & Seashore, S. E. (1967). *Management by participation.* New York: Harper & Row.

Mayo, E. (1933). *The human problems of an industrial civilization.* New York: Macmillan.

McGregor, D. (1960). *The human side of the enterprise.* New York: McGraw-Hill.

Moore, F. G. (1953). *Manufacturing management.* Homewood, IL: Irwin.

Morgan, G. (1986). *Images of organization.* Beverly Hills, CA: Sage.

Owens, R. G. (1987). *Organizational behavior in education* (3rd ed.). Englewood Cliffs, NJ: Prentice-Hall.

Sherif, M. (1962). *Intergroup relations and leadership.* New York: Harper & Row.

Taylor, F. W. (1911). *The principles of scientific management.* New York: Harper & Row.

chapter 2

Organizations from a Cultural Perspective

Culture carries with it many images. Typically we think of culture as something to do with the arts—symphony orchestras, classical music, art exhibits, and plays. Some associate it with travel and visiting historical sites and quaint landmarks. For organizations culture takes on a different meaning. When culture is linked to social groups such as organizations, it is seen in the anthropological sense as a prevailing set of beliefs and customs that guide the actions of persons within that group. Those who have participated in tight social cliques (fraternities, sororities, street gangs, Scouts, etc.) know firsthand how the influence of the group transcends the influence of any single individual. Czarniawksa-Joerges (1991) describes an organization's culture as a bubble that surrounds the organization and separates it from outside groups and individuals. Frost, Moore, Louis, Lundberg, and Martin (1985) refer to it as the glue that holds the organization together. Moore (1985) describes it as a form of magnetism drawing members of the organizations. In any regard, culture is omnipresent and ambiguous at the same time. Its presence is felt but even for the long-term insider it is often difficult to pin down. It is what we do and value that we often do not question or fully comprehend.

This chapter illuminates the metaphor of culture as applied to organizations. Related concepts will provide a framework to isolate elements that typically describe an organization's culture. Using these elements of ritual, symbol, story, hero and heroine, and others, we will explore how to study one's own organizational culture. Finally, we will explore the practical and moral implications of trying to "manage" an organization's culture. The idea of managing an organizational culture is linked, as we will see, to Mountain View School District's (MVSD's) effort at creating a five-year plan in part through the efforts of "ambassadors of culture."

NEED FOR ORGANIZATIONAL CULTURE

It may seem obvious, but we might wonder why groups form cultures in the first place. Is there something innate to human beings in groups that necessitates the drive for establishing a set of prevailing norms? Weick (1969) suggests that groups are predominantly emotional: "Group members are persuaded more by emotional than by intellectual appeals, because feelings are the primary means by which members are linked" (p. 15). It seems that because of our emotionality we are predisposed to seek emotional support; a group often provides such support through its culture.

The propensity to form a culture in an organization, particularly school organizations, can in part also be attributed to the notion that organizations are loosely coupled (Weick, 1982). Sergiovanni states:

> The cultural perspective is particularly important in understanding loosely structured organizations. Such organizations are characterized by a great deal of breathing room for individuals and units despite managerial attempts to tighten and structure things by applying conventional management theories. In loosely structured organizations coordination is difficult, controls are adhered to more by letter than spirit with little effect, and, whether intended or not, individuals enjoy a great deal of discretion. Workers operate independent of each other; thus close supervision is difficult to practice. (Sergiovanni & Corbally, 1984, p. ix)

The breathing room discussed by Sergiovanni is typical of educational organizations, as illustrated in our case study organization. At MVSD we observed the difficulty the superintendent and the associate superintendent had garnering support for their policy changes. The so-called breathing room or relative autonomy, in part a consequence of separating students by grade levels into independent school buildings managed by semi-autonomous building-level administrators, makes it difficult to gain support and/or cooperation across the entire system. On the other hand, if the proposed changes can be linked to the culture of the organization or total system then the culture can serve as the silent supervisor. In other words, in order to prevent a drift toward chaos or, to state it more positively, in order to see that something is shared in common, a cultural bubble needs to exist. Cultural norms provide an opportunity to commit ourselves emotionally to some common good that is often encouraged by supervisors but cannot be mandated. The experiences of the superintendent and associate superintendent at MVSD after imposing a new cultural diversity policy in the district reflect the limits of top-down mandates.

Also, we observed that MVSD members had different needs to be fulfilled within the cultural context of the district. To some students and parents open access to school facilities helped form a sense of community. The teachers worried about academic leadership and their role in determining curriculum content and teaching methodology. The new superintendent wanted to create a vision that stretched this complacent community to reach new heights in spite of its traditional low-income student population. These were common ideas to which different members of the organization could align themselves and find purpose for their membership in the school system. They reflect an emotional desire for a sense of identification and meaning that seems to exist in most educational organizations that operate with ambiguous goals and multiple means of attaining them.

Rosen (1991) points out that "the knowledge structure through which reality is interpreted and thus created is socially constructed. This knowledge structure is what anthropologists and other social constructionists construe as 'cultural'" (p. 273). These constructions take many forms and are often expressed in symbols. Rosen further suggests that symbols are the "objects, acts, relationships, or linguistic formations that stand *ambiguously* for a multiplicity of meanings, evoke emotions, and impel men [*sic*] to action" (p. 273). We create meaning in a variety of ways in order to maintain our attachments to and sense of connection with others in organizations. The continued disintegration of two-parent families and declining church membership place even more responsibility on other settings, such as the workplace, for developing a sense of identity and emotional support. Educational organizations, by meaning different things to many people, have the potential to provide that support.

The power and potential that exist in an organization's culture reinforce the importance of critical theory as espoused by Jürgen Habermas (1971). Habermas suggests that knowledge, or "knowledge-constitutive interest," is not value-free but is constituted in three different interests: technical interest (a deductive technical model), practical interest (an inductive interpretive model), and emancipatory interest (critical theory). According to Frost et al. (1991), when critical theory is "applied to organizational symbolism, his [Habermas's] approach shows how the contributions of symbolism have led to developments in the practical interest but severe underdevelopment of the emancipatory interest" (p. 315). These authors remind us that there is a danger in rushing to make use of the practical payoffs of culture (e.g., increased worker productivity) while overlooking its potential to either free or oppress persons in organizations.

The dangers of overemphasizing the technical and practical interests of an organization's culture while ignoring the emancipatory interests can be observed in the MVSD case. The superintendent and her associate superintendent had noble goals for the school district. They took bold action where they felt it necessary (e.g., new cultural diversity and student disciplinary policies) and developed a planning process (Plan for Cultural Change at MVSD and Ambassadors of Cultural Change). Unfortunately, some members of the system, particularly teachers and students, felt dominated and their freedom threatened.

As we move forward in our understanding of the qualities normally associated with organizational culture, it is important to keep in mind its pitfalls as well as its promise. We have come to appreciate the important need that an organizational cultural can fill. But as systems theorists and economists like to remind us, there is no free lunch. In our pursuit of emotional support we may put at risk our individual autonomy. How we view and try to resolve this conundrum is relevant to our understanding of an organization's culture.

DEFINITIONS AND RELATED CONCEPTS

Definitions of Culture

In the opening paragraph of this chapter, we observed how an organizational culture can be both omnipresent and ambiguous at the same time. This is a paradox of sorts but reflects the difficulty of discerning or defining one's workplace culture. Rousseau (1990) summarizes eight definitions of culture.

Source	Definition
Becker & Geer (1970)	Set of common understandings, expressed in language.
Kroeber & Kluckhohn (1952)	Transmitted patterns of values, ideas, and other symbolic systems that shape behavior.
Louis (1983)	Three aspects: (1) some content (meaning and interpretation) (2) peculiar to (3) a group.
Martin & Siehl (1983)	Glue that holds together an organization through shared patterns of meaning. Three component systems: context or core values, forms (process of communication—for instance, jargon), strategies to reinforce content (such as rewards, training programs).
Ouchi (1981)	Set of symbols, ceremonies, and myths that communicate the underlying values and beliefs of the organization to its employees.
Swartz & Jordon (1980)	Pattern of beliefs and expectations shared by members that produce norms shaping behavior.
Uttal (1983)	Shared values (what is important) and beliefs (how things work) that interact with an organization's structures and control systems to produce behavioral norms (the way we do things around here).
Van Maanen & Schein (1979)	Values, beliefs, and expectations that members come to share. (D. M. Rousseau, "Assessing Organizational Culture: Case for Multiple Methods," in B. Schneider [Ed.], *Organizational Climate and Culture,* 1990, Jossey-Bass, San Francisco, CA. Reprinted with permission of Jossey-Bass.)

As she suggests, "Notions of shared values, common understandings, and patterns of beliefs and expectations underlie our views on the nature of culture" (p. 154). Or to put it more directly, it is the way things are done in an organization.

Types of Cultures

To understand the similarities and differences among definitions of organizational culture, Martin and Meyerson (1988) provide a framework based on three dominant perspectives: the *integration* perspective, which portrays the culture as being consistent and organizationwide; the *differentiation* perspective, which stresses inconsistency but *sub*cultural consensus; and the *fragmentation* perspective, which stresses ambiguity as a pervasive aspect of contemporary life. This last perspective illuminates the lack of consensus and the presence of both consistency and inconsistency in organizations.

When applying this framework to the MVSD case study, we can observe the validity of all three perspectives to some degree. The superintendent's goal of creating an organizationwide, consistent culture through her vision of the MVSD's potential to become "preeminent among moderate-sized school districts in the state" reflects the integration perspective. However, the factionalism observed by the special committee on sexism reflects the differentiation perspective. The committee identified subcultures that exhibited consensus within their respective groups but resulted in inconsistency across the entire organization. Finally, the fragmentation perspective is illustrated by the high degree of ambiguity felt in the community as to the MVSD's mission (e.g., should it stress academics and thus serve college-bound students or emphasize vocational relevance and serve low-income students?). Both a lack of consensus and mixed messages contributed to the unstable culture in the MVSD.

Ambiguity and Culture

The fragmentation perspective, in Meyerson's (1991) judgment, has not received enough attention. Typically more attention is given to organizationwide cultures and subcultures within organizations, with little recognition and/or acceptance of organizational ambiguities. It is Meyerson's opinion that "a formulation of culture that acknowledges ambiguities will more likely recognize and potentially legitimate a diverse chorus of voices, interests, and perspectives that potentially exists within an organization. . . . This view, which sees culture as dynamic and multivocal, represents a radical departure from those views that depict culture as a mechanistic, hierarchical system of stable relationships and universal symbols" (p. 260). Meyerson's observation links well to the MVSD's experience. The superintendent was operating under a set of assumptions that were consistent with the integration perspective of an organizational culture. It is interesting to speculate what effect acceptance of the fragmentation perspective by the superintendent might have had on her leadership efforts.

The MVSD's struggle illustrates the tensions between the forces contributing to conflict and those stressing order. Trice (1991) believes that "we need an operational definition of culture that includes both the forces of integration and ambiguity as well as the intermingling of the two" (p. 305). There seems to be a continuous struggle between the need for order and regularity and the existence of underlying variety and complexity. Order does not totally prevail, nor should it. This tension can be understood by the concept of cultural centers and peripheries.

Center and Periphery Influences

Trice (1991) summarizes the theory of centers and peripheries: A "set of ultimate ideologies appears to consistently emerge at the center where there is considerable consensus about each one even though they may conflict among one another. These, in turn, radiate outward from the center toward the periphery in varying degrees of consensus to diverse segments of the periphery. This process tends to make for a motley and tangled skein of meanings loosely held together by a distinct center" (p. 306).

The MVSD's superintendent struggled to establish a consistent and distinct culture at the center. However, she faced resistance there that led to resignations of other central office administrators. The periphery became even more tattered and fragmented due in part to the lack of consensus or consistency at the center.

Occupational Cultures within Organizations

Trice (1991) points out yet another factor which has been given scant attention and in his judgment is a major influence on the nature of an organization's culture: occupational cultures. That is, important occupational groups, especially in educational organizations (e.g., administrators, teachers, counselors, custodial and support staff) have their own views as to how organizations like schools should operate. These points of view can lead to various levels of accommodation and/or conflict. An interesting consequence of occupational cultures is the forging of different kinds of coalitions. As mentioned in the MVSD case study, the superintendent received backing from the district's support staff (i.e., secretaries and custodians), who had felt left out by past administrations in solving the problems of the district; this superintendent made an effort to seek input from this occupational group, which in turn had an opportunity to express their expectations for the MVSD.

Rosenholtz's (1989) research on teachers' culture within school organizations provides additional insight into the way differing organizational cultures affect the members of the system. She found that in high-consensus schools teachers shared a common definition of teaching and their instructional goals were a high priority. As a result, the teachers had significant impact on other members in the organization (e.g., their colleagues and students). Rosenholtz observes, "Their [teachers'] sense of community and their own identity led most of them to persist unassailably in their goals of student learning. Teachers spoke boldly, nobly, building big hurrahs of ideas for classroom instruction, tending to create for their students and themselves beginnings instead of endings. Student mastery of basic skills appeared the common factor that united them, the force that welded all the separate autonomous teachers into one common voice" (p. 207).

In low-consensus schools, however, there was little sense of shared community and, worse yet, a reluctance to challenge school norms of self-reliance. The nature of teachers' work became more random, tending to follow individual instincts. In these cases, there was more evidence of listlessness and a greater sense of futility.

While occupational groups within an organization can have their impact on an organization's culture, it appears equally possible that supranorms of the organization will compromise or minimize this influence. In other words, influence has many edges. For example, as Rosenholtz found in her research, teachers can affect their organizations through either activism or withdrawal; the first approach alters existing norms, whereas the other permits existing norms to prevail.

Environmental Influences on Organizational Culture

In addition to internal factors, organizational cultures are also shaped by external or environmental influences. Drawing on the thinking of Davies and Weiner (1985), Figure 2.1 provides a framework for examining the complex array of influences on educational organizations, particularly from professional associations of teachers and administrators.

As shown in Figure 2.1, the subcultures of educational organizations are linked to and interact within a broader context. Rosenholtz's (1989) research demonstrates

FIGURE 2.1 Interactive relationships between organizational culture and the broader cultural context

SOURCE: R. J. Davies & N. Weiner, "Cultural Perspective on the Study of Industrial Relations," in P. J. Frost et al. (Eds.), *Organizational Culture*, p. 365, copyright 1985 by Sage Publications, Inc. Reprinted by permission of Sage Publications, Inc.

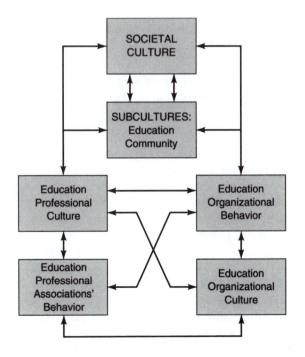

that the organizational behavior of teachers has a direct affect on the organizational culture of their schools. However, the organizational behavior (particularly teachers' behavior) is dependent on and interactive with other important influences. Societal values and expectations, as sustained by education at large and communities in general, can influence teachers' behavior and their organizational culture. In addition, there is an exchange of influences and points of view with the education professional culture and the education professional associations. The strength and clarity of these ties can exert tremendous influence on how a local school and its teachers will view their professional work and the kind of school environment they wish to create.

The MVSD case study illustrates external influences on various occupational groups in the school district. The superintendent brought with her a set of values honed by years of studying educational systems (e.g., commitment to academic excellence); already in place were the values of our present-day society and its preoccupation with the notion of excellence. The professional cultures of the faculty and principals, however, introduced a tension regarding both the superintendent's vision and the means of attaining it. The various administrators who either volunteered or were forced to resign expressed frustration over how little voice they had in shaping and implementing the superintendent's vision. The teachers initially supported the superintendent's cause because they interpreted her commitment to academic excellence as beneficial to improving their status in the school district, which had suffered somewhat under the authoritarian behavior of the previous superintendent. Unfortunately, this congruence of expectations split apart when the faculty became divided over the forced resignations of former colleagues, many of whom had loyal supporters in the teacher ranks. These loyalties soon took precedence over dreams of academic excellence.

To summarize, there are different ways to think about organizational culture. Several points made in the preceding discussion are worth reemphasizing:

- Organizational cultures are not necessarily integrated
- Considerable ambiguity can exist in an organization
- Different views of the organization are held by members at the center and periphery of the organization
- An organization exists in a larger environment that helps to define its culture
- Occupational group cultures and their linkage to outside parent organizations can transcend an organization's culture

These concepts provide a vantage point to explore more specific ways of getting to know one's own workplace culture.

WAYS TO STUDY ORGANIZATIONAL CULTURE

Much of the research on organizational culture is done by sociologists and anthropologists who are outsiders looking into a particular organization or organizations. Members of school organizations do not typically engage in this kind of activity; however, in order to better understand one's organizational culture some form of self-exploration is needed. This self-exploration is congruent with the concept of reflective practice developed by Argyris and Schon (1974) and discussed in chapter 1. Seeing and understanding something as subtle and ambiguous as the culture of an organization can be very challenging. Failing to do so, however, can lead to the calamity revealed in the MVSD case. Developing and using alternative methods for examining the culture of an organization are skills organizational leaders can ill afford to be without.

The methods for examining an organization's culture can be divided generally into two categories: quantitative and qualitative. Those with a bent toward the positivisitic paradigm may favor measurement devices such as surveys and structured interviews, whereas those favoring the paradigms of interpretism and criticism may prefer methods that rely more on direct observation, review of documents, and unstructured interviews. Some researchers argue that the complexity of organizational cultures requires the use of multiple methods, and that a qualitative approach is more appropriate.

Schein (1985) offers a systematic process to "expose oneself to the culture [of an organization] in a natural way" (p. 114):

1. *Entry and focus on surprises.* Particularly when new to an organization, one's attention is caught by events that seem out of the ordinary. One example would be the incident reported in the MVSD case of students threatening physical harm to a student they suspected of intending to burn the American flag. This and other incongruent behaviors may give some hint to deep cultural values.

2. *Systematic observation and checking.* Through careful and systematic observations one can attempt to verify "surprises" as reflective of the culture and not random or idiosyncratic events.

3. *Locating a motivated insider.* Often in an organization there are persons in important positions who are very concerned about patterns of behavior they see as disturbing. These persons may be of assistance in clarifying and further deciphering patterns and underlying assumptions.

4. *Revealing the surprises, puzzlements, and hunches.* Once a rapport has been established with a motivated insider, it may be appropriate to share one's observations, reactions, and hunches about what seems to be going on in the organization's culture. This should be done in a manner that is not accusatory but rather in a process of mutual exploration and understanding.

5. *Joint exploration to find explanations.* With the assistance of the concerned insider, systematically explore hunches for their underlying assumptions and patterns among them. Care needs to be taken to minimize defensiveness of the insider, but at the same time an attempt needs to be made to gather essential information and insights that may be taken for granted.

6. *Formalizing hypotheses.* As a consensus emerges about what seems to be going on with the culture and some underlying assumptions behind certain behaviors, tentative hypotheses should be formed about these basic as-

sumptions. You and the insider(s) should determine what data are needed to confirm or disprove your tentative hypotheses. For example, are the students of the MVSD truly concerned about patriotism or are they using such an incident as an opportunity to vent their frustration over other concerns?

7. *Systematic checking and consolidation.* With the hypotheses as a focus, further gathering of information is needed. A variety of methods are worthy of consideration, including formal interviews, systematic observations, content analysis of documents, and gathering of stories and other artifacts.

8. *Pushing to the level of assumptions.* The most difficult part of this process is to go beyond stated values and attempt to understand the deeper layer of assumptions beneath.

9. *Perpetual recalibration.* As a clearer picture emerges about the underlying assumptions, these conclusions can be shared and discussed with a wider audience. The purpose of these discussions is to further test the accuracy of the conclusions to stimulate reflection by important members of the organization. Again care is needed to minimize defensiveness and/or embarrassment. These discussions should provide important information and aid in fine-tuning or revising conclusions.

10. *Formal written description.* The ultimate test is whether the insights garnered can be articulated clearly and concisely in writing. The statement should be checked for accuracy by participating insiders. The written analysis serves as an important record subject to further revisions and new insights. It can also serve as a basis for planning changes. (pp. 113–19)

Schein stresses the importance of a historical perspective and the exploration of critical incidents. (Critical incidents are events that heighten people's attention and may cause a considerable amount of reflection.) He also emphasizes the concept of triangulation, or multiple perspectives, for developing inferences about an organization's culture.

Rousseau (1990) suggests that organizational culture is a "continuum from the unconscious processes to highly observable structures and patterns of activity . . . " (p. 159). Her continuum begins with fundamental assumptions in the center and moves outward through values, behavioral norms, patterns of behavior, and artifacts. Hidden assumptions are the most subjective and deepest elements of culture, and thus are more difficult to decipher, whereas artifacts, at the perimeter of this continuum, are more observable and may include rituals, routines, dress, logos, and slogans. Rousseau's continuum suggests a linkage between the most observable artifact and an underlying assumption.

For example, the routine of a school principal walking around the school at certain times of the day could reveal certain aspects of the school's culture; in other words, underlying what seems to be a benign routine may be a discernible pattern of behavior. An observer can notice, for example, how the routine is conducted, the amount of time involved, who is or is not spoken to, what is said, and any variability in the routine from day to day. From these observations one can surmise the behavioral norms that influence this activity. Members of the organization may expect the principal to be seen nearly everywhere in the course of the day and to engage teachers and students in brief conversations. These norms suggest the importance to members of the school of direct contacts with the principal and the value they place on the personal reinforcement that comes from these contacts. One of the underlying assumptions of this routine is that the principal will be better informed and, as a result, will be more in tune with what is going on and, hopefully, more responsive to the needs of the school.

Deal and Peterson (1990) argue for "sizing up the situation" or reading the culture by "watching, sensing, listening, interpreting, using all of one's senses, and employing intuition when necessary" (pp. 16–17). They suggest starting the process by examining the history of the organization: its past heroes and heroines and the stories and special events that people remember. At the same time, a principal must listen to the key voices of the present and identify the dreams and aspirations that members hold for the organization that may permit a consensus in engaging desirable changes. Their suggestions (pp. 17–19) for "reading the culture" include recognizing

- "priests" and "priestesses" who "minister" to the needs of the school
- storytellers who re-create the past and personify contemporary exploits
- gossips who keep everyone current on contemporary matters of importance and trivia as well
- spies, counterspies, and moles who carry on subterranean negotiations that enable an equilibrium to be maintained between the power brokers of the school

The information generated by these observations should increase an administrator's understanding of the nature of the informal networks within the organization and the underlying assumptions that are of most importance to the organization's key members.

This sizing-up process may be aided by Whyte's (1961) symbolic interaction approach of participating in events, observing behavior firsthand, and interviewing (or having numerous informal discussions). Whyte employs four concepts: interaction, activities, sentiments, and symbols. In observing interactions among individuals one looks for frequency, duration, and origination. In activities one looks for what people do when working, during breaks, at lunch, and during horseplay. Sentiments are not always directly observable but can be inferred from what people say or do; they give some indication of how people feel about themselves, other people, their work, and the organization. Symbols include words, objects, conditions, acts, and characteristics of people that help explain relationships between people and their environment; physical appearance, cleanliness, and use of space can symbolize what people value in an organization. When linked together these concepts can reveal much about an organization's culture.

Bryman (1991) reminds us that when using these qualitative methods, it is most important to "[*see*] *through the eyes* of one's subjects. In a sense this is the *sine qua non* of qualitative research" (p. 206). In other words, as we observe the various interactions within and objects of our organization, we attempt to "walk in the other person's shoes." It helps to speculate on what others see, think, feel, and assume in regard to a variety of symbols. For example, we may not personally become very emotional when hearing or singing our national anthem, but we can observe tears and pride in others. We can gain more insight about what people feel and value by accepting their emotionality in events we may consider less significant.

According to Schein (1985, pp. 128-35), viewing an organizational culture through the eyes of its participants can be achieved through group interviews. His approach includes providing members of the organization with some general understandings of various dimensions to culture and leading group members through a discussion of these dimensions with prompting questions.

1. *The organization's relationship to its environment:* Who are we? What is our core mission? our justification for survival? What and who are relevant environments (e.g., economic, political, technological, sociocultural)? What is our position vis-à-vis these environments (e.g., dominating, symbiotic, dominated)?

2. *The nature of reality and truth, the basis for decisions:* What are the organization's basic assumptions about physical, social, and subjective reality? How do members of the organization determine when something is "true" or "real" (e.g., by tradition, religious/moral dogma, revelations by authorities, rational/legal means, open debate, trial and error, and/or scientific test)?

   a. *The nature of time:* What are the organization's basic assumptions about the nature and structure of time (e.g., the past, present, and future; linear, monochronic, polychronic, cyclical; length of cycles)?

   b. *The nature of space:* What are the organization's basic assumptions about the nature of space, its availability, its symbolic meaning, and norms of "distance"?

3. *The nature of human nature:* What basic assumptions are held about human nature (e.g., humans are basically "bad," "good," or neutral)? How are these assumptions applied at the employee and managerial levels (e.g., humans are basically fixed at birth, or mutable and perfectible)?

4. *The nature of human activity:* What assumptions are implicit in the problem-solving approaches adopted by a group?

5. *The nature of human relationships:* What are the basic assumptions about how relationships should be conducted so that basic needs of love and aggression are constructively managed (e.g., lineally, collaterally, or individually)? What assumptions underlie the management of power, control, influence, intimacy, and affection (e.g., autocracy, paternalism, consultation, participation, delegation, and collegiality)?

In addition to these probing questions, for each of the five dimensions Schein provides relevant concepts for interpreting group comments, analytical methods to use in group discussion, and in some cases alternative methods.

Time, patience, and caution are needed when trying to identify underlying assumptions about an organization's culture. The need for multiple methods and cross-checking of observations is self-evident. Then, if one assumes that members can get a reasonable handle on the nature of their organization's culture, what happens next?

MANAGING AN ORGANIZATIONAL CULTURE

Whether management of an organization's culture is possible is linked in some ways to how one views the concept of culture. Smircich (1983) suggests that theorists tend to conceptualize culture in one of two ways: organizations *as* cultures or organizations *have* cultures. According to the first view, the culture of an organization is intrinsic in nature and somewhat immutable, whereas the view that organizations have cultures suggests that these cultures are more easily manipulated and changed. In any regard, persons in leadership roles who need to improve an organization's performance and/or its health will tend to gravitate to the latter view, in part because it encourages greater use of the organization's culture as one important strategy to guide needed changes. As Weick (1985a) explains,

> If beliefs, values, and exemplars diverge and become more idiosyncratic [in an organization], there is a great necessity for detailed planning. But there is also a greater possibility that the detailed plans will not be implemented as intended, because they will be interpreted in diverse ways and lead to divergent actions. Thus the substitutability of culture for strategic plans may be asymmetrical. Culture can substitute for plans more effectively than plans can substitute for culture. (p. 383)

Bolman and Deal (1991) raise an additional issue concerning the culture of an organization and its relationship to management. Their concern is whether the culture of an organization shapes its leaders or the leaders shape the culture. It is the old chicken-or-egg debate: Is an organization successful because of its culture, or does a cohesive culture result from an organization's success? In any event, Bolman and Deal suggest that "managers who take the time to understand symbolic forms and activities and then go on to encourage their use can help create an effective organization if what the organization stands for is isomorphic with the challenges of the environment or marketplace" (p. 269). A good fit is critical, as demonstrated by the MVSD superintendent's experience in trying to create a new culture of excellence. As noble as this vision was, it did not match well with the existing culture or subcultures.

Also we must appreciate that most administrators inherit their organization's already existing culture unless they have had the unusual opportunity to start up a brand-new operation or school:

Most principals must work with a cultural tapestry that is already woven. They must somehow reinforce thin spots or tears, shape it to cover different or changed surfaces, or even try to reverse the fabric without unraveling the shared meaning. There is a delicate balance between a principal's doing nothing and doing harm. The Chinese call this balance *wei-wu,* the place between inaction and undue force. This balance is at the center of effective leadership and cultural change. (Deal & Peterson, 1990, p. 14)

The advice of Deal and Peterson is well supported by the research of Rossman, Corbett, and Firestone (1988). In their case studies of three secondary schools they uncovered the importance of core values and the difficulty in altering them. They concluded, "Some norms are untouchable and exempt from tampering, and others are more pliant" (p. 125). For example, in one school teachers described the importance of the classroom's being a private sanctuary not to be violated by external forces. In another school, the mission of producing good citizens was considered almost sacred. Interestingly enough, in each of these schools these values were not held by a vast majority, but rather were believed fervently by a small but influential minority to which the majority tended to defer. Rossman, Corbett, and Firestone used the metaphor of a high priest and a close circle of believers to describe the influence and control exhibited by these small but powerful groups.

In their book *The Principal's Role in Shaping a School Culture,* Deal and Peterson (1990) provide a number of concrete suggestions principals can use to shape or reinforce a school's existing culture. Thinking of the principal as symbol, potter, poet, actor, and healer, Deal and Peterson explore a number of insights suggested by these metaphors.

1. The principal as *symbol:*   affirm values through dress, behavior, attention, routines.
2. The principal as *potter:*   shape and be shaped by the school's heroes, rituals, ceremonies, symbols.
3. The principal as *poet:*   use language to reinforce values and sustain the school's best image of itself.
4. The principal as *actor:*   improvise in the school's inevitable dramas.
5. The principal as *healer:*   oversee transitions and change in the life of the school. (p. 20)

Deal and Peterson stress further that "Shaping the culture is *not* an exact science. Shaping a culture is indirect, intuitive, and largely unconscious" (p. 20).

Prince (1989) shares the view that the culture of a school and its community is an "invisible force" that can block the best intentions of school reformers. He introduces "the idea that change may be considered as a process that can be managed by changing cultural attitudes" (p. 5). He coins the phrase *systemic cultural renorming* to describe his strategy for creating new norms. Essentially the strategy builds on the importance of developing choices for people in an organization that emerges from a systematic process of organizational self-examination. He draws on the methodology associated with organization development (Fullan, Miles, & Taylor, 1978; and Callan & Trusty, 1987) and the use of systems theory (Klir, 1985; Pugh, 1969; and Immegart & Pilecki, 1973) for approaching the change process.[1] Even though Prince stresses a more organized and rational approach to renorming a school or school district, as compared with Deal and Peterson's "indirect, intuitive and largely unconscious" approach, they do share the same goal of shaping and developing new norms in one's organization.

ETHICAL IMPLICATIONS OF ORGANIZATIONAL CULTURE

Those involved in shaping and developing a new culture in an organization face a possible moral dilemma. This dilemma arises in part from how much the culture is intrinsically woven into the fabric of the organization and the degree to which people are invested in it. Any efforts at removing old symbols and substituting new ones go to the heart and soul of persons in the organization. Such changes place a burden of responsibility on persons who are interested in creating a new culture. It is not a choice that one person can or should take lightly or make unilaterally. As Jones (1985) reminds us, "Change is reprehensible when it disregards the value of what preceded and when it becomes a value—an alleged good—for its own sake, without consideration of the consequences. . . . What makes conduct 'wrong' and therefore unethical, is that someone suffers embarrassment, harm, or deprivation because of others' actions" (pp. 242–43).

Culture is often closely associated with personal meaning and identity. Weick (1985b) observes: "There is no shortage of attention to money. Unfortunately, the same cannot be said for meaning. This is why the concept of culture is significant" (p. 388). The upside of culture is its potential to be supportive and reinforcing to individuals in an organization; the downside is that certain people's rights can be abused or neglected, particularly if the process is one of imposition by authority or only superficially democratic.

Whether democratic or consensus-based change processes are used, sensitivity to the ethical dimensions is still in order. Mirvis (1985) suggests that ethical and practical conflicts can emerge when cultural intervention is attempted over issues of rights to privacy, free and informed consent, and freedom from harm. Jones (1985) helps put in perspective the decision to intervene in an organization's culture. He suggests the goal for such efforts should be "to participate in efforts to improve life in the workplace whenever one's assistance can contribute to designing environments that *provide pleasant social and sensory experiences, purvey good will*, and *promote a sense of well-being*" (p. 252; emphasis added).

---

[1] Organization development (OD) is an organizationwide, systematic problem-solving process that draws on social science theories and research for identifying needs and implementing needed changes.

CONCLUSION

Organizational culture as a metaphor opens the door to understanding many subtle dimensions of an organization, helping us more fully appreciate the emotional attachment we and others have to our school, college, or agency. However, to gain the emotional support that an organization's culture can provide, we must give something in return. Our membership fee is often a diminution of individual autonomy, reduced through our compliance with certain norms and expectations. In organizations with an integrated culture there is even greater pressure for conformity. The more differentiated or fragmented the culture, the greater likelihood of balancing the gains against the costs of membership. But then again, the stress of coping with competitive subcultures may wipe out any perceived gains.

Thinking of organizations as cultures permits a greater appreciation for ambiguity, which often is viewed as something to be reduced or eliminated rather than acknowledged and accepted. The celebration of diversity and the legitimation of voices seldom heard can be important benefits to accepting ambiguity as a natural phenomenon.

Although we often are quick to recognize the influence of the environment on an organization, the concept of organizational culture demonstrates the impact clearly. For example, we can see how occupational groups can have an impact on shaping an organization's culture; teacher organizations have certainly played a significant role in defining the type and quality of education offered in a school. Other important beliefs also permeate our schools and play a role in how we organize or view the school; for instance, generally accepted beliefs about the importance of individuality, uniqueness, and creativity make schools in the United States different in some respects from schools in Japan, where there tends to be a greater emphasis on group values and compliance.

Organizational culture also helps to explain the idiosyncratic nature of individual schools that exist in a common milieu. We often puzzle at how two schools in the same community with essentially the same conditions and resources will vary so greatly from one another. A closer look reveals many subtle differences that can be attributed to the belief systems, common understandings, and expectations within each school. The leadership styles of the principals may in part explain these differences, but we should keep in mind that leadership style is often a proxy for the school's culture; from a cultural perspective, leaders and group support are inextricably linked in a mutually causal relationship.

To better understand a particular organization's culture, it is necessary to go beyond the more obvious artifacts and ferret out underlying assumptions. We also can try to see events and rituals through a different set of lenses. Stories, for example, take on more meaning when we place them in a cultural context; they can be quite revealing of what people value most in the past, present, and future. Patterns of behavior (e.g., gift giving, coffee breaks, presence at special events) send a message to various members of the organization. These behaviors and other activities often appear random and unconnected; however, the process of examining one's own organizational culture provides the opportunity to see these events as artifacts of subtle but important value systems.

Being armed with many new insights about what makes an organization tick does not give us license to act as we may. Our knowledge carries with it responsibility for how we put this knowledge to use. Some self-awareness of what we personally value in our relationships with people in an organization is needed in order to value the relationships and aspirations of others. We may grow to appreciate the long-term importance of creating and/or preserving a healthy environment based on mutual respect. Rosenholtz (1989) came to a similar conclusion based on her research in schools: "Finally, in successful schools, regardless of all past history, shared principles govern. We find most often in successful schools a capacity to cherish individuality and inspire communality that is the hallmark of our loftiest institutions" (p. 221).

MVSD CASE REVISITED

It is speculative, but one cannot help wondering how the superintendent of the MVSD might have approached the school district differently, so that the clash of wills was avoided. It is interesting to think about the additional range of insights and options that might have come from thinking of the MVSD in cultural terms. For example, would the superintendent have benefited more from an understanding of the history of the MVSD, past efforts at improving itself, and aspirations people had for the future? Would she have discovered some common ground that could have been used to avoid the conflict she experienced with other administrators? Did she rely too much on her intellectual credentials and academic reputation to overpower people whom she felt were less competent and supportive? How open and inclusive was her vision of academic excellence? Did her stress on academic excellence trample upon other sacred values, such as a sense of community and personal loyalty?

It is clear her five-year plan to transform the culture of the MVSD came too late, given the dissension and polarization that already existed. It placed considerable emphasis on a rational approach that was tightly controlled at the center and where outside experts were more valued than the contributions of people from within. The strategy placed the members who were on the periphery and in the various subcultures in a position of having to defend their values. The students decried the restrictions on access to school facilities because their sense of community was threatened.

The foregoing plausible explanations represent but a sample of insights that can be identified by examining the MVSD case from the metaphor of organizational culture. The discussion questions and suggested activities that follow provide an opportunity to develop additional insights.

DISCUSSION QUESTIONS

1. If a colleague asked you to define organizational culture, how would you respond?
2. As an educational practitioner, what methods do you believe would best allow you to better understand your organization's culture?
3. Again thinking about the culture of your organization, what aspects do you believe are worthy of preserving and what aspects should be changed? Why?

4. Assuming some aspects of your organization's culture are in need of change, how would you suggest going about making these changes? What responses should you anticipate? How would you work with these responses?

5. What, if any, ethical problems or issues do you see in changing an organization's culture?

SUGGESTED ACTIVITIES

1. Drawing on the organizational culture concepts proffered in this chapter, revisit the MVSD case and identify additional plausible explanations for the superintendent's eventual downfall.

2. Assume for the moment that you are the superintendent of Mountain View School District. Develop a set of strategies congruent with concepts of organizational culture that you would follow to improve the current situation.

3. As mentioned in the introduction to section 1, diagnostic reading can help in discerning the character of a situation. For some specified period of time, become a participant-observer (continue to be an active participant while attempting to observe the behavior of others in a conscious, systematic way) of your workplace and diagnose its culture. Draw upon the definitions, concepts, and methods for examining an organization's culture outlined in this chapter, and develop and implement a plan for discovering specific aspects of your organization's culture.

4. Conduct a class debate on the ethical implications of altering an organization's culture. One group should argue for correctness of intervening and changing an organization's culture. A second group should argue against taking such action. Follow up the debate by generating some general ethical principles that should guide our actions in dealing with an organization's culture.

5. Identify a recent critical incident in your organization and analyze it from an organizational culture perspective.

6. Identify four or five cultural guideposts that you believe are important ideas to keep in mind as you go about performing your daily duties as a member of an organization.

7. Think of your organization's current culture. What should be publicly acclaimed? What should be changed? What new symbols should be added? Why?

REFERENCES

Argyris, C., & Schon, D. A. (1974). *Theory in practice.* San Francisco: Jossey-Bass.

Bolman, L. G., & Deal, T. E. (1991). *Reframing organizations: Artistry, choice, and leadership.* San Francisco: Jossey-Bass.

Bryman, A. (1991). Street corner society as a model for research into organizational culture. In P. J. Frost, L. F. Moore, M. R. Louis, C. C. Lundberg, & J. Martin (Eds.), *Reframing organizational culture* (pp. 205–14). Newbury Park: Sage.

Callan, M. F., & Trusty, F. M. (Eds.). (1987). *Organizational development.* Bloomington: Phi Delta Kappa.

Czarniawska-Joerges, B. (1991). Culture is the medium of life. In P. J. Frost, L. F. Moore, M. R. Louis, C. C. Lundberg, & J. Martin (Eds.), *Reframing organizational culture* (pp. 285–97). Newbury Park: Sage.

Davies, R. J., & Weiner, N. (1985). Cultural perspective on the study of industrial relations. In P. J. Frost, L. F. Moore, M. R. Louis, C. C. Lundberg, & J. Martin (Eds.), *Organizational culture* (pp. 355-72). Beverly Hills: Sage.

Deal, T. E., & Peterson D. (1990). *The principal's role in shaping a school culture.* Washington, DC: U.S. Department of Education, Office of Educational Research and Development.

Frost, P. J., Moore, L. F., Louis, M. R., Lundberg, C. C., & Martin, J. (Eds.). (1985). *Organizational culture.* Beverly Hills, CA: Sage.

Frost, P. J., Moore, L. F., Louis, M. R., Lundberg, C. C., & Martin, J. (Eds.). (1991). *Reframing organizational culture.* Newbury Park: Sage.

Fullan, M., Miles, M., & Taylor, G. (1978). *OD in schools: The state of the art.* Toronto: Ontario Institute for the Study of Education.

Habermas, J. (1971). *Knowledge and human interests.* Boston: Beacon Press.

Immegart, G. L., & Pilecki, F. J. (1973). *An introduction to systems analysis for the educational administrator.* Reading, MA: Addison-Wesley.

Jones, M. O. (1985). Is ethics the issue? In P. J. Frost, L. F. Moore, M. R. Louis, C. C. Lundberg, & J. Martin (Eds.), *Organizational culture* (pp. 235-52). Beverly Hills: Sage.

Klir, G. J. (1985). *Architecture of systems problem solving.* New York: Plenum Press.

Martin, J., & Meyerson, D. (1988). Organizational culture and the denial, channeling, and acknowledgement of ambiguity. In L. R. Pondy, R. J. Boland Jr., & H. Thomas (Eds.), *Managing ambiguity and change* (pp. 93-126). New York: Wiley.

Meyerson, D. E. (1991). Acknowledging and uncovering ambiguities in cultures. In P. J. Frost, L. F. Moore, M. R. Louis, C. C. Lundberg, & J. Martin (Eds.), *Reframing organizational culture* (pp. 254-70). Newbury Park: Sage.

Mirvis, P. H. (1985). Managing research while researching managers. In P. J. Frost, L. F. Moore, M. R. Louis, C. C. Lundberg, & J. Martin (Eds.), *Organizational culture* (pp. 201-32). Beverly Hills: Sage.

Moore, M. (1985). Culture as culture. In P. J. Frost, L. F. Moore, M. R. Louis, C. C. Lundberg, & J. Martin (Eds.), *Organizational culture* (pp. 373-78). Beverly Hills: Sage.

Prince, J. D. (1989). *Invisible forces: School reform versus school culture.* Bloomington: Phi Delta Kappa.

Pugh, D. S. (Ed.). (1969). *Systems thinking: Selected readings.* Baltimore: Penguin.

Rosen, M. (1991). Scholars, travelers, thieves: On concept, method, and cunning in organizational ethnography. In P. J. Frost, L. F. Moore, M. R. Louis, C. C. Lundberg, & J. Martin (Eds.), *Reframing organizational culture* (pp. 271-84). Newbury Park: Sage.

Rosenholtz, S. J. (1989). *Teachers' workplace.* White Plains, NY: Longman.

Rossman, G. B., Corbett, H. D., & Firestone, W. A. (1988). *Change and effectiveness in schools.* Albany: State University of New York Press.

Rousseau, D. M. (1990). Assessing organizational culture: Case for multiple methods. In B. Schneider (Ed.), *Organizational climate and culture* (pp. 153-92). San Francisco: Jossey-Bass.

Schein, E. H. (1985). *Organizational culture and leadership.* San Francisco: Jossey-Bass.

Sergiovanni, T. J., & Corbally, J. E. (1984). *Leadership and organizational culture.* Urbana: University of Illinois Press.

Smircich, L. (1983). Concepts of culture and organizational analysis. *Administrative Science Quarterly, 28*(3), 338-58.

Trice, H. M. (1991). Comments and discussion. In P. J. Frost, L. F. Moore, M. R. Louis, C. C. Lundberg, & J. Martin (Eds.), *Reframing organizational culture* (pp. 298-308). Newbury Park: Sage.

Weick, K. E. (1969). *The social psychology of organizing.* Reading, MA: Addison-Wesley.

Weick, K. E. (1982, June). Administering education in loosely coupled schools. *Phi Delta Kappan*, pp. 673–76.

Weick, K. E. (1985a). The significance of corporate culture. In P. J. Frost, L. F. Moore, M. R. Louis, C. C. Lundberg, & J. Martin (Eds.), *Organizational culture* (pp. 381–90). Beverly Hills: Sage.

Weick, K. E. (1985b). Sources of order in underorganized systems: Themes in recent organizational theory. In Y. S. Lincoln (Ed.), *Organizational theory and inquiry* (pp. 106–36). Beverly Hills, CA: Sage.

Whyte, W. F. (1961). *Men at work*. Homewood, IL: Dorsey Press/Richard D. Irwin.

chapter 3

Organizations from a Political Perspective

If organizations have cultures, then organizational politics are inevitable. As suggested in chapter 2, people in organizations form allegiances and close personal relationships often held together by shared values. This cohesiveness among various subcultures in an organization can contribute to a we–they feeling, which in turn can lead to further polarization among various groups of employees. Hazard Adams (1976) used the metaphor of academic tribes to describe competing groups in universities. The question is not whether politics should occur in organizations but rather what kind of politics should prevail. Bolman and Deal (1991) write:

> Politics can be and often is sordid and destructive. But politics can also be the vehicle for achieving noble purposes, and managers can be benevolent politicians. Organizational change and effectiveness depend on such managers. The constructive politician recognizes political realities in organizations and knows how to fashion an agenda, build a network of support, and negotiate effectively both with those who might advance and with those who might oppose the agenda. (p. 224)

From Bolman and Deal's perspective, politics is not a four-letter word. Indeed, they go so far as to suggest that good politics and political leadership in organizations are essential. In this chapter we will explore various dimensions associated with politics, including definitions and related concepts, focusing particularly on power and conflict. In addition, we will discuss how politics may be better understood or studied in an organization with an eye toward how administrators may be more effective political leaders. We will revisit the Mountain View School District (MVSD) case to demonstrate how organizations may be viewed from the metaphor of politics.

NEED FOR ORGANIZATIONAL POLITICS

Are politics inevitable? This question is often asked by persons uncomfortable with the idea of politics in part because they perceive politics in the worst light. With the advent of television, the opportunity to observe in prime time raucous debates, public posturing, and deception creates a longing for a better way. As negative as this image may be, however, it does not represent the whole picture of politics, especially in an organizational context. In fact, this kind of negative image often prevents members of an organization from more fully appreciating how politics work in their organization. The twin influences of political cynicism and naïveté can seriously impair the capacity to reframe a variety of organizational situations that are political in nature.

The question of the inevitability of politics can best be answered by examining the underlying causes of political behavior. Political scientists use the concept of zero-sum conditions to explain political behavior; that is, in most organizations, resources (e.g., money, space, expertise, and competence) are limited and must be shared. Nonzero-sum conditions suggest unlimited resources and minimize the need to compete for them. Educational organizations can aptly be described as working often under zero-sum conditions. It is rare to encounter a school in which there are not problems associated with shortages of funds, space, and qualified personnel. The presence of transportable buildings on school lots provides testimony to the consequence of zero-sum circumstances.

In addition, educational organizations, particularly schools, are relatively flat organizations; that is, proportionately there are a limited number of positions in the hierarchy to which persons may aspire for promotion and higher status. Many schools, particularly small-sized schools, have only one or two administrative positions to covet by persons desiring upward mobility and recognition. The limited number of opportunities can result in the "politics of getting ahead" in an organization.

A third influence on the political conditions of schools takes us back to organizations as cultures. Because of the presence of multiple value systems, reasonable people can disagree over both ends and means. These disagreements over goals and ways of attaining them can take many forms. For example, in the Mountain View School District there was an initial agreement between some faculty, students, and the new superintendent to develop a school district with an excellent academic reputation. As the superintendent moved forward on this agenda, however, disagreements emerged over her methods: Students questioned the relevance of academics to their aspirations to find a job after graduation, and teachers worried when some administrative colleagues were forced to resign. The harder the superintendent pushed her vision, the greater the rift. In educational organizations, the means for attaining goals can be as important as the goals themselves: "Organizational goals arise not from fiat at the top, but from an ongoing process of negotiation and interaction among the key players in the system" (Bolman & Deal, 1991, p. 189). The superintendent of the MVSD did not take into account this point of view.

The debate over ends and means manifests itself in the establishment of goals for American education and the curricula to be taught in our schools. Klein's (1991) *The*

Politics of Curriculum Decision-Making explores the sociopolitical influences on the content and materials used in schools. In that book Goodlad (1991) writes:

> In sociopolitical arenas the interests of the decision makers transcend ideas, even when debate often appears to be focused on getting the "best" decisions. The tools of power usually dominate over the rules of discourse. . . . Becoming players in these [political] arenas creates some troublesome problems for educators. But to become a bystander and to simultaneously expect decisions to be made in the best interests of children and youth and those who teach them in schools is to be naive. (p. 13)

Goodlad lays before us a reality that many in education wish not to engage: macrolevel politics at federal and state levels determining the curricula of American schools. The school often is caught in the cross fire of unresolved political debates and becomes a microcosm of the larger society. For example, the MVSD felt the pressure on schools to address our societal concerns of cultural diversity; but teachers had different views on this problem, and some became quite resistant to the new policy directions.

Politics seem to be ubiquitous and thus difficult to avoid or escape. Morgan (1986) suggests that "it is useful to remember that in its original meaning, the idea of politics stems from the view that, where interests are divergent, society should provide a means of allowing individuals to reconcile their differences through consultation and negotiations" (p. 142). At the organizational or micro level, it can be argued that schools need to provide their members a means by which they can resolve their differences. This, unfortunately, is often lacking, and it is left to each person's ingenuity to figure out how to cope with inevitable conflicts. Some persons come up with creative and effective ideas, but quite often conflicts go unresolved and begin to affect morale and organizational performance. Yet many organizations eschew any recognition of natural competition and consequently methods for finding productive outlets. Typically our educational organizations provide little or no formal guidance in dealing with the pluralistic views that swirl in and around a school.

The conditions of limited resources and conflict over ends and means set the stage for political activity. It is not predetermined that members in an organization must resort to unbridled competition in order to satisfy their expectations or needs. Other styles, such as cooperation, can emerge, as is observable in the *Hope Springs Eternal* case in section 3. In Western culture, however, we seem to cherish competition and stress the importance of winning and being number one. Our obsession with big time sports, especially with unlimited television coverage of football, baseball, basketball, and hockey, reinforces this cultural value. Competition and the need to win, sometimes at all costs, are so integral in our everyday experiences that it requires a conscious effort to minimize the negative impact of these excesses. It is hoped that our examination of important political concepts can open the door to a more balanced view and a positive use of politics in organizations.

DEFINITIONS AND RELATED CONCEPTS

Definitions of Organizational Politics

Politics can trace its origin to the Greek word *polis* or an "aggregate of many members." According to Aristotle, politics provides an opportunity for "creating order out of diversity while avoiding forms of totalitarian rule" (Morgan, 1986, p. 142). Aristotle also claimed, "It is evident that the state is a creation of nature, and that man is by nature a political animal" (quoted in Ross, 1954, p. 45).

Gray (1984) defines politics as being "concerned with the deliberate and purposeful attempt to change the balance of power in an organization, usually in favour of the protagonist" (p. 113). The notion of power in politics is implied by Bacharach and Lawler (1980) when they state that "politics is a series of competitive tactical encounters. These encounters entail an assessment of the situation (that is, an evaluation of one's power vis-à-vis that of significant competitors), and a selection of countertactics by which to thwart the competitors' tactics" (p. 7). Parker (1984) takes a slightly different approach when he links politics to culture by suggesting that "politics in organizations is more the manipulation of symbols and metaphors, myths and legends; the interpretation of facts rather than facts themselves" (p. xiii).

These views suggest that sociopolitical arenas (such as schools) often engage in activities that can be described as political. These activities are designed to gain influence over events and decisions in order to maximize one's share of the resource pie or to influence the ends and means of the organization. In the pursuit of interests by individuals and/or groups, conflict may naturally occur and power is needed to maintain order in the organization.

Many important and related concepts of politics emerge when considering the implications of the foregoing definitions. The concepts of partisan groups, pluralism, coalitions, power, conflict, and negotiations are some examples.

Pluralism and Partisan Groups in Organizations

Gamson (1968) focuses on two major players in an organization: authorities and partisans. Persons in authority positions basically have the legal power to make binding decisions. Gamson describes the relationship between authorities and partisans as follows: "Authorities are the recipients of targets of influence, and the agents or initiators of social control. Potential partisans have the opposite role—as agents or initiators of influence, and targets or recipients of social control" (p. 76).

In schools, the principal is often the recipient of lobbying by teachers and parents who seek a judgment in their favor, and the principal seeks ways to control the actions of teachers. For example, the time allocations for different subjects at the elementary school level are enforced by administrators and monitored through the review of lesson plans. Such policies and practices are designed to ensure teachers' compliance. Teachers, in turn, attempt to influence these policies by drawing attention to the different needs of various age levels and the need for setting priorities for what is taught. Primary teachers are known for their emphasis on reading and math over science. Intermediate-level teachers tend to desire more time on science and less on direct instruction in reading. These preferences reflect what might be called a "dance" between authority (principal) and partisans (teachers) in determining acceptable policies and practices.

We observed the dynamics of partisan groups and authorities in the MVSD case. The superintendent and associate superintendent attempted to address issues of cultural diversity by imposing a policy requiring teachers to give attention to these issues. The teachers balked at this level of control and attempted through group action and resistance to alter the new cultural diversity policy; they felt they could not rewrite the policy per se but could resist its implementation and by doing so force a compromise.

The task of authorities in organizations is to attain a level of social control and predictability. When partisan groups, however, are not enamored with the efforts at control, they rely on a variety of tactics to reduce or change the controls. In this dynamic interchange between control and resistance, the authorities' greatest fears are having their authority undermined and having partisan groups polarize. Unfortunately, this is what happened to the superintendent of the MVSD; her experience illustrates the delicate balance authorities must achieve in bringing about control.

Power in Organizations

Korda (1975) suggests that "all life is a game of power" (p. 3). This notion may be overwhelming at first, but Korda attempts to challenge our conventional thinking and help us realize the degree to which power plays a part in our lives:

> Some of the best players I know developed their basic techniques [of power] in such places as fruit markets, where the choice of the individual pieces of fruit one wants as contrasted to those being palmed off on one, can be used to study such concepts of resistance under pressure, feigned hesitation, whining and compromise. Childhood itself teaches us many useful techniques— playing one parent off against the other, withholding affection, throwing up when all else fails—but most people forget these valuable techniques in the process of becoming adults. School, on the other hand, provides lessons in the power game which are seldom forgotten by anyone, particularly the ability to look busy and industrious when one is in fact doing nothing, and the essential knowledge of how to deal with bullies, or becoming one. (pp. 5-6)

Daily experiences in schools provide direct opportunities not only for students to learn about power but for their teachers as well. We do not have to look far to see teachers being very successful in garnering special favors or unquestioned support from their colleagues or administrators. Administrators often find themselves outmaneuvered by highly respected teachers who enjoy a great deal of admiration in the school and the community. Power and influence take on several dimensions in school situations.

McClelland (1975) points out two aspects of power: the negative aspect of exploitation and dominance, and the positive aspect that can enable the creation of visions and collective goals. The negative view tends to be more observable and possibly more prevalent in educational organizations. It is important, however, to find a balance between the realities of self-interest and viable social goals. Positive uses of power can act as a fulcrum in balancing selfish tendencies against a greater social good. It is important to understand that power is an integral part of a school organization and thus needs to be garnered for its potential benefits. It is not a question of whether power exists but rather how it is used. Boulding (1989) writes, "For individual human beings, power is the ability to get what one wants. The term *power* is also used, however, to describe the ability to achieve common ends for families, groups, organizations of all kinds, churches, corporations, political parties, national states, and so on" (p. 15).

Kotter (1985) puts the power issues in a specifically political perspective when he suggests that managers become "benevolent politicians." He says, "Beyond the yellow brick road of naivete and the mugger's land of cynicism, there is a narrow path, poorly lighted, hard to find, and even harder to stay on once found. People who have the skill and the perseverance to take that path serve us in countless ways. We need more of these people. Many more" (p. xi).

Bolman and Deal (1991) proffer three major areas in which these politician-managers should develop skill and understanding: (1) agenda setting (create a vision and strategy for change), (2) networking and coalition building (build relevant and supportive relationships), and (3) bargaining and negotiating (invent options for mutual gain).

The politician-manager can be further helped by understanding sources of power. Being in a position of power as an administrator in a school is but one source and may not be strong enough to counterbalance power sources that other members of the organization enjoy. The superintendent of the Mountain View School District quickly learned that she had lost position power; she had fallen victim to other power centers. Morgan (1986) identifies 14 sources of power:

1. formal authority
2. control of scarce resources
3. use of organizational structure, rules, and regulations
4. control of decision processes
5. control of knowledge and information
6. control of boundaries
7. ability to cope with uncertainty
8. control of technology
9. interpersonal alliances, networks, and control of "informal organizations"
10. control of counterorganizations
11. symbolism and the management of meaning
12. gender and the management of gender relations
13. structural factors that define the stage of action
14. the power one already has (pp. 158–85)

The MVSD case provides some insight on these power sources and how they influenced the events there. As mentioned, the superintendent initially enjoyed formal authority that gave her legitimate power by virtue of her being the chief administrator in the school district. She had the legal authority to make final decisions as dictated by state law and by policies of the state department of education. This can provide enormous power because it connects to other sources of power as well. For example, as superintendent of schools, she had

- control over the use of discretionary funds
- a major voice in the interpretation of rules and regulations, which tend to be written in ambiguous language
- some discretion in restructuring the central administration of the district (which she attempted and which created a backlash when she overextended her power by forcing some popular administrators to resign)
- potential to influence the outcomes of decision-making processes, which potentially includes postponing crucial decisions and fostering decisions that support one's own agenda (e.g., changing the policies concerning use of buildings)
- the opportunity to serve as a gatekeeper in the sharing of knowledge and information by filtering, summarizing, and analyzing such in a manner that was in accordance with her views
- boundary management potential by virtue of her central office position, which allows the opportunity and legitimacy to be kept informed and to influence what various groups become involved in
- the opportunity to influence the school district's symbols and their meaning for the community, which she exercised in part by her four-year "Plan for Cultural Change at Mountain View School District" and by creating "Ambassadors of Cultural Change"
- an opportunity as a female administrator to appeal to supporters favoring sex equity and to develop respect for her style of management
- credibility as a knowledgeable person and scholar, thus the ability to exercise some influence over academic standards, curriculum, and instruction for the school district

As card players know, a good hand in any game has face cards, aces, and high trump cards. You are not always assured of winning, but at least at the beginning you are playing from a position of strength. In many ways the superintendent of the MVSD was dealt a good hand. Of the 14 sources of power, she had 9. As with cards, not all sources of power are equal, and these sources can shift over time depending on the nature of new conditions and how effectively the so-called power cards are played. For example, being a female administrator gave her an opportunity to manage gender relations from a female perspective and to garner support from those who shared similar views. Initially she was praised for her consultative style, which contrasted dramatically with the authoritarian style of the previous superintendent, who was a male. For unknown reasons, however, the gender card did not play well as a source of power, at least not in the long term, although the gender issue prevailed as a strong argument for her reinstatement as superintendent. She was able to portray herself as a victim of a male conspiracy to resist her authority and to force her resignation; this argument won in the court and was persuasive with the board of education. Meanwhile, as the ad hoc committee on sexism discovered, the charge of sexism was in fact polarizing the community and threatening "the attrition of teachers, especially women."

There were other cards of power that were not in her hand to begin with and in many ways countered her initial strong position of power. Some examples include the ability to cope with uncertainty, control of informal organizations, control of counterorganizations, and control over the stage of the action. Each of these compromised her capacity to influence and maintain control. For example, the ability to cope with uncertainty did not appear to be one of her strongest suits: She attempted to reduce uncertainty through her four-year plan and through the purging of administrators associated with the previous administration. But these efforts were not well received and contributed to her eventual demise. Another circumstance over which she had little control was the stage of action. Most administrators prefer more private conditions, out of the spotlight, in which to debate and resolve issues. Once she initiated her lawsuit, however, it was impossible for her to control the publicity, the subsequent media attention, and the public airing of dirty laundry that a court hearing often engenders.

Eventually the other power sources gained momentum, particularly the informal networks and counterorganizations. The teachers became quite influential through their petition drive, with over 700 signatures calling for the resignation of the superintendent and the associate superintendent. Soon these forces gained sufficient strength to call into question the capacity of the superintendent to reestablish control and leadership. It became increasingly clear to the superintendent that her powers at the MVSD were greatly reduced; in effect, she felt she had no other choice but to resign. She had lost the power game.

Power struggles are endemic to organizations, especially educational organizations that are often the battleground for community conflicts and differing value systems. Power goes with the territory whether we accept its presence or not. Korda (1975) eloquently concluded that "the more mechanical and complicated our world is, the more we need the simplicity of power to guide us and protect us. It's the one gift that allows us to remain human in an inhuman world—for 'the love of power is the love of ourselves'" (p. 261). Power may not be everything, but it is certainly important in getting people to cooperate in attaining common goals in spite of their personal differences.

Conflict in Organizations

The context of American schools continues to undergo significant changes, placing many unresolved conflicts at the schoolhouse doorstep. There are debates over whether schools are properly structured to provide quality education for all children, whether schools are being adequately and equally funded, whether teachers are being properly recognized and supported, whether shifting demographics are contributing to the erosion of public support in schools, and so on. Schools continue to be on the national political agenda, and the halls of government echo with calls for change (cf. Boyd & Kerchner, 1988).

These external, macrolevel conflicts have a way of spilling over into the operation of schools. Administrators and teachers often find themselves confronted by parents and community leaders who believe the school is expecting too much or too little of their children, using or not using the latest curriculum or instructional innovation, or asking for too much money to operate the school. One consequence of these conflicting expectations of a school's community is the division it engenders in the staff. Soon teachers and administrators become locked in debates on the justice of these criticisms and of the calls for various changes (cf. Dow, 1991). These debates lead to conflict and the need for political leadership.

Morgan (1986) takes the position that conflict in organizations is inevitable and offers some insight on its origins:

> Conflict may be personal, interpersonal, or between rival groups and coalitions. It may be built into organizational structures, roles, attitudes, and stereotypes, or arise over a scarcity of resources. It may be explicit or covert. Whatever the reason, and whatever the form it takes, its source rests in some perceived or real divergence of interests. (p. 155)

Hanson (1990) makes a similar point:

> Conflict, in varying degrees and situations, is present in all organizations. When decisions must be made to the satisfaction of some and not to others, conflict will be present or perhaps lurking around the corner. Neither a natural enemy nor inherently bad, conflict should not be repressed or fueled. Rather, it should be managed. (p. 282)

Understanding that conflict is part of the fabric of organizations in general and particularly endemic to educational organizations should alert leaders and administrators to the need for skill in managing these conflicts. Educational leaders and administrators need to be able to read developing situations and analyze interests, understand how these contribute to conflict, and appreciate the respective power relations that exist or that are emerging.

WAYS TO STUDY ORGANIZATIONAL POLITICS

When caught in power struggles or stressful conflict, it is very difficult to step back and analyze what's going on and what options are available. And yet, that is exactly what leaders and administrators must do. Ideally there is no better cure for these conditions than to avoid them in the first place, but this is not always possible, particularly when attempting to make needed changes or redress past wrongs. It is still possible, however, to anticipate conflicts and detect which, and even when, members of the organization will become upset by certain decisions and/or events.

There are some parallels between the study of an organization's culture and the study of its politics. There are methods that are more formal and quantitative and there are approaches that are more natural and qualitative; the major difference is the lens that is being used. In other words, politics are about special interests, competition, use of power, and conflict. The culture of the organization is important because of its role in setting expectations for how the politics are to be played. We should anticipate

- the special interests people have in the organization
- the linkage among these interests to different individuals and respective partisan groups
- the way people typically exercise influence
- the sources of power
- the potential for bargaining and compromise

As with understanding the culture of an organization, the history of an organization plays an important role in predicting future behavior. How people will respond to decisions or opportunities to participate in certain change efforts can in part be understood from how they responded in the past. Past critical events (e.g., hiring of upper-level administrators, settling of teacher contracts, purchasing new and costly equipment, deciding on a new textbook series, parent complaints) reveal who gets involved, what motivates their involvement, what influence different persons had, and, if any conflict emerged, how it was resolved. Informal discussions with different persons over what happened in the past or direct observation of current events can be quite revealing about the organization's politics and political leadership.

These less formal methods help identify key informal leaders, their tactics in gaining influence and control, and their sources of power. Conclusions here should be tentative; nevertheless, such information can help guide the actions of the thoughtful and benevolent politician-manager.

MANAGING ORGANIZATIONAL POLITICS

Important information concerning past political events and the general nature of current politics in one's organization can provide a foundation for exerting political leadership. As stated earlier, a leader or administrator needs a repertoire of skills and approaches to manage the politics of an organization. One important area that will test the best of political leaders is conditions of conflict.

Hanson (1990, pp. 283–85) discusses tactics of conflict management:

- *Expand resources*, which may help to eliminate one possible cause of friction and conflict
- *Establish an appeals system* by providing a formal process for redressing perceived wrongs and which can serve as a relief valve

- *Change interaction patterns* by getting opposing parties together to encounter other points of view
- *Modify reward systems* by giving out rewards for preventing problems and encouraging the feeling of everyone being a winner
- *Create new mergers* by breaking up conflicting units or enlarging units to enable the identification of newer, superordinate goals
- *Clarify role expectations* by reducing ambiguity over responsibilities and duties, resulting in a further reduction of confusion and tension
- *Involve an outside, neutral party* who can bring a sense of rationality to the process, which may open people to compromise
- *Become a conflict sponge* by absorbing responsibility for the conflict, which in turn may help people to lighten up and become more flexible

In addition to these tactics, Thomas (1976), in an often-cited work on conflict management, suggests that in dealing with conflict in an organization, a person should attempt to satisfy his or her own concerns as well as the concerns of others. He advances five styles for dealing with conflict:

- *avoidance* by slowing or ignoring the conflict and hoping that with more time the problem may take care of itself
- *domination* by being highly competitive and determined to win at the possible expense of others
- *accommodation* by appeasement and giving way to others, possibly at one's own expense
- *compromise* by negotiating and looking for deals and trade-offs
- *collaboration* by integrating opposing views, building trust, and finding solutions that enable persons involved to feel they're in a win-win situation

Situations will arise in which different styles will be more or less potent. For example, based on the views of 28 chief executives (Thomas, 1977), when faced with an emergency requiring decisive action, domination and competition against those who may be trying to take advantage of the situation are most appropriate. On the other hand, when faced with issues that are more trivial or of a lesser priority, some cooling off time is needed, and gathering more information is in order; then avoidance is the best option. Accommodation fits well in situations where others are more invested and one desires to minimize one's losses and collect credits for the future. Collaboration fits well in situations where there is no clear answer to the issues, maintenance of relationships is important, and there is time to work through feelings and points of view. Compromise can serve as a backup when collaboration bogs down and there is some pressure to find an expedient or temporary solution.

These political leadership styles, except possibly domination, rely in part on the negotiating skills of leaders and/or administrators. Lax and Sebenius (1986) maintain that "Managers negotiate with those whom they cannot command but whose cooperation is vital, including peers and others outside the chain of command or beyond the organization itself. Managers even negotiate with subordinates who often have their own interests, understandings, sources of support, and areas of discretion" (pp. 1–2). Their description of subordinates resonates well with the nature of educational institutions. Educational administrators are confronted with the reality that the people they supervise do have a degree of autonomy and control that transcends their own authority. The incidents of the MVSD case illustrate this point very well and suggest how valuable bargaining skills would have been for the superintendent in resolving the school district's conflicts.

In Lax and Sebenius's (1986) judgment most people have a limited view of the negotiating or bargaining process (terms they use interchangeably); often negotiations are viewed too formally and seem to apply only within the context of collective bargaining. Bargaining as a metaphor can contribute to resolving conflict in less formal situations. The central issue facing persons in a conflict situation is how to manage the potential value of cooperation for the mutual benefit of many or to compete and maximize the benefits for a few. Lax and Sebenius see four important ingredients in a negotiating situation: interdependence, some perceived conflict, opportunistic interaction, and the possibility of agreement. They summarize, "We characterize negotiation as *a process of potentially opportunistic interaction by which two or more parties, with some apparent conflict, seek to do better through jointly decided action than they could otherwise*" (p. 11).

Lax and Sebenius (pp. 12–23) advocate a manager-as-negotiator metaphor; to successfully function in this role, they suggest the following:

- Deal outside the chain of command by engaging in indirect management
- Deal with subordinates by moderating demands, by managing the system resources to benefit shared interests, and by emphasizing cooperation
- Deal with superiors by emphasizing mutual dependence and identifying zones of possible agreement

Lax and Sebenius acknowledge some risks in promoting this view: Such a role may threaten traditional views of status, authority, and control; it also may suggest that solutions to organizational problems can be solved only through bargaining, whereas more technical and thoughtful analyses would work better. In spite of these limitations, they counter:

> Some standard images of good management leave little room for "inside" bargaining. To recognize its existence is inevitably to recognize some indeterminacy of outcomes as well as mutual dependence and conflict. Certainly, some tough managers will argue, effective command, control, or careful manipulation of subordinate routines should drive out these pathologies. And, the successful shaper of organizational culture achieves consensus on values, norms, purposes; not conflict, opportunistically employed discretion, and unpredictability. Because the existence of bargaining seems to imply a

failure of management when viewed through such common lenses, some may miss the existence and even virtues of manager-negotiators. (p. 24)

Bargaining must be more than merely executing trade-offs; as a process for facilitating shared interests and purposes, it should incorporate a mix of cooperation and competition. And it should be considered integral to the role of leaders and/or administrators of educational organizations.

ETHICAL IMPLICATIONS OF ORGANIZATIONAL POLITICS

A common reason for resisting organizational politics is the feeling that politics is unethical and immoral. Those who participate in politics are often seen as people who engage in deception and self-promotion at the expense of others or of the common good. Unfortunately, there is evidence that these attitudes and behaviors do exist in many of our organizations. On the other hand, often hidden from our view and not fully appreciated are "political" persons who reach above negative politics to enhance the health of the total organization.

While there are potential ethical problems in applying political behaviors to organizations, there are also many potential benefits; in fact, ethical application of political behavior can actually prevent an organization from becoming divisive and dysfunctional. As administrators and leaders, we are faced with a dilemma: to become politically active and so enhance the quality of the political process, or to remain on the sidelines while the political activity seeks its own level of discourse.

One of the risks in playing the political game is the danger of manipulation and exploitation of people in an organization. This is in part due to the varying levels of sophistication and experience persons have in dealing with issues and influencing their outcomes. Efforts must be made to ensure that policies, structures, and procedures exist that promote empowerment and informed choice.

Another ethical dilemma built into politics in an organization is how to deal with adversaries. In playing the political game there is the danger of overreacting to one's enemies and resorting to behaviors that are more appropriate to surviving gang warfare in an urban neighborhood. Block (1987) offers four steps for freeing up your emotional engagement with your opponents and moving on:

1. telling them your vision for the organization
2. stating as neutrally as possible your perception of their position
3. identifying your own contribution to the problem
4. ending your conversation by telling them what you are going to do but without placing any demands on them

Such an exchange removes some of the tension, unravels miscommunications, and can engender mutual respect that empowers both participants to approach their differences in a more mature and professional manner.

Lax and Sebenius (1986) state that bargaining by its nature is fraught with ethical issues: "(1) the appropriateness of certain tactics, (2) the distribution of value created by agreement, and (3) the effects of negotiation on those not at the table (externalities)" (p. 147). They provide a number of questions to help determine whether an action is ethical:

- Are the "rules" known and accepted?
- Can the situation be freely entered and left?
- Would you be comfortable if your coworkers, colleagues, and friends were aware that you had used a particular tactic?
- How would you feel if someone did it to you?
- Would you be comfortable advising another to use this tactic?
- How would you rule on this tactic if you were an arbitrator or even an elder in a small community?
- What if everybody bargained this way? Would the resulting society be desirable?
- Are there alternative tactics available that have fewer ethical ambiguities or costs? (pp. 148–50)

Finally, Lax and Sebenius advise us of the merits of taking a broader view: "First, there is a powerful tendency for people to focus on conflict, see a 'zero-sum' world, and thus confront the problems associated with claiming value in negotiation . . . yet, . . . we showed that such a focus on claiming results from an inherent dynamic of the process, stunts creativity, and often causes significant joint gains to go unrealized" (p. 150).

Organizational politics pose a challenge to keeping relationships among members from deteriorating into vicious back-stabbing. No doubt there is a hidden hand to prevent the dark side of politics from dominating people's lives in an organization for too long. Ethical political leadership, however, may be the most important resource an organization can draw on and can keep the organization from wallowing too long in negativism. Better yet, ethical and informed political leaders can play a major role in preventing this downward spiral from ever beginning.

CONCLUSION

Politics affects our lives in organizations whether we choose to play or not. Some organizations are more benevolent than others; in these cases there is less motivation to get politically involved. To some degree these are individual choices and each of us rationalizes our choices differently. In this chapter we took a broad and comprehensive look at ways to perceive and get involved with political activities in one's own organization. Hopefully, politics in organizations can be appreciated for their potential to create opportunities for involvement, for understanding sources of power and influence, and for learning how to resolve inevitable conflict.

People working in educational organizations are particularly vulnerable to external, macrolevel politics that soon get reflected in internal, microlevel politics. Educational systems require significant resources, particularly as our political leadership increases pressure by suggesting that our schools are falling behind our foreign competitors'. In addition, schools are being perceived more and more as a place where our society looks for cures to our social ills. As was portrayed in Anywhere, U.S.A., in chapter 1, there seems to be no end to requests that our schools are asked to fulfill. As educators, we are often eager to address important social issues through educational processes, but noble as this is on our part, there is often a price to pay. This higher profile places us in the limelight, and soon individuals are using schools as a platform for their own political agenda. School leaders need to be aware of these conditions and be prepared to counter the extreme behavior of self-interested individuals.

As schools attempt to define their role and the means for achieving their goals, conflict is bound to emerge. School leaders must accept conflict, but more importantly they need the ability to anticipate and minimize the impact of these disagreements. School administrators are in a position to recognize the special interests of people in the school, and their sources of power, and have the legal authority to change conditions to reduce interpersonal tensions. The manager-as-negotiator is one metaphor for school administrators trying to manage conflict.

As school administrators become more involved in the politics of their organization, the number of dilemmas and paradoxes they face increases proportionately. School administrators are not innocent bystanders with no stake in the outcomes of various decision-making bodies and individuals. Being morally and ethically clear about who the clients are, what their needs are, and whose aspirations should be supported is essential during political battles. As Bolman and Deal (1991) explain, "managers inevitably encounter a dilemma that is both practical and ethical—when to adopt strategies that are open and collaborative and when to choose tougher, more adversarial approaches. They will need to consider the potential for collaboration, the importance of long-term relationships, and most importantly, the values and ethical principles that they endorse" (p. 224).

As a political leader in an organization, having a clear sense of self and comfort with the politics of the organization will open up opportunities often precluded by rationality alone. Political behavior is not a substitute for competence; on the other hand, effective leadership rests heavily on the acquisition of political skills.

MVSD CASE REVISITED

As we speculated along the way in this chapter, the superintendent of the MVSD seemed ineffective in part because she lacked important political skills. From our review of the literature on power, we can see that the superintendent had a number of power sources at her disposal. It appears, however, that she may have relied too heavily on formal authority and did not have a self-image as a political leader. We see little evidence of informal bargaining and other conflict-resolution approaches. It seems the superintendent and the associate superintendent of schools felt so convinced of the

rightness of their cause that they did not take the necessary time to develop support for their proposed changes. Worst yet, as the resistance mounted, greater force was applied, only to result in threats and anti-Semitic attacks.

There is no doubt that the superintendent was caught in circumstances not of her own choosing. There was a legacy of authoritarian rule by the previous superintendent that resulted in conditions in which trust was difficult to establish. The superintendent was chosen in part because of her academic and humanities credentials; yet historically the MVSD was a district that had shifted priorities from the humanities to more career-oriented programs. In addition, the district had a strong commitment to serving the needs of its low-income population. The superintendent's call for academic excellence and her humanities background no doubt raised concerns with some partisan groups about the new directions the district was taking; when leaders opposed to the superintendent's vision resigned or were asked to resign, these concerns were more strongly reinforced.

The superintendent was doing what she felt she was hired to do. As she pursued her goals, however, she was not prepared for the resistance that emerged and did not know how to handle the opposition. She resorted to adversarial methods, making matters worse. Reframing her problem and drawing upon the political metaphor may have given her additional insights on how to handle the conflict that she had not intended to create.

When she agreed to the board of education president's request to resign she must have felt she had lost the struggle. Then the outburst of initial unanticipated support from teachers, students, and parents caught her by surprise and subsequently resulted in her lawsuit to recover her job. The state court judge found her testimony concerning the conditions of her "resignation" convincing and ruled in favor of reinstatement. This was a setback for the partisan groups who were unhappy with her agenda and her leadership style.

For reasons that are unclear, the superintendent was unable to convert her legal victory into a strategy for support and for a reduction in internal conflicts. Possibly her claims of sexism did not go down well with some members of the school community, or she misread the support for her reinstatement as a mandate for her academic excellence agenda. We do know that her cause was not well served by the style and actions of the associate superintendent of schools. The superintendent stood by her associate superintendent when the teachers began to resist the cultural diversity policy; had the superintendent been in a more powerful position she may have prevailed in her support, but when the going got rough, her position of weakness became more clear and soon the problems of the associate superintendent were linked to the problems of the superintendent's leadership.

The MVSD case portrays a sociopolitical environment in which the metaphor of politics enables an understanding of many of its dynamics. Our review of political tactics and strategies provides valuable insight on how this superintendent could have handled the situation differently. It provides an opportunity to explore a number of "what ifs": What if she had taken the time to identify the partisan groups and entered into a bargaining process? What if she had recognized her other sources of power and used them more fully to enhance her influence in the school district when conflict be-

gan to emerge? What if she had employed a variety of conflict-management tactics? and finally, What if she had shown more of the olive branch to her "enemies" and attempted to expand her style to include accommodation, compromise, and/or collaboration? Instead of employing these various political management options, however, she resorted to a rational management style and proposed a four-year, long-range plan. And as is often the case, this proposal was met with mixed reviews and did little to resolve the conflicts and concerns people were expressing at that time. This was a situation in which long discussions and deliberations by task forces with outside experts made little sense, at least at the time. The situation was crying out for political leadership and an appreciation of the politics being engaged by various members of the MVSD and beyond.

DISCUSSION QUESTIONS

1. If you were asked to give a simple and straightforward definition of organizational politics, what would it be? How would you define political leadership in an organizational context?
2. If you were confronted by a colleague who complained about the politics of your organization, how would you respond? Could you portray its virtues? Why or why not?
3. In your judgment, what are the underlying ethical problems with organizational politics?
4. Think of a recent conflict in your organization and how it was handled. If it could be relived, what strategies of power and/or conflict resolution would you suggest based on the ideas in this chapter?
5. Are politics inevitable in organizations? in your organization? Why or why not?

SUGGESTED ACTIVITIES

1. Revisit the MVSD case. Using the political concepts of this chapter, develop an explanation for why the superintendent of the MVSD was unsuccessful and had to resign. Following this analysis, develop a strategy that will enable a new superintendent to restore order and create a healthy environment for subsequent needed changes.
2. Develop a role-play situation in which members of your group can take different roles and positions on any of the critical issues in the case, for example, the teachers' reactions to the newly proposed cultural diversity policy. Persons might assume different roles (e.g., white classroom teachers, teachers of color, building principals, parents of minority background, students both of white and of minority backgrounds, past victims of racial abuse, etc.) and points of view inferable from the MVSD case (e.g., for cultural diversity, against cultural diversity, for cultural diversity but against imposition of policy by the administration) and any other permutations that would help demonstrate the complexities surrounding the establishment and implementation of a cultural diversity policy in a community with a sizable minority population. After roles and points of view have been assigned and persons have a chance to reflect on their role, set up a group-meeting simulation in which a discussion of the cultural diversity policy is to take place with the hope of developing some consensus on the problem(s) and what can be done (assume features to this policy that are typical of school districts faced with a similar challenge). Following the simulation, take time to discuss what transpired and its implications for political leadership.

3. Structure a debate on the pros and cons of political leadership and the value of the metaphor of politics for analyzing organizational situations. Following the debate, generate some general ideas about understanding educational organizations.

4. Identify a political situation in your organization and analyze it from an organizational political perspective.

5. In discussion with others develop a set of ethical guidelines that you believe all members, most importantly you, should follow when engaging in political action within your organization.

REFERENCES

Adams, H. (1976). *The academic tribes*. New York: Liveright.

Bacharach, S. B., & Lawler, E. J. (1980). *Power and politics in organizations*. San Francisco: Jossey-Bass.

Block, P. (1987). *The empowered manager: Positive political skills at work*. San Francisco: Jossey-Bass.

Bolman, L. G., & Deal, T. E. (1991). *Reframing organizations: Artistry, choice, and leadership*. San Francisco: Jossey-Bass.

Boulding, K. E. (1989). *Three faces of power*. Newbury Park, CA: Sage.

Boyd, W. L., & Kerchner, C. T. (Eds.). (1988). *The politics of excellence and choice in education*. New York: Falmer Press.

Dow, P. B. (1991). *Schoolhouse politics: Lessons from the Sputnik era*. Cambridge, MA: Harvard University Press.

Gamson, W. A. (1968). *Power and discontent*. Homewood, IL: Dorsey Press.

Goodlad, J. I. (1991). Curriculum making as a sociopolitical process. In M. F. Klein (Ed.), *The politics of curriculum decision-making* (pp. 9-23). Albany: State University of New York Press.

Gray, H. L. (1984). The politics of educational institutions. In A. Kakabadse & C. Parker (Eds.), *Power, politics, and organizations* (pp. 109-26). New York: Wiley.

Hanson, E. M. (1990). *Educational administration and organizational behavior* (3rd ed.). Boston: Allyn & Bacon.

Kakabadse, A., & Parker, C. (1984). *Power, politics, and organizations* (pp. xi-xiii). New York: Wiley.

Klein, F. M. (Ed.). (1991). *The politics of curriculum decision-making*. Albany: State University of New York Press.

Korda, M. (1975). *Power!* New York: Random House.

Kotter, J. P. (1985). *Power and influence: Beyond formal authority*. New York: Free Press.

Lax, D. A., & Sebenius, J. K. (1986). *The manager as negotiator*. New York: Free Press.

McClelland, D. (1975). *Power: The inner-experience*. New York: Wiley.

Morgan, G. (1986). *Images of organization*. Beverly Hills: Sage.

Parker, C. (1984). Introduction. In A. Kakabadse & C. Parker (Eds.), *Power, politics, and organizations* (pp. ix, xiii). New York: Wiley.

Ross, W. D. (Trans.). (1954). *Aristotle: Ethics, book 1, and politics, book 1*. Chicago: Henry Regnery.

Thomas, K. W. (1976). Conflict and conflict management. In M. D. Dunnette (Ed.), *Handbook of industrial and organizational psychology* (pp. 889-935). Chicago: Rand McNally.

Thomas, K. W. (1977). Toward multi-dimensional values in teaching: The example of conflict behaviors. *Academy of Management Review, 12*, 484-90.

Organizations from a Theatrical Perspective

$\mathbf{A}$s suggested in the previous two chapters, if there is culture there are politics, and if there are both culture and politics in organizations then there must be theater. Ceremonies for which schools are so well known often reflect more than the culture of a school; ceremonies such as graduation exercises or public meetings of a newly appointed superintendent can be political in nature by virtue of whose values get displayed at these exercises and whose do not. At the public meeting honoring the appointment of the MVSD superintendent, she used the opportunity to enunciate her philosophy on academic excellence and received accolades for her presentation. Her presentation took on more meaning than just a cultural event; it was also political and theatrical, spiced with humor and sprinkled with quotes from the humanities. By all accounts she gave a stunning performance.

However, setting aside for a moment the metaphors of culture and politics and substituting the theater metaphor, we can begin to appreciate another perspective on not only obvious and dramatic events but also other more subtle forms of discourse in an organization. Hare (1985) suggests some parallels between everyday life and theater:

> In everyday life, as people react to an idea either positively, negatively, or indifferently, some are moved to take roles in support of the idea, others to take roles that are critical of the idea, and some to remain neutral. If the idea that is presented is not the espouser's own, there may be someone similar to a playwright behind the scenes who created the idea. There may also be someone who facilitates the presentation of the idea like a director. There is always a stage, or action area, where the activity takes place. Persons who are outside this action space form the audience. The time during which

a presentation takes place is always limited. It may be only a few minutes or it may be a lifetime; an actor, however, cannot hold the stage forever. (p. 8)

Theater as a metaphor provides us with the opportunity to observe and understand the dynamics—the obvious and the subtle—surrounding human behavior in organizations. As Burns (1972) states, "The theatrical metaphor suggests that in ordinary life, as on the stage, we take parts and fit into situations and scenes that are part of a large scheme of action" (p. 126). Organizational ceremonies and events can often beguile us and prevent closer scrutiny of the more subtle message(s) and the backstaging that may be going on. The theater metaphor provides a means by which we can articulate a number of our organizational observations and possibly prevent ourselves from being "taken in." As Mangham and Overington (1987) explain,

> It is this reflective awareness which we want to claim as a *theatrical consciousness;* we want to have it as a recognition that there is an actor "behind" a character, a playwright "behind" a script, a stage "behind" a performance, a reality "behind" the appearance. (p. 49)

In this chapter we shall explore several dimensions of theater, including the need for theatrical behavior in organizations, theater and dramaturgical concepts, ways to study organizational theater, how to manage the theatrical dimensions of an organization, and the ethical implications of applying theater concepts within an organizational context (with a side trip into humor and its role in organizations).

NEED FOR THEATRICAL BEHAVIOR IN ORGANIZATIONS

A recent *Calvin and Hobbes* comic strip illustrates the importance of theater in organizations. Calvin, a primary-school-aged student, raises his hand in response to his teacher's request for questions. He asks, "What's the point of human existence?" His teacher responds that she was looking for questions "about the subject at hand." To which Calvin replies, "Frankly, I'd like to have the issue resolved before I expend any more energy on this." Wouldn't we all! In the meantime, however, as they say in the theater, "The show must go on." Theater, as a metaphor, provides a way to understand the need to perform our respective roles in organizations and in life in general, even in spite of sometimes not knowing why.

Theater also provides a means to explain and interpret the multiple layers involved in human action within an organizational context. According to Mangham and Overington (1987),

> A theatrical event is a communication between actors and audience in the context of a meta-communication about the framing of this event as a theatrical *staging* of action. Theatre is an opportunity for mundane opportuni-

ties to be inspected as appearances in order to consider their meanings. As such, theatre creates space for awareness. (p. 101)

This theatrical awareness allows us to see and appreciate the multiple meanings of performances in an organization. As illustrated in Figure 4.1, we can explore the dynamic interrelationships involved in a performance and the underlying layers that contribute to it. It allows us to speculate about who the audience is, the director, what script is being enacted, and so forth.

Performance is a matter of creating realities and links well to reflective thinking, which stresses the importance of understanding our actions. Theater permits the exploration of the mysteries of life and invites us to think about them. Mangham and Overington (1987) claim that "as characters we are the result—and only the result—of a process of creating, presenting, interpreting and being interpreted" (p. 143).

Theater allows an organization to portray itself both internally and externally. Space, costume, and setting have meanings that serve to organize social relations. Bolman and Deal (1991) emphasize that "organizational structures, activities, and events are more than simply instrumental. They are part of the organizational theater, an ongoing expressive drama that entertains, creates meaning, and portrays the organization to itself" (p. 274). Organizations can create impressions that help tell their story and influence judgments about their strengths as an organization. Organizations and their leaders are often judged not by their actions but by appearances.

In summary and paraphrasing from Hare (1985), studying organizations from a dramaturgical perspective

- helps determine the meaning of behavior
- allows one to sense one's individuality
- recognizes the importance of variability in performance
- helps to predict future actions
- highlights the interplay between the context (stage) and the culture (normative script)
- views human beings as fundamentally communicators
- recognizes interaction and situations, not individuals, as the locus of motivation
- views human beings as consciously rationalizing, not consciously rational (p. 144)

An exploration of related dramaturgical concepts will aid in clarifying these perspectives on organizations as theater.

FIGURE 4.1 Performance continuum

self-actor-role-script-stage-director-audience-performance

DRAMATURGICAL CONCEPTS

In our everyday conversation we often use theatrical terms in an unthinking manner. Words like *role, performance, appearance, acting, script, drama, rehearsal, critic, props, costumes, stage fright,* and so forth are part of our lexicon for describing situations in social settings such as organizations. When these concepts are used in a more conscious and organized manner, they can elicit insights that tend otherwise to lie buried. If we begin to think of a school as a setting or stage; the architecture as scenery; furniture, pictures, and plants as props; clothing as costumes; policies and curricula as scripts; the principal as a director; teachers and students as actors; classroom and other interactions as drama, then we may begin to appreciate the potential theatrical concepts have to show us afresh our everyday world.

Figure 4.1 illustrates a means for identifying a basic set of concepts and their interrelationships, but there is a multiplicity of concepts with many layers to each. At the heart of these relationships is the interplay between the individual as manifested in self and actor and the group as manifested in the role and script. Hare (1985) offers an explanation of this relationship: "The roles we play have two main goals, one to achieve group goals efficiently and the other to achieve personal reward in the form of validation of self, self-esteem, and reinforcement from others" (p. 155). As we examine each of these dramaturgical concepts, keep in mind their mutual interdependence.

Self, Actor, and Role

The interrelationships of self, actor, and role beg the question concerning the congruence of self and performance. As we consider people like the superintendent of schools for the MVSD, we may wonder to what degree she was performing according to the expectations of the role of a superintendent and when we were seeing her true self. Reflecting on self and role offers the opportunity to muse about this interrelationship and to appreciate the range of options one has in fulfilling an organizational role. As Mangham and Overington (1987) explain, "For us the actor, the individuality, is bound up with the roles; the unitary being . . . is a unity of actor and performance— who he *is* and what he *does*" (p. 152).

The actors on the stage must draw from their inner experience in order to present the image required by the role being played. A large repertoire of experience enables the actor to give greater depth of character and to struggle less with understanding the nature of the role. That is, more experience enables the actor to become one with the role.

Actors operate on two levels: One level is acting the part as required and interpreted by others and oneself; the other is a form of self-monitoring and being aware of the image being projected. However, as the actor grows in comfort with the part being played and/or can draw from a range of experiences in similar roles, these two levels become blurred. The self-consciousness needed to monitor the performance is diminished and the actor is able to project an image that is credible and appears authentic.

Acting is a process of discovery and fit. Certain roles and scripts that define these roles have expectations attached to them. At the same time, the actor comes with a sense of self (i.e., a personality) that attempts to blend and fit with these expectations. As the actor becomes more aware of the expectations and is able to fit the role, his or her performance may be judged appropriate. The actor does discover that there are limitations to acceptable images that can be projected for a role. As described by Barish (1981), "Our efforts of self-definition consist of our attempts to cope with this amphitheater of gazes . . . forced to improvise our identities as we go along . . . we may opt for 'role-making' or 'role-taking'" (pp. 476-77). In reality, what works is a mixture of altering the role and accepting it at the same time.

Hare (1985), borrowing from symbolic interactionism, defines *role* as a "set of activities that are expected of a person who fills a given position in a group" (p. 19). As we are socialized to a role, we learn of its rights and duties and we choose roles in light of our definition of the situation. Of course, some situations allow a greater range of interpretations by the actor and other situations discourage such interpretations. Figure 4.2 illustrates the balance between self and role and different roles that permit more or less choice in acting out certain behaviors. A university professor has a higher degree of influence in playing out his role of professor than a first grade student, who is under considerable pressure to conform to certain role expectations of his or her teacher. Persons do influence how a role is played; it is, however, a matter of degree and in some organizations persons receive greater pressure to conform to others' expectations (e.g., a private in the army or an inmate in a correctional center).

According to Polti (1977) there are 36 types of dramatic situations which, however, require only two basic role types for plot and supporting actors. The central roles include protagonists who guide action and antagonists who oppose them. Serious situations of tragedy and melodrama have their heroes, heroines, and villains; in comedy

FIGURE 4.2 Self–role interface

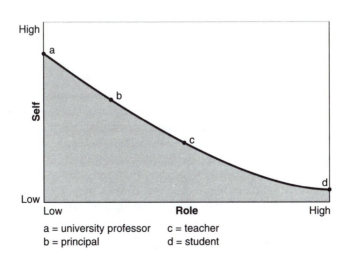

a = university professor   c = teacher
b = principal   d = student

and farce there are fools. Supporting (auxiliary) players may play individual or group (chorus) roles in support of either protagonists or antagonists.

The MVSD case illustrates a situation of melodrama containing these basic role types. Regardless of the issue chosen (e.g., reinstatement of the superintendent, imposition of a new cultural diversity policy, or forced resignations) there was a mixture of protagonists, antagonists, and auxiliary members. The case also demonstrates that these roles are not fixed: People may shift back and forth depending on the issue and the situation at hand. We witnessed the teachers and staff, in their auxiliary roles, acting in support of the new superintendent. As the situation changed, however, many shifted their loyalty to antagonists. The dramaturgical approach requires the observer to consider the roles being played by group members at the moment of their action. As Perinbanayagam (1985) observes, "dramas contain persons acting on each other, and by such acting generate the reality that is relevant for them . . . while allowing for the possibility that reality may be altered at any moment in the future" (p. 59).

Persons in leadership roles would be wise to recognize the episodic nature of their context and be prepared to adapt or to encourage shifts in attitudes.

Script, Stage, and Playwright

Obviously roles do not occur in isolation; they are guided by a context made up of, among other things, script and setting (stage). Hare (1976) suggests the following influences on role performance:

- role expectations
- role location
- role demands
- role skills
- self-role congruence
- audience
- complex role phenomena (pp. 148–50)

These multiple influences on role performance illustrate the challenge facing persons in organizational roles, particularly those subject to more public exposure and scrutiny. For example, the superintendent of the MVSD was confronted with a complex context that illustrates each of these influences on her performance. The role expectations defined her rights (e.g., to hire and fire her top-level administrators) and duties (e.g., represent and explain school district policies), which are enacted in various role locations that help clarify such questions as Who am I? and Who is she? As the actor, the superintendent discovered a great deal about herself as she confronted situations in a variety of role locations. These situations clarified the range of possible role behaviors required of a superintendent in a given situation (role demands) and her physical and psychological readiness to perform some of the tasks at a given level of competence (role skills). She was ready to articulate a new vision of academic excellence, but one wonders about her level of understanding of the variety of contradictory and conflicting demands a person faces as school superintendent and her skill level for coping with these circumstances.

The success of any leader rests with self-role congruence; that is, role enactment is more effective when self characteristics are congruent with role requirements. The superintendent of the MVSD not only needed the capacity to envision an academically excellent school district, she also needed to cope with antagonists and choruses who would resist her proposed changes. Her personal and academic background may not have given her the opportunity to acquire the role skills necessary for dealing with resistance and open conflict.

She may not have realized it, but she also may have been playing to the wrong audience. (The audience is a reference group and may not actually be present.) The superintendent's perceived audience may have been an oligarchy of influential persons who were instrumental in hiring her and who shared her vision for academic quality; however, the audience to which she eventually had to be accountable was the teachers, staff, and students. Audiences provide consensual reality for the role, provide cues to guide performance, give social reinforcement, and contribute to its maintenance over time. Choosing the right audience and being able to respond to its cues are critical to successful role enactment.

The superintendent of the MVSD was not ready for the complex role phenomena swirling around the position. As she discovered, the superintendent of a school district is not only an instructional leader but must also be a conflict manager, a political figure, a symbol, a counselor, and more—all of which contribute to confusion over role expectations and make apparent the need for a vast repertoire of skills for carrying a very entangled and visible role.

To further our understanding of role we must better understand the script that contributes to the role requirements. The concept of script(s) in organizations raises many subtle questions about who is or are the playwright(s) and what are the different levels of scripts in an organization (e.g., obvious, subtle, and subtextual).

We know that at one level, unlike the case of a play, there are no written scripts that members of an organization must follow. On the other hand, organizations do try to reduce uncertainty through a variety of means that approximate written scripts. These scripts are known as policies, regulations, directives, job descriptions, and guidelines, which lay out procedures that members of the organization are required to follow. These are the more obvious scripts and are more or less effective in determining actor behavior.

Paradoxically, these obvious scripts can contribute to mindlessness as they become routinized and reduce the need for high-level cognitive alertness. These scripts can cause failures in vigilance to the aspirations of an organization and failure in authenticity in the interpersonal contacts of an organization. Formal as well as informal interactions and structured episodes are likely to rely on such scripts. According to Ashforth (1988), a script is a "cognitive structure that specifies a typical sequence of occurrences in a given situation" (p. 306). Unfortunately scripts can negatively affect the decision-making process and cause premature closure, superfluous learning, and inconsistencies between attitudes and behavior. The challenge to us is to discover these various scripts and understand their influence on our conscious and unconscious thinking and related behavior. The theater metaphor challenges us to look beyond the observable and ferret out the underlying messages, the subtexts. To discover these subtexts we have to move beyond the action displayed frontstage and give attention to what is going on backstage and offstage. These subtexts are offered up by a number of different playwrights who are interested in pushing a particular script (i.e., an agenda) within the context of other discussions and issues. Observations outside the setting of action can help us appreciate the drama that exists and how various actors contribute to its unfolding.

The execution of a special event, like the special meeting that honored the new superintendent's appointment, illustrates the dynamics of script and staging. The obvious script was the public display of symbols and people to represent the values important to a school district like the MVSD. Also, the script called for the superintendent to act as visionary and to articulate a vision for the MVSD during her superintendency. In her speech she talked about making the MVSD "preeminent among the moderate-sized school districts of this state." Humor and thoughtful reflection emanated from her speech and actions. This is what was observable frontstage.

We must ask, however, what was going on backstage (probably nervous chatter and rapid heartrates, brought on by some anxiety over how well the event would go over in the presence of so many community leaders and other notables) and offstage, before and after the meeting. What kinds of discussions did the superintendent have before she wrote her speech and after she gave her speech? Was her speech more or less predetermined by the deliberations in executive session of the school board at the time of her selection and subsequent appointment? Did people at the reception following her speech offer support and reinforcement? It is unlikely that antagonists had formed or begun to articulate a position in opposition to her script of academic excellence. Clearly, it was too early to anticipate the implications of her speech and the actions she might take to carry out her dream.

Over time, however, it did become more evident that a new script was being written for the MVSD, and actors who had difficulty performing according to these ideas were being asked to step down from the stage. Presumably, they were to be replaced by actors more capable of accepting the new script. The subtext perceived by some persons at the MVSD was: Either buy into the new vision or your services are no longer needed. Various role incumbents had little or no choice but to act as the script required. This inflexibility in allowing more interpretation by the actors led to the superintendent's downfall.

Director, Audience, and Performance

In the theater, the director is the person who prepares the play for the stage. According to Miles-Brown (1980), the director must perform the following tasks:

- find the theme
- observe the plot, subplot, and subtext

- locate the dramatic climaxes
- understand the style, the characters, and the relationships
- visualize the staging (p. 22)

Once the play is in progress, according to Spolin (1977), the director coaches the actors from the wings, before they go on stage or before leaving it, and critiques the performance after the audience has left.

In organizations, in the course of normal activities, the "director" may or may not be very obvious. Special events and/or crises make it easier to determine the director. In the MVSD situation, being new to the position and having a strong interest in writing a new script for the organization made the superintendent's role as director more evident. In many ways a change agent, such as a school superintendent, acts like a director in the theater in exposing people to possibilities of "playing different roles in different plays, of giving them the vocabularies and strategies to abandon old plays for new ones" (Perinbanayagam, 1985, p. 82).

The audiences in theaters and organizations share some common characteristics. They tend to be passive unless extra effort is made to draw them into the play as an active participant. Audiences do support, reinforce, and in some cases can alter the behavior of actors based on subtle and nonverbal cues of head nodding, eye contact, alertness, smiles, applause, or the lack of any of these. We can observe these same kinds of influences in school meetings, in classrooms, and at related ceremonies.

Mangham and Overington (1987) talk about the tension of theatrical performances that emerges from the intentions of the actors, the director, and the audience. Directors, working with actors, hope to present a theatrical event that emotionally involves the audience. Their goal is to have a performance that proves funny or moving or horrifying; "they are not interested in having the audience feel it is 'as if' the drama were 'funny,' were 'moving,' were 'horrifying.' On the other hand, the audience is pulling away from this kind of involvement, trying to hang on to their framing of the events as theatrical. It is somewhere between these two positions—in the tension which is created—that theater works" (p. 50).

Further, it is between these two positions that change in organizations works. That is, as audience, the uninvolved members of the organization watch events unfold and as a consequence they are either irrevocably drawn into the change process or struggle to remain outside it. As they become more involved, however, they cease being audience and become participant. We observed in the MVSD case that various members quickly lost their audience status as certain events (e.g., forced resignation of the superintendent, reinstatement of the superintendent, and forced resignations of central office administrators) became more prominent and compelling in nature.

Performance, according to Goffman (1974), "is that arrangement which transforms an individual into a stage performer, the latter, in turn, being an object that can be looked at in the round and length without offense, and looked to for engaging behavior, by persons in an 'audience'" (p. 124). Performance crosses the line demarcating the safe haven of the audience and is the sum total of the self interacting with a script on stage under some direction and in the presence of an audience. The challenge for modern-day leaders, often placed in a director's role, is to move persons from the status of audience to that of participant in a play that can be mutually crafted (script and staging) and presented to those still left in the audience.

Plays, Themes, and Drama

According to Hamilton (1939), a play is "a representation, by actors, on a stage, before an audience, of a struggle between individual human wills, motivated by emotion rather than the intellect, and expressed in terms of objective action" (p. 17). Sounds somewhat like a faculty meeting at which there are underlying emotions being suppressed but which influence the so-called objective discussion of school-related issues.

Plays permit the staging of a range of human emotions and experiences in dramatic form. Drama historically has been limited to four types. In two types—tragedy and comedy—the characters control the plot; in the other two types—melodrama and farce—the plot controls the characters. Tragedy and melodrama typically are serious and have unhappy endings, whereas comedy and farce have a lightness of style and a happy ending. Fry (1962) distinguishes the differences between comedy and tragedy. Both deal with the truth but "comedy is an escape, not from truth but from despair: a narrow escape into faith. . . . In tragedy we suffer pain; in comedy pain is a fool, suffered gladly" (p. 68).

Present-day performances may be a blend of these different types of drama and may be more reflective of the realities of organizational life. That is, as we examine the MVSD case, we might conclude that this is an example of melodrama with a sad ending. However, organizations often do not have endings without new beginnings: Life goes on and organizations go through cycles (explored in more detail in chapter 13) that might be described as a particular type of drama in a specified period of time. Today things are different in the MVSD and the melodrama that was so prominent during the reign of the previous superintendent has given way to a new administration whose character is yet to be determined.

Many themes have been addressed by theatrical plays and performances. Burns (1972, pp. 220–27) provides a review of the major themes in theater over time: In medieval times, religious drama addressed a person's relationship to God and the struggle between God and the devil for his or her soul. In secular drama of the sixteenth and seventeenth centuries, the themes were primarily focused on the relationship between people. In Shakespeare's tragedies, accident plays an important part, and in his comedies, accident and coincidence are intermingled in humorous ways.

Since Shakespeare, Western European drama has placed emphasis on choice and accident rather than on inevitability and consequence. Tragic dramatists of the late nineteenth century (e.g., Ibsen, Strindberg, and Chekhov) dealt with themes of control of society and erosion of individual freedom, themes of conformity, self-deception, and alienation. Ibsen worked with traditional themes of heroic sacrifice for a principle, the fate of the social outcast, and the struggle for eminence and maintenance of power. He also introduced newer themes, including the search for definitions of reality and the implicit search for identity. Freud influenced the themes of the individual dealing with the dichotomy of good and evil, the force of liberation, and the force of conservative repression. The traditional themes of honor and vengeance, ambition, power, and love are eternal and thus relevant to present-day conditions.

Contemporary theater is a blend of old and new themes. Present-day social values permit a wider range of subjects to be addressed in a more blunt and forceful way. Themes of sexuality, greed, and prejudice, such as racism, are concerns that will keep theatergoers and members of our society preoccupied for some period of time. As Burns (1972) points out,

> The theatre is always a place in which symbols, whether stressed or unstressed, can be displayed in a form that is more potent than that of other kinds of literature. . . . When a play . . . makes some of the audience laugh, some unhappy, some angry, some shocked and some merely puzzled, it exposes the discrepant values of the audience, but it can still be effective because of its semiotic complexity. (p. 228)

Theater reminds us of our complex human emotions that are often denied or suppressed. Experiences in organizations—the multiple and daily face-to-face contacts, rituals, and ceremonies—create numerous opportunities to experience drama and related themes of human existence. Coworkers' experiences display elements of tragedy, comedy, and even farce. As we are drawn into these experiences the fine line between theater and life becomes blurred. Dramaturgical concepts provide a means by which these emotions can be appreciated and better understood. According to Hare (1985),

> [for] those subscribing to humanist, symbolic interactionist, or dramaturgical views, the important aspect of life is to be found in its comic nature, when persons can stand apart from interaction, even as they engage in it, to discover its meaning. They enjoy life because . . . they do not escape from truth, but from despair. (p. 42)

HUMOR IN ORGANIZATIONS

Comedy in theater can provide needed relief and permit examining awkward themes in a more comfortable, less threatening manner. Comedy in organizations is often manifested in the form of humor, from practical jokes to witticisms to farcical blunderings of well-meaning people. Most organizations have their jesters or persons with "a sense of humor" who foster humorous exchanges of human foibles experienced daily in any organization. As Duncan (1989) observes, "the single most important reason that joking behavior is a universal part of work is that joking, more than anything else, makes people feel they belong" (p. 29).

Krohe (1987) talks about humor in the workplace and how laughter eases tension, creates bonds, and provides a gentler language for criticism; jests, at one's own expense, make a person more accessible. He suggests that "laughter is subversive of authority, or pretense, or pomposity [but] . . . while humor can grease the wheels at work, it doesn't often rearrange them" (p. 35). Joking can also take on some tentativeness in mixed company (mixed by gender, race, culture, or ethnicity).

There is power in combining humor with ritual. For example, an organization reportedly participated in an annual ritual of literally burying its members' mistakes: Descriptions of mistakes were written on pieces of paper that were ceremonially placed in a cigar-box coffin; this in turn was buried on the grounds of the workplace, complete with a grave marker. Such a display of humor can rid persons of needless guilt and develop the capacity to forgive and forget.

Timing and sincerity are important ingredients in such ceremonial attempts at humor. "Humor," as Duncan (1989) says, "lubricates social relations" (p. 29), and Hertzler (1970) suggests that laughter around the ambiguity of authority produces "a shortcut to consensus between incumbents of different statuses" (p. 126). Maybe it is too much to suggest that the superintendent of the MVSD should have engaged in a similar ceremony when some of her early proposals hit a wall of resistance. Humor may have eased the tension and enabled her to take the initiative in the struggle between the protagonists and antagonists.

Jaffe (1990) discusses examples of the ways in which humor and fun increase productivity and profit. His examples include theme days, casual days, a graffiti board, and the best joke of the week. According to Jaffe, when workers feel good, morale increases and so does worker satisfaction. Humor and fun feel good, and "workers who have fun treat customers well" (p. 60). Schools may not have customers in the typical sense, but they do have students and parents, many of whom appreciate humor and would benefit from a school staff's feeling good about their work.

Consalvo (1986) found in his research of small task-oriented groups in human service organizations that humor came in five basic patterns: (1) episodic humor, (2) corrective humor, (3) outgroup and self-disparaging humor, (4) speaker laughter or remark with a laugh, and (5) humor occurring as part of the decision-making process. He also found that ambiguity, uncertainty, imperfection, and paradox are rich sources for stimulating humor. Consalvo observes that "The density of humor's capacity to convey meaning combined with the detachment and emotional safety it provides, permits playful seriousness to encompass the ambiguities and paradoxes of organizational experience in ways that direct seriousness simply cannot" (p. 164).

Humor is difficult to define, though it is something we intuitively recognize. According to Ziv (1984), there are two dimensions to humor: humor as creativity, which refers to the ability to perceive relationships among people, objects, or ideas, and humor as appreciation, which refers to the ability to understand and enjoy humor. He goes on to discuss the functions of humor that permit people to deal with difficult subjects, such as sex, and to provide an outlet for aggression, much like sports. Humor can have a social function in the form of social criticism, as expressed in satire and comedy, which can illuminate areas needing change. "Gallows" or "black" humor can help us deal with things that frighten us. Finally, Ziv sees humor as intellectual, permitting an escape "from the bondage of rationality" (p. 3). It permits solving problems in a pleasurable way.

Consalvo (1986) and Ziv (1984) both point out that humor can have a down side. Consalvo addresses the use of humor to ossify an organization and to keep persons from suggesting new ideas. Ziv discusses how persons can be rejected from a group by humor: They are treated as the victim or scapegoat and can become the brunt of jokes and biting remarks.

In spite of its potential negative uses, however, humor offers interesting opportunities to leaders who are coping with controversial issues and threatened individuals. As Ziv (1984) states,

> Humor has some characteristics that remind one of mercury. It looks like a unified whole until the moment someone touches it. Then it breaks up and scatters into tiny droplets that roll away separately and then draw near again, creating a new united body. Like mercury, humor also has a spark of light within it. It brightens, shines on, and enriches all the factors that compose the dynamics of group life. (p. 38)

The superintendent of the MVSD displayed some flashes of humor in her speech at the special meeting; unfortunately, these did not continue as the conflicts and tensions began to mount. Kushner (1990) discusses the value of humor in managing conflicts. He points out that often the message is lost during clashes but the relationship is remembered: Humor or anger will outlast our ability to recall what was said. Kushner suggests reframing conflicts with humor: "Humor, because of its ability to put things into perspective, provides an important frame for creating new meanings in conflict situations" (p. 110). A good sign that a quarrel is over is when laughter can be heard. Unfortunately, laughter was not heard in the halls of the central office of the MVSD; instead, anger and frustration began to take hold and dominate the dialogue.

To illustrate reframing with humor, Kushner reports several incidents where persons caught in rather difficult circumstances used humor to rescue them. He describes the predicament of a Canadian governor-general's being confronted by a group of striking maintenance workers during a ceremonial visit to a public school. He did not like the idea of crossing a picket line, nor did he like the idea of backing down and having his authority diminished. As the pickets gathered around him, he reframed the problem and said, "How very nice of you to turn out to see me! Thank you. Shall we go in?" By the time the strikers stopped laughing, the governor-general had entered the school. Bolman and Deal (1991) describe a panicked school principal who called his superintendent asking for help because he had 25 armed Black Panthers outside his office. The superintendent told him to think of them as "pink panthers" and hung up. Apparently this new image permitted the principal to see his situation differently and he was able to defuse the situation.

Humor can create a new image of a situation in which there is tension or stress. It may be a needed relief for all parties and permit new creative solutions to emerge. Hansot (1979) argues that we should not ask why people in organizations are humorous; rather we should wonder why they are so serious.

WAYS TO STUDY ORGANIZATIONAL THEATER

As was suggested earlier, in the minds of some theorists theater and life are one and theater is more than a metaphor. Dramatism as defined by Burke (1968) is a depiction of human reality; it "is a method of analysis and a corresponding critique of terminology designed to show that the most direct route to the study of human relations and human motives is via a methodological inquiry into cycles or clusters of terms and functions" (p. 7).

To guide the study of drama, Burke (1962) offers the following questions:

- What was done? (Act)
- When or where was it done? (Scene)
- Who did it? (Agent)
- How did he do it? (Agency)
- Why was it done? (Purpose) (p. xvii)

These questions provide some structure for sorting the dynamics surrounding an event or series of events. The questions also allow us to step back from the field of action and sort through the multiple layers of human exchanges, symbols, and activities. According to Perinbanayagam (1985), these questions identify the basic elements of a situation: "They are used, wittingly and unwittingly, by all actors to both create and interpret situations and to engage in the production of appropriate social acts" (p. 66).

Mangham and Overington (1987) introduce the notion of a subtext in the exchange between persons in an organization. They suggest that in certain exchanges one may detect a clear separation between the surface dialogue and a deeper subscript that is not fully acknowledged but is inferable from inane comments or gestures like avoidance of eye contact or silent pauses. An example is a two-person scene in which one person is avoiding stating true feelings toward another person, while the second person is trying to discern what those feelings are and why they are being experienced but not expressed. Such a typical scene, regardless of the players (e.g., supervisor/supervised, teacher/student, teacher/parent), provides an opportunity to observe the interplay between obfuscation and prodding. When such exchanges occur, whether between individuals or in groups, they signal the presence of a subscript. The observer is challenged to speculate and delve into other cues (e.g., history, personal motivations, and unresolved conflicts) in order to tap into the unspoken message of the subscript. As Mangham and Overington observe, "The words and phrases used may give us a clue, but the action is always and inevitably embedded in a context which has dimensions stretching backward and forward in time, just as in the theatre a scene may both echo and foreshadow that which has been or is to be" (p. 165).

Moving from the sublime to the more or less obvious, Hare (1985) suggests the use of diagrams to illustrate what is going on in various scenes or dramatic events over time. In chapter 2 (see Figure 2.1), we discussed the impact of the environment and external cultures on an organization's subcultures. Using theatrical language, Hare describes these relationships as reference groups helping "to sustain role performance even though members may not be part of the organization under analysis" (p. 29). Regardless of the type of organization, he sees both groups and individuals in the roles of directors, protagonists, auxiliary players, and audiences in a stage setting. Figure 4.3 displays these respective roles in formal organizations and informal networks or events.

We need to keep in mind that individuals are capable of performing many roles and can shift from one to the other rapidly depending on the circumstances. As helpful as it is to identify persons and particular roles during certain events or under certain thematic conditions, conditions do not remain static and the analyst must repeat

FIGURE 4.3 Roles and relationships in organizations

SOURCE: A. P. Hare, *Social Interaction as Drama: Applications from Conflict Resolution*, p. 30, copyright 1985 by Sage Publications, Inc. Adapted by permission of Sage Publications, Inc.

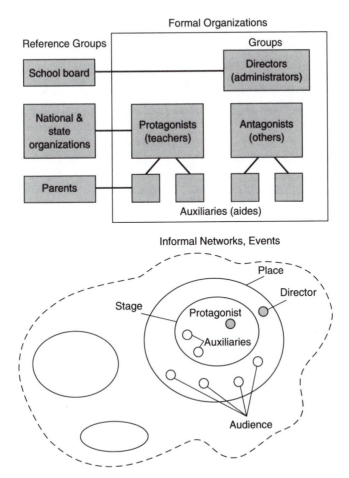

these observations at different times. Repeated observations and graphic representa-
tions help us appreciate the dynamic flow of persons, roles, and actions over time.

Hare (1985) offers a visual approach to dramaturgical analysis of an event. The
first diagram is a field diagram, which "indicates the relative positions of the actors or
images in the four-dimensional space (upward-downward, positive-negative, serious-
expressive, and conforming-anticonforming)" (p. 68). According to Hare, this diagram
allows the identification of different roles, such as protagonist, antagonist, director,
auxiliaries, and audience. Figure 4.4 illustrates the different roles played by persons
associated with the surprise resignation of the MVSD's superintendent and subsequent withdrawal followed by court action to regain the position. In this situation, the
school board president (P) is faced with a difficult situation and attempts to play the
role of director in a serious and positive manner. The superintendent (SU) takes on
the role of protagonist, attempting at first to resign, then on reflection to seek reinstatement. Her role is viewed as serious but negative. The role of antagonist to the superintendent's resignation is played by a variety of persons, teachers and staff, who

FIGURE 4.4 Field diagram of MVSD superintendent's resignation

SOURCE: A. P. Hare, *Social Interaction as Drama: Applications from
Conflict Resolution,* p. 31, copyright 1985 by Sage Publications, Inc.
Reprinted by permission of Sage Publications, Inc.

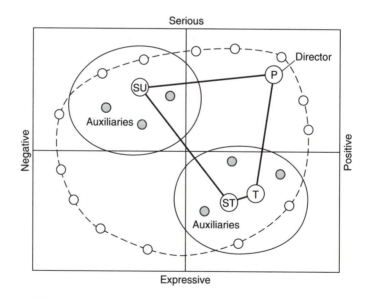

SU = superintendent
P = president of school board
T = teachers
ST = students

are shocked and dismayed at the resignation. Their roles are seen as positive and expressive. Auxiliaries are those who secretly complained about and resisted the new superintendent's directives, as well as those, such as the support staff, who were less active in this conflict but who supported the superintendent's return. The audience was made up of less active faculty and students, people in the community, and the state commissioner of education, who eventually became an active player.

Hare's field diagram has additional optional features built into it; for simplicity, Figure 4.4 does not display the dimensions of dominance and conformity to role or lines of polarization and balance. Together these additional features add richness to the description of an event and a way to sort out relationships among principal actors. However, this description is limited to a single event, and as conditions change, the roles of director, protagonist, antagonist, and so forth will shift. This was the case when the scene of the dispute over the superintendent's reinstatement was shifted to the courtroom: The judge became the director and the board president the antagonist while the superintendent remained as protagonist. Her script also shifted from wishing to escape to wishing to be in control.

The field diagram graphically represents the self-images of antagonists and protagonists and their images of one another. These impressions can be gathered through observations and/or interviews of various participants. The diagram also indicates the relative positions of actors or images during each "scene" or "act."

The second diagram (Figure 4.5) depicts "variations over time in the amount of involvement and creativity of the main individual and group theme carriers during the course of the action" (Hare, 1985, p. 68). The left-hand vertical scale of 0 to 5 indicates the levels of involvement/creativity of the main individuals or groups. The bottom horizontal line is a time line plotting the changes in these dimensions at different times (e.g., minutes, hours, days, etc.).

Applying Hare's diagram to the MVSD resignation/reinstatement situation, as shown in Figure 4.5, we can observe the flow of involvement/creativity of various actors or groups over time. At Time 1 the superintendent decided to resign; the board president accepted her resignation at Time 2. As the teachers and staff grasped the significance of the superintendent's actions (Time 3), they saw the superintendent as victim and confronted the board president with charges of forced resignation (Times 4 and 5). The superintendent reconsidered her decision and requested reinstatement (Time 5), which the board president denied, forcing the superintendent to seek resolution through civil court (Time 6). The judge held sway during the trial; the board president was put on the defensive and lost credibility in the process. Eventually the judge ruled in favor of the superintendent's reinstatement (Time 8), which was subsequently confirmed by the board of education of the MVSD. The superintendent returned to her position the conquering heroine and was greeted with enthusiasm and warm embraces. The board president was vanquished; he would have to wait for another day to exercise his influence over the superintendent's tenure. The activism of the teachers and staff and their confrontation with the board president were rewarded, but slowly they faded into the background as auxiliary players and/or members of the audience (Time 9). As we know, this was all to change as the events unfolded and time moved along.

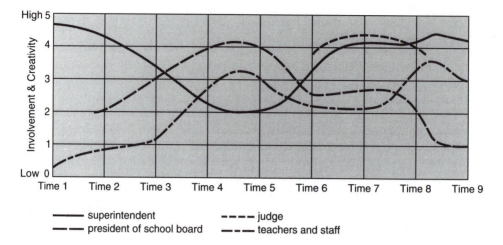

FIGURE 4.5   Theme carriers surrounding the superintendent's resignation and reinstatement events

SOURCE: A. P. Hare, *Social Interaction as Drama: Applications from Conflict Resolution,* p. 70, copyright 1985 by Sage Publications, Inc. Reprinted by permission of Sage Publications, Inc.

Hare (1985) maintains that with any theory, the dramaturgical perspective forces the analyst "to consider systematically how the various aspects of the action fit together in terms of the theory" (p. 71). With the theory grounded in the action of the major players, we can begin to anticipate reactions and possibly future actions of various members of the organization. For example, after observing the activism of teachers and staff, it would have been possible to forecast that they would employ this strategy again, which, of course, they did when the superintendent's new initiatives were not to their liking.

MANAGING ORGANIZATIONAL THEATER

Mangham and Overington (1987) write, "The management of organizations is a performing art, an important aspect of that is the shaping of direction and the marshalling of support through appropriate rhetoric" (p. 164). Leaders in organizations are called upon to fulfill many theatrical roles, from scriptwriter to director to actor. In the process of change, some leaders write scripts for other members of the organization to follow; other leaders act as directors, eliciting from actors a performance as near to the new script as possible. In all cases, we leaders must also be convincing actors, with a minimum of distance between our feelings, our spoken words, and our actions. Effective managers, in theatrical terms, are credible actors whose performance is in keeping with the script written for their role and audience expectations.

In addition to the triad of script, director, and actor is the importance of appearances. People in organizations are expected to maintain appearances that are in keeping with the nature of the organization and the public's expectations. Presidents of colleges and universities are expected to be formal, intellectual academicians temporarily serving in an administrative position. Superintendents in suburban school districts are expected to be bright, energetic, sociable, and well versed in recent educational innovations. Principals in rural areas are expected to be casual and personable and to know each child and parent on a first-name basis. Male presidents usually wear three-piece, pinstriped suits and female presidents wear comparable formal apparel. Their liberal arts faculty wear jeans, sweaters, and for men an occasional Harris Tweed jacket. Some schools even go so far as to specify proper dress codes for teachers and students. We are conditioned and in some cases coerced into accepting certain costumes with certain kinds of roles in different settings.

Persons in formal leadership positions are in a fishbowl and are expected to maintain appearances regardless of personal preferences. A good actor understands this and is skillful in fulfilling these expectations; by doing this, he or she gains greater credibility and respect. The new superintendent or the MVSD understood this and by all appearances had a great gift for being a leader and intellectual at the same time, a potent combination. Unfortunately, she was not able to maintain this image and began appearing less a leader and more like an ordinary person struggling to survive.

Bolman and Deal (1991) speak to the importance of appearances when they state: "From the vantage point of the symbolic frame, organizational structures, activities, and events are secular theatre. They express our fears, joys, and expectations. They arouse our emotions and kindle our spirit. They reduce our uncertainty and soothe our bewilderment. They provide a shared basis for understanding events and for moving ahead" (p. 275). These authors discuss our expectations for the physical appearance of churches and mental health clinics. There are similar expectations for schools. School designs are boxlike or egg-carton-shaped; the main office is usually near the front entrance of the building and often has a bench or chairs and counter. In elementary schools children's art is usually displayed in the corridors. During the sixties there was a movement to build schools without interior walls between classrooms; this design was short-lived and those that were built have been refitted with portable partitions or permanent walls.

The message is loud and clear: If a school wants the public's support, it must look like a school. To deviate carries with it many risks. Meyer and Rowan (1978) argue that a school must be able to answer three questions if it is to enjoy the public's support:

1. Does it offer appropriate subjects?
2. Are the topics taught to age-graded students by certified teachers?
3. Does the school look like a school (with classrooms, a gymnasium, a library, and a flag near the front door)?

Managers of organizational theater should not underestimate the importance of appearances and should realize that an image that runs counter to these expectations may prove costly. This may be viewed as bad news. The good news, however, is that if appearances are well managed, leaders may gain important support and resources vital to the success of their organization. For example, wealthy suburban communities quite often pride themselves on having first-rate schools with the latest in educational technology and curricular offerings. Wise administrators in these systems understand this phenomenon and make proposals and seek grants and tax support to provide for the latest innovations. In doing so, they are able to increase the educational opportunities of their students and provide faculty resources that ensure their success and high motivation. Managing these appearances may be just as important if not more than being knowledgeable in the latest theories of human development and/or student learning. As Bolman and Deal (1991) observe, "Leadership, therefore, is less a matter of action than of appearance. And when leaders do make a difference in a more proactive sense, it is usually by enriching and updating the script for the organizational drama—by constructing new myths that alter beliefs and generate faith among members of their audience" (p. 288). Getting appearance right is important. Getting it wrong is like putting a gun rack in a Volvo.

Managing humor can also serve an organizational leader well, particularly in situations of conflict. Being able to draw humor into the fray may take steel nerves and a cool head but also may turn a sour situation sweet. Kushner (1990) says that when facing a heated confrontation, we should try to diffuse it by making an unexpected joke. He suggests focusing on areas of agreement, making a joke about the competition, working conditions, or current events—whatever will induce laughter and a brief cooling-off period. Even a bad joke may help break the rhythm of the conflict and move it to a new plane.

Leaders in organizations have great opportunities to use their consciousness of dramaturgical concepts to observe, understand, and interpret the myriad of human interactions. With these new insights, leaders can begin to revise scripts, offering new symbols to uplift the spirit and hopes of members of the organization. If humor can be sprinkled in along the way, all the better.

If organizations are theater, then their leaders are actors who understand very well their role and its script. Their performance will be judged worthy of an Oscar by auxiliary and audience members as they perform and maintain appearances of what is generally expected of "leaders." Language, gestures, costumes, settings, and props all play a part in carrying out this performance and in conveying the qualities of leadership. The challenge is to find a good script and director that will prevent the play from becoming a melodrama or tragedy.

ETHICAL IMPLICATIONS OF ORGANIZATIONAL THEATER

As with any good strategy, this one can be subject to abuse. Humor can be used at the expense of certain people in an organization. Scripts can be written that effectively close out certain members and along with them their points of view and energy. Unscrupulous leaders can use appearances and symbols to hide devious motives and cover unethical behavior. Persons can be typecast and not allowed to challenge these assumptions about their character and abilities. All of these happen from time to time in organizations and can have very negative and debilitating effects. An ethical consciousness is needed when experimenting with theatrical concepts. Pragmatically, Perinbanayagam (1985) argues:

> Dramatization of my intentions, dispositions, feelings, attitudes, my past experiences, and my anticipations, etc., are courtesies that I extend to those who have to interact with me, exemplars of my *thoughtfulness* rather than Machiavellian ploys to take advantage of the others. In fact, it could be said that one who dramatizes his intentions, identity, etc., more or less accurately is the sincere person and that one who dramatizes inaccurately does so at the peril of one's continued relationship with the relevant audiences. (p. 81)

No doubt there is a hidden hand of retribution for those who attempt to be devious in their intentions. Time is not on their side. Lincoln is credited with saying that "you may fool all the people some of the time . . . but you can't fool all of the people all of the time." This aphorism is apropos those who have ulterior motives and sends the cautionary message that deception has its limitations. To put it more positively, there may be a universal ethical standard that applies as the ultimate script in judging the quality of one's ethical performance as a leader. Over time audiences can become quite discerning and sophisticated critics of the quality of a leader's performance, particularly on the more delineated stage of an organization.

CONCLUSION

In the final analysis, according to Mangham and Overington (1987) the theatrical metaphor allows us

> to explore the nature of others and their roles, enables us to comment upon performance everywhere. It enables us to ask questions about the nature of our commitment; do we play roles on both the social and organizational stages which are representations of our real selves, expressive . . . of some "deep structure," or are we simply role players simulating some sense of self? Is the actor an empty creature attuning himself [*sic*] to the winds of situations or is there something more to us than that? In the literature of both the stage and social life, the actor is seen as both authentic performer and as empty vessel. (p. 152)

The MVSD case, as a play, carries this theme to its final act when the superintendent resigns suggesting that there is something rotten in the state of the MVSD. Evil in the form of sexism and anti-Semitism won out and the good (i.e., academic excellence) that she had hoped to create at the MVSD would have to wait for another day. She was willing to "die" for her principle and fought the evil forces to the bitter end. These are often the ingredients of good theater and of life as well.

MVSD CASE REVISITED

One could view the MVSD case as a melodrama with an unhappy ending. Hopes for ushering in a new era gave way to tragic mistakes with long-term negative consequences. At the beginning, however, many individuals were captured by her vision and style, as was apparent at the special meeting for the new superintendent. No doubt her appointment was an attempt by many persons to write a new script for the MVSD, which for many years had been viewed as a struggling school system saddled with a large percentage of low-income students. The entrance of the new superintendent fostered new hope of the MVSD's becoming a district known for its excellence. The opening act was a tough act to follow.

Subsequent acts and scenes turned hope into an uncomfortable reality. At the beginning people were allowed to enjoy their own image of excellence; however, these images soon gave way to the reality of the superintendent's decisions, including, for example, the resignations of upper-level administrators. The previously held vision of a small and very personable school system was being replaced by a more impersonal and driven vision. The transition to a system based on principles of academic excellence brought many obstacles and challenges about which many persons soon grew uncomfortable.

We are not privy to what took place backstage and offstage between the superintendent and various key leaders of the MVSD: We can only speculate from what transpired onstage. Onstage, there were complaints of arbitrary and dictatorial behaviors by the superintendent, and we saw persons either voluntarily resigning or being forced to resign. We can assume many conversations, no doubt some of them quite heated, debating the virtues of the excellence vision and ways of achieving it. The subscript that began to emerge was the abuse of power and a disregard for personal worth. The audience began to feel that the superintendent was not acting as a leader but more like a dictator.

The theater metaphor and its lens allow an appreciation of how the events in this case can be seen as a series of acts and scenes linked together to provide an overall script befitting a melodrama. In addition, the dramaturgical concepts provide insight into the various roles being played by the major actors at various times. For example, we can observe the traditional theme of heroic sacrifice for a principle (i.e., academic excellence), which the superintendent no doubt felt was her raison d'être and worth her struggles with members of the MVSD. Maybe the superintendent needed to develop the ability to stand "apart from interaction, even as [one is] engaged in it to discover its meaning" (Hare, 1985, p. 42). Often a good actor must do this in order to give an outstanding performance.

DISCUSSION QUESTIONS

1. Is there a difference between theater and life in organizations? If yes, in what ways are they different? If no, in what ways are they the same?
2. What dramaturgical concepts do you find most interesting and relevant to your organizational experiences?

3 What implications do the dramaturgical concepts have for leadership in organizations?

4. We explored the symbolic importance of appearances both for the organization and for leaders in the organization. What is your position on appearances? Are they more important than substance? Can they substitute for substance in an organization?

5. In Figure 4.1, Performance Continuum, are displayed several interrelated dramaturgical concepts from self to performance. Does this make sense at a personal level? Why or why not?

SUGGESTED ACTIVITIES

1. Revisit the MVSD case and apply various dramaturgical concepts to its events.

2. Take a recent event in your organization and apply various dramaturgical concepts. Using Figure 4.4 and 4.5 as references, diagram this event. What inferences are reasonable from this analysis?

3. Take the same event or another and rewrite the script for it. What new theme(s) would you like to portray? What characters would you need? Who would be your protagonists, antagonists, and auxiliary players? Who would you cast from your organization into which roles? What props, costumes, gestures, and so forth would you use? For what audience would you like to perform?

4. Select one of the more promising scripts from activity 3 and have members of the class perform it. Provide time for learning the script and for rehearsal. Following the performance, discuss the experience and its implications for understanding organizational behavior.

5. Review some of the themes portrayed in the theater, past and present. Discuss their relevance to the challenges and paradoxes often faced in present-day organizations.

6. An organizational consultant claimed that he would be "hanged" in his state if he ever engaged the idea that organizations are like theater. Why is this notion so threatening? Would some individuals abhor such a comparison between organizations and theater? What is driving this point of view and what are its implications for creating effective organizations? Request members of the group to express arguments on both sides of this question (i.e., appropriateness of comparing organizations to theater). Maybe some member(s), as a course project, would be willing to capture these views in a play format that could be performed at end of the course.

REFERENCES

Ashforth, B. E. (1988). The mindlessness of organizational behaviors. *Human Relations, 41,* 305-29.

Barish, J. (1981). *The antitheatrical prejudice.* Berkeley: University of California Press.

Bolman, L. G., & Deal, T. E. (1991). *Reframing organizations.* San Francisco: Jossey-Bass.

Burke, K. (1962). *A grammar of motives and a rhetoric of motives.* Cleveland: World Publishing.

Burke, K. (1968). Dramatism. *Encyclopedia of the Social Sciences,* 445-51.

Burns, E. (1972). *Theatricality: A study of convention in the theatre and in social life.* New York: Harper & Row.

Consalvo, C. M. (1986). *Humor in task-oriented management meetings.* Unpublished dissertation, University of Vermont, Burlington, VT.

Duncan, W. J. (1989). No laughing matter: Patterns of humor in the workplace. *Organizational Dynamics, 17*(4), 18-30.

Fry, C. (1962). Comedy. In S. Barnet, M. Berman, & W. Burto (Eds.), *Aspects of the drama: A handbook.* Boston: Little, Brown.

Goffman, E. (1974). *Frame analysis: An essay on the organization of experience.* New York: Harper & Row.

Hamilton, C. (1939). *The theory of the theatre: And other principles of dramatic criticism.* New York: Holt, Rinehart, & Winston.

Hansot, E. (1979). *Some functions of humor in organization.* Unpublished paper, Kenyon College, Gambier, Oh.

Hare, A. P. (1976). *Handbook of small group research* (2nd ed.). New York: Free Press.

Hare, A. P. (1985). *Social interaction as drama: Applications from conflict resolution.* Beverly Hills, CA: Sage.

Hertzler, J. O. (1970). *Laughter: A socio-scientific analysis.* New York: Exposition Press.

Jaffe, C. A. (1990). Management by fun. *Nation's Business, 1,* 58–60.

Krohe, J. (9187). Take my boss—please. *Across the Board, 24,* 31–35.

Kushner, M. L. (1990). *The light touch.* New York: Simon & Schuster.

Mangham, I. L., & Overington, M. A. (1987). *Organizations as theatre: A social psychology of dramatic appearances.* New York: Wiley.

Meyer, J., & Rowan, B. (1978). The structure of educational organizations. In M. W. Meyer et al., *Environments and organizations: Theoretical and empirical perspectives.* San Francisco: Jossey-Bass.

Miles-Brown, J. (1980). *Directing drama.* London: Peter Owen.

Perinbanayagam, R. S. (1985). *Signifying acts: Structure and meaning in everyday life.* Carbondale: Southern Illinois University Press.

Polti, G. (1977). *The thirty-six dramatic situations.* Boston: Writer.

Spolin, V. (1977). *Improvisation for the theatre: A handbook of teaching and directing techniques.* London: Pitman.

Ziv, A. (1984). *Personality and sense of humor.* New York: Springer.

chapter **5**

Organizations from a Brain Perspective

Behind culture, politics, and theater are brains that consciously or unconsciously determine the behaviors associated with these metaphors. Thus it is fitting that we leave to the end the source of ultimate rationality *and* subjectivity—the brain.

An article in *Newsweek* reporting the latest research on the brain concluded that "as an organization, the brain is a society of specialists" (Gelman, Rosenberg, Kandell, & Crandall, 1992, p. 72). This image captures the complexity of the brain's structure, with its relatively discrete sections, and provides an apt metaphor for describing most educational organizations. Specifically, most neurobiologists describe the brain as having three major parts: the old or visceral brain, and the new brain made up of right and left hemispheres. MacLean (1964) refers to these as the primitive reptilian brain, paleomammalian (limbic system), and neomammalian (neocortical system), respectively. The visceral brain is concerned with basic biological thought processes and basic value systems. The limbic system or right brain is concerned with creative thought processes and latent value systems. The left brain or neocortex controls conscious, cognitive thought processes and temporal value systems.

Public school organizations and their curricula reflect, in part, these three major sections of the brain. From an organizational perspective the school administration represents the conscious cognitive functions of the organization; the teachers and their pupils respond in more personal, creative, and emotional ways, sustaining the latent values of the school; and the support personnel carry out specific and basic routines to maintain a safe and predictable environment.

In terms of the curricula of a school, it does not require much imagination to apply each of the parts of the brain to academic subjects and activities. Subjects like math and science have a strong emphasis on orderly and rational thinking, associated with the left brain. The arts—music, visual arts, theater, and dance—draw heavily on right-brain thinking. Sports, particularly contact sports, and skill-related activities can be associated with the visceral brain. In many ways schools and other educational organizations are more obviously reflective of the brain's structure than other types of organizations. This may be due in part to the educational institutions' general purpose of developing persons of reason *and* creativity.

Even as we look beyond the simple structure of the brain, we discover other similarities. For example, research on the brain and how it functions reveals a holographic phenomenon; that is, parts of the brain tend to reflect the whole of the brain. This characteristic makes it possible for persons with serious brain injuries to replicate certain functions in other parts of their brain. In educational organizations, such as the Mountain View School District (MVSD), we can observe this redundancy of functions to the lowest level of the institution; for example, teachers carry on many of the same functions of disciplinary control, public relations, and staff development, as does the school administration. At the same time, in organizations as in the brain, there are discrete functions in certain parts that cannot be easily replicated in other parts. Administrators do not typically take over the instructional functions, and teachers do not typically take over budget allocations and approval of expenditures.

Obviously, to maximize the metaphoric or reframing potential of the brain in discovering certain features of educational organization, we need to examine other characteristics associated with brains. This leads us to differentiate the mind from the physical structure of the brain and explore areas of thinking, ways of knowing, learning, control, boredom, and neurosis and addiction. However we choose to reduce the parts of the brain or mind, we are cautioned by Bessinger and Suojanen (1983): "Remember that the three minds of man [*sic*] operate concurrently as *one total system*. Anything we do, anything we say, anything that we think (whether we are sick or well) is the composite result of these three minds operating together" (p. 188; emphasis added).

The image of the brain as a total system with interacting and interdependent parts links well to systems thinking. In this chapter we shall explore a number of concepts of the brain and systems that can help illuminate the behavior of educational organizations. We will first explore the need for organizations as brains and then launch into a number of brain- and systems-related concepts. In addition to the brain concepts mentioned above, we will explore related systems concepts of autopoiesis, hologamy, cybernetics, and mutual causality. As it has been our practice in previous chapters, we will discuss ways to study organizations as brains and how to manage organizational learning. We will close out the chapter with a revisit to the MVSD case and some suggested activities that will help us appreciate the power of reframing organizations as brains.

NEED FOR ORGANIZATIONS AS BRAINS

In many ways, the earlier chapters stressed right-brain thinking. We examined the emotional and value-laden aspects of organizations as cultures and politics and the creative dimensions of organizations as theaters. Viewing organizations as brains brings a certain balance to this and an awareness that other aspects of organizational life exist, such as the powers of logical thinking and reason. However, as Goldberg (1989) stresses: "Emotion and intellect are not separable. Nor should they be. Rather we need to understand and appreciate the essential unity and complementarity of the two. Healing this dualism can significantly enhance our survival as individuals and as a race. Failure to do so can equally be harmful" (p. 146). As a metaphor the brain provides an opportunity to integrate these seeming opposites of reason and emotion.

Further, the brain as a metaphor stresses the importance of information processing. The brain has been compared to a master control system, a neurocybernetic system, that monitors all functions of the body and various signals in the environment, processes this information, stores and retrieves data, and stimulates various forms of response or behavior. Morgan (1986) observes: "Rational action is not undertaken blindly but in an awareness that is appropriate" (p. 78). It is this capacity to observe-think-do-reflect that is unique about the human brain and serves well as a model for structuring and examining organizational functions.

The capacity to process information and to learn from the process is crucial to individual development as well as the development and effectiveness of organizations. There is a fine line separating learning by individuals in an organization and organizational learning: It is possible for persons to learn from their individual actions while the overall organization continues its modus operandi unaware of errors or need for change. When individual learning becomes integrated into corporate learning the organization can reflect on and modify its behavior. The brain metaphor helps us appreciate the need for synthesizing many independent learnings over time into a new theory of action. As Argyris (1978) states, "Organizational learning occurs when members of the organization act as learning agents for the organization, responding to changes in the internal and external environments of the organization by detecting errors and correcting errors in organizational theory-in-use, and embedding the results in their enquiry in private images and shared maps of organization" (p. 29).

One of the major functions of the brain is learning, a point that should not be ignored by educational organizations; as they grapple with changes in a turbulent and unpredictable environment, a capacity to react, reason, emote, and create will be indispensable.

Learning is dependent on how we think and, as has been suggested, specifically how we process information. How we come to think about people and situations in organizations is a consequence of social cognition. According to Sims and Gioia (1986), social cognition "is based on the fundamental assumption that thinking and thought are the lifeblood of organizations, that social cognition lies at the heart of decision making, communication, strategic action, interpersonal behavior, organization design, and virtually every other important organizational process" (p. ix).

Understanding social cognition within an organizational context permits greater insight as to how administrators and other members are affected by complex internal and external social forces. A further probing of this function of the brain can help to build the link between cognition and action. To quote Goethe: "Thinking is easy, acting difficult, and to put one's thoughts into action, the most difficult thing in the world." The brain metaphor acknowledges this difficulty and offers further insight into the connection, or misconnection, between thought and action.

Social cognition also has different sides to it. According to Belenky, Clinchy, Goldberger, and Tarule (1986), women's cognition is different from men's. Their research on women from various social and economic backgrounds enabled them to appreciate the qualities of women's ways of knowing. Using the metaphor of voice, these researchers discovered the developmental pattern women typically experience in moving from having a limited sense of self to being able to express their perceptions and feelings. Schaef (1991) describes women's reality as different from men's reality: "In the Female System, there is no right or wrong. It is possible to be different and still be all right. There can be two—or more—answers to the same question, and all can be right. None has to be wrong" (p. 21). She challenges the myth that it is desirable to be totally logical, rational, and objective; illogical, subjective, or intuitive thoughts or behaviors should not have to be denied or suppressed. (Chapter 13 devotes more attention to feminist theory and its implications for understanding organizations.)

The brain metaphor opens the door to insights on conditions ranging from rational to emotional to visceral built into our organizations. It permits seeing and discovering common but also unique characteristics. In the next section, we will explore some of these special features in greater detail.

BRAIN-RELATED CONCEPTS

The brain and its functions offer fertile ground for identifying a variety of concepts. Our purpose, of course, is to link these concepts to school organizations and discover their explanatory powers. As discussed, the brain has three major parts, each of which performs special functions; at the same time, the brain is capable of duplicating functions in its different parts. These seem to be contradictory phenomena and defy simple explanations. We shall begin our review of related concepts by first recognizing the brain as a total system with holographic features. Following our exploration of systems concepts, we shall explore concepts of the major subsystems of the brain, often referred to as the left, right, and visceral brains.

The Brain as a Total System

There is considerable interdependence and interconnection among the major subsystems of the brain, and it is very difficult to separate these parts when attempting to explain the behavior of individuals. In the case of organizations, it is difficult to explain organizational behavior by examining any one subsystem within the larger system. In the same way, there is often a tendency to explain the behavior of an individual based on his or her personality and overlook the variety of other influences that act on this individual. For example, we may attribute a number of personal characteristics to the Mountain View School District superintendent to explain her commitment to academic excellence while overlooking a number of other influences. Clearly her drive for excellence was in part a response to messages received from a number of sources (e.g., board of education members, teachers, and students) and resonated well with her own values and background as a respected scholar. Separating out a single cause for the superintendent's interest in academic excellence would violate the interlocking relationships that combined to create a force in favor of some change.

According to Flood and Jackson (1991), "the concept of 'systems' is used not to refer to things in the world but to a particular way of organizing our thoughts about the world" (p. 2). This new mode of thought is needed to counter the effects of mechanistic thinking, which relies on reductionism. It is becoming increasingly evident that social behavior cannot be easily reduced to independent parts and single, one-way causes. Early systems thinking borrowed heavily from biological analogies such as survival, adaptability, development, growth, flexibility, and stability. More recently, systems have become known as a "complex and highly interlinked network of parts exhibiting synergistic properties—the whole is *greater than* the sum of its parts" (Flood & Jackson, 1991, p. 4).

Systems thinking, according to Senge (1990), "offers a language that begins restructuring how we think" (p. 60). He explains the importance of a "shift of mind from seeing parts to seeing wholes, from seeing people as helpless reactors to seeing them as active participants in shaping their reality, from reacting to the present to creating the future" (p. 60). Part of this shift of mind is the capacity to view events in a mutually causal way or to think in circles rather than straight lines. In systems thinking, actions are both cause and effect. According to Senge, performing simple tasks like filling a glass with water from a faucet is often viewed as a linear and one-way causal event: "I fill the glass with water." What is overlooked is how this process unfolds and how the various elements—you as observer, you as actor, the faucet, glass, water flow, and water level—are interlinked in a circular and mutually causal relationship. We might observe, for example, that it is the water flow into the glass that controls the person's hand on the faucet; that is, it is the structure of the system, its component parts and their relationships, that control how a person plays a part, but only a part, in filling a glass of water. The individual has not caused the glass to fill but rather is part of a system to fill a glass with water; he or she is in part controlled by water flow, the nature of the glass, the position of the faucet, and the ability to observe the filling of the glass. A sudden rise in water pressure helps to remind us that we are not in total control but are only one element of the system. As Senge (1990) observes, "From the systems perspective, the human actor is part of the feedback process, not standing apart from it. This represents a profound shift in awareness. It allows us to see how we are continually both influenced by and influencing our reality" (p. 78).

Systems Dynamics.   Causal loops, as in the example of filling the glass, have led to extensive research and development of a subfield in systems thinking known as systems dynamics. According to Roberts (1978), "Systems dynamics is the application of feedback control systems principles and techniques to managerial, organizational, and socioeconomic problems" (p. 3). Systems dynamics recognizes our natural tendency to think in the form of mental models when it comes to understanding our social context. Our mental models, however, tend to be very fuzzy, imprecise, and intuitively faulty (cf. Forester, 1971) when it comes to explaining social system behavior. Systems dynamics, with the use of computer programs such as DYNAMO or STELLA, attempts to represent our mental models in more precise ways. According to Meadows,

Richardson, and Bruckman (1982), computer models surpass mental models in rigor, accessibility, comprehensiveness, logic, and flexibility. On the other hand, critics question the computer model's capacity to factor in less precise variables such as human subjectivity and emotions (cf. Flood & Jackson, 1991). In any regard, systems dynamics illustrates the connectiveness of variables, including oneself, and demonstrates features parallel in many ways to the structure of the brain. There is further exploration of systems dynamics later in this chapter when we examine its relevance to studying organizations as brains.

Holography.   Reliance on computers in systems dynamics reminds us how often the brain is associated with being a command center made up of a complex computer. This helps reinforce the image of the brain as an information-processing system. The brain appears to have enormous capacity for storing and retrieving information. More recently, the brain has been compared to a holographic system (Morgan, 1986). A hologram recorded on a photographic plate re-creates original images across the entire surface; that is, if a hologram is broken, any single piece will reflect the entire image. As Morgan (1986) explains, "Everything is enfolded in everything else, just as if we were able to throw a pebble into a pond and see the whole pond and all the waves, ripples, and drops of water generated by the splash *in each and every one of the drops of water thus produced*" (p. 80). With holography the whole is encoded in all its parts and every part represents the whole. It has been suggested by neuroscientists that the human brain functions on holographic principles: The brain appears to store memory in many of its parts and can reconstitute it from any of them.

When applying holography to organizations, certain principles, such as learning to learn, requisite variety, minimum critical specification, and redundancy of functions, are emphasized (Morgan, 1986). School organizations often reflect holographic features, particularly redundancy. Semi-autonomous teaching teams and multi-age groups duplicate several functions within the teams and among the other teams in the school; this enables learning-related activities to move forward even if one member of the team is absent. Overlapping and shared responsibilities reflect holographic characteristics.

Autopoiesis.   According to the theoretical work of Maturana and Varela (1980), the concept of autopoiesis has taken systems thinking to yet another level. Simply, autopoiesis means self-producing. As Maturana and Varela observe from their study of living cells, "In our common experience we encounter living systems as unities that appear to us as autonomous entities of bewildering diversity endowed with the capacity to reproduce" (p. 73). This capacity is actually for *infinite* self-reproduction. Beer (1980) concludes, "Autopoiesis says that something that exists may turn out to be unrecognizable when you next observe it" (p. 67).

The importance of this concept for organizations is explored by Mingers (1989). He suggests that

humans are autopoietic entities and, as such, autonomous and independent. Traditional types of organizations, however, treat them purely as components within the system, that is, they treat them as allopoietic. Not only is this wrong in the moral sense, but it is also not necessarily good systems design. Autopoiesis shows how systems can function in a decentralized, non-hierarchical way purely through the individual interactions of neighboring components. (p. 173)

Autopoiesis challenges the viewpoint that the environment dictates the nature and survival of organizations. In this system, organizations have the self-reproducing capacity to draw resources from the environment and adapt sufficiently so that they continue to survive as an entity.

This concept offers an interesting perspective as we think of various efforts to reform education in the United States, including efforts to create new organizations outside the public education system. When we look at school reform efforts in section 3, we will revisit the concept of autopoiesis and its implications for sustaining existing school organizations in spite of extreme pressure from outside to significantly "restructure."

The Brain as Subsystems

As described earlier, the brain is made up of three distinct parts, although these parts are highly interactive and interdependent: the visceral brain, the right brain, and the left brain. An exploration of each of these will permit us to examine related concepts to further illuminate the subtleties of organizational life.

To help us appreciate the differences in these three subsystems, Bessinger and Suojanen (1983) compare the parts of the brain to the characters from the original episodes of *Star Trek*: Mr. Spock, Dr. McCoy, and Capt. Kirk. Mr. Spock is left-brain dominant: analytical, quantitative, intellectual, verbal, and rational. McCoy, on the other hand, is right-brain dominant: synthesizing, creative, artistic, normative, and spatial. And to Trekkies, it is no surprise to see Capt. Kirk associated with the visceral brain.

Visceral Brain.   The animal behavior of human beings is dominated by the search for pleasure. Kirk is seen often under the influence of the visceral brain's pleasure areas, which send chemical "yes" messages in response to pleasure. By contrast, the left and right brains send chemical "no" messages. When these are in balance, Kirk makes realistic decisions. However, when the pleasure areas of the visceral brain dominate, the result is hedonistic pursuit.

As we know, this imbalance can lead to addiction in individuals; organizations can become addictive as well. Schaef and Fassel (1988), in their book *The Addictive Organization*, point out that addictions can be to a substance or a process: "This is because the purpose or function of an addiction is to *put a buffer between ourselves and our awareness of our feelings*. An addiction serves to numb us so that we are out of touch with what we know and what we feel. Moreover, we often get so taken up with the addiction—an addictive relationship, for example—that we have no energy for or awareness of other aspects of our life" (p. 58; emphasis added).

Addiction can be subtle and reinforced in ways we are not aware of, particularly within an organizational context. Schaef and Fassel (1988, pp. 68-73) outline six processes involved in an addictive system:

- *the promise* (provides temporary relief from the here and now)
- *the pseudopodic ego* (projects an illusion of openness and flexibility while at the same time perpetuates the system's rigidness intact)
- *the external reference* (influences people to behave as others would have them and results in being less able to sense one's own true feelings)
- *invalidation* (is being capable of knowing other points of view but not allowing them inside one's frame of reference)
- *fabricating personality conflicts* (helps avoid having to deal with conflicting information by the illusion of a conflict with its source)
- *dualism* (allows us to relegate a very complex and ambiguous universe to two simplistic choices)

Addictive systems are perpetuated by a silent conspiracy of co-dependence. Co-dependent individuals or groups avoid confronting the addictive behavior of others and, worse, will lie about its negative aspects even if presented with an opportunity to comment openly. True feelings about the addictive behavior are denied; instead, there is often an expression of public approval.

Organizations can unknowingly reinforce employees' addictive behavior. One way is through promises. Organizations make many promises of getting ahead—with power, money, influence—and belonging—by being part of one big happy family. A well-articulated mission can often seduce members into believing they are serving some greater cause. According to Schaef and Fassel (1988), persons working in the "helping" professions are most vulnerable to the promises associated with their dedicated careers. Unfortunately, what persons are committed to and what they experience can be quite different:

> The organization becomes the addictive substance for its employees when the employees become hooked on the promise of the mission and choose not to look at how the system is really operating. The organization becomes an addictive substance when its actions are excused because it has a lofty mission. We have found an inverse correlation between the loftiness of the mission and congruence between stated and unstated goals. When this lack of congruence exists, it is more probable that the organization will enter into a rigid denial system with concomitant grandiosity. (Schaef & Fassel, 1988, p. 123)

Organizations can act as an addictive substance particularly for those who are already substance abusers or are children of substance abusers. Of course, work can provide a platform for finding one's identity, but an overidentification with work can lead to a destructive form of behavior: workaholism. It is unfortunate that in our society workaholic behavior is socially accepted and reinforced in a variety of ways: Persons who are willing to sacrifice their personal life for their job are often praised, rewarded, and given public recognition for their extensive productivity.

Workaholics who totally immerse themselves in their work speak of an altered state of mind or of experiencing an adrenaline rush often associated with drugs; in fact, workaholics frequently suffer from other addictions to alcohol, food, or drugs. Like any other addiction, workaholism can lead to a loss of spirituality and to losing touch with one's morality.

An addictive organization often displays

- *communications* that usually appear indirect, vague, confused, secretive, and ineffective
- *thinking processes* that are distorted and result in a loss of corporate memory or forgetfulness
- *management and personnel processes* that include denial and dishonesty, isolation, self-centeredness, judgmentalism, perfectionism, confusion and crises orientation, seduction, setting up sides, and manipulating its consumers or clients
- *structural components* that engender competition, heighten control, apply punishment, guarantee predictability, and make accomplishing its mission very difficult (Schaef & Fassel, 1988, pp. 137-76)

We will revisit some of these characteristics of addictive organizations when we explore ways to study organizations as brains later in this chapter. At this juncture, suffice it to say that both organizations and individuals can act in addictive ways that appear to be commonplace, everyday behavior. We often fail to recognize these behaviors as extreme and controllable. The visceral brain, as a reality and as a metaphor, alerts us to the extremes to which individuals and organizations may extend themselves in the pursuit of "pleasure" and in the avoidance of everyday problems or concerns. We may wish to consider other forms of healthy behavior as substitutes, including flexibility, honesty, multiple options, and intrinsic rewards.

Right Brain. Bessinger and Suojanen (1983) describe the right brain as associated with sensing, feeling, and creating: It uses lateral thinking, which is nonsequential, need not be accurate at each step of the way, and is not restricted to only relevant ideas. This portion of the brain favors art and sculpture, poetry and literature, architecture and music.

Metaphoric thinking—seeing the forest rather than the trees—and reframing processes—generating new observations and new explanations—are right-brain oriented. Right-brain thinking gives way to the "art" and practice of administration as opposed to the left-brain "science" of administration. A major theme of this text is right-brain development in ourselves and in our organizations.

Left Brain. The left brain performs the judging, controlling, and assessing functions to support the scientific method. If the right brain is the research and development functions of our thinking, the left brain performs the tests and evaluations. The left brain is rational and specializes in vertical thinking, which is stepwise, correct, and relevant. It is often associated with management science and operations research or hard systems thinking. Left-brain functions that work in concert with right-brain thinking create a powerful combination and need to be appreciated for their synergistic potential.

Frontal Lobes. It appears that the right and left brains do collaborate. According to Bessinger and Suojanen (1983), our planning function occurs in the frontal lobes of both sides of the brain. The frontal lobes appear to operate jointly when expectancy is involved. The front of the brain is like a trusted adviser who handles public relations and planning. Evoked responses may be an indication that the right and left brains are preparing for joint action. Bessinger and Suojanen conclude, "It is clear that the truly creative individual is one in whom a balance exists between the cerebral hemispheres" (p. 171).

On the other hand, we are aware that affective (right brain) and cognitive (left brain) processes can break down or work in conflict with one another. Affective influences on managerial decisions, for example, can be subtle, insidious, and pervasive. As Park, Sims, and Motowidlo (1986) suggest, "Better insight into the affective and cognitive processes involved should point the way toward strategies and interventions to help managers avoid the potentially dysfunctional effects of affective and emotional states on information processing, judgment, and decision making" (p. 231).

Yet, others might argue just the opposite. That is, we should not allow information, judgment, and decision making to go unchecked and unexamined by our values and affective senses, particularly our sense of right and wrong. As Goldberg (1989) suggests, "That emotions can hold the key to reason is something of a paradox. Yet we consistently downgrade and demean our emotional instincts" (p. 146).

Butcher (1985) describes what can go awry when a sense of right and wrong becomes confused or ignored. He describes his shock when he discovered that his two-and-a-half-year-old-son was diagnosed with aplastic anemia caused by the dyes in his crayons. His child's doctor informed him that some crayon manufacturers use harmful dyes that contain benzene even after being informed of its danger to young children, who often eat the crayons. Butcher was left wondering, "If antisocial business behavior is not necessary to make a profit, and if it is not a necessary part of human nature, why does it keep occurring?" (p. 275).

Organizations can unwittingly or consciously do harm to their members and to their "customers." Morgan (1986) explores the dark side of organizations when he elaborates on organizations as psychic prisons. He states, "Human beings have a knack of getting trapped in webs of their own creation" (p. 199) and discusses the traps of success (sense of superiority), organizational slack (excessive inventory), and group processes (groupthink). Freud, according to Morgan, believed "that in order to live in harmony with one another humans must moderate and control their impulses, and that the unconscious and culture were thus really two sides of the same coin, giving hidden and manifest form to the 'repression' that accompanied the development of human sociability" (p. 203). Recognition of this dark side can give birth and hope to our creative side, helping us to change and move away from harmful unconscious thinking. Our potential for mitigating negative impulses is evident in school environments that reflect a healthy attitude toward their members and serve as exemplars of what we are capable of creating. These positive examples can serve us well as we contemplate the reformation of schools.

An equally important point, according to Gardner (1983, 1993), is to respect the multiple intelligences of individuals and how these can make unique contributions to our lives. Gardner claims that for too long we have considered intelligence as a single property of the human mind. He advocates "a far wider and more universal set of competencies than we have ordinarily considered" (1983, p. x) and goes on to define intelligence as the ability to solve problems or create products that are valued in one or more cultural settings. This definition places greater emphasis on the capacities to learn and act as opposed to some intrinsic, narrowly measured characteristics of our capacity to think. He describes seven intelligences: linguistic and logical-mathematical (which dominate most school curricula), musical, spatial, bodily-kinesthetic, and two forms of personal intelligence, one directed at other persons and one directed at oneself. Gardner's work provides yet another rich metaphor for increasing an organization's potential to improve: the recognition of multiple intelligences and capacities to problem-solve and produce something of value.

WAYS TO STUDY ORGANIZATIONS AS BRAINS

Systems Perspective

The previous section provided a number of concepts for thinking of organizations as brains. Systems concepts, for example, prompt attention to the degree to which the organization is cybernetically linked.

Viable Systems. Beer (1979, 1981, 1985), in his development and application of the Viable Systems Model (VSM), emphasizes the dynamic relationships of organizational functions that address the needs for communications and control processes. Essentially, Beer outlines five systems for an organization to be "viable" or to survive: "Survival is the function of the *total organization* of any system that does survive, and includes its capacity to learn, to adapt, to evolve. A system that does all these things is called a *viable system*" (1979, p. 334). Beer defines the five systems:

- *System 1* is concerned with implementation and connects to the environment
- *System 2* coordinates parts that make up System 1 and dampens uncontrolled oscillations between parts
- *System 3* acts as a control function that maintains internal stability and interprets policy decisions of higher management
- *System 4* is the intelligence-gathering/reporting function of the total system and rapidly transmits urgent information from Systems 1, 2, and 3 to System 5
- *System 5* is responsible for policy and represents the total system to the environment and other systems

These five systems and their related functions need to be attended to at all levels of an organization if it is to avoid drift and eventual collapse. If we relate these functions to the Mountain View School District, we can appreciate how they get distributed in an organization. For example, we would expect that the goals of the institution are implemented in each of the schools in the MVSD and in the actions of their teachers; they would be responsible for System 1 functions. System 2 functions would rest with school administrators, including department chairs and project leaders. Systems 3 and 4 would be seen operating at the superintendent's level and System 5 at the school board level. Although it is tempting to view these systems in a hierarchy, Beer (1979) says the "VSM is not essentially hierarchal, it is essentially an intersection of subsystems" (p. 335).

It is important to keep in mind that these functions are recursive (that is, each viable system contains and is contained in a viable system) throughout the organization and that information flows through appropriate communication links connecting the various systems and its environment. Shared information ranges from a regard for the attainment of goals to the condition of employee morale.

Using VSM as a conceptual framework allows us to peel back layers of complexity in some orderly fashion and identify breakdowns in communications and control. It should also allow us to ascertain the degree to which each of the subsystems works in harmony with the others for the benefit of the total system. Frequently, a major problem is that the information gathered and communicated has little to do with performance, or, if the information is appropriate, it is not shared in a timely manner, rendering it obsolete. In sum, Beer (1989) offers four pithy questions when applying the VSM to organizations:

1. Is management presiding over a "viable system"?
2. Does subsystem 5 truly represent the entire system within the context of larger, more comprehensive and more powerful systems?
3. Do managers often fail to understand the need for subsystems 2 and 4?
4. Do the 3, 4, and 5 subsystems need to form a 3-4-5 subsystem to encourage "synergy" and interactivity? (pp. 27-28)

Systems Dynamics.   Other systems metaphors or models can aid us in studying organizations. Systems dynamics, discussed earlier in this chapter, provides a methodology for analyzing "problem situations." According to Richmond and Peterson (1992), "We *are* capable of meeting the challenges we face. However, to do so, we must learn to 'think smarter'" (p. 4). To do this, Richmond and his colleagues designed a software program called STELLA that guides the user through a thinking process by (1) constructing mental models, (2) making comparisons between models, and (3) resolving conflicts between these models by making appropriate adjustments to currently held mental models. The STELLA software moves the user from a pencil sketch of a mental model of a situation with principal variables and their interactions to a computer-constructed representation of these relationships, which is equally visual and capable of displaying movement or change over time.

Richmond and Peterson use the situation of a college campus bookstore to illustrate the potential of the STELLA software. The bookstore was faced with an enormous problem of overload of student customers, all wanting to buy their books during similar time periods. The STELLA software isolated the various factors that created this situation and the flow of students over the first week of the semester. Once this flow was diagrammed the bookstore manager simulated "what if" scenarios, enabling the manager to discover a workable solution: Students would receive colored tickets that allowed access to the store at specified times. This simple policy permitted a wider distribution of the student load over a longer time period and limited the number of students in the store at any one time.

The STELLA software basically extends the thinking and creativity of the problem solver, allows simulation of prospective solutions, and minimizes the risks of taking action that might exacerbate a condition. The problem solver can focus on identifying and understanding the various factors influencing a situation and allow the computer program to manipulate these factors and their interrelationships and project the effects of probable changes. As Flood and Jackson (1991) write, "Given sound reasoning and understanding of structure in the development of a SD [systems dynamic] model, it is assumed that high quality prediction and control can be achieved" (p. 64). If prediction and control cannot be fully achieved, at least a greater appreciation of the internal dynamics of the problem and the probable effects of different solutions can be anticipated.

Organization Addiction

Thus far we have discussed ways of drawing upon the various parts of the brain, particularly the left and right sides, to better understand a complex condition. Schaef and Fassel (1988) explore ways to understand an organization from the perspective of addiction, a primal- or visceral-brain problem, using the organizational variables of communications, thinking, management and personnel processes, and structure.

Communications. Communications in all organizations tend to be a problem, but communications problems in an addictive organization are more exaggerated. Often, they include extreme forms of communications

- that tend to be conducted in more indirect ways often through third parties
- that are usually vague, confused, and ineffective
- that include lots of gossip and "secrets"
- that break down but are not accidental

Thinking Processes. Addictive symptoms showing up in thinking processes include

- a loss of corporate memory, or forgetfulness, distorted thinking, and dualism
- externalization of issues by placing them on others so that the source does not have to deal with them or assume any responsibility
- organizational projection, which involves blaming others or outside conditions for the organization's problems

- dualistic thinking, which sees people as being either good or bad
- seeing competitors as the enemy, with little or nothing to teach

Management and Personnel Processes. Management and personnel in addictive organizations engage in a number of damaging behaviors. Schaef and Fassel (1988) define one of them: "Denial is not allowing oneself to see or know what is really going on. It is a type of dishonesty. Dishonesty is related to lying to or misleading the self and others" (p. 150). Denial in an organizational context can lead to the refusal to recognize or deal with aberrant or extreme conditions.

Other symptoms include

- judgmentalism: makes no attempt to separate the person from his or her behavior
- perfectionism: perpetuates the illusion of perfection while the person is experiencing internal chaos
- self-centeredness: accounts for unrealistic job descriptions and excessively lofty goals
- crisis orientation: used to bring people in line and to give an inordinate amount of power to management
- seduction: plays a role in getting people to do things that they ordinarily might not feel is right for them
- superficial relationships: used as a substitute for closer and more intimate relationships
- setting up either/or conditions: forces members to take sides around issues

Structural Components. Schaef and Fassel (1988) point out that "structurally, control is built into every level of the addictive organization" (p. 167). Addictive behavior is manifested structurally in the following ways:

- Greater emphasis is placed on controlling the image of the organization by enforcing dress codes, appearances at certain social functions, and on creating the right impression
- Planning is overemphasized in order to maximize control
- Planning is prescriptive and attempts to rigidly apply goals and objectives as though they were predictions of the future
- A small oligarchy, with minimal outside participation, makes use of power and politics in order to demand conformity to the plans

The aforementioned addictive behaviors exist individually to varying degrees in all organizations, but when their intensity is great and their aggregation dense the organization is sick and in need of help. No doubt a fine line exists between acceptable and unhealthy, self-destructive behavior. The pursuit of pleasure or escape is not bad per se; when done in the extreme, however, or when such pursuits become an end in themselves, it is time to sound the warning bells. Organizations must establish a proper balance among competing needs and work to focus resources away from satisfying addictive needs toward meeting the needs of clients. Learning more about an organization's behaviors should be a high priority; it will help point the way toward recovery from addictive habits so that organizations can be healthy environments for both members and clients.

MANAGING ORGANIZATIONAL LEARNING

The metaphor of the brain applied to an organizational context helps us to see the learning capacity that exists in our organizations. As the brain seems to have unlimited potential in acquiring new insights, so it seems reasonable to assume organizations have similar potential. Heirs and Pehrson (1982) observe that "individuals and organizations both function through a combination of thought and action. Therefore we believe it is accurate and practical to recognize that an organization possesses a 'mind' of its own, that is, a *collective* mind that includes but transcends the combined individual minds of the executives and employees who work and think together to make an organization function" (pp. 4-5).

Heirs and Pehrson argue that when people make decisions in an organization they engage in a thinking process involving asking and answering questions. This process goes through four stages:

1. *question*—formulating a question to answer
2. *alternatives*—gathering information in order to identify and create alternative answers to the question
3. *consequences*—predicting the potential consequences of acting on each of the alternative answers
4. *judgment/decision*—making a judgment/decision concerning which alternative is the best answer to the question

Heirs and Pehrson make a distinction between the organization as a brain and the organization as a mind: The brain is capable of storing and retrieving information; the mind, however, is capable of thinking. The organizational mind is the "collective and collaborative thought processes of the minds of the individuals who think on behalf of the organization" (p. 24). Individuals are asked on behalf of the organization to answer the questions Why? What? When? Who? Where? and How? The challenge for management is to stimulate individuals to think on behalf of the total organization and its future.

Sims and Gioia (1986) argue that getting employees to think in this way is a "function of ability and motivation, within environmental constraints" (p. 281). They offer four suggestions:

1. *Increase the amount and immediacy of useful feedback.* Emphasis should be on the expected benefits of innovations, which are often based on intu-

ition and quasi-rational, analytical thinking. They would like to see measurement of relevant variables that the intervention is expected to impact or change.

2. *Create a social environment that requires learning.* The role of the "devil's advocate" should be institutionalized. For any major decision a person should present reasons why the course of action may be wrong or why a rationale may be faulty; this person should generate alternatives and in doing so will contribute to organizational learning. Although such efforts may not succeed, they may have greater impact on future decisions.

3. *Hire and train employees to be experts in both substance and process.* Learning to do the dance of the "what" *and* "how" is of great importance. Persons should be encouraged to become more knowledgeable in their area of practice. At the same time, however, they should develop the methodological skills to ask questions and get feedback on crucial areas of concern.

4. *Don't expect infallibility.* According to the old saw, "Everyone wants to learn, but nobody wants to be wrong." Penalties should not be imposed for being wrong but for refusing to learn. Burying mistakes, as mentioned earlier, may be a way of reducing a fear of failure. Sims and Gioia argue for the value of job rotation and promotion from within as means for increasing the learning opportunities for individuals and for the organization without taking great risks.

Sims and Gioia (1986) summarize by arguing that their strategies do not "mean that an organization must be paralyzed by interminable study of each and every action. Rather, action and evaluation should be linked, so that whether a decision is made quickly or not, its consequences may be evaluated, the basis for the decision considered, and the *next* decision made better. That is, after all, what learning is about" (p. 284).

Argyris (1978) provides a set of questions to test whether organizational learning has taken place:

1. Did individuals detect an outcome which matched or mismatched the expectations derived from their images and maps of organizational theory-in-use?

2. Did they carry out an inquiry which yielded discoveries, inventions, and evaluations pertaining to organizational strategies and assumptions?

3. Did these results become embodied in the images and maps employed for the purposes such as control, decision, and instruction?

4. Did members subsequently act from these images and maps so as to carry out new organizational practices?

5. Were these changes in images, maps, and organizational practices regularized so that they were unaffected by some individual departure?

6. Do new members learn these new features of organizational theory of action as part of their socialization to the organization? (p. 20)

Each of these questions can help identify a capacity for or sources of failure in organizational learning. They may help to determine the openness of the organization to participate in double-loop learning, discussed in chapter 1. Argyris (1982) claims that there is a predisposition of organizations to inhibit double-loop learning by theories of action "with which most people are acculturated in modern industrial societies" (p. 4). Present-day administrations are challenged to overcome this propensity for action with little desire for reflection. Seeing organizations as brains and minds with the capacity to learn shows us that we may be doing ourselves a great harm by not taking the time to think and examine our obsession for action.

Senge (1990) recognizes that learning takes time: "One useful starting point for all managers is to look at their time for thinking" (p. 305). He questions whether it is our work schedules or our natures that inhibit us from taking time. Either way, how we resolve the time bind says a great deal about our commitment to learning. Given that the primary mission of educational organizations is learning, it is strange that those in charge (administrators and teachers) do not take the time to learn from their organizational experiences. There may exist a significant gulf between what we espouse for our youthful learners and what is our theory-in-practice.

Senge believes it may be a problem of leadership in developing learning organizations: "The new view of leadership in learning organizations centers on subtler and more important tasks. In a learning organization, leaders are designers, stewards, and teachers. They are responsible for *building organizations* where people continually expand their capacities to understand complexity, clarify vision, and improve shared mental models—that is, they are responsible for learning" (p. 340).

These new concepts of leadership will be explored in more depth in the leadership section of this text. Here it is sufficient to say that those of us who have opportunities to provide leadership in our organizations may profit from viewing them as brains and minds with a strong emphasis on thinking, reflecting, and learning.

ETHICAL IMPLICATIONS OF ORGANIZATIONS AS BRAINS

As has been discussed in various sections of this chapter, persons and organizations can do harm to themselves and to others for reasons that are not always apparent. Thinking of organizations as brains conjures up the image of interdependence and wholeness; that is, organizations need to see themselves as a collective system capable of creating both healthy and unhealthy, ethical and unethical, environments. For example, organizations can exploit their members and clients: Addictive organizations treat people as objects whose energies and talents are abused for some grander scheme of satisfying the organization's addiction. Greater consciousness of how workaholism is being reinforced and other forms of unethical behavior is essential if a healthy environment is desired.

A second ethical problem for organizations as brains is the need for balance among the forces of rationality, emotionality, and pleasure. Historically and in today's schools, rationality has been given high priority, often resulting in overlooking or suppressing other concerns and needs. Heavy emphasis on efficiency (i.e., lower costs by creating larger classes and larger school units) has resulted in overlooking other needs of closer personal relationships and a sense of community. In some schools, the un-fettered pursuit of athletics provides an escape and substitutes for dealing with other unmet needs in the organization. Internal politics and emotional conflicts can also tip a school's priorities. The result of any of these behaviors, if taken to the extreme, is losing sight of a school's potential for creating a healthy environment in which there is a genuine respect for the individual and the organization at the same time. As Gold-berg (1989) says,

> Acknowledging the existence of polarizing dualistic forces is a necessary first step in perceiving the essential unity of these forces and is an essential prerequisite to striking a balance between them. . . . The fantasy that reason and intellect alone can provide solutions to essentially value-based dualistic tendencies is naive and potentially dangerous. (p. 153)

It is no easy task finding these balances among opposing and often self-destruc-tive forces. On the other hand, to ignore potential harm and drift toward undesirable behaviors that can reign unopposed in an organization is a fault of leadership. Open-ness, flexibility, and involvement are crucial but cannot guarantee that awareness and learning will emerge as more dominant values. A strong sense of ethics anchored in fundamental values of optimizing a person's and the organization's potential good is a necessary starting point.

CONCLUSION

The brain is an amazing organ capable of performing many, often contradictory, func-tions simultaneously. It is a system of interacting and interdependent parts whose re-lationships, at some level of balance, are important to the development of a healthy person. Imbalance can occur as the brain struggles with impulses and thoughts from its subsystems. Thinking of organizations as brains allows us to consider a number of factors when trying to understand how our organizations function and what their problems may be.

The brain as a metaphor for organizations is not a road map to solving organiza-tional problems, but it does provide a means for reframing these problems and appre-ciating what might be some of the underlying causes or related factors. Our excursion into systems thinking has shown us practical implications of interdependence and holism. We are challenged with the inescapable reality that we are an integral part of the problem, one of the factors contributing to the conditions under observation. At the same time, however, we must acknowledge that we are only a part and not in total control or able to will certain outcomes unilaterally. Systems thinking presses us for a paradigm shift, to look at the system as being more than a collection of individuals; rather it is capable of behaving in ways that transcend individual parts. We are con-fronted with the dilemma of not being in total control as an individual actor while at the same time being a contributor to the overall persona of the organization.

The brain as metaphor provides us with an image of what an organization can look like when it is out of balance and takes on addictive behaviors. The desire to escape problems, anxiety, and fears is part and parcel of all of us. These individual apprehensions can aggregate to such a level that an organization behaves much like a person engaged in substance abuse. We explored many of the symptoms of addiction and co-dependence that offer a frame for examining behavior in our respective organizations.

Finally, we switched to the positive message that comes from viewing an organization as a brain: the notion of learning. The ability to learn from experience is not guaranteed; we are, it seems, destined to repeat errors of the past. According to Feldman (1986), the inability to see errors, self-fulfilling prophecies, hindsight biases, and social influences all play a role in stultifying the awareness of a need to learn. The survival of an organization is ultimately dependent on its capacity to learn from errors, accept feedback, and increase the exchange of information regarding performance. None are simple tasks, but all are necessary for the future well-being of the organization.

MVSD CASE REVISITED

The Mountain View School District case manifests multiple characteristics inferable from the brain metaphor. We are witnesses to rational, emotional, and visceral behaviors. We can also observe a leader and an organization displaying characteristics of addiction and co-dependence. Further, we see an organization finding its voice and breaking from its addiction. Let's explore some examples of each.

First, a broad view of the MVSD from rational, emotional, and visceral perspectives produces some interesting observations, both pro and con. For example, on the rational side we see an institution attempting to carve out a new future with a vision of excellence and a leader whose credentials offer credibility for moving the school district in this direction. At the emotional level we observe pride in and excitement about the new superintendent at the special meeting to honor her appointment and happiness at her reinstatement following the court case. At the visceral level we see threats of violence aimed at dissenters and anti-Semitism directed at the associate superintendent of schools. We also see an effort to find a balance among these conflicting forces by putting together a four-year comprehensive plan for the school district. Unfortunately the MVSD's climate had deteriorated to such a level that this effort was viewed with skepticism, mistrust, and charges of elitism.

Second, before the final altercations of petition drives and threats of violence, a number of addictive conditions at the MVSD and in its superintendent could be observed. For example, the superintendent's high level of scholarly productivity in a relatively short period of time (3 books, 2 edited books, and 25 articles,) suggests a person of workaholic tendencies. The school board may have reinforced her addictive tendencies by making promises to support her mission of excellence and may have seduced her into believing she was serving a great cause by accepting the superintendency. She may have been more vulnerable to these promises because she was dedicated to an ideal and because she had previously served in a more protected environment as a faculty member at a higher education institution.

In addition to promises, other addictive processes can be observed in the superintendent and the school district as a whole. The school board's deference to the external reference of the excellence movement across the United States and in the private sector blinded their ability to see the needs of the clients and personnel of the MVSD. The superintendent projected an illusion of being open and flexible in pursuing the goals of excellence while firing some people and forcing others to resign. She seemed to be acknowledging other points of view but was actually refusing to bend or compromise. Toward the end of her reign and during the purging of central-level administrators, the majority of whom were males, the superintendent may have fabricated fundamental personality conflicts with charges of antifeminism. A dualistic climate existed where some people, particularly the teachers, were pitted against the administration, particularly the superintendent and associate superintendent, if they did not support the new cultural diversity policy.

In this dualism, we can sense that people were beginning to break from their codependent relationships and were willing to challenge the authority of the superintendent and associate superintendent. The no-confidence petition drive by the teachers provided ample evidence that members of the school district were attempting to take charge of their lives. Even though there were tensions and threats of violence, the high school graduation ceremony went according to plan without any disruptive incidents. Subsequently, the superintendent must have sensed her isolation and so resigned.

It is hard to predict the future of the MVSD, but a willingness to confront problems and to challenge addictive behaviors suggests a beginning step on the road of recovery. Hopefully, members of the school system learned from this experience and will be able to build a better future. Conflict, though unpleasant, does enable people to see various sides to their behavior. This self-awareness and exposure of hidden feelings are important precursors to gaining control of visceral impulses and developing the ability to find a balance between rational and emotional drives. Time will tell the degree to which these new learnings result in the development of a healthier environment and a willingness to face problems in a more mature, open, and honest manner.

DISCUSSION QUESTIONS

1. When thinking of your organization, what features of it match characteristics and functions of the brain?
2. When considering the primitive reptilian (visceral) brain, paleomammalian (right) brain, and neomammalian (left) brain and their respective thought processes, are there persons within your organization who reflect behaviors associated more with one type than another? What behaviors can you observe? What effect do they seem to have on the organization?
3. Discuss the characteristics of the viable systems model and systems dynamics. How might they help improve communications or problem solving within your organization?
4. Is your organization an addictive organization? Why or why not?

5. What are your views on the effect of co-dependent behavior in an organizational context?
6. When does addictive behavior cross the line of balance and become a problem to an organization?
7. How can one determine whether an organization is capable of becoming a learning system?

SUGGESTED ACTIVITIES

1. Explore some of the concepts associated with organizations as brains and reflect on your organization specifically. What are some general observations you can make and what areas are worthy of further diagnosis?
2. Reflect on the variables of communications, thinking, management and personnel processes, and structure. To what degree does your organization manifest some of the addictive qualities associated with each of these variables?
3. Investigate systems dynamics more thoroughly or acquire a copy of the STELLA software and apply these concepts and procedures to a problem situation in your organization.
4. Investigate the concept of learning systems or organizational learning. If you were to take a stance that this was needed in your organization, how would you go about transforming your organization into a learning system?

REFERENCES

Argyris, C. (1978). *Organizational learning: A theory of action perspective.* Reading, MA: Addison-Wesley.

Argyris, C. (1982). *Reasoning, learning, and action.* San Francisco: Jossey-Bass.

Beer, S. (1979). *The heart of the enterprise.* Chichester, England: Wiley.

Beer, S. (1980). Preface. In H. R. Maturana & F. J. Varela, *Autopoiesis and cognition: The realization of the living* (pp. 63–76). Holland: D. Reidel.

Beer, S. (1981). *Brain of the firm.* Chichester, England: Wiley.

Beer, S. (1985). *Diagnosing the system for organizations.* Chichester, England: Wiley.

Beer, S. (1989). The Viable Systems Model: Its provenance, development, methodology, and pathology. In R. Espejo & R. Hernden, *The Viable Systems Model* (pp. 11–37). New York: Wiley.

Belenky, M. F., Clinchy, B. M., Goldberger, N. R., & Tarule, J. M. (1986). *Women's ways of knowing.* New York: Basic Books.

Bessinger, R. C., & Suojanen, W. W. (Eds.). (1983). *Management and the brain.* Atlanta: Business Publishing Division, College of Business Administration, Georgia State University.

Butcher, C. (1985). Unethical business behavior must be understood. In P. J. Frost, L. F. Moore, M. R. Louis, C. C. Lundberg, & J. Martin (Eds.), *Organizational culture* (pp. 271–76) Beverly Hills: Sage.

Feldman, J. (1986). On the difficulty of learning from experience. In H. P. Sims & D. A. Gioia (Eds.), *The thinking organization* (pp. 263–92). San Francisco: Jossey-Bass.

Flood, R. L., & Jackson, M. C. (1991). *Creative problem solving.* New York: Wiley.

Forester, J. W. (1971). Counterintuitive behavior of social systems. *Technological Forecasting and Social Change 3*, 1–22.

Gardner, H. (1983). *Frames of mind.* New York: Basic Books.

Gardner, H. (1993) *Multiple intelligences:The theory in practice.* New York: Basic Books.

Gelman, D., Rosenberg, D., Kandell, P., & Crandall, R. (April, 1992). Mapping the brain. *Newsweek*, 66-72.

Goldberg, M. A. (1989). *On systemic balance.* New York: Praeger.

Heirs, B., & Pehrson, G. (1982). *The mind of the organization.* New York: Harper & Row.

MacLean, P. D. (1964). Man and his animal brains. *Modern Medicine, 32*, 111-12.

Maturana, H. R., & Varela, F. J. (1980). *Autopoieses and cognition:The realization of the living.* Holland: D. Reidel.

Meadows, D., Richardson, J., & Bruckman, G. (1982). *Groping in the dark.* New York: Wiley.

Mingers, J. (1989). An introduction to autopoiesis—implications and applications. *Systems Practice, 2*(2), 159-80.

Morgan, G. (1986). *Images of organization.* Beverly Hills: Sage.

Park, O. S., Sims, H. P., & Motowidlo, S. J. (1986). Affect in organizations: How feelings and emotions influence managerial judgment. In H. P. Sims & D. A. Gioia (Eds.), *The thinking organization* (pp. 215-37). San Francisco: Jossey-Bass.

Richmond, B., & Peterson, S. (1992). *STELLA II: An introduction to systems thinking.* Hanover, NH: High Performance Systems.

Roberts, E. B. (Eds.). (1978). *Applications of system dynamics.* Cambridge: MIT Press.

Schaef, A. W. (1991). *Women's reality.* New York: Harper Paperbacks.

Schaef, A. W., & Fassel, D. (1988). *The addictive organization.* San Francisco: Harper & Row.

Senge, P. M. (1990). *The fifth discipline.* New York: Doubleday.

Sims, H. P., & Gioia, D. A. (1986). *The thinking organization.* San Francisco: Jossey-Bass.

Section 1 Summary

Viewing organizations from a metaphoric orientation is like examining paintings in an art gallery or studio. As we wander past the displays, suddenly, for reasons we are not sure of, our attention is captivated by a certain painting. We stop and gaze. At first our attention is focused on a feature or two that caused us to stop in the first place. The particular scene or the colors or the flow of lines seems to trigger an initial reaction. We may linger a bit, or this fanciful flight subsides and we move on. On the painting to which we feel a stronger reaction, however, our attention becomes more fixed. Whatever attracted us initially is more thoroughly explored, and soon we find ourselves observing other features that we find equally captivating. After a while we become aware of how this image before us is holding our attention and that we are experiencing a rush of different and unexplainable feelings. Somehow this painting has surfaced memories or emotions that have not been explored for some time, and we may find ourselves looking at some old and unresolved feelings, possibly for the first time. Art offers an opportunity to reflect and discover thoughts about ourselves and others that may result in new insights worthy of further contemplation. As it is with art at a personal level, so it is with metaphors at the organizational level. Flood and Jackson (1991) observe that "the process of creative thinking can be prompted not only through the ideas of 'likeness' [of the metaphor to an organization] but also by adopting a dialectical approach: asking when particular metaphors break down in practice and comparing and contrasting the different visions provided by alternative metaphors" (p. 56). They suggest that metaphors, individually or mixed and remixed, should be used to enrich and challenge perceptions.

In the previous chapters, we explored four major metaphors of culture, politics, theater, and the brain. Each of these metaphors allows us to examine a number of concepts and ideas that have implications for how we view the nature of organizations. The case *A House Divided* enabled us to explore these metaphors and related concepts in the organizational context of the Mountain View School District.

The purposes and uses for which metaphors may be applied are modest. We can hope that they enable us to see the value of generating new viewpoints of situations that initially may not seem complicated and/or appear easily explainable. By exploring these viewpoints we may grow to appreciate multiple perspectives, the value of reframing, and the contradictions and paradoxes that often exist in organizations. In the process, we may discover an antidote to perceptual self-entrapment and habits of the mind that lock us in and minimize our creative, flexible, and adaptive abilities.

No doubt, like paintings in art galleries, some metaphors resonate better than others and will vary in their impact from time to time. Specific organizational circumstances may prompt some reflection from only one point of view (e.g., political, theatrical) or whatever seems to fit best. Each of the metaphors explored in section 1 may individually surface new insights; however, to accomplish a comprehensive diagnosis, the use of all four on a rotating and remixing basis is desirable. Figure S1.1 provides a framework for viewing these four metaphors interactively.

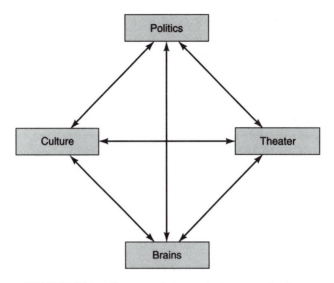

FIGURE S1.1 Framework for analyzing organizations

To assist the diagnostic process, the questions below have been formulated to help us explore each metaphor by building on related concepts in more depth. Following this, a brief revisit to the case will help us consider the insights that can surface from the use of the respective metaphors and the general themes suggested overall.

The questions provided for each of the metaphors are not intended to be all-inclusive; no doubt more can be added and others can be rephrased. It is not clear whether any sequence of questions is better than any other, nor should one expect to get "correct" or unambiguous answers. The questions should, however, prompt insights that may go undiscovered in a more casual, superficial diagnosis. At a minimum, we might consider the use of these questions as a first step in the reflection and reframing process.

DIAGNOSTIC QUESTIONS

Organizations as Culture

1. What is the theme/glue that appears to connect parts of this organization?
2. What are the overarching cultural norms for this organization?
3. What "meaning" do persons take from this organization?
4. What is the dominant culture of this organization? How does it treat minority cultures?

5. What are the common and core values, understandings, beliefs, and expectations in this organization?

6. To what degree is the culture integrated, differentiated, and/or fragmented in this organization?

7. How do cultures differ in this organization at the center and periphery? between occupational groups?

8. What external, environmental cultures (e.g., general society, region, local community, and professional organizations) affect this organization? What is the nature of its relationship with external cultures?

9. What historical values are emphasized in this organization? past heroes/heroines?

10. What are the organizational ambiguities in this organization?

11. What "incidents" of a recent nature seem to capture and hold the attention of people in this organization?

12. What are the patterns of interactions, activities, sentiments, and symbols in this organization?

Organizations as Politics

1. To what degree must people compete for resources in this organization?

2. To what degree is the "politics of getting ahead" played out in this organization?

3. To what degree is there conflict or agreement over the major goals and means of attaining these goals in this organization?

4. What "debates" are being engaged in this organization? From whence do these issues seem to emerge and why?

5. What conflicts exist in this organization? How are these conflicts typically handled or resolved?

6. To what degree are societal and local community conflicts played out in this organization?

7. Who are the partisan groups in this organization? How different from one another are their views?

8. How is power distributed and used in this organization?

9. To what degree are varying power sources drawn on in this organization?

10. How is the long-term agenda established in this organization?

11. To what degree is there networking and coalition building in this organization?

12. To what degree do persons engage in bargaining and negotiations in this organization?

13. What special interests (groups) exist in this organization? What is the nature of these interests?

14. To what degree are persons in this organization willing to compromise?

15. Does an explicit governance and appeal process exist in this organization?

16. To what degree are issues avoided, dominated, accommodated, compromised, or collaborated on in this organization?

17. To what degree do administrators model negotiating behavior in this organization?

18. To what degree are people manipulated or exploited in this organization?

19. What are people's attitudes toward politics in this organization?

20. Do adversarial relations exist in this organization?

Organizations as Theater

1. Who is/are the playwright(s) in this organization? the director(s)? reference groups?

2. What script is being followed in this organization? subscript? plot? subplot?

3. Where is/are the stage(s) where this organization acts out its script and subscript?

4. What are the typical costumes worn by persons in this organization? Why?

5. How are spaces decorated or arranged in this organization? Why or what explanations are offered?

6. What drama seems to exist in this organization? What type of drama (tragedy, comedy, melodrama, or farce) seems to prevail or is most dominant?

7. To what degree is there role-taking or role-making in this organization?

8. Who are the protagonists and antagonists in this organization? auxiliary and chorus members? Do these roles change over time? How?

9. How good is the performance of this organization? How are appearances maintained? Are there rehearsals?

10. To what degree is humor evident in this organization? What form does it take? How is it used (e.g., to ease tension, create bonds, facilitate criticism, surface awkward subjects, in decision making, scapegoating, or for self-disparagement)?

Organizations as Brains

1. How are the primal, rational, and subjective forces balanced in this organization?

2. To what degree are holographic principles or redundancies practiced in this organization?

3. Does this organization operate as a total system or as a collection of fragmented subsystems?

4. How are intellectual reasoning and emotional feelings balanced in this organization?

5. What evidence is there of organizational learning (e.g., use of feedback, reflection, supportive social climate, practicing what is preached, and being open to making mistakes) in this organization?

6. How well are communications handled in this organization?

7. How is information processed in this organization?

8. Is there an awareness of gender differences in this organization?

9. What mental models or maps exist in this organization?

10. Is this organization looking forward and backward at the same time?

11. How is this organization engaging in self-renewal?

12. Who are the Spocks, McCoys, and Kirks in this organization?

13. To what degree does this organization engage in addictive processes (e.g., promises, invalidations, fabricating personality conflicts, and contrived dualism)?

14. To what degree is workaholism evident in this organization?

15. Is this organization having problems with communications, thinking processes, management and personnel processes, and structural components?

16. Are viable systems (Systems 1–5) operating in this organization?

17. Does this organization engage in problem solving using simulation and systems dynamics techniques?

MVSD CASE REVISITED

Each metaphor offers a different perspective on the Mountain View School District and the tensions described in this case study. Below are some general observations surfaced by the respective metaphors.

Culture

- The superintendent of schools either misread or did not care about the MVSD's cultural heritage and core values.
- The superintendent attempted to impose the values of the "excellence movement" upon the school system.
- There was a clash between center and periphery values.
- Fragmented cultures and subcultures existed at the institution.

Politics

- The superintendent was naive or lacked insight about the nature of the politics at the MSVD.
- The superintendent mismanaged her sources of power.
- The superintendent relied too heavily on the use of authority and adversarial methods to resolve conflict.
- Lack of trust and suspicion became prevalent over time.

Theater

- The superintendent was performing for the wrong audience.
- The superintendent seemed to lack the skill and knowledge for performing a complex role as a school district superintendent.
- The MVSD case was a melodrama with a sad ending.
- The superintendent's performance did not match expectations for an educational leadership role.
- The superintendent exhibited a willingness to sacrifice her livelihood for principle.

Brains

- The MVSD engaged in addictive processes and co-dependent behavior.
- The MVSD was unable to recognize and address organizational problems.
- Focus was put on the promise of the "excellence movement" rather than coping more directly with the problems of violence and abuse.
- Toward the end of the MVSD's conflicts, visceral and emotional feelings outweighed rational thinking.

These observations are general; each could be fleshed out to elicit its implications for the MVSD situation and to offer insights for change. They produce some contrasting perspectives and show how complex a situation may become. They also provide a knowledge base for considering what went wrong and how one might adjust to prevent these circumstances from being repeated.

GENERAL THEME AND SUBTHEMES

The MVSD case and the overall use of the metaphors allow us to study some general needs of organizations. These needs can be clustered under the general theme of the paradox of coping with the needs of the individual and of the organization simultaneously. Through their emphasis on serving a common good, often expressed as goals, organizations place pressure on individuals to suppress their individual preferences. Individual adjustment to organizational demands is complicated even more by changing priorities, changes in leadership, and an uncertainty in the organization's environment. At the same time, individuals are often unwilling to change or feel they can go only so far in suppressing or sacrificing their personal needs to meet the needs of the organization. In order to get the desired level of individual commitment, the organization must allow and support individuals' personal needs and desires. It is no easy task to determine how this balance can be achieved. In our next section on leadership, we will look at other metaphors related to this dilemma.

In addition to the main theme of individual versus organization, two subthemes are inferable from the reading thus far: the notion of healthy organizations and the importance of ethical practices. In educational organizations there is often confusion and ambiguity over goals and the means for attaining them. We often search for prevailing needs or universal conditions that should prevail regardless of desired organizational outcomes. The two themes of healthy organizations and sound ethical practices should prevail regardless of specific goals; that is, persons who devote a major share of their lives, time, and energy to educating our youth should have a minimal guarantee of healthy and ethical conditions in which to practice as professionals.

Admittedly the concepts of a healthy and ethical environment in an organizational context, such as a school, are ambiguous at best. Yet, leaders who have a vision or consciousness of these two subthemes are more likely to advocate for conditions that reflect these ideals. In section 2, Leadership Perspectives, the main theme of balancing organizational and individual needs and desires plus the subthemes of healthy and ethical conditions will provide a context for examining alternative metaphors of leadership.

REFERENCE

Flood, R. L., & Jackson, M. C. (1991). *Creative problem solving.* New York: Wiley.

section 2

Leadership Perspectives

$\mathbf{A}$s with organizations, the phenomenon of leadership is complex and must be examined from several perspectives. Over time, theories of leadership have evolved in ways similar to the shifts in organizational theories. To place views of leadership in an evolutionary context, this section presents a brief historical review of leadership theory from the early 1900s to the present. In addition, an overview of the respective chapters of section 2 presents an introduction to three metaphors of leadership. Following this overview, a case, *The Telephone Stopped Ringing*, serves as a context for exploring the concepts presented in these chapters. As we explore various insights on leadership, keep in mind that

> perspectives are images of reality and not truths in themselves. Since educational administration and organizational behavior are linked to human conventions, perspectives of practice are not truth seeking in the traditional sense but rather to enhance one's understanding and to illuminate one's view of the world. (Sergiovanni, 1984, p.10)

In order to enhance our views of leadership, section 2 provides alternative theories, research, and concepts for the leadership metaphors of transformation, dialectic, and democracy. Section 2 chapters explore writings that are interdisciplinary in nature and reflect current thoughts on leadership.

HISTORY OF LEADERSHIP THEORY

Shifts in major orientations to leadership parallel the shifts concerning the nature of organizations. Again, as with the historical review of organizational theories, the following time periods are somewhat arbitrary but do help discriminate major trends in thinking and help us understand the historical roots of contemporary leadership

123

theories. We should also keep in mind that approaches to understanding leadership in an earlier period often resurface at a later time. The intent of these time periods is not to represent a linear progression of theories per se but to provide an orientation to major ideas over time. The four time periods are 1900-1930, classical leadership theory; 1930-1950, human relations approach to leadership; 1950-1975, behavioral approach to leadership; and 1975-present, sociocultural approach to leadership.

Classical Leadership Theory

Depending on how far back we wish to go, leadership has been a topic of interest for many people. Feudal traditions, according to Fiedler and Garcia (1987), regarded "leadership as a highly personal relationship between the leader and the led" (p. 13). A bond of loyalty was assumed and religiously reinforced. Persons from upper-class, royal, and religious backgrounds where assumed to be better qualified to be leaders. We can still observe the remnants of the feudal tradition, particularly in family-owned businesses and in the higher ranks of government in many European countries. It is not unusual for present-day managers and school administrators, like leaders in feudal times, to expect a certain degree of loyalty from their employees. These feudal practices of birthright and special privilege linked to early theories of leadership, labeled the "great man" theories. Earlier, and even into the present time, studies focused on great leaders and their style as a source for developing theories of leadership. According to Lipham (1973), "The philosophy underlying these works was heavily oriented toward the viewpoint that leaders were born and not made, that nature was more important than nurture, and that instinct was more important than training" (p. 2). Such studies tended to enshrine leaders rather than explain leadership.

The great man approach to the study of leadership provided an impetus to researchers early in the twentieth century to "concentrate almost solely on the personal traits of leaders" (Mazzarella & Grundy, 1989, p. 10). Since leadership and abilities such as intelligence were believed to be inherited, it made sense to study the special traits of leaders. Terman's (1904) research of characteristics of playground leaders was typical of these early studies. In addition to IQ, other studies focused on birth order, childrearing experiences, and socioeconomic background. Mazzarella and Grundy (1989) concluded from reviews of these studies that none of these characteristics—high IQ, birth order, status, liberal parents—is a guarantee of leadership ability. Nor are these the only qualities correlated with leadership. The most that can be said is that research shows that many—but not all—leaders have these qualities (p. 16).

Knowing the traits of potential leaders reveals only part of the story. There was a need to understand how leaders related to others in group situations. This led to the next era of research, often referred to as the human relations period.

Human Relations Approach to Leadership

Recognizing that personal characteristics did not tell the whole story concerning what makes leaders, researchers shifted their focus from the characteristics of the leader to characteristics of the group: size, productivity, decision making, satisfaction, intimacy, autonomy, cohesion, stability, drive, and participation. From these studies, Lipham (1973) concluded "that if the analysis of leadership were limited to situational factors, then the study of leadership, per se, was at a dead end" (p. 3). He judged that the transferability of leaders to and from different situations was difficult to explain and overlooked the determination or will of leaders to lead.

By the late 1930s, employers began experimenting with new management practices as a way of minimizing strikes, and these new practices provided an impetus for human relations approaches to leadership. Possibly the most notable research during this period was the work of McGregor (1944) and his development of Theory X and Theory Y. He stressed the importance of leaders' examining their underlying assumptions about those persons they hoped to lead and the effects of these assumptions in shaping relationships with the led. The Theory X mode of leadership was most common during this period; it assumed that workers were primarily motivated by economic gain and security. McGregor urged that leaders give more consideration to a Theory Y orientation of leadership, which assumed that employees were self-motivated, shared common interests in the success of an organization, and required less supervision. Although McGregor's ideas prevail to some degree to the present, Bennis pointed out in 1961 that Theory Y does not work all the time and so other strategies are often needed.

Behavioral Approach to Leadership

In the behavioral approach to the study of leadership, the focus shifted to leaders' behavior in context. Lewin, Lippitt, and White's (1939) often-cited work provided the foundation for this approach. These researchers explored different leadership styles or behaviors (autocratic, democratic, and laissez-faire) and their affect on group performance. Their findings revealed that democratic, participative behavior involving members of the group resulted in higher group performance.

Research conducted at Ohio State University (Hemphill & Coons, 1957) identified two dimensions of leadership—initiating structure and consideration—as having a positive influence on followers' behavior. Initiating structure includes establishing patterns of organization, channels of communications, and methods of procedure; consideration involves dimensions of friendship, trust, respect, and warmth. Halpin (1956) applied this theory and survey research methods to a study of 50 school superintendents and found those administrators who were perceived as effective by their school boards and staffs also had high scores on these two dimensions. Ineffective superintendents had low scores.

Fiedler (1967) challenged the assumption that a leader can balance people's needs and work concerns. His thinking gave rise to a contingency theory of leadership. He developed the dualism of task orientation and relationship orientation and argued that leaders could not have both at the same time. Depending on the amount of control the leader had over circumstances, either orientation could be effective. His research showed that those leaders who were at the extremes—very influential or very uninfluential—were more effective with a task-oriented style of leadership. Leaders with a relationship-oriented style were more influential in situations that were moderately controllable.

Sergiovanni and Elliott (1975) cite additional contingencies that influence leadership styles: job demands, nature and distribution of power and authority, and expectations held by significant others. They judge that human relations styles are more likely to be effective in schools.

The study of styles and contingencies raises a practical question: What is the degree to which leaders know and can alter their leadership styles to fit a situation? Alternatively, should they look for a more compatible situation to fit their style? Hersey and Blanchard (1969, 1982) hypothesized that leaders can adapt their styles to meet the need of group members. Blake and Mouton (1985) developed a managerial grid and process to enable leaders to determine the nature of their leadership style. These researchers concluded that leadership stressing flexibility is more likely to be effective in situations that are ambiguous and unstable. However, as Reddin (1970) points out, flexibility has a negative side; leaders seen as too flexible are perceived to be overwhelmed by events and without a mind of their own.

Sociocultural Approach to Leadership

Some writers, notably Downton (1973) and Burns (1978), felt that there was more to leadership than the dimensions of initiation and consideration or balancing task and individual needs. Burns was particularly critical of past leadership research; in his judgment there was a crisis of leadership. As he stated, "Leadership is one of the most observed and least understood phenomena on earth" (p. 2). He felt that leadership theories up to the mid-seventies lacked an ethical/moral dimension.

Burns builds on exchange theory in which followers play a central role in defining leadership. This theory is based on power relations and requires bargaining, trading, and compromising among leaders and followers. This transactional model of leadership is politically based and recognizes the need to examine the sociocultural influences that act on the leader-follower relationships.

Sergiovanni (1984) describes leadership within a cultural perspective as having

> a more qualitative image; of less concern is the leader's behavioral style, and leadership effectiveness is not viewed merely as the instrumental summation of the link between behavior and objectives. Instead, what the leader stands for and communicates to others is considered important. The object of leadership is the stirring of human consciousness, the interpretation and enhancement of meanings, the articulation of key cultural strands, and the linking of organizational members to them. (p. 8)

Leaders operate within realms of values, sentiments, and beliefs which necessitate awareness of an organization's symbols, culture, philosophical roots, and historical experiences. Leaders are challenged to link the past with the future and build new meanings and possibilities while preserving what seems "good." Rost (1991) echoes this challenge: "Leadership scholars need to develop a new leadership narrative with the revised myths and rituals that fit the postindustrial paradigm. And practitioners of leadership need to adopt postindustrial leadership models that help them make sense of what they do as leaders and followers in the postmodern world of the twenty-first century" (p. 36).

Section 2 will begin this conversation about adapting new images and perspectives on leadership to help potential members of organizations appreciate the phenomenal dynamics surrounding leadership efforts.

CHAPTER HIGHLIGHTS

In the chapters that follow in section 2, we will examine three orientations to leadership and view them as processes as opposed to fixed characteristics. We have already seen the complexity of leadership and the need to resist reducing it to the presence or absence of one characteristic at a single point in time. The focus on process emphasizes that leadership is not a single event or happening at only one point in time, but rather is emergent, ongoing, and incremental in nature. Leadership is very dynamic, highly interactive, and, depending on the circumstances, may be shared by different people at different times; it may be viewed as a total of experiences that work to move ideas and people.

The perspectives in section 2 stimulate or reinforce images that have relevance in light of trends and needs of educational organizations. In some cases the ideas presented reinforce the theories of earlier writers, and in other cases they are intended to be more provocative. Each chapter presents a process or an approach that exemplifies some of the dimensions associated with the leadership metaphor presented. Chapter concepts are highlighted by a case study of a community (Valley View) and its elementary school's encounter with efforts to pass a school bond issue. The principal and other members of the community provide experiences that help illustrate various dynamics of leadership.

Chapter 6: Leadership as a Transformational Process

The emphasis in this chapter is on change and how persons in leadership positions must address the need for change. A clear distinction is drawn between what is traditionally viewed as management and what is currently viewed as new leadership. Concepts explored, as part of transformational leadership, include charisma, vision, trust, and empowerment. The Total Systems Intervention (TSI) approach provides a framework for illustrating how transformational leadership can be implemented. TSI is applied to the Valley View case and helps to illustrate change through a process of interactive planning.

Chapter 7: Leadership as a Dialectical Process

This chapter explores the implications of paradoxes, dilemmas, and dualisms for leadership. Hard choices often confront persons in organizations, both their official and unofficial leaders. This chapter argues for embracing opposite views and finding ways of incorporating them into a single strategy. Ancient Chinese philosophy provides a beginning to understanding the value of blending opposites; from this early perspective, there is an exploration of contemporary views, including Marx's dialectical theory. These views illustrate the importance of a moral framework to guide actions under conditions of great ambiguity and conflicting choices. Attention is given to concepts of dialectical analyses, dialectical dimensions of leadership, competing value systems, and moral imagination. Drawing on another application of TSI, there is an explication of a critical systems heuristic as a means by which the assumed values underlying proposals for change can be properly surfaced and examined.

Chapter 8: Leadership as a Democratic Process

The final chapter in section 2 explores various philosophical dimensions of democracy and their implications for educational organizations such as schools. A major issue explored concerns the role of schools as support for democratic and community values. Democratization of schools offers an opportunity to enhance local control, provide firsthand experiences in democracy for both teachers and students, and provide a framework for coping with moral issues of the day. Concepts explored in this chapter include micropolitics of schools, collaborative schools, workplace democracy, participatory democracy in schools, and communitarianism. The leadership application for this chapter includes a strategic management approach.

CASE: *THE TELEPHONE STOPPED RINGING*

Introduction

Using the same approach followed in section 1, Organizational Perspectives, a case is presented up front to contrast concepts with real life experiences. The case chosen for examining and discussing various leadership metaphors and concepts involves an elementary school, grades K–6. The school's small size and the rural nature of its community permit observation of multiple interactions and interconnections that either go unnoticed or are difficult to observe in larger schools. Many writers describe rural communities and schools as fishbowl environments in which the actions and thinking of individuals are difficult to hide. This is the case with Valley View Elementary School and the community of Valley View. The Valley View case will permit viewing leadership and its context at the same time.

 The Telephone Stopped Ringing is a case study of how a real school and its community were able to unlock their struggle to upgrade the school. The case traces over time how its principal worked with the staff of the school and members of the community to accomplish a number of significant changes. The true identity of the community has been changed and actual names of persons involved have been omitted.

VALLEY VIEW ELEMENTARY SCHOOL

Nestled in a valley surrounded by gentle wooded hills is Valley View Elementary School and its community of Valley View. Down the middle of the valley flows a stream that is the envy of any trout fisherman. This natural beauty, however, belies the economic stress that faces this community, though in spite of this region's weak economy, its natural beauty encourages persons to relocate to the area. The town has experienced two waves of immigration, one in the early 1960s and another in the 1980s. These newcomers have not always seen eye to eye with old-time residents, particularly when it came to deciding what should be done about the school. On the other hand, even before new persons moved in, there seemed to be a strong rivalry among certain families in the community. Thus, part of Valley View's legacy had been community conflict and its perpetuation with the entrance of new residents.

Valley View is a community of about 1,200 residents. There is no local industry. Historically this community was a center for dairy and vegetable farms, but with the federal buyout of dairy herds and the demise of small family farms, this source of employment has dwindled appreciably. A large number of persons commute to work in neighboring communities or eke out a subsistence-level existence by working locally in auto repair shops, carpentry, logging, and/or by receiving social welfare benefits. Many families in the area are multigeneration families that have survived on welfare benefits or other inventive means of earning income.

The present Valley View Elementary School is an attractive new school facility located on a bluff overlooking the town. Its old facility, built around 1900, was located in the center of town and was the focal point of much debate and conflict in the community. Approximately five years ago, before the construction of the new school, conditions were pretty bad. The school's relationship with the community was tense. The citizens were rejecting school budgets and complaining about teachers and principals. There was, as well, a division in its three-member school board. The school facility was overcrowded, there was no space for special classes and support services, no space for a kindergarten program which was housed in a local church basement, the septic system failed, and the spring providing water for the school went dry. The teachers were paid among the lowest salaries in the area, a teacher and two principals were forced to resign, one principal lasting only two years, and the school board elections became mudslinging events. As one parent observed, "It could not have been worst. We could only go up."

Getting things back on track was not easy. The first stop was the board's appointment of a new principal; with some initial reservations they appointed a woman. This person grew up in the community and had many relatives residing there, including her parents. In fact, her mother was a previous chair of the school board during its tumultuous times, and the new board members wondered if this would be a political problem. Also, the previous principal was a woman and had experienced some serious personnel problems with male members of the teaching staff.

The new principal, who was a former secondary school teacher in a nearby community, was tuned into Valley View's culture and politics and understood from the start how carefully she had to proceed in order to turn things around. She initiated her administration by taking the faculty and staff to lunch at a local restaurant. This occasion allowed the principal to build some rapport, break down barriers between staff members, and open communications concerning what was needed to improve the school. Many suggestions emerged; more importantly, many of these suggestions were acted upon at the opening of school.

The principal also began a campaign with the school staff and community, stressing the centrality of students to the mission of the school and the importance of meeting their needs in spite of trying conditions. Approximately 40 percent of the students were eligible for free or reduced lunch, and over a three-year period, on average 80 percent of the students scored below the thirtieth percentile on a standardized achievement test. Some resolution of staff differences was achieved by focusing the debate on what was best for the kids.

To help make the community feel more welcomed and a part of the school, she rescinded an unpopular visitors' sign-in policy and replaced it with a new open-door policy. The new policy encouraged parents and community members to visit the school at any time. She also initiated and distributed a newsletter of school activities and events, not only to parents but to all members of the community.

The principal was quoted in a local newspaper article soon after her appointment: "My philosophy of school administration is that the child is the bottom line. When I make a decision I consider what's best for every child whatever the learning level. My goal is to maximize learning and make school a pleasant place to be for each child. This requires a positive school climate. Parents, teachers, and kids need to work together to enjoy each other. School should be a caring, friendly place."

In spite of past traumas in the community, within one month of being principal and at her first school board meeting she discussed the need to build a new school. After considerable discussion, the board approved a school facilities assessment process. Ten community members were invited to complete a school facilities evaluation; staff members completed a staff component of the evaluation. The facility's shortcomings were highlighted by the process. In late fall a facilities study committee was formed to explore ways to resolve the space problems. Every identified organization within the community was invited to send a member to the committee. State officials' attendance at the committee's meetings confirmed the difficulties involved in renovating the existing structure.

In the spring of the principal's first year, the facilities study committee made its recommendation to the school board: to build a new school rather than add on to the existing facility. Their recommendation was supported by expert advice and extensive data about comparative costs. The board accepted the report and gave the go-ahead to the committee to work on plans for a new facility and a new site.

While the principal was working with the staff of the school to improve internal and external relations, she also worked in the background with a group of citizens who supported a bond issue to build the new school. After the school board set a bond vote for the following fall, a well-organized and quiet campaign was initiated. The principal and staff members cooperated to provide support and information about the needs of the school, but they also were careful not to cross the line and appear to be pushing the school bond vote. In the fall of the next school year (year two for the principal), a bond vote passed by a slim margin of eight votes.

In part because of the closeness of the vote and quiet manner of the campaign, the anti-school-bond people were caught by surprise. They quickly organized a recall vote and managed to defeat a second bond vote in January by nine votes. Their main concerns were related to costs and whether the community could afford an expensive new school facility. The pro-school-bond folks, with behind-the-scenes support of the principal, hit upon a strategy that they thought would help their cause: They suggested expanding the school board membership from three members to five. In a subsequent school board election, two members of the school bond opposition group were elected to the school board and a third member of this group was defeated by one vote. This brought the opposition within the inner circle; in doing so, they were forced to confront the major school issues as accountable insiders rather than unaccountable, critical outsiders.

The following fall (the principal's third year) a new bond issue was approved by 35 votes. Not only was the bond passed by a larger margin than in the past but the school plans were expanded to include additional space. A modest increase in state aid and reimbursement rates on bond indebtedness no doubt played some role in garnering a positive response. The state funding changes were dramatized by the governor's symbolically signing the new school funding legislation into law at Valley View.

Throughout the debate over the school's needs for a new facility the principal worked tirelessly to promote the needs of her students and express pride in the community. She helped people see what a new facility could do for both the students and members of the community by advocating for additional space for (1) a library open to the community, (2) spare rooms to tutor individuals and small groups, (3) a kindergarten classroom, and (4) an all-purpose room that could serve the needs of the school during the day and the recreational needs of the community in the evening.

Whenever an opportunity arose the principal took advantage of it. One example was the purchase of school buses by the school board. Previously the school system rented buses to provide transportation for their students living in outlying areas. Unfortunately this service was sub par, and there were horror stories of kids being stranded for long hours on back roads in the middle of winter. The principal urged the school system to buy their own buses, train their bus drivers, install two-way radios, and clearly label the buses with the Valley View name. All this was done, and the board received many favorable comments from parents and other members of the community.

While waiting for the completion of the new facility, the principal worked with the staff to define a vision for the new school. They adopted a slogan—Quality and Equality: Excellence for All. She stressed teamwork and shared decision making as the staff prepared for the new school.

Finally the students and teachers, with help from the community, moved into their new facility in February (the principal's fourth year). The move went smoothly—except for a minor misunderstanding that left the principal locked in a bathroom for three hours on a Sunday afternoon. The fire department came to the rescue.

Soon after being in the building and adjusting to their new surroundings, school members found that there was more work to be done. Much of their energy over the past several years had been devoted to planning, arguing, dreaming, and lobbying for the new school. Now water was dripping from the ceiling throughout the entire school, necessitating placing water buckets in strategic places. These leaks and the effort to keep the water under control seemed to symbolize the school's new predicament. The principal, out of frustration, exclaimed, "Nirvana has leaks!" It was probably at this moment that she and others realized that getting their new school was not an end but rather a beginning. She observed further that "in many ways it was easier to facilitate the building project than it is to lead a restructuring of the human systems."

After settling into the new facility the principal began a focused effort on "restructuring." She expressed a desire to develop a program of instruction that matched the positive impression provided by the new facility. She viewed the process that she, the staff, and the community had gone through over such a long stretch of time as a model for how they needed to view important organizational changes in the future. Moreover, the school symbolized an important change and a source of pride for the community. She concluded from their experience "that any other change efforts will need to remain gradual and low-key." This set the context for future changes.

A number of changes came slowly and deliberately. A sampler includes

- adding another full-time teacher and two full-time aides without an appreciable increase in student enrollment
- dramatically increasing resource materials for classroom instruction
- classroom teachers and learning specialists (special education and Chapter I) agreeing to team-teach language arts in the classroom with an eye toward a "marriage" of regular and special education (This change, in June of the principal's fifth year, proved a testing ground for the staff's determination to change how the school operated. After coping with the time pressures and frustrations of their proposed changes, some teachers advocated returning to the traditional self-contained classroom and pull-out student services model. Even the state department of education got in the act by suggesting their proposed changes were not in confor-

mance with Chapter I regulations. Through patience, adaptation, and further experimentation they managed their way out of these and other subsequent problems.)

- with input from teachers, designing and implementing a new staff development program that included instructional aides and focused on intensive training in collaborative group work and conflict resolution

- participating as a team (made up of the principal, a classroom teacher, an aide, a special educator, and a Chapter I teacher) in a summer institute that focused on ways to integrate support services within schools and meet the needs of all children

- starting a retired senior volunteer program in the school

It is clear that Valley View had done more than build a new school facility: They developed a new school culture as well. As the principal explained,

> I need to keep the concept of shared leadership clearly in focus. Whenever possible, new knowledge which will enhance our restructured school should be presented by someone else on the staff. As part of my staff development plan, I hope to have teams present their programs to the school board throughout the year. This will help the board develop an understanding of our approach, and it will also turn the board's attention to other staff members as educational experts. Being a principal of Valley View has been a challenging, exciting, and rewarding experience. We built a beautiful building. It has some quirks, but with time and patience we are resolving them. We are also restructuring the human systems in ways that will better bring maximum learning and a good life to all within its walls. The restructured systems also have some quirks, but these are nothing that cannot be resolved with "more than enough time."

As an indicator that conditions had improved significantly, a school board member said, "My telephone has stopped ringing." In six years the Valley View principal had managed, along with everything else, to quiet a telephone that constantly rang with complaints during the era prior to her appointment.

With this case as a context, we shall examine alternative metaphors for leadership, including transformation, dialectic, and democracy, and use them to reframe the experiences of Valley View.

REFERENCES

Bennis, W. G. (1961). Revisionist theory of leadership. *Harvard Business Review, 39,* 146–50.
Blake, R. R., & Mouton, J. S. (1985). *The managerial grid III.* Houston: Gulf.
Burns, J. M. (1978). *Leadership.* New York: Harper & Row.
Downton, J. M. (1973). *Rebel leadership.* New York: Free Press.

Fiedler, F. E. (1967). *A theory of leadership effectiveness.* New York: McGraw-Hill.

Fiedler, F. E., & Garcia, J. E. (1987). *New approaches to effective leadership.* New York: Wiley.

Halpin, A. W. (1956). *The leadership behavior of school superintendents.* Columbus: Ohio State University.

Hemphill, J. K., & Coons, A. E. (1957). Development of the leader behavior description questionnaire. *Leader behavior: Its description and measurement.* Columbus: Ohio State University.

Hersey, P., & Blanchard, K. (1969). *Management of organizational behavior: Utilizing human resources.* Englewood Cliffs, NJ: Prentice-Hall.

Hersey, P., & Blanchard, K. (1982). *Management of organizational behavior: Utilizing human resources* (4th ed.). Englewood Cliffs, NJ: Prentice-Hall.

Lewin, K., Lippitt, R., & White, R. K. (1939). Patterns of aggressive behavior in experimentally created social climates. *Journal of Social Psychology,* 10, 271-301.

Lipham, J. M. (1973). Leadership: General theory and research. In L. L. Cunningham & W. J. Gephart (Eds.), *Leadership: The science and the art today.* Itasca, IL: F. E. Peacock.

Mazzarella, J. A., & Grundy, T. (1989). Portrait of a leader. In S. C. Smith & P. K. Piele (Eds.), *School leadership.* Eugene, OR: ERIC Clearinghouse on Educational Management.

McGregor, D. (1944). Conditions of effective leadership in the industrial organization. *Journal of Consulting Psychology,* 8, 55-63.

Reddin, W. J. (1970). *Managerial effectiveness.* New York: McGraw-Hill.

Rost, J. C. (1991). *Leadership for the twenty-first century.* New York: Praeger.

Sergiovanni, T. J. (1984). Cultural and competing perspectives in administrative theory and practice. In T. J. Sergiovanni & J. E. Corbally (Eds.), *Leadership and organizational culture.* Urbana: University of Illinois Press.

Sergiovanni, T. J., & Elliott, D. L. (1975). *Educational and organizational leadership in elementary schools.* Englewood Cliffs, NJ: Prentice-Hall.

Terman, L. M. (1904). A preliminary study of the psychology and pedagogy of leadership. *Pedagogical Seminary, 11,* 413-51.

chapter **6**

Leadership as a
Transformational Process

Present-day conditions of schools and their communities suggest an environment that is becoming increasingly pluralistic, unsettled, and uncertain. Traditional orientations to educational leadership are being called into question and new forms are being suggested. One of these new orientations is transformational leadership. In this chapter, we shall explore the origins of transformational leadership, contemporary definitions and related concepts, related characteristics and skills, and associated applications. We also draw on the real life experiences of the people of Valley View to illustrate various concepts presented in this chapter.

BACKGROUND

J. McGregor Burns (1978), in his seminal work, called for a new form of leadership. Leaders, in Burns's thinking, should reach beyond the basic emotional tools of fear, jealousy, and greed and do more than provide persons with pay, status, and other material rewards in exchange for their loyalty and support. According to Burns, transformational leadership is a process where "leaders and followers raise one another to higher levels of morality and motivation" (p. 20). It is a relationship that appeals to the deeper emotional needs and desires of both leaders and followers.

Interestingly the roots of transformational, or charismatic, leadership, as it is often referred to in the literature, can be traced to the earlier work of Weber (1948). Weber, often better known for his theories and research associated with bureaucracies, explored the contrast between formal authority by virtue of rank in an organization and personal authority as derived from personal qualities of the individual leader. Weber was impressed by how charismatic leadership provided for order and direction in complex organizations that were neither bureaucratized nor tradition bound.

Burns's and Weber's work raises the question of the differences between those who provide leadership in an organization and those who attempt to manage or administer an organization. For Burns, it is the difference between transactional management and transformational leadership. Kotter (1988, 1990) has given serious study to these distinctions. In his judgment, leadership and management are both very important processes that can work together; however, conventional wisdom often treats leadership as "good" and management as "bad." Table 6.1 reflects Kotter's comparisons of management and leadership.

As Kotter (1990) observes,

> any combination other than strong management and strong leadership has the potential for producing unsatisfactory results. When both are weak or nonexistent, it is like a rudderless ship with a hole in the hull. But adding just one of the two does not necessarily make the situation much better. Strong management without much leadership can turn bureaucratic and stifling, producing order for order's sake. Strong leadership without much manage-

TABLE 6.1 Comparing management and leadership

	Management	**Leadership**
Creating an agenda	Planning and Budgeting—establishing detailed steps and timetables for achieving needed results, and then allocating the resources necessary to make that happen	Establishing Direction—developing a vision of the future, often the distant future, and strategies for producing the changes needed to achieve that vision
Developing a human network for achieving the agenda	Organizing and Staffing—establishing some structure for accomplishing plan requirements, staffing that structure with individuals, delegating responsibility and authority for carrying out the plan, providing policies and procedures to help guide people, and creating methods or systems to monitor implementation	Aligning People—communicating the direction by words and deeds to all those whose cooperation may be needed so as to influence the creation of teams and coalitions that understand the vision and strategies, and accept their validity
Execution	Controlling and Problem Solving—monitoring results vs. plan in some detail, identifying deviations, and then planning and organizing to solve these problems	Motivating and Inspiring—energizing people to overcome major political, bureaucratic, and resource barriers to change by satisfying very basic, but often unfulfilled, human needs
Outcomes	Produces a degree of predictability and order, and has the potential of consistently producing key results expected by various stakeholders (e.g., for customers, always being on time; for stockholders, being on budget)	Produces change, often to a dramatic degree, and has the potential of producing extremely useful change (e.g., new products that customers want, new approaches to labor relations that help make a firm more competitive)

SOURCE: J. P. Kotter, *A Force for Change: How Leadership Differs from Management,* Free Press, New York, 1990, p. 6. Reprinted with permission of Macmillan Publishing Company.

ment can become messianic and cult-like, producing change for change's sake—even if the movement is in a totally insane direction. (pp. 7–8)

In the field of education, Louis and Miles (1990) support Kotter's conclusion of the equal importance of leadership and management. In their study of successful urban high schools, they found that leadership involves articulating a vision, shared ownership, and evolutionary planning, whereas management involves negotiating demands and resource issues with the environment and coordinated and persistent problem coping. Louis and Miles suggest that management of change is as important as leadership through change.

Other research (Hall & Hord, 1987; Smith & Andrews, 1989; and Wilson & Corcoran, 1988) reinforces and expands on the findings of Louis and Miles. These findings suggest that effective educational leaders are those who inspire followers to a higher purpose while simultaneously taking specific actions that enable the process to move forward toward some expressed or articulated ideals. Leithwood and Jantzi (1990) studied principals who were particularly successful at school improvement, as compared with their less effective peers; these principals

- strengthened the school's culture
- used a variety of bureaucratic mechanisms to stimulate and reinforce cultural change
- fostered staff development
- engaged in direct and frequent communication about cultural norms, values, and beliefs
- shared power and responsibility with others
- used symbols to express cultural values (p. 22)

Fullan (1991) concluded from these educational studies that "the larger goal [for principal leadership] is in transforming the culture of the school" (p. 161). In his vision, principals who are successful in creating a culture that is collaborative in nature allow change to be a natural process widely shared across the organization.

The theory and research cited thus far set the context for examining leadership as a transformational process in greater detail. There is a consensus view that the organizations of the future, in their struggles with a rapidly changing environment, will need leaders and followers invested in a transformational process. According to Bryman (1992), such a process includes the themes of visionary leadership, communicating the vision, empowerment, organizational culture, and trust. An exploration of these and other concepts is next as we discover the ingredients of transformational or charismatic leadership.

DEFINITIONS AND RELATED CONCEPTS

As implied earlier, there is a fine line, if any line at all, between transformational and charismatic leadership. To some, these terms are interchangeable; to others, charisma is considered a component of transformational leadership. Trice and Beyer (1990) claim the distinction is one of purpose: "Charismatic leaders typically create new organizations (and hence new cultures) whereas transformational leaders are concerned to change existing organizations and their cultures" (p. 105). Bass (1990) concluded from his research that charisma is a major component of transformational leadership. Other researchers (Bennis & Nanus, 1985; and Tichy & Devanna, 1990) treat transformational leadership as an approach that articulates a vision that in turn animates followers and creates intense loyalty and trust. Nadler and Tushman (1989) write about "magic leadership," which reflects many of the qualities outlined thus far. Bryman (1992) integrates these concepts under the title of "new leadership." Table 6.2 contrasts old and new leadership themes.

Bryman concludes,

> There is little doubt that there is the possibility of conceptual confusion becoming rife in this field. A number of terms are currently being used to describe what are essentially very similar phenomena. Increasingly, leadership is extolled which exhibits vision, empowers others, inspires, challenges the status quo, and adopts a proactive stance. Such actions are seen as highly motivating and as greatly enhancing people's commitment and performance. (p. 113)

For our purposes, thinking of leadership as a transformational process captures these important qualities and emphasizes leadership meeting changes over time in an organizational context.

Charisma

Some believe charisma is something one has or does not have; others believe it exists only in the eyes of the beholder. Normally we associate charisma with persons who are inspiring, flamboyant, powerful speakers, and who have the capacity to make their message seem very important. As mentioned earlier, efforts at understanding

TABLE 6.2   Themes in new leadership literature

Less emphasis needed on	Greater emphasis needed on
Planning	Vision/mission
Allocating responsibility	Infusing vision
Controlling and problem-solving	Motivating and inspiring
Creating routine and equilibrium	Creating change and innovation
Power retention	Empowerment of others
Creating compliance	Creating commitment
Emphasizing contractual obligations	Stimulating extra effort
Detachment and rationality on the part of the leader	Interest in others and intuition on the part of the leader
Reactive approach to the environment	Proactive approach to the environment

SOURCE: A. Bryman, *Charisma and Leadership in Organizations,* p. 111, copyright 1992 by Sage Publications, Inc. Reprinted by permission of Sage Publications, Inc.

charisma can be traced to the early work of Weber (1968), who distinguished types of authority based on rational grounds, traditional grounds, and charismatic grounds. He saw charismatic authority based on "devotion to the exceptional sanctity, heroism or exemplary character of an individual person, and of the normative patterns or order revealed or ordained by him [*sic*]" (p. 215).

Weber also understood the dependence of a charismatic leader on support from his or her followers. Persons are willing to follow such leaders as long as their "magic spell" remains intact or the mission to which they swore allegiance is attained or sufficient benefits are derived from its pursuit. This all suggests that charisma can be an unstable phenomenon: Once leaders fall out of favor their charismatic influence is quickly dissipated. Leaders who understand this find ways of renewing the spirit and keep loyalty to the cause as a high priority. The Valley View principal was able to keep people focused on the benefits of a new school, and once they were in the new building, she found a new cause—renewed commitment to meeting the needs of all their youthful charges.

Bryman (1992), who explores the nature of charisma, observes that "We may depict the charismatic leader as someone who is viewed as extraordinary and special by followers. These followers allow the charismatic leader to have power over them and they submit willingly to his or her commands. The followers view the charismatic leader with a mixture of reverence, unflinching loyalty and awe" (p. 41). What underlies these feelings toward leaders is less clear. It may be some combination of being captivated by personal traits (e.g., knowledge, kindness, forcefulness) and projecting one's own needs onto the leader (e.g., for guidance, comforting authority, security) and the viability of the leader's mission (e.g., important cause, intrinsic reward, status and recognition).

Most importantly, charismatic persons are able to create some excitement for their followers. Berlew (1974) discusses three forms of behavior that contribute to this excitement: (1) creating a common vision for the organization, (2) creating value-related opportunities and activities within this common vision, and (3) making members of the organization feel stronger and less powerless. The principal of Valley View Elementary School managed to spark excitement with all three behaviors, particularly her emphasis on giving voice to teachers through involvement and responsibility for restructuring the school.

House (1977) specified a number of effects of charismatic leadership:

- followers' trust in the veracity of the leader's beliefs
- creation of similarity of belief between followers and the leader
- affection for and obedience willingly given to the leader
- emotional involvement of followers in the leader's mission
- enhanced follower performance in relation to task
- a belief among followers that they will contribute to the mission's consummation

He further stresses that certain personal characteristics contribute to charismatic leadership, including a high level of self-confidence, a tendency to dominate and a need to influence others, and a strong conviction in the integrity of one's own beliefs.

Conger and Kanungo (1987), however, debunk the notion that charisma is a mystical quality. While admitting that leaders differ in their capacity to transmit a vision, they believe we are dealing with a fairly mundane universe of behaviors that enhance the likelihood of being deemed charismatic and that are learnable by many leaders. Some of these behaviors are revealed in our discussion of further concepts relating to transformational leadership.

Vision

A major component to the transformational process and to possessing charisma is the capacity to develop and articulate a vision of what is possible and that challenges the status quo. Conger (1989) defines vision "as an idealized future goal that the leader wishes the organization to achieve" (p. 29). Members of an organization are challenged to contrast such an ideal with present goals. This helps set a context for motivation for change, particularly if this new vision matches well followers' aspirations.

According to Hunt (1991), visionary leadership consists of "focusing attention on the vision; communicating the vision personally; demonstrating trustworthiness; displaying respect; and taking risks" (p. 196). In the Valley View case, the principal demonstrated these behaviors by helping members of the school and community see the need to create a new self-image. No doubt the past history of conflict and deteriorating school conditions made it easier for some persons to accept a new vision; on the other hand, it is likely that there were feelings of cynicism and negativism that could have derailed any effort at accepting a new vision for the Valley View Elementary School. Members of the school and community had to see this vision as being attainable in spite of their reservations. The principal was successful in getting individuals (within and outside the school) to believe in the need and potential for a new school building. Her personal investment of time and energy made it evident that she was willing to take some risks and in turn enabled her to garner respect and to build trust. In addition, her family connections and having grown up in the community enhanced the viability of her leadership and her vision.

It is clear that vision is important to the transformation process, but it is a somewhat ambiguous concept. Conger (1989) attempts to demystify vision: "Once the initial direction is in place, the leader is essentially involved in a constant process of collecting relevant information from multiple perspectives. At the same time, he or she is employing conceptual skills to create a gestalt of emerging opportunities or shortcomings that an [outcome] might fulfill. While the leader may have an endpoint in mind, the evolution to that point is opportunistic" (p. 64). Conger stresses the importance of a leader's intuition as a process of handling and synthesizing lots of information from a variety of sources, weeding out the less useful, and conceptualizing a coherent picture. He states that it is "essentially a creative process" (p. 65), and "while chance may from time to time play a role, it favors the prepared mind" (p. 66). The principal of Valley View appreciated this and slowly and incrementally prepared and discussed her vision for a new school. Not even the recall vote on the bond issue dissuaded her from this vision.

Building a vision is akin to the notion of framing, which is stressed throughout this text. As defined by Conger (1989), "Frames are symbolic structures that we use to make sense of our personal and social experiences—the perspective from which we interpret experience. And in a larger sense, they also provide a map for action" (p. 85). Frames, or visions, help create a sense of the possible, but this does depend on the degree to which our frames cause us to stretch and test new behaviors. New visions challenge our willingness to trust in the capacity of ourselves and others to meet the perceived requirements.

Trust

Transformational leaders are able to convince those involved that they are capable of transforming their ideals or vision into a reality. Conger (1989) explains that leaders are able to convince subordinates that they have the skills necessary to achieve goals "by appearing to be an extraordinary individual and by demonstrating an extraordinary level of personal commitment to the vision" (p. 94). This is accomplished by being perceived as having the answers or knowing how to go about accomplishing the vision, being capable of referencing significant past successes, and having personal talents including skills of persuasion.

Conger further states that transformational leaders build trust through expertise, both in content (what) and in process (how); through commitment, demonstrated by the willingness to take great risks (e.g., possible loss of power, authority, or personal reputation) or by symbolic means (e.g., personal and hands-on involvement, visible excitement when speaking about related goals or activities); and by setting an example, exhibiting the behaviors that subordinates are being encouraged to perform.

This orientation of trust is at a slightly different level than is typically addressed. Trust is often thought of in terms of being able to rely on others to do things they promise or to follow rules mutually agreed on. Clearly these behaviors are important; however, trust within the context of transformational leadership is concerned with helping followers believe in themselves and their leader and that they have the wherewithal to implement desired changes. At the Valley View school the principal developed a school restructuring process after they moved into the new facility. Assigning support personnel to classrooms to assist in language arts instruction was desirable but also overwhelming at times and caused the teachers to want to back off from their innovation. The principal was willing to accept this decision but urged the teachers to give it one more try; in doing this she conveyed her belief that they had the ability to problem-solve this new situation and come up with adaptations that would make their innovation workable. Her trust was rewarded when the change effort was kept alive, but perhaps more important, the teachers discovered that they could meet this new challenge: They discovered the meaning of empowerment.

Empowerment

Empowerment is about efficacy. Believing in one's capacity to influence circumstances in positive ways is critical to feeling empowered. Bandura (1986) identifies four sources for developing a sense of efficacy: actual accomplishments, verbal persuasion, emotional arousal, and observation of others.

Seeing progress while involved in a difficult task enables individuals to discover their ability to prevail in spite of obstacles and problems. Being verbally persuaded by a leader in face-to-face discussions plays an important role in reinforcing the perceptions that a change is doable. Comments that express confidence and praise are important in helping followers keep negative thoughts from crowding out positive thoughts about their change efforts. Expressive or emotional displays stemming from changing conditions can ignite the emotions of others. For example, individuals in high spirits treat others more amiably; this generates positive experiences. Bandura reminds us that "seeing models express emotional reactions tends to elicit emotional arousal in observers" (p. 50). Considerable positive or negative learning is derived from observing others. When it comes to feeling empowered about the change process, it seems wise to emote the positive.

In chapter 4 we discussed dramaturgical concepts for understanding organizations; Conger (1989) adds that "another empowering practice by charismatics is the element of play or drama" (p. 117). He sees effective charismatic leaders building empowerment in an organization by staging dramatic events, or what he calls "up sessions." Using special events to support and motivate involved persons recharges them about the worthiness of their cause and maintains their fidelity to the change effort. Such events can also encourage the use of humor or introduce the element of play, so that persons can have some fun while getting the tasks accomplished.

Howell (1988) distinguishes between socialized and personalized forms of charismatic leadership and their impact on the empowerment of followers. The latter form, a more personalized approach, is directed at empowering individuals to be capable of pursuing a desired vision independently of the leader. This was exactly what the Valley View principal did by deferring the responsibility of working out the design and modifications of Valley View's restructuring program to the teachers. She was attempting to remove a socialized dependency on her as principal in solving implementation problems. She recognized that the success of their change efforts would depend greatly on whether the teachers believed that they could accomplish their goals without the principal's direct guidance and authority. Moving this sense of power or ability to influence the course of events to the followers is a basic ingredient in charismatic or transformational leadership.

A TRANSFORMATIONAL LEADERSHIP MODEL

Thus far we have seen an image of transformational leadership that places the importance of facilitating change in an organization. We can see the importance of having and articulating a vision, creating enthusiasm and support through charisma, building trust, and enabling empowerment to emerge in those taking on the task of implementing change. As worthy as these concepts are, it is difficult to picture how they are linked together in a deliberate or conscious effort at implementing change over time. In this section, we will explore an application or model for organizing the transformation process discussed thus far. It is important to keep in mind, however, that these concepts cannot be mechanically implemented without an appreciation for social, political, cultural, and psychological dynamics.

The Total Systems Intervention (TSI) approach allows a transformational process to unfold in an organizational context. TSI offers potential as a strategy for leadership as a transformational process for several reasons. First, TSI, reflecting the underlying themes in *Reframing & Reform,* includes the notion of reframing situations with the use of metaphors, recognition of the influence of subjectivity in managing organizations, and the need for a total and comprehensive systems approach. Second, TSI grows out of and links to current theories and research on leadership and organizations that fit well with the concepts being explored throughout this book. Third, TSI encourages creativity by potential users and strongly supports the desire to adapt strategies to the unique conditions of an organization. Finally, the concepts of vision, charisma, trust, and empowerment provide a firm footing for the application of TSI.

Total Systems Intervention (TSI)

Flood and Jackson (1991) in their text *Creative Problem Solving* developed the components of TSI. They argue that our society and organizations are faced with "messes" (a set of interacting problems) for which there is not a "super-method" that will address them all. On the other hand, they are uncomfortable with reverting to a heuristic, trial-and-error approach. Thus, they attempt to strike some middle ground, offering an approach to guide the selection of a problem-solving method that fits best with the conditions being addressed. As they state, "The key to the successful use of the 'Total Systems Intervention' (TSI) approach . . . is to choose an appropriate methodology for tackling the problem situation as it is perceived, but always to recognize that other possible perceptions of the problem situation are possible" (p. xi). Not only possible but, from a reframing perspective, desirable.

Total Systems Intervention is just what its words imply. *Intervention* speaks to pursuing appropriate activities that will lead to change. TSI enables all kinds of changes, from the very beginning of implementing TSI to those less visible effects of learning by virtue of using new ideas in organizational and social orders. *Systems* represents a reliance on systems thinking and provides an underpinning for the various methodologies suggested by TSI. *Total* suggests the use of the vast knowledge base available in systems and management sciences to address a whole array of organizational and societal problems involving all persons caught in the web of TSI-related activities. Flood and Jackson say, "In modern systems approach, the concept 'systems' is used not to refer to things in the world but to a particular way of organizing our thoughts about the world" (p. 2).

There are seven principles embedded in three phases of TSI:

- Organizations and problems are too complex to be tackled by one management model and/or the "quick fix"
- Organizations should be investigated from a range of systems metaphors

- Systems metaphors can be linked to appropriate systems methodologies to guide intervention
- Different systems metaphors and methodologies can be used in a complementary fashion
- It is possible to appreciate the strengths and weaknesses of different systems methodologies
- TSI follows a systemic cycle of enquiry with iteration back and forth between the three phases
- Facilitators, clients and others are engaged in all phases of the TSI process (p. 50)

The three phases of TSI are creativity, choice, and implementation. Figure 6.1 outlines these three phases and related tasks, tools, and outcomes. In the creativity phase, the objective is to help involved persons to think creatively about their organizations. The systems metaphors that offer new perspectives include organizations as machine, organism, brain, culture, team, coalition, and prison.

The choice phase is focused on choosing an appropriate intervention methodology that matches the organization's situation as revealed by the creativity phase. This phase guides persons to classify their situation according to two dimensions: systems, the relative complexity (simple or complex) of the system; and participants, relationships (unitary, pluralist, or coercive) between individuals within the system. These dimensions result in six classifications:

- simple-unitary
- complex-unitary

FIGURE 6.1   The three-phase TSI methodology

SOURCE: R. L. Flood & M. C. Jackson, *Creative Problem Solving,* 1991, Wiley, New York, p. 54. Reprinted by permission of John Wiley & Sons, Ltd.

Creativity

Task	—to highlight aims, concerns and problems
Tools	—systems metaphors
Outcome	—"dominant" and "dependent" metaphors highlighting the major issues

Choice

Task	—to choose an appropriate systems-based intervention methodology (methodologies)
Tools	—The "system of systems methodologies"; the relationship between metaphors and methodologies
Outcome	—"dominant" and "dependent" methodologies chosen for use

Implementation

Task	—to arrive at and implement specific change proposals
Tools	—systems methodologies employed according to the logic of TSI
Outcome	—highly relevant and coordinated intervention

- simple-pluralist
- complex-pluralist
- simple-coercive
- complex-coercive

As seen in Table 6.3, Flood and Jackson identify systems methodologies that best fit with particular problem contexts and underlying metaphors.

The implementation phase is targeted at using a systems methodology or methodologies "to translate the dominant vision of the organization, its structure, and the general orientation adopted to concerns and problems, into specific proposals for change" (p. 52). This phase is devoted to the use of procedures and processes suggested within the respective systems methodologies listed in Table 6.3. Each offers a special approach that is somewhat unique and different from its counterparts. Chapter 5 discussed systems dynamics and viable system diagnosis. The interactive planning methodology is explored later in this chapter. An exploration of critical systems heuristics is in chapter 7.

We should keep in mind that TSI is a systemic and iterative methodology. Each phase informs the next but also vice versa. TSI is not to be thought of as a highly se-

TABLE 6.3   Systems methodologies related to systems metaphors

Systems Methodology (Examples)	Assumptions Problem Contexts	Underlying Metaphors
System dynamics	S-U	Machine Team
Viable system diagnosis	C-U	Organism Brain Team
SAST (strategic assumption surfacing and testing)	S-P	Machine Coalition Culture
Interactive planning	C-P	Brain Coalition Culture
SSM (soft systems methodology)	C-P	Organism Coalition Culture
Critical systems Heuristics	S-C	Machine/Organism Prison

S=simple
C=complex
U=unitary
P=pluralist
C=coercive
SOURCE: R. L. Flood & M. C. Jackson, *Creative Problem Solving*, 1991, Wiley, New York, p. 53. Reprinted by permission of John Wiley & Sons, Ltd.

quential and linear process; rather it should be viewed as a series of circles following the ideas of mutual causality developed in chapter 5.

APPLICATION OF TSI TO THE VALLEY VIEW SITUATION

To understand how TSI may be useful in an actual situation, we will consider its application to the Valley View case. We should keep in mind that this is being done retrospectively for demonstration purposes; there was no evidence that the Valley View principal in fact used any formal model, such as TSI. The implications of this we will discuss shortly; for now, however, let's look at the TSI phases and their possible relevance to Valley View.

Creativity Phase

This phase is designed to highlight the aims, concerns, and problems inherent in the situation. We should try to determine which metaphors best reflect people's thinking about the nature of the organization, which metaphors best capture what is desirable for the organization, and which metaphors best explain the organization's difficulties and concerns.

Going back in time is risky and speculative, but one metaphor suggested by the school's early organization and its relationship with the community is the metaphor of a prison. Persons were locked in rigid positions in a situation that could be described as a coercive political system. Considerable negativism and mistrust existed, and people were using political power to get their way with school authorities. Budget defeats, repeated complaints, and forced resignations portrayed an environment that barred people from using other approaches to solving their problems. Coercive behaviors, often used to keep prisoners (or in this case, the school board) in line, also prevented the pursuit of other avenues of problem solving.

When we consider which metaphors might make sense of Valley View's difficulties and concerns, organism and coalition come to mind. The organism metaphor suggests an open systems view that allows an open exchange between the school and its community and between groupings within the school. This metaphor would suggest, for example, the inappropriateness of a visitor sign-in policy, particularly with its overtones of coercion. The coalition metaphor suggests a pluralistic political system in which varying factions get to work out their respective viewpoints and forge necessary compromises so that the organization can function and accomplish its stated goals. The school bond votes and expansion of the school board from three to five members demonstrated the vitality of political action leading to compromise and compliance with majority rule.

The metaphor of the brain captures best what can be achieved with this school and its community. The brain, as we examined in chapter 5, suggests a learning system perspective. Applied to Valley View, it shows that persons within and outside of the school could learn from their experiences and forge ahead in new directions that would increase the well-being of members of the school and the community. This learning process could potentially create a new culture for the community. The culture metaphor emphasizes norms and values. With appropriate leadership and involvement, Valley View could move away from a culture of negativism to a culture of mutual well-being, symbolized in a new school/community facility.

Through the use of different metaphors, the creativity phase enables us to capture the essence of Valley View's problems and aspirations. The outcome of this phase is to select a dominant metaphor "which highlights the main interests and concerns and can be a basis for a choice of an appropriate intervention methodology" (Flood & Jackson, 1991, p. 51). The metaphors that offer future direction and potential for change are the brain, coalition, and culture.

Choice Phase

This phase targets the selection of an appropriate intervention strategy. Table 6.3 provides a guide in the selection of a systems methodology. As can be observed, the underlying metaphors of brain, coalition, and culture suggest a complex-pluralist problem context, which in turn suggests the systems methodologies of interactive planning and SSM (soft systems methodology). According to Flood and Jackson (1991), "These methodologies are designed to tackle contexts in which there is a lack of agreement about goals and objectives among the participants concerned, but where some genuine compromise is achievable (a pluralist situation)" (p. 39). Both methodologies provide a framework for permitting open dissent and debate. They also recognize the political nature of the change process and provide methods for allowing a consensus among participants to emerge. For purposes of this exercise, we will assume that the interactive planning methodology should be selected. Again, this was not the case in the Valley View situation, but for our simulation of the application of TSI, the interactive planning methodology has some relevance.

Implementation Phase

In this phase we are interested in using a chosen systems methodology to "translate the vision of the organization, its structure, and the general orientation adopted to concerns and problems, into specific proposals for change" (Flood & Jackson, 1991, p. 52). Essentially our challenge is to operationalize the vision of Valley View as contained in the dominant metaphor, which in this case is the brain. The principal of Valley View Elementary School intuitively may have sensed the value of creating a learning system environment. This metaphor or vision could be seen as enabling a break with the past, as those persons involved came to know or learned of new possibilities.

The *interactive planning methodology* is anchored in the theories of Russell Ackoff (1974, 1978, 1981), who is known for many insightful ideas, not the least of which is the idea of problems being better understood as "messes." As this word implies, problems are not neat little packages that can be clearly delineated and then neatly wrapped in a rational planning process. Messes are made of multiple problems intermingled and multilayered, in various stages of confusion, and are ubiquitous in nature. Solving messes is like picking raspberries from a dense thicket of thorny bushes. It can be done but has to be done very carefully and with some forethought, particularly if you are dressed in shorts.

Three operating principles underlie interactive planning: the participative principle, the principle of continuity, and the holistic principle. The participative principle states that the process of planning is more important than the product of planning, and that those affected by planning should be involved in it. This principle claims that persons involved will come to understand their organization and its potential by actively discussing its problems and vision.

The principle of continuity recognizes that a system is not static but is undergoing changes while the planning process is in progress. Flood and Jackson (1991) write that "no plan can predict everything in advance, so plans, under the principle of continuity, should be constantly revised" (p. 149).

The holistic principle addresses the need to "plan simultaneously and interdependently for as many parts and levels of the 'system' as is possible" (p. 149). This principle stresses the importance of coordination between units, often where problems arise, and the importance of integration across levels of the organization, because decisions at one level usually affect other levels.

There are five phases to interactive planning:

- formulating the mess
- ends planning
- means planning
- resource planning
- design of implementation and control

Formulating the mess includes systems analysis, which details how the organization works; obstruction analysis, which outlines obstacles; and future projection, which projects where the organization is headed if nothing is done.

Ends planning is concerned with specifying the ends desired in terms of ideals, objectives, and goals. It is a process of selecting an idealized design in three steps: selecting a mission, specifying desired properties of the design, and designing the system.

Means planning addresses what is needed (e.g., planning, policies, and proposals) to fulfill the desired future suggested by the ends planning phase. Alternative means should be explored and evaluated for their potential to achieve the desired ends. A means strategy should be selected in this phase.

Resource planning addresses what resources are needed for the chosen means, when they are required, and how they can be obtained. Potential resources to consider include inputs (e.g., materials, supplies, energy, and services), facilities and equipment, personnel, and money.

The final phase of design of implementation and control focuses on who is to do what, when, where, and how. Outcome information during the implementation phase needs to be fed back in order to allow those involved to learn from their experiences and to make necessary changes and improvements in the planning effort.

Although Valley View leaders did not use interactive planning in an explicit or formal way, we can retrospectively overlay the five phases onto their more informal planning process. The "messes" of Valley View and its school were long-standing and complex in nature and included low teacher morale, administrative turnover, community conflict, deteriorating facilities, a crowded school, and water and septic problems. The old school facility, citizen resistance to support a tax increase, and polarization of political views were major obstacles to overcome. It was clear to many that to do nothing about their school would only allow conditions to get worse, and no doubt the public approval standards of the state would put this school in real jeopardy.

A vision and mission came into focus: a new school facility that allowed space for the daytime instructional program and nighttime recreational use by the community (library and gymnasium). Once this vision became clearer for many members of the community, including the school principal and school board, means and resource planning began to unfold. However, not all went according to plan; the recall vote forced the pro-school-bond coalition to be more creative, which in turn resulted in their proposal to expand the board from three to five members. As we know, eventually the plan for approving a school bond vote and constructing a new school was successful. What we do not know is how various coalitions operated, how consensus developed, and how a sufficient majority of voters was convinced to support the new school bond. We do know that a transformational process with the principal playing a leadership role did unfold in Valley View.

CONCLUSION

In this chapter we explored the dimensions of leadership as a transformational process and explicated the important concepts of change, vision, charisma, trust, and empowerment. Although these concepts help us appreciate the terrain of transformational leadership, they do not necessarily help us know how to get there—to develop or implement a transformational process. We saw that the Total Systems Intervention strategy could provide a road map to enable persons in an organization to develop a clearer understanding of their problems or messes, to develop a vision of what is possible, and to develop a strategy for improving their situation. The application of TSI to the Valley View situation surfaced two potential systems interventions. The interactive planning intervention approach allowed us to observe the potential (at least retrospectively) of being more clear about one's messes, articulating an end mission, exploring appropriate means and resources, and adapting one's plans as conditions unfold.

The Valley View situation illustrates that leadership as a transformational process is more than the efforts of a single person or a single event. There is little doubt, however, that the principal played an important role and was supportive throughout. Her willingness to articulate a vision of a new school facility in a period of low morale and negative support for the school was bold and imaginative. Her willingness to take risks was needed to trigger the transformational process; this allowed others to join the cause and to provide additional leadership and energy. And once there was momentum the rest was history.

DISCUSSION QUESTIONS

1. How would you define transformational leadership?
2. If you were to envision transformational leadership within your educational context, what form would it take? Would there be support for it? Why or why not?
3. Have you worked with persons you would describe as transformational or charismatic leaders? To what extent did they exhibit some of the characteristics discussed in this chapter?
4. In your judgment what role should followers play to support leadership as a transformational process?
5. Do you believe that you could be a transformational leader? Why or why not?

SUGGESTED ACTIVITIES

1. Identify a recent effort at change in your organization. Describe this effort in some detail and analyze it in light of the concepts discussed in the chapter.
2. Take a position on the following statement and be ready to debate with others your point of view: What we need today for the future well-being of our educational systems are more transformational leaders.
3. Do a case study on a person you consider a prototypical transformational leader.
4. Using TSI and its three phases of creativity, choice, and implementation, develop a strategy for change in your organization.
5. Write a concept paper on the merits and demerits of embarking on change in your organization.

REFERENCES

Ackoff, R. L. (1974). *Redesigning the future.* New York: Wiley.
Ackoff, R. L. (1978). *The art of problem solving.* New York: Wiley.
Ackoff, R. L. (1981). *Creating the corporate future.* New York: Wiley.
Bandura, A. (1986). *Social foundations of thought and action: A social-cognitive view.* Englewood Cliffs, NJ: Prentice-Hall.
Bass, B. M. (1990). *Bass and Stogdill's handbook of leadership: Theory, research and managerial applications,* 3rd ed. New York: Free Press.
Bennis, W. G., & Nanus, B. (1985). *Leaders: The strategies for taking charge.* New York: Harper & Row.
Berlew, D. E. (1974). Leadership and organizational excitement, *California Management Review, 17:* 21–30.
Bryman, A. (1992). *Charisma and leadership in organizations.* Newbury Park, CA: Sage.
Burns, J. M. (1978). *Leadership.* New York: Harper & Row.
Conger, J. A. (1989). *The charismatic leader.* San Francisco: Jossey-Bass.
Conger, J. A., & Kanungo, R. N. (1987). Towards a behavioral theory of charismatic leadership in organizational settings, *Academy of Management Review, 12:* 637–47.
Flood, R. L., & Jackson, M. C. (1991). *Creative problem solving.* New York: Wiley.
Fullan, M. G. (1991). *The new meaning of educational change,* 2nd ed. New York: Teachers College Press.

Hall, G. E., & Hord, S. (1987). *Change in schools: Facilitating the process.* Albany: State University of New York Press.

House, R. J. (1977). A 1976 theory of charismatic leadership. In J. G. Hunt & L. L. Larson (Eds.), *Leadership: The cutting edge* (pp. 89-102). Carbondale: Southern Illinois University Press.

Howell, J. M. (1988). Two faces of charisma: Socialized and personalized leadership in organizations. In J. A. Conger & R. N. Kanungo (Eds.), *Charismatic leadership: The elusive factor in organizational effectiveness* (pp. 213-36) San Francisco: Jossey-Bass.

Hunt, J. G. (1991). *Leadership.* Newbury Park, CA: Sage.

Kotter, J. P. (1988). *The leadership factor.* New York: Free Press.

Kotter, J. P. (1990). *A force for change: How leadership differs from management.* New York: Free Press.

Leithwood, K., & Jantzi, D. (1990). *Transformational leadership: How principals can help reform school culture.* Paper presented at American Educational Research Association annual meeting.

Louis, K., & Miles, M. B. (1990). *Improving the urban high school: What works and why.* New York: Teachers College Press.

Nadler, D. A., & Tushman, M. L. (1989). What makes for magic leadership? In W. E. Rosenbach & R. L. Taylor (Eds.), *Contemporary issues in leadership.* Boulder: Westview.

Smith, W. F., & Andrews, R. L. (1989). *Instructional leadership: How principals make a difference.* Alexandria, VA: Association for Supervision and Curriculum Development.

Tichy, N. M., & Devanna, M. A. (1990). *The transformational leader.* New York: Wiley.

Trice, H. M., & Beyer, J. M. (1990). Cultural leadership in organizations, *Organizational Science, 1,* 139-45.

Weber, M. (1948). Politics as a vocation (1921). In H. H. Gerth and C. W. Willis (Eds.), *From Max Weber: Essays in sociology* (pp. 77-128). London: Routledge & Kegan Paul.

Weber, M. (1968). *Economy and society* (1925), 3 vols. G. Roth & C. Wittich (Eds.). New York: Bedminster.

Wilson, B., & Corcoran, T. (1988). *Successful secondary schools: Visions of excellence in American education.* Philadelphia: Falmer Press.

chapter 7

Leadership as a Dialectical Process

The consequence of pluralism and uncertainty in our society, which we alluded to in chapter 6, is often crushing paradoxes, dilemmas, and dualisms. Today's educational leaders face an unusual assortment of conflicting choices that often leave them paralyzed and seeking refuge in the fantasy of a more serene environment. Having to face difficult choices is certainly not a new phenomenon; however, it seems that in the present context the consequences of these choices carry heavier threats and burdens. The audiences for school leaders' decisions are not as passive and willing to defer to authority as they were in the past; a growing skeptical and suspicious public places educational leaders in a fishbowl environment in which people are quick to challenge decisions that are not seen as favorable to their beliefs, values, and expectations. It should not come as any surprise that fewer people can be enticed into school leadership positions. Yet, there may be ways of recognizing and dealing with (or reframing) these difficult and trying conditions, rather than avoiding or withdrawing.

In this chapter we will explore leadership as a dialectical process and examine ways to "balance" conflicting choices of equal value or goodness. This is obviously a big challenge but also vital to the well-being of our educational enterprises. We will develop some background first and then explore in more depth what is meant by dialectical leadership and important and related concepts. In addition, we will explore a related application called critical systems heuristics. Throughout the chapter we will reconnect to the Valley View case in order to demonstrate or illustrate various concepts.

BACKGROUND

To appreciate how uncertainty has preyed upon many generations of leaders, we might reach back in time, to around 500 B.C., and into another culture. Over time the Chinese collected words of wisdom in the *I Ching, or Book of Changes.* The gist of this ancient Chinese book is that life is filled with constant change and uncertainty. Goldberg (1989) writes, "Traditional Western analytic and scientific approaches to learning and knowledge are quite contrary to the philosophy of the *I Ching.* The only constancy in the universe is to be found in change. The only certainty is the prevalence of the unknown and the unknowable" (p. 47).

According to the *I Ching,* change is a process that is inseparable from human reality and the human perception of reality which is in process of change. These Chinese philosophers believed that life is neither predetermined nor under the control of free will. In sharp contrast, the Western mind often assumes control is possible and desirable through direct, nonequivocal answers to life's problems and that there are ways to obtain immediate results. It is a condition that can create a pressure cooker for school leaders.

Figure 7.1 illustrates the Chinese philosophy of blending or accepting opposites. It is a familiar symbol which has been popularized and commercialized in a variety of ways. It does, however, have relevance for understanding dialectical thinking. The symbol, called T'ai-chi Tu, or Diagram of the Supreme Ultimate, represents the two forces of *yin* (the passive or female element) and *yang* (the active or male element) and their dynamic relationship in affecting change. To add complexity to our understanding of the relationship of these forces is the presence, as represented in the two small circles, of some *yin* in *yang* and vice versa. To fully appreciate the complexities of human behavior is to recognize the presence of these opposing forces and their influence within each other. This philosophy stresses that many human situations can be balanced and improved by influencing the relationship between opposing elements.

According to this theory, the challenge is to reframe our thinking to permit the coexistence of opposites. In developing management strategies for an organization, for example, we might be willing to accept the virtues of scientific management and its emphasis on control along with the virtues of artistic management and its emphasis on creativity and spontaneity: the sweet and sour sauce of dialectical leadership.

These early Chinese philosophers provided a philosophical base for the dialectical thinking of Western philosophers. For example, they had a strong influence on

FIGURE 7.1   Yin and yang relationships

Hegel, a nineteenth-century German philosopher, and on Karl Marx. These thinkers recognized that the internal tensions between opposites had a potency for a theory of social change. In *Capital,* Marx used a dialectical method to expose how economic and social contradictions within a society provided a basis for self-transformation. According to Morgan (1986, p. 258) Marx's dialectical theory of social change reflects three principles:

1. the mutual interpenetration (struggle, or unity) of opposites
2. the negation of the negation
3. the transformation of quantity into quality

The first principle makes the power of opposites evident by the countereffect of a change strategy. The seeds of counterchange are sown in the implementation of the change. An example of this was the attempt by the pro-school-bond people to outmaneuver the anti-school-bond advocates in Valley View. Their success on the first school bond vote was short-lived and provided the impetus for the anti-school-bond folks to get their act together and to rescind the first vote. This in turn moved the pro-school-bond people to suggest a change in the membership of the school board. And so on. We can observe how the school bond process changed direction and strategy as a consequence of the tensions brought on by actions and counteractions of the two opposing factions.

The second principle posits that "change may become developmental in the sense that each negation rejects a previous form, yet also retains something from that form" (Morgan, 1986, p. 258). As with the series of school bond votes, each new iteration of events rejected the previous actions but also retained some of its features, eventually resulting in the citizens' approval of a bond for not only a new school but one with more space than requested in the original proposal.

The third principle sets the context for revolutionary change. In the efforts at control and countercontrol, the school bond vote eventually ran its course and led to a new phase of collaboration rather than confrontation. Eventually a consensus emerged with the expansion of the school board, which permitted sufficient support to surface not only for approval of the school bond but to support an increase in the size of the new school. These changes set a context for greater cooperation and consensus building than was the case in the earlier efforts at getting approval of the bond. As Morgan states, "Cumulative changes in society may thus provide the platform for a revolution that changes the underlying basis of that society" (p. 258).

These three principles permit a richer and more complex understanding of the nature of change. The experiences of Valley View, in its attempts to get voter approval of a new school facility, illustrate these three principles and their interactive relationship. No doubt citizen and school personnel morale was on a roller coaster as the school bond voting events unfolded. On the other hand, the eventual outcome had strong support and set the stage for a new era of cooperation in creating a new school environment and addressing issues of school effectiveness.

Kets de Vries (1980) defines organizational life as full of dilemmas that stem from day-to-day activities: "Managers will be confronted with many paradoxical encounters which at first glance might seem irrational and lack obvious answers. But there is some kind of logic behind these behavior patterns which warrants further investigation. We can not just ignore these paradoxes met in interpersonal relationships. They raise important questions about human motivation, individual and organizational action, the nature of decision making, and the problem of change" (pp. 1–2). He suggests that there is a "twilight zone" in which we need to understand better the blurring of boundaries that separate rationality and irrationality. There is a tendency on our part to ignore or dismiss these vagaries of organizational life and hope they will go away. More careful reflection and analysis of these paradoxes and their underlying causes may help us appreciate the irrational as well as the rational side of organizations and develop empathy for our fellow human beings. For Kets de Vries, management is a balancing act and change poses constant conundrums for managers. Leaders in organizations must deal with basic human drives of love and aggression and with feelings and attitudes of dependency and control, conflict and compromise, and hostility and compassion. Our effectiveness is dependent on our adaptive capacity for handling shifting conditions brought on by many opposing forces.

Goldberg (1989) states that "it is the striking of a healthy dynamic balance between the opposing elements that makes for a stable world and worldview. Simplistic either/or reasoning should be replaced by frameworks that value both choices and strike a balance between them" (p. 87). He claims that the exploration of dualisms and paradoxes opens up the possibility of seeing new questions and new answers. The dualistic view allows for comprehending wholes by looking for the opposite element in the pairs of elements. Some examples he provides are the dualisms of analysis/synthesis (neither method will suffice), generalist/specialist (we need both engineers and poets), and individual rights/societal rights (trade-offs should be considered).

Dualisms and paradoxes can often place an educational leader between the rock and hard place of moral and ethical dilemmas. The limited fiscal resources of educational organizations, for example, lead to having to make choices concerning how these resources will be distributed. School leaders have the unenviable task of determining whose needs will be met or ignored. The list must seem endless for school leaders who have to face many and conflicting choices. Issues of accessibility, best instructional practices, grouping or tracking of students, control and freedom for students, meeting individual and group needs, balancing success and failure, and balancing change and stability have unlimited potential for presenting leaders with ethical dilemmas.

For example, the principal of Valley View Elementary School faced the dilemma of seeing the need for a new school but needing to be careful not to appear supportive of one parent group over another. She and her staff walked the fine line of explaining the problems of the school without giving one group more special treatment or more access to information. She acknowledged her ethical bind and called on a sense of professionalism to handle the situation. Her experience demonstrates the need for both an awareness of potential dilemmas and an ethical or moral framework to guide behavior in these kinds of situations.

The combined effect of paradoxes, dualisms, and dilemmas is a need for leadership that is dialectical in nature, is anchored in an examined and articulated value framework, and recognizes the need for artistry. Maxcy (1991) introduces the notion of leadership as best manifested by the metaphors of the philosopher-leader and the artist-leader: "If research on leadership reveals anything it tells us that all leadership must involve teaching and learning. Thus, in educational settings in particular, leaders qua teachers, as creative and innovative thinkers, will be necessary if we are to make the kinds of significant reforms in education today and in the future" (p. 50). Leaders teaching and learning more about the dialectical process may be able to lead in an environment of pluralistic values and conflicting choices.

DEFINITIONS AND RELATED CONCEPTS

Early views (Blau & Scott, 1962; Lourenco & Glidewell, 1975; Weinstein, Weinstein, & Blau, 1972) essentially saw the dialectical process as an ongoing one through which dilemmas are confronted and partly resolved only to be confronted again in modified form. Benson (1977) further developed a dialectical view of organizations:

> A dialectical view is fundamentally committed to the concept of process. The social world is in a continuous state of becoming—social arrangements which seem fixed and permanent are temporary, arbitrary patterns and any observed social pattern are regarded as one among many possibilities. Theoretical attention is focused upon the transformation through which one set of arrangements gives way to another. Dialectical analysis involves a search for fundamental principles which account for the emergence and dissolution of specific social orders. (p. 3)

Dialectical analysis, according to Benson, is guided by four principles: social, construction/production, totality, contradiction, and praxis. The social construction/production principle states that people are continuing to construct their social world, often guided by concrete, mundane tasks of everyday life. The existing social structure tends to favor certain individuals or groups and acts as a constraint on them and others. The old order in Valley View favored those who had conservative views and used the school as a forum to debate and reinforce these views; the new order favored more liberal views that supported efforts at change. Time will tell if this new social construction and what it produces can balance the opposing needs and/or give way to another construction.

The principle of totality involves studying social phenomena relationally with attention to multiple interconnections. The dialectical analysis stresses looking at wholes and recognizing the partial autonomy of its components. Totality stresses the emergent nature of a social system that is caused in part by the tension of new socially constructed realities and the status quo of semi-autonomous components. As Benson, (1977) states, "The totality, conceived dialectically then, includes newly emergent social arrangements as well as those already in place" (p. 4). The new school in Valley View reflects a new order, but at the same time there are conservative remnants with their emphasis on the acquisition of basic skills and competencies in the instructional program.

The contradiction principle recognizes that new patterns of social order must always run against established interests. The variability and semi-autonomy of various levels and layers within the social order almost guarantee an unevenness and disconnection in the social production of a new order. These social contradictions have numerous and somewhat constraining effects upon new innovations and include occasional dislocations and crises brought about by unusual combinations of people and values. The side effect can be to facilitate or thwart change or limit certain changes to a particular period of time or within a given subsystem. Valley View Elementary School's restructuring effort at integrating support services with classroom instruction has had its fits and starts and no doubt will continue to reflect the tugs and pulls of the inevitable contradictions of specialized and integrated services.

The final principle of praxis is defined as "the free and creative reconstruction of social arrangements on the basis of a reasoned analysis of both the limits and the potentials of present social forms" (Benson, 1977, p. 5). In other words, persons can be active in rethinking or reconstructing their social relations based on an ethical commitment to the liberation of human potential.

To summarize: "Dialectical analysis contributes to [the process of reconstruction] in part by dereifying established social patterns and structures—points out their arbitrary character, undermines their sense of inevitability, uncovers the contradictions and limits of the present order, and reveals the mechanisms of transformation" (Benson, 1977, p. 6).

Dimensions to Dialectical Leadership

Dialectical leadership involves, according to Benson (1977), "[t]he mobilization of participants to pursue their interests and to reach out for alternative structural arrangements" (p. 9). This mobilization provides commitment and resources to various groups often disenfranchised in an organization and empowers them to become actively involved in the reconstruction of the organization. In some ways, it is an effort at capturing and harnessing the energy flow in the organization and establishing processes that link various participants to each other so that they can jointly engage in the principle of praxis.

Hodgkinson (1991) reinforces Benson's thinking by linking praxis to the dichotomy of theory and practice in his "*tri*chotomy" of theory, practice, and praxis. In his view, "administration [or leadership] is not art or science, nor is it art and science, it is art, science, and philosophy" (p. 42). He is also interested in creating an intersection of interests, particularly of administrators, teachers, and students. The intersection reveals the overlaps and potential conflicts of interests between these groups. But also, these overlaps have the potential to intensify interests and organizational synergy, in keeping with Benson's notion of mobilization of various participants. It is through the process of praxis with multiple participants and their respective interests that leadership can be best exercised.

Hodgkinson describes praxis as a "duality in action, two 'moments': one of consciousness or reflection in the first moment and one of action and commitment in the second moment" (p. 43). Praxis goes beyond the mere reflex or habitual response to stimuli: It presses leaders to be consciously reflective and intentional in their actions. Certainly this is a tall order when considering the frenetic pace of present-day school leaders, and yet being more than a reactor to external forces requires it.

The principal of Valley View Elementary School could have stayed with the status quo and assumed the construction of a new school was impossible and impractical. Having grown up in the community she understood the forces for and against such an effort and no doubt reflected at some length before she boldly suggested to the school board that they address the need for a new school facility in spite of strong community opposition. She realized on the one hand that she would be risking support and understanding from the more conservative parents and citizens of the community; she also knew that the school board was not eager to take on the task of promoting a new school bond issue. On the other hand, she knew that the school was substandard, overcrowded, and had little or no space for special subjects and support personnel.

As Kets de Vries (1980) points out, managers have to disentangle the web by finding "a workable solution out of situations which, at first sight, appear as double binds." The Valley View principal exhibited "the skill of balancing trade-offs" (p. 55). Kets de Vries writes further that it is a question of asking which choice is more stress inducing. The choices for the principal were to say nothing and operate the school as best she could while absorbing complaints from staff and some parents, or to press the school board to study the issue and be exposed to questions and complaints by the conservative element in the community and by those who felt they could not afford higher taxes.

According to Kets de Vries (1980), managers can reduce ambiguity and modify stress levels by embarking "on a continuous process of accurate self-observation and reality testing. This will necessitate a regular re-evaluation of life goals and achievements, and an examination of reactions to disappointment" (p. 56). This form of honesty can keep rationalizations to a minimum. Managers often have to make a choice between reality and rationalization and hope they can tell which is which and when to do what. The role of leaders is to be able to break the impasses, provide motivation, and give directions, even in highly paradoxical situations with competing value systems.

Competing Value Systems

Quinn (1988) has developed a schema for understanding the nature of competing value systems that often plague leaders in organizations. A series of studies (Quinn & Rohrbaugh, 1983) collected judgments of organizational theorists and researchers concerning similarity and dissimilarity between pairs of organizational effectiveness criteria. Figure 7.2 provides a theoretical framework summarizing their findings. The two axes create four quadrants ranging from flexibility to control (vertical axis) and internal to external focus (horizontal axis). Each of the quadrants represents one of four major models in organizational theory. The human relations quadrant stresses criteria of cohesion, morale, and human resource development. The open systems model in the upper right quadrant stresses flexibility, readiness, growth, resource acquisition, and external support.

The remaining quadrants of the rational goal model and the internal process model have criteria opposing the two previously mentioned models. For example, the open systems model is characterized by flexibility and external focus, counter to the internal process model that emphasizes control and internal focus. Also parallels can be observed, with the human relations model and open systems model sharing an emphasis on flexibility. Similarly the internal process model and rational goal model share an emphasis on control.

As Quinn (1988) explains,

> This scheme [Figure 7.2] is called the *competing values framework* because the criteria seem to initially carry a conflictual message. We want our organizations to be adaptable and flexible, but we also want them to be stable and controlled. We want growth, resource acquisition, and external support, but we also want tight information management and formal communication. We want an emphasis on the value of human resources, but we also want an

FIGURE 7.2   Competing values framework: Effectiveness

SOURCE: R. E. Quinn, *Beyond Rational Management: Mastering the Paradoxes and Competing Demands of High Performance*, 1988, Jossey-Bass, San Francisco, CA, p. 48. Reprinted with permission of Jossey-Bass Inc., Publishers.

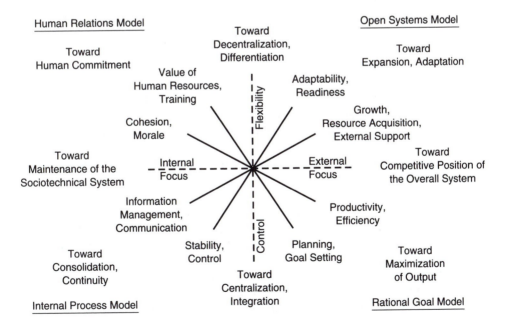

emphasis on planning and goal setting. The model does not suggest that these oppositions cannot mutually exist in a real system. It suggests, rather, that these criteria, values, and assumptions are oppositions in our minds. We tend to think that they are very different from one another, and we sometimes assume them to be mutually exclusive. (pp. 49–51)

Quinn and his associates designed a questionnaire based on this framework to serve as a diagnostic tool and assist members of organizations to interpret their organization's competing values. The content provides a basis for discussion and consensus building concerning desirable changes and/or maintenance of existing conditions. Quinn's competing values framework helps make concrete and explicit the differing assumptions of members of an organization. This approach also permits addressing competing values and integrating these into a blend or balance of opposites.

Hodgkinson (1991) developed a value paradigm as a conceptual tool for supporting the praxis process or for resolving conflicts of values in a practical context. Value conflicts are inevitable: "Because of the radical difference between fact and value, it is both possible and likely for two observers to attribute two divergent values or sets of values to the same piece of objectivity or fact. Indeed they must do so, if only for the simple reason that everyone experiences the world from a different angle. No one can occupy the same life-space as another. The world comes up differently each time for each person. Therefore, in some very fundamental sense values are always in conflict" (p. 90). Hodgkinson stresses that telling the difference between facts and values is not easy and that in most cases we are talking about values. Those of us who aspire to leadership roles in education are faced with value choices and we are often forced to choose. We may rely on the culture of the organization to guide us, or we may draw on our own sense of what is right or wrong; we may be guided by values derived from hedonism, ambition, or careerism or by the prejudices of our colleagues. A big question for leaders is on what grounds one should choose. Hodgkinson poses additional questions:

- What values are the *right* values?
- How are the values of the case before us to be ordered?
- How are we to achieve that degree of certainty which can imbue us with a sense of philosophical satisfaction and psychological security? (p. 93)

To guide us through these difficult questions, Figure 7.3 presents Hodgkinson's analytical model for classifying values.

The first step in sorting values is to break apart the concept of value between *right* (deontological) and *good* (axiological). Good refers to what is enjoyable, likable, or pleasurable, whereas right is proper, moral, and duty-bound. Good is already known by our preferences and does not have to be explained to us. It is basically hedonistic, part of our psychology of seeking pleasure and avoiding pain; it suffers from little inner conflict but can cause conflict externally in interpersonal relations.

The dimension of right is less clear-cut and can be troublesome. We have a moral sense or sense of collective responsibility sometimes referred to as our superego. This

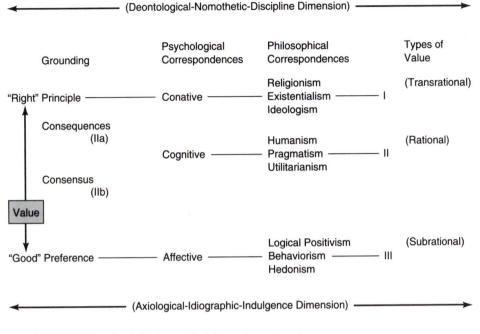

FIGURE 7.3   Analytical model of the value concept

SOURCE: C. Hodgkinson, *Educational Leadership: The Moral Act*, State University of New York Press, Albany, NY, p. 97.

often leads to conflict at the personal level when we are attempting to resolve two equal desires—the pull of the affect and the demands of the situation. We often displace our self-indulgent desires by accepting more nomothetic, or group, demands. We sort through these numerous demands and establish or ground our values in one of four ways. The first column of Figure 7.3 introduces the groundings of *principle* (Type I), *consequences* (Type IIa) and *consensus* (Type IIb), and *preference* (Type III).

Type III values are self-justifying and grounded in an individual's affect. Something is good because we like it and we like it because we like it. Value is difficult to justify beyond our feelings and is often taken for granted.

Moving up the hierarchy, there are three ways (Types I, IIa, and IIb) to judge whether something is right. Type IIb values concur with the will of the majority and are grounded in a consensus of a collectivity. Second, it is a Type IIa value if, after some analysis, the consequences anticipated are held to be desirable. According to Hodgkinson (1991), "Type II values enlist the reason, the cognitive faculty, whether it be to count heads (IIb) or to assess contingencies (IIa); the grounds are *social* for they depend upon collectivities and collective justification" (p. 98).

Type I values are grounded in the metaphysical, in principles that take the form of ethical codes, injunctions, or commandments (e.g., Thou shalt not kill). They are neither verifiable by the techniques of science nor justified by logical argument. Type

I values are "based on the will rather than upon the reasoning faculty; their adoption implies an act of faith, belief, commitment" (Hodgkinson, 1991, p. 99). Because of their normative orientation, Type I values link to the phenomena of loyalty, commitment, guilt, conscience, and responsibility but go beyond mere consensus.

In organizational situations we can sense the tugs and pulls across these value types. Little is predetermined except the degree to which we accept without question Type I or Type III values. Without reflection, we may not fully appreciate the influence of these two levels and our capacity to control Type III values or to question Type I values. Hodgkinson's analytical model provides a way of sorting through values that play a subtle but significant influence as we grapple with multiple choices and day-to-day events. It also provides a framework for conducting a praxis in sorting through and deciding on a course of action.

Moral Imagination

According to Greenfield, "Education is a deeply moral enterprise. How can the administration of such an enterprise be any the less moral?" (cited in Hodgkinson, 1991, p. 140). The challenge for leaders is to develop a moral vision to guide the affairs of educational enterprises. Others (Smith & Blase, 1987) suggest that leadership needs to be distributed among key players in schools and argue that moral vision should be replaced by value-driven human relations psychology with an emphasis on policy and practice of a caring nature.

Maxcy (1991) argues a third perspective or a middle of the road approach that avoids the extremes of the moral imagination and the human relations views. He stresses the importance of leaders helping "followers identify and further what is of value" and being imaginative in the sense of being "inspirational, creative, innovative, and problem-solving in nature" (p. 12).

Maxcy explores four distinct meanings to moral imagination:

- discovery (identifying a hypothetical state of affairs that can serve as visions of the future)
- moral authority (possessing superior moral knowledge and certitude)
- a faculty of the mind (acting as a sixth sense that is profound and beyond rational monitoring or correction)
- super science (substituting for traditional research paradigms) (pp. 116–20)

There are limitations to each of these orientations in the practice of the moral imagination of educational leaders. Maxcy would like to see the private dimensions of moral imagination be turned into something he terms the public democratic critical imagination. As Maxcy explains it, "The critical and pragmatic perspective on leadership that is advanced here finds democracy to be the most congenial social arrangement, or way of life, offering a middle ground between abstract moralizing found in the moral imagination view and the atomistic individualism of the personal relations model" (p. 129).

We will explore some of these democratic principles in chapter 8. Suffice it to say that schools are special organizations with cultures in which values and caring play important roles (a reemerging theme that was explored in chapter 2). A need exists for members of a school and its community to be guided by democratic values that permit open access to shaping and reshaping a school's vision and overarching values. The previous principal at Valley View imposed restrictions on parents' and community members' access to the school during the school day. These restrictions caused considerable consternation and stress between the community and the school. The new principal quickly dropped this policy and was particularly concerned with opening the school to parents. She even included all members of the community in the distribution of the school's newsletter. She fully supported the democratic process that enabled deliberation over the school's facilities needs and citizens' right to choose. She advocated for the well-being of her youthful charges but was careful not to dictate the value principles which eventually prevailed in the school bond approval.

Constructing a moral context for guiding school decision making is critical to resolving alternative or conflicting choices. There is, however, a danger of elitism or restrictive participation in the formulation of this framework, and it can result in sorting people as winners and losers. A democratic process built on open and full participation of all members of a community should safeguard against the creation of more restrictive visions that are imposed on weaker or less represented members of the community. It is through the debates, so integral to the democratic process, that value conflicts, paradoxes, dualisms may be aired and resolved.

AN APPLICATION OF DIALECTICAL LEADERSHIP

As discussed in chapter 6, Flood and Jackson (1991) conceptualize a Total System Intervention (TSI) model in which alternative strategies for problem solving and change can be guided. TSI provides a metaframework for selecting the most promising interventions for specific problem contexts. Assumptions about problem contexts (e.g., simple, complex, unitary, pluralist, and coercive) and underlying metaphors (e.g., organism, coalition, culture, machine) suggest an a priori intervention that seems to fit best the particular situation. The systems methodology of critical systems heuristics (CSH) fits well in problem contexts that are simple and coercive in nature and can be best described by the underlying metaphors of machine/organism and prison. Although these characteristics do not fully fit the Valley View situation, CSH does provide a method by which a critique of proposals to solve existing problems may be carefully scrutinized.

CSH is based on Ulrich's work (1983) and philosophy of emancipation (gaining freedom from oppression) and reveals the underlying value assumptions involved in an intervention strategy. According to Flood and Jackson (1991), CSH "enables us to reveal the 'true' interests and motivations underlying . . . proposals, assists with challenging the proposals and constructing counter proposals, and insists that no plans are rational which have not been approved by the 'affected but not involved'" (p. 198).

Each of the words of CSH has special meaning: *Critical* refers to the practice of making transparent the normative content of proposed interventions; *systems* refers to the totality of relevant conditions; *heuristics* is a process for uncovering deceptions and revealing messy issues through critical reflection. A dialectical process validates an intervention or design solution for implementation; this involves a dialogue of those affected but not necessarily involved. For example, school reform plans or designs so often have little or no input from students. The dialectical solution is to "bring the systems rationality of the planners directly into contact with the 'social rationality' of those who have to live in and experience social systems designs" (Flood & Jackson, 1991, p. 202).

Four principles guide CSH: purposefulness and three "quasi-transcendental" ideas—systems idea, moral idea, and guarantor idea. Purposefulness refers to the importance of adequately designing a social system intervention's intended purposes. The purposeful system produces knowledge of desired purposes and encourages debate about them; all plans are assessed in terms of their normative content. The systems idea is concerned with the comprehensiveness of plans; the moral idea raises the question of the ethical adequacy of those plans; and the guarantor idea is concerned with democratic involvement.

The heart of CSH methodology is 12 "critically heuristic categories." These categories permit the posing of critical questions about designs or potential designs for change. They can serve as an outline for ordinary persons being impacted by proposed changes to structure a rational discourse with leaders of the change. When leaders introduce new ideas and schema for change, it is assumed that they operate within a discretionary value context in which they choose to include or exclude certain options. The 12 categories permit formulating boundary questions to determine the break-off points used by leaders. As Flood and Jackson (1991) explain, "Anyone who understands the concept of boundary judgments, knows that planners who justify their proposals on the basis of expertise, or 'objective necessities' are in fact employing boundary judgments, whether cynically or simply unreflectively. So if planners [leaders] can be made to discuss basic boundary judgments, they are put in a position where they are not better off with their knowledge and expertise than ordinary affected citizens [followers]" (pp. 205–6).

The 12 boundary questions are divided evenly into four categories. The questions probe sources of motivation behind a designed intervention or its value assumptions, sources of control or its basis of power, sources of expertise or its basis of guarantee, and sources of legitimation.

The questions are asked within an "is" mode and "ought" mode that permit contrasting answers. For example, the first question addresses who the client "is"; in the "ought" mode it is a matter of who "ought" to be the client. Figures 7.4 and 7.5 display the 12 questions in these two respective modes.

These questions make more explicit underlying assumptions and values that are guiding or have guided a projected plan or innovation. This normative content permits a more open discussion than a situation where value assumptions are obfuscated

1. Who *is* the actual *client* of S's [the system's] design, i.e., who belongs to the group of those whose purposes (interests and values) are served, in distinction to those who do not benefit but may have to bear the costs or other disadvantages?
2. What is the actual *purpose* of S's design, as being measured not in terms of declared intentions of the involved but in terms of the actual consequences?
3. What, judged by the design's consequences, is its built-in *measure of success?*
4. Who is actually the *decision taker*, i.e., who can actually change the measure of success?
5. What *conditions* of successful planning and implementation of S are really controlled by the decision taker?
6. What conditions are *not* controlled by the decision taker, i.e., what represents *"environment"* to him?
7. Who is actually involved as planner?
8. Who is involved as *"expert,"* of what kind is his expertise, what role does he actually play?
9. Where do the involved see the *guarantee* that their planning will be successful? (e.g., In the theoretical competence of experts? In consensus among experts? In the validity of empirical data? In the relevance of mathematical models or computer simulations? In political support on the part of interest groups? In the experience and intuition of the involved?, etc.) Can these assumed guarantors secure the design's success, or are they false guarantors?
10. Who among the involved *witnesses* represents the concerns of the affected? Who is or may be affected without being involved?
11. Are the affected given an opportunity to *emancipate* themselves from the experts and to take their fate into their own hands, or do the experts determine what is right for them, what quality of life means to them, etc? That is to say, are the affected used merely as means for the purposes of others, or are they also treated as "ends in themselves" (Kant), as belonging to the client?
12. What *worldview* is actually underlying the design of S? Is it the worldview of (some of) the involved or of (some of) the affected?

FIGURE 7.4 The 12 critically heuristic boundary questions in the "is" mode

SOURCE: R. L. Flood & M. C. Jackson, *Creative Problem Solving*, 1991, John Wiley & Sons, New York, p. 206. Reprinted by permission of John Wiley & Sons, Ltd.

or merely not consciously reflected on. It also permits those who will be affected by a planned intervention to validate its potential consequences.

If we applied just the first question to Valley View's plans to gain citizen approval in raising local property taxes to fund the construction of a new elementary school building, we can appreciate the effect such questions may have in sorting value choices in what appears at first blush to be a straightforward school bond vote. The first question deals with the notion of who is or who ought to be the actual client of S's (the system's) design. As outlined in Figure 7.4, we are interested in whose purposes are served as distinct from those who do not benefit but may have to bear the costs. This question illustrates perfectly the dilemma facing school leaders in getting citizens to support tax increases for services that they may not perceive as being of direct benefit to them. The actual clients in this situation are the children and the teachers who will benefit from improved surroundings. As far as who ought to be the client, here we can appreciate the principal's desire to articulate the concept that the school should serve the "community" as well as the children and staff of the school. Thus, she proposed that the school library become a resource for both the school and community. Also the increase in square footage netted a larger all-purpose room, which included a kitchen and gymnasium with ample space for adult recreational activities.

1. Who ought to be the *client* (beneficiary) of the system S to be designed or improved?
2. What ought to be the *purpose* of S, i.e., what goal states ought S be able to achieve so as to serve the client?
3. What ought to be S's *measure of success* (or improvement)?
4. Who ought to be the *decision taker*, i.e., have the power to change S's measure of improvement?
5. What *components* (resources and constraints) of S ought to be controlled by the decision taker?
6. What resources and conditions ought to be part of S's *environment*, i.e., not be controlled by S's decision taker?
7. Who ought to be involved as *designer* of S?
8. What kind of *expertise* ought to flow into the design of S, i.e., who ought to be considered an expert and what should be his role?
9. Who ought to be the *guarantor* of S, i.e., where ought the designer to seek the guarantee that his design will be implemented and will prove successful, judged by S's measure of success (or improvement)?
10. Who ought to belong to the *witnesses* representing the concerns of the citizens that will or might be affected by the design of S? That is to say, who among the affected ought to get involved?
11. To what degree and in what way ought the affected be given the chance of *emancipation* from the premises and promises of the involved?
12. Upon what *worldviews* of either the involved or the affected ought S's design be based?

FIGURE 7.5   The 12 critically heuristic boundary questions in the "ought" mode

SOURCE: R. L. Flood & M. C. Jackson, *Creative Problem Solving*, 1991, John Wiley & Sons, New York, p. 207. Reprinted by permission of John Wiley & Sons, Ltd.

This simple question of who the client is demonstrates the value choices hidden from view in choosing a design for a new school. So often school authorities come to the public asking for support on behalf of their children, which is noble but does not tell the full story. There are other potential clients, such as parents and citizens at large, whose needs could be incorporated in the plans of a new school without sacrificing or trading off the needs of the students. So often school designs are driven by past practices and unexamined assumptions about who the client is and what needs should be met. We do not know for sure what effect these proposals had in the eventual passing of the Valley View bond vote, but it is reasonable to suspect that some members of the community voted yes because they saw some direct benefits in the new school design.

The 12 critically heuristic boundary questions can clarify the options in a new school design. A discussion of these questions with school and community leaders should elicit many of their underlying assumptions and values concerning the options being promoted. Without the 12 questions, it is business as usual and a dialectical opportunity lost.

CONCLUSION

Leadership as a dialectical process is the willingness to face the ambiguities and subjectivities of choice and consciously acknowledge that with any choice there are potential opposites of equal value. Leadership that begins with this premise and proceeds through a thoughtful process of reflection and dialogue with others should make more explicit the opposing value choices. Goldberg (1989) explains that "by acknowledging the existence of the dualism as an entity in its own right, the struggle for supremacy of one element over the other vanishes, and our attention is focused on reconciling the opposites through acknowledging and balancing them, not through eliminating one of the opposing elements" (p. 87).

Notwithstanding this advice, it is no easy task sorting through and choosing among competing values. We did, however, explore some value frameworks that help explain the complementary and interrelated nature of values. This perspective allows for the merger or integration of values as opposed to their being irreconcilable opposites.

Conflicting values do prompt the need for a broader value framework to guide choices and the integration of choices. Moral imagination, a process through which multiple and competing values can be discussed and a consensus can be agreed upon, is very important. Schools in particular can easily become a battleground where value choices clash and where often more heat than light is produced. The earlier condition of Valley View was such a situation. The new principal's leadership helped reframe many of these issues and a new consensus, albeit shaky, emerged. Interestingly, as the conflict over the school bond faded into the background, the principal and school staff began to discuss how they could make the school experience better for their pupils. Applying Greenfield (1987) to the case, we can say that the Valley View Elementary School principal and teachers began to act morally by "the application of some standard of goodness that illuminates the discrepancy between the present and what is possible, and better" (p. 62). He continues:

> Vision, then, results from the exercise of moral imagination. The latter is a process that involves observation of the current state of affairs in a school and the making of a judgment as to whether or not the current state is satisfactory. Implicit in the activity of making a judgment is the application of some standard of goodness. It is a consideration of what is observed in light of the standard applied that results in the decision to leave things as they are, or to try and change them for the better. Engaging in this process is thus requisite to the development of a "vision" of what be both possible and better, in a particular school situation. (p. 62)

New plans or ideas within this dialectical framework should be examined according to what value assumptions are being used or overlooked. The critical systems heuristic provides us with 12 questions to scrutinize a proposal in terms of its design and what ought to be considered in its design. These 12 questions serve as a practical tool for reflecting on emancipatory concerns and assuring that a small and often voiceless minority will not suffer at the hands of the more powerful majority. To state it more positively, within the context of a dialectical process, the answers to these questions may provide a vision of how *all* values can be appropriately integrated into a planned change.

Goldberg's (1989) goal captures a superordinate value that is worth remembering when dealing with dualisms: "My goal is to outline more flexible, adaptive, and healthy human behaviors, the kinds of behaviors on which we can build flexible, adaptive, and healthy societies" (p. 133-34). The success of leadership as a dialectical process is dependent on flexible, adaptive, and healthy leaders.

DISCUSSION QUESTIONS

1. If a colleague asked you, "What is this dialectical thing?" how would you answer, particularly as it applies to the leadership process?
2. How do you feel about morals being part of the school decision-making process? What morals or ethical standards do you believe schools should be all about?
3. How would you define *dilemma, paradox,* and *dualism*? How are these concepts similar? How are they different? Can you apply them to your own organization?
4. What does the idea of *praxis* mean to you? How does this relate to reflective practice discussed in chapter 1? Why is it a significant link to reframing and reform?
5. How do concepts of dialectical leadership overlap with transformational leadership? How are they different?

SUGGESTED ACTIVITIES

1. Generate a list of contradictions, dilemmas, paradoxes, and dualisms that are representative of your organization. Compare your list with others'. How are they similar? How are they different? What are the implications of these items?
2. Identify a colleague or administrator who in your opinion best represents characteristics of a dialectical leader. What attributes or behaviors does this person have? How is he or she able to blend "opposites"? If you cannot identify someone, why do you suppose this is the case?
3. No doubt you recently or are presently being confronted with an effort to change something in your organization. Apply the 12 boundary questions in Figures 7.4 and 7.5 to this change effort. What general inferences can you draw from your answers to these questions? Are they helpful in clarifying the value assumptions built into the change effort you identified? What are the implications of your observations?
4. With your colleagues, create a moral framework that you believe should guide the actions and decisions of you and other members of educational organizations in general. What are the implications of this framework for your organization?
5. Write a paper on the importance of morals to the educational process.

REFERENCES

Benson, J. K. (1977). Organizations: A dialectical view. *Administrative Science Quarterly, 22*: 1-21.
Blau, P. M., & Scott, R. (1962). *Formal organizations.* San Francisco: Chandler.
Flood, R. L., & Jackson, M. C. (1991). *Creative problem solving.* New York: Wiley.
Goldberg, M. A. (1989). *On systemic balance.* New York: Praeger.

Greenfield, W. (1987). Moral imagination and interpersonal competence: Antecedents to instructional leadership. In W. Greenfield (Ed.), *Instructional leadership: Concepts, issues, and controversies* (pp. 56-74). Newton, MA: Allyn & Bacon.

Hodgkinson, C. (1991). *Educational leadership: The moral art.* Albany: State University of New York Press.

Kets de Vries, M. F. R. (1980). *Organizational paradoxes.* New York: Tavistock.

Lourenco, S. V., & Glidewell, J. C. (1975). A dialectical analysis of organizational conflict. *The Administrative Science Quarterly, 20*: 489-508.

Maxcy, S. J. (1991). *Educational leadership: A critical pragmatic perspective.* New York: Bergin & Garvey.

Morgan, G. (1986). *Images of organization.* Beverly Hills, CA: Sage.

Quinn, R. E. (1988). *Beyond rational management.* San Francisco: Jossey-Bass.

Quinn, R. E., & Rohrbaugh, J. (1983). A spatial model of effectness criteria: Toward a competing values approach to organizational analysis. *Management Science, 29*(3), 363-77.

Smith, J., & Blase, J. (1987). Educational leadership as a moral concept. Unpublished paper. Athens: University of Georgia.

Ulrich, W. (1983). *Critical heuristics of social planning.* Berne: Haupt.

Weinstein, M., Weinstein, D., & Blau, P. (1972). Blau's dialectical sociology and dialectical sociology comments. *Sociological Inquiry, 42*: 173-89.

chapter 8

Leadership as a Democratic Process

In the section 1 summary, a review of alternative metaphors for organizations revealed a prevailing or metaparadox of balancing individual needs and organizational needs. It is fitting, therefore, to return to this theme and to understand this dilemma from a leadership perspective. That is, how can leadership processes practiced within an organizational context permit the recognition of individual needs and organizational needs at the same time? Thus far in our leadership chapters in section 2, we have discussed the importance of leadership as a process of change and as a process for solving paradoxical situations. In this chapter, we shall explore a logical extension of these leadership orientations and discuss yet another metaphor for leadership: leadership as a democratic process.

To help us understand the need for more democratic processes in our educational organizations, we shall examine the literature on the micropolitics of schools. Although we did review organizations as politics in chapter 3, in this chapter we will try to understand the nature of these politics within school organizations specifically and their implications for leadership. With micropolitics as a backdrop, we will explore concepts concerning workplace democracy, particularly with emphasis on participation in decision making and the development of community. To assist us in connecting democratic processes that can lead to self-actualization and integration of personal and public interests, we will investigate a strategic management process. Also, as our discussion permits, we will revisit the Valley View case and its implications for leadership as a democratic process.

BACKGROUND

As we have seen in previous chapters, particularly in chapter 7, there are many paradoxes that confront leaders. But there probably is not a more basic problem for leaders than having followers wishing for solutions to problems for which there are no apparent solutions. In reality, most leaders in social organizations quickly realize that they cannot resolve difficult conditions without the involvement and participation of those who are most affected by these conditions. Heifetz and Sinder (1988) suggest that there are "only a very limited number of problematic situations [that] can be resolved by a leader providing solutions; and therein lies the trap. Even in situations where solutions can be given, the very act of providing them will reinforce the group's presumption that leaders can be relied upon to find solutions and should be expected to do so" (p. 184).

To illustrate their point, Heifetz and Sinder discuss the analog of the physician-patient relationship. Often the physician's role is to provide solutions to our health problems; he or she is expected to diagnose, treat, and cure the illness. Heifetz and Sinder describe three types of typical doctor-patient situations. In Type I situations physicians fulfill the role of being the diagnostician and prescriber of treatment. These are situations where the diagnosis is more or less straightforward and is in keeping with the physician's knowledge of diseases and treatments that are not totally dependent on the patient's involvement. Combating an infection with an antibiotic prescription is an example, even though this does require some patient cooperation in taking the medicine in the prescribed manner. It is the Type II and Type III situations that are more analogous to organizational situations and have implications for leadership. In Type II situations, there are no clear-cut technical solutions and the physician can offer only treatments but no cures. Heart disease is a prime example. The patient's involvement is crucial to a successful treatment of this disease, which will most likely involve long-term medication, exercise, a diet program, stress reduction, and more. In these situations, doctors can diagnose and prescribe but the patient has to judge the pluses and minuses of the treatment plan.

In Type III situations, the problem is less clear and no technical fixes are available. Serious chronic cases or impending death from diseases such as cancer are examples of Type III situations. In such situations, there is a need to separate the problem from the medical condition or diagnosis. If cancer is seen as the problem, then the focus is on getting rid of the disease, as opposed to focusing on the reality that the patient has to make significant lifestyle adjustments that go beyond the health problem per se. For example, the patient may need to give more thought to making the most of life, considering the impact of death to significant others, and completing important tasks. In Type III situations the doctor cannot provide the "fix."

According to Heifetz and Sinder (1988), "the alternative definition of the physician's job—'helping the patient to do his work'—would serve in each of the situations" (p. 187). In Type I situations the doctor helps the patient face the problem situation and recommends appropriate treatment. Type II situations require more patient evaluation and life adjustments and thus will require some education and persuasion to gain the patient's support and cooperation. Type III situations are far more complex and treatment is unclear. Type III requires the patient (not necessarily the doctor) to define the specific problems and solutions within a broader context. In all situations, the goal of the doctor (or leader) is to help patients (or followers) to do their work.

The analogy of doctor as teacher as opposed to problem solver provides an alternate way of understanding a leader's position in relation to problems being faced by other persons. The analogy is not totally comparable to organizational situations since leaders are more embedded in the problem situation and, as a consequence, are a part of both the problem and its solution. In any case, the analogy does provide an alternative view for persons who find themselves being called upon to solve others' problems that are not necessarily of their own making but where there exists a high expectation for them to provide the "cures."

Preventing the overreliance upon leaders to solve an individual's or group's problems speaks to the need for empowerment of employees in an organization. Clark and Meloy (1989) discuss the imbalance of control over employee freedom in educational organizations. They see an inconsistency between the rights we enjoy as citizens in a democracy and how these rights are denied in bureaucracies like schools: "The Declaration of Independence is built solely on assumptions about persons. Bureaucracy assumes that organizational structure can be considered 'without regard for persons.' Once the structure is considered apart from people, the consent of the governed in the designation of leaders is inappropriate, because election reduces 'the strictness of hierarchical subordination.' Domination and power assume precedence over liberty and the pursuit of happiness . . . " (p. 274).

A side effect of the stress for control and domination of persons in an organization is the undervaluing of their potential and their ability to contribute to their own well-being *and* that of the organization. Teachers, for example, are seen as the problem rather than the solution; they are labeled as uncaring, incompetent, and self-centered, which provides a basis for rationalizing greater controls and required in-service training. This often results in failing to get the consent or advice of the governed. Clark and Meloy (1989) urge a more democratic structure for leadership in schools. They offer the following propositions:

- Schools must be built on the assumption of the consent of the governed
- Schools must be built on shared authority and responsibility, not delegation of authority and responsibility
- The staff of a school must trade assignments and work in multiple groups to remain in touch with schools as a whole
- Formal rewards to the staff—salary, tenure, forms of promotion—should be under the control of the staff of the school as a whole
- The goals of the school must be formulated and agreed to through group consensus. The professional staff is responsible for negotiating the acceptability of the goals to the school community (pp. 291–92)

The concern for democratization of schools goes even deeper than the apparent inconsistencies of individual rights in our society and the absence of such rights within the school organization. Giroux (1992) describes a broader, more comprehensive need for democratic conditions:

We need a language in our leadership programs that defends schools as democratic public spheres responsible for providing an indispensable public service to the nation; a language that is capable of awakening the moral, political and civic responsibilities of our youth. Public schools need to be justified as places in which students are educated in the principles and practices of democracy, not in a version of democracy cleansed of vision, possibility, or struggle. (p. 15)

Giroux extends his concerns for creating democratic institutions beyond the involvement of teachers in decision making: He wishes to get to the heart of preparing future citizens in an environment that provides direct experiences in the democratic process. He sees the school as a small community of teachers, students, and parents coming together and addressing its problems and possibilities.

The democratization of schools can potentially combat what Kirst (1989) considers to be the shifting of power over school matters to nonlocal sources. He observes that "the discretionary decision zone of the local superintendents and the boards has become squeezed progressively into a smaller and smaller area during the last two decades" (p. 67). He sees this trend created by the growth of the federal government, the state government, the courts, private interest groups, professional reformers, and interstate organizations. All of these groups, through mandates and/or political clout, have impacted the local school agenda and created a number of expectations that may have limited relevance to local schools. For example, the so-called accountability movement resulted in proliferating basic competencies and testing procedures. A great deal of time and money was spent by local schools to devise specific competencies, appropriate measurements, record keeping procedures, and revision of curricula. But over time these policies and practices faded from view. Once again, local schools had been sold a bill of goods and externally directed to address their perceived failures.

Something is amiss with the governance of local schools. It has become bureaucratized and outer-directed by powerful interest groups who are forcing their perceptions of the problems and solutions. The challenge is to build the responsibility for recognizing school-related problems at the lowest level possible and create a governance structure that results in shared governance sensitive to local needs.

Further examination is in order to understand the micropolitics of schools and how they influence relationships within the school's context. Following this review we will explore the dimensions of democratization of schools and how this effort fits well with our current needs as a democratic society.

DEFINITIONS AND RELATED CONCEPTS

The relationship of education and its institutions, particularly schools, to sustaining and supporting a democratic society has been vague at best and confused at worst. Students and their teachers live lives within the context of schools that are often contradictory to lifestyles outside of school. Outside of schools, as adults in a free society, there are opportunities to participate in the political process, notwithstanding non-legal barriers of prejudice and economic disadvantage.

Within the context of schools, these same adults face hierarchical, authority-driven bureaucracies that may provide little or no opportunity to practice birthrights guaranteed in a constitutional democracy. These seemingly contradictory experiences raise the question of how effectively our schools support and prepare their youthful charges for living in an open, participatory democracy. One message was consistently expressed by the principal of Valley View: She stressed the importance of community members and teachers having full opportunity to participate in decisions that affected their futures and, at the same time, taking responsibility for these actions in the best interests of their pupils. Barber (1992) takes a straightforward position on the role of education and educators in a democracy when he argues that "in democracies, education is the indispensable concomitant of citizenship. Where women and men would acquire the skills of freedom, it is a necessity. . . . And in a democracy, there is only one essential task for the educator: teaching liberty" (p. 15).

Micropolitics of Schools

Unfortunately, the curricula for teaching liberty in our schools is left primarily to chance with a heavy reliance on academic subjects and few experiential opportunities. Lack of a democratic framework often leads teachers, students, and parents to filling the void with what Ball (1987) and Blase (1991) refer to as the micropolitics of schools. Blase (1991) defines micropolitics as

> the use of formal and informal power by individuals and groups to achieve their goals in organizations. In large part, political actions result from perceived differences between individuals and groups, coupled with the motivation to use power to influence and/or protect. Although such actions are consciously motivated, any action, consciously or unconsciously motivated, may have political "significance" in a given situation. Both cooperative and conflictive actions and processes are part of micropolitics. Moreover, macro- and micropolitics factors frequently interact. (p. 11)

Micropolitics grow out of the social dynamics of schools and their diverse value systems, often leading to conflict. Ball (1987) views schools as "arenas of struggle; to be riven with actual or potential conflict between members; to be poorly co-ordinated; to be ideologically diverse" (p. 19). In part, these conflicts exist because power is not equally distributed, persons are forced to be reactive and protective against abuses of power, and there are very few rules and/or sanctioned forums in which members have an equal voice and opportunity to be heard.

Micropolitics can result in persons playing different roles and experiencing different levels of involvement. Baldridge (1971) studied the micropolitics of New York University and identified four types of actors: officials, activists, attentives, and apathetics. The officials are committed to the task of running the organization and are politically involved by virtue of their formal positions in the organization. The principal of Valley View Elementary School would fall in this category. Activists "are a relatively small body of people intensely involved in the university politics" (p. 177). The Valley View citizens' committees that formed around the school bond vote were very active and played a major role in influencing the decisions concerning the construction of a new school. The attentives tend to watch from the sidelines. They get involved when issues become hot and affect them personally. They can play a significant role in swaying the direction to be taken by officials. Certainly many of the taxpayers of Valley View were drawn into the conflict over the school bond as the contest became protracted by multiple votes. The final group is the apathetics, who rarely participate and in general seem to care least about what is going on. These persons are marginalized for a variety of reasons but essentially stay out of the politics of the organization. In Valley View, these would be the persons who did not exercise their right to vote and deferred to those who did.

Micropolitics can have interesting influences on leadership and school change. Ball (1987) discusses four types of leadership that emerged from his case studies of British schools: interpersonal, managerial, and political, which is divided into adversarial and authoritarian. Ball explains each of these styles: "Interpersonal heads [principals] rely primarily on personal relationships and face-to-face contact to fulfill their role. In contrast, managerial heads have major recourse to committees, memoranda and formal procedures. The adversarial tends to relish argument and confrontation to maintain control. Whereas the authoritarian avoids and stifles argument in favour of dictat" (p. 87).

Hargreaves (1991) explores the implications of micropolitics for establishing collegiality in a school environment and its effects on team-teaching efforts. From his research, he finds "there are substantial differences in values and beliefs among the teachers involved" (p. 51), and he offers four plausible explanations for this.

First, teachers are like sculptors who are willing to share ideas about their sculpting but because of differences in beliefs and approaches would never work on the same piece of marble. Second, there is the classic struggle in schools of the rights of the individual and their protection in light of group pressure. Teachers desiring to work alone and who feel they can plan better by themselves are often ostracized by their colleagues.

Third, the micropolitical perspective raises the question of when the emphasis on collaboration becomes co-optation. Co-optation minimizes one's own ideas and becomes a method for persuading one to implement the ideas of someone else. Co-optation through in-service activities, for example, can "cultivate emotional commitment to externally mandated changes at the expense of rational deliberation and critique about their worth and applicability" (Hargreaves, 1991, p. 52).

Fourth, the micropolitical perspective urges the need to raise critical questions about different forms collaboration can take, who supports these different forms, and whose interests are being served by different approaches. The concern is one of control and whose values get served. Hargreaves cites research (Quicke, 1986; and Rudduck, 1991) in which teachers were observed forcing more bureaucratically contrived and administratively controlled forms of cooperation among children over the more natural and spontaneous forms of cooperation anchored in their culture. According to Hargreaves, "these reforms [e.g., active learning and cooperative learning] pass the locus of control over cooperation from the pupil to the teacher, from the community to the school, draining it of much of its richness, spontaneity, and unpredictability" (p. 52).

The issue is not whether teachers and parents should create collaborative relationships, but rather what are the dangers of advocating such efforts from a micropolitical perspective. It is important to consider the degree to which individuality is properly balanced by group expectations and how such collaborative interventions can in fact give greater power to local schools in charting their own destinies. It also raises the question of the willingness of persons (e.g., politicians, state educational bureaucrats, special interest groups) who sit some distance from the local school scene to permit these schools autonomy in defining their own problems and solutions, as opposed to being forced to accept outside renditions.

Collaborative Schools

One model for greater local school control by teachers is suggested in the concept of a collaborative school that builds on the concept of a collegium. Shulman (1989) explains that "a collegium is a setting in which individuals come together with a shared mission" (p. 181). Smith and Scott (1990) provide a summary of literature on collaborative schools. They conclude that the primary goal of a collaborative school is educational improvement, although they recognize side benefits such as staff harmony, mutual respect, and a strong focus on instructional effectiveness. As they see it, the most important "dynamic comes from teachers working together to improve their practice of teaching. It is the informally and formally structured interaction among teachers about instruction that distinguishes the collaborative school from earlier models of democratic management and participative decision making, even though it incorporates elements of these concepts" (p. 3).

In helping to clarify a collaborative school they discuss also what it is not:

- It does not seek discussion for its own sake
- It does not require administrators to abdicate their authority
- It does not reduce teachers' accountability (pp. 4–5)

Keith and Girling (1991) also support the spirit of participation in the management of education. For them, the benefits of greater participation include clarity of purpose, greater commitment to and coordination of decisions, effective conflict resolution, ability to adapt to changing circumstances, and renewal. Keith and Girling argue that at the core of effective schools is the notion of "participation, teacher involvement, and teamwork" (p. 47).

A weakness of both collaborative schools and participatory management is that they do not deal with the involvement of parents and the community in the collaborative process. Nor do they speak to the implications of participatory efforts for democratization of the classroom. We will explore these issues more fully after developing more understanding of democratic applications to the workplace environment.

Workplace Democracy

A vision for establishing collaborative schools can be obtained from the private sector's efforts at workplace democracy and self-management. Cozzens (1993) reminds us why democracy is so important:

> Why democracy? Because people matter. It is easy to forget this simple value in the complex arguments of democratic theory. Democracy is desirable because individuals are unique and because our decisions cannot take uniqueness into account unless we listen to others. Democracy is about giving voices to people, because people matter. (p. 9)

Pateman (1976) echoes these words when she discusses the value of democracy within the workplace. She believes that workplace democracy "is not primarily concerned with productivity, efficiency, better relations (even though these things may even result from organizational democracy); rather it is to further justice, equality, freedom, the rights of citizens, all familiar democratic aims" (p. 22–23). These are values that link well to sociopolitical life in our society, and the opportunity to participate in their use within the workplace provides continuity and less alienation with the society as a whole. She is clear, however, that organizational democracy needs to be more than representational participation, which is normally part of a liberal democratic state.

Our society is well imbued with the notion that managers manage and representatives govern; this simple notion breeds workers' dependence. Thus there is a need for more direct participation in everyday matters that concern employees within the workplace. Experience at self-management bodes well for developing skills, expertise, and confidence for being a full participant in making decisions about the organization and in the greater society. Rotating persons through leadership positions is a simple example of creating opportunity to acquire more experiences in leadership and participatory democracy. (The case study of Country View in section 3 provides an example of this approach.) In the final analysis, according to Pateman (1976), "the importance of voting for the individual is that, exercised within a context of organizational and self managing democracy, it allows the collective democratic control by citizens of their own lives and environment" (p. 28).

Mickunas (1993) supports this view by suggesting that there are two historical and fundamental concepts within Western tradition that are a philosophical basis for ideals associated with democracy. He refers to the classical Greek concept of human equality and the more modern view of personal autonomy. He also argues that the autonomy of individuals is structured by three conditions: (1) Everyone is an autonomous source of law; (2) all laws are proposed and discussed in order to reach consensus; and (3) all laws apply equally to everyone (p. 181). Thus, one does not have full license within a democratic environment to do whatever seems to fit one's purposes, but rather one has a right to express these desires and seek group understanding as to the appropriateness of such actions.

Barber (1984) summarizes five types of democracy:

- authoritative democracy—resolves conflict through deferring to representative executive elite that employ authority (power plus wisdom) in pursuit of the aggregate interests
- juridical democracy—resolves conflict by deferring to a representative judicial elite who are guided by constitutional norms in arbitrating differences
- pluralist democracy—resolves conflict by bargaining and exchange among free and equal individuals and groups
- unitary democracy—resolves conflict through community consensus
- strong democracy—resolves conflict by a participatory process of ongoing, proximate self-legislation and the creation of a political community capable of transforming dependent private individuals into free citizens (pp. 140-51)

Deetz (1992) builds upon Barber's ideas and reinforces the need for providing democratic opportunities in everyday life, reflective of Barber's "strong democracy." The fulfillment of this ideal is in part being constrained by problems of communications and in establishing a connection of the person to a community. As Deetz defines it, "Democracy is a moral issue. Democracy involves the collective decision of what we willfully or unwittingly become. It opposes arbitrary privilege or one-sided considerations in that determination. Filling out such a base requires both a concept of democracy and an analysis of communication processes to sustain it" (p. 159).

Fischer (1990) addresses the concern of democratic elitism and the role of expertise in making democratic decisions. He explores the uncomfortable relationships of social scientists' direct involvement in policy research, which is often used by political elites to dominate and influence policy decisions. He echoes Waltzer's (1983) words that "citizens [should] arrive at [a] 'forum with nothing but their arguments.' They must leave all of their 'non-political goods . . . outside: weapon and wallets, titles and degrees.'" This vantage point may help ensure that democratic decisions are "founded on the most persuasive argument" (p. 347).

In an organizational context this would suggest that supervisors and upper-level managers need to submit their ideas and proposed policies to scrutiny and discussion by workers at the lowest levels. This organizational elite should not be permitted to hide behind their formal positions and authority. Mason (1982) makes a crucial distinction: "Democracy relates to the process of decision making, not to its content. This may be illustrated convincingly by the fact that a democracy and a dictatorship may pursue the same policy. Process, however, will influence content. Through the connection between a participatory process and content, participation not only benefits individual development, but also creates community benefits as well. Participatory democracy produces better decisions" (p. 185).

The principal at Valley View Elementary School understood this, and from the beginning of her tenure as principal she made an effort to convey the importance of faculty, citizen, and student participation in decisions that affected their lives. Judging from the dramatic turnaround made in this community and its outlook toward its school, it appears she did the right thing.

Garson and Smith (1976) speak to the need of codifying workplace democracy by establishing a workers' bill of rights. In broad strokes they recommend the following rights:

- the right of freedom of information and corporate accountability (includes placing labor and public representatives on the board of directors to act as ombudscommittee)
- the right to formal national labor standards (includes an annual social audit on social costs of enterprise operations conducted by an independent auditor)
- the right of employee participation in decision making (includes the establishment of and inclusion of employees on committees for health and safety, job organization, and human resource development; work on these committees shall be considered paid time according to regular employee rates)
- other potential rights for working people include the right to be awarded 50 percent of the seats on the board of directors; the right to elect the personnel director or equivalent; and/or creation of worker councils at various levels or divisions of the organization

Garson and Smith (1976) are against piecemeal changes and favor major structural change integrated into public policy requirements. As they caution, "Rather than abandon jurisdiction to authoritarian private governments, a democratic state should act to guarantee the rights of workers to the democratic organization of work" (p. 135).

Participatory Democracy in Schools

Several writers speak to the importance of democratic practices in schools and other community organizations. Mason (1982) finds that workers who are also parents and who themselves experience workplace democracy will naturally request a more participatory environment for their children in the public schools. As Mason states, "After all, if schools are doing their job in preparing young men and women for productive and meaningful work, then they certainly should be preparing young adults for the new participatory workplaces" (p. 192). He does not see this as unique to schools; he maintains that all public institutions, as well as the private family unit, will be under pressure to ensure greater participation as workers experience workplace democracy.

Murphy and Choi (1993) discuss opening the classroom to democratic procedures. They are concerned at the cost associated with greater disciplinary controls or increased parent supervision. They believe education is placing too much emphasis on conformity and narrowing of students' interests rather than developing more insights about "ambiguity tolerance, reconciliation of differences, open discussion, and other themes essential to democracy" (p. 173).

Democratization of the classroom should include several elements, according to Murphy and Choi (pp. 173–74):

- Biases of teachers and experts should be exposed; professionals should be understood to reflect a value base
- Assumptions that influence tests should be thoroughly discussed
- Efforts should be made to demonstrate that authorities are not omnipotent
- Experiences of students should be elevated in importance

The goal of education should be to transform differences into assets and to permit students greater freedom to "explore, challenge, and invent realities, as opposed to accepting and mastering a universally recognized body of information" (p. 174). As stated earlier in this chapter, democracy is better served by providing experiences in the classroom and in the governance of the school; this will better equip young people to become active members of a democratic society. Part of this preparation is understanding the importance of balance between the needs of the community and individual freedom.

Communitarianism

The pursuit of individual freedom and liberty suggests to many the obliteration of responsibilities to others, our communities, and our environment, but slowly a realization is emerging that individual freedom must be balanced by community needs. The same paradox that appeared in section 1 has resurfaced; we must attempt to better understand this dilemma of balancing individual needs with society's or organizational needs. Unfortunately our Constitution speaks only obliquely of the public good when it speaks of a "more perfect Union" or the need to "promote the general welfare." According to Etzioni (1993) and other communitarians, we must bring into greater focus a sense of individual responsibility toward one's friends and neighbors.

Etzioni's concern is with developing a higher level of moral conduct that does not abridge the rights of others or do them harm. He feels that higher-order values should guide practical decisions affecting communities and social groups. He describes these values as "values that we all should share as a society, or even humanity, values that prescribe rules of behavior such as 'Do unto others only as you wish others would do unto you'" (p. 37). The rights of minority members and individuals should be protected by the values of the larger community.

Communitarians are also concerned with how well we value children in our society. In 1991, the National Commission on Children called for a reevaluation of our treatment of children and raised the question of whether we are capable of sacrificing in order to create opportunities for children. Etzioni quotes a 1985 study by the University of Maryland in which it was reported that parents spent an average of 17 hours per week with their children as compared with 30 hours in 1965. In Etzioni's judgment, "A community that is respectful of children would *make parenting a less taxing and more fulfilling experience*" (p. 64).

Etzioni concludes, "If the moral infrastructure of our communities is to be restored, schools will have to step in where the family, neighborhoods, and religious institutions have been failing" (p. 89). This notion resonates well with the notion of inculcating the values of democracy that we have discussed thus far and providing experiences, not lectures, that are consistent with these values. Schools need to address the development of basic personality traits that characterize effective individuals and to help in their acquisition of core community values. This needs to be done, of course, without overly simplifying these qualities nor abusing the cultural values that children may bring from their families and ethnic or racial groups. Providing opportunities for teachers to bond with students is providing more quality time (as opposed to the factory assembly-line model of secondary schools, which makes it difficult to learn much about students beyond their names) for developing a moral sense among students.

Communitarians, however, are not suggesting that schools and teachers unilaterally assume responsibility for the moral development of a community's youth. Schools need to involve parents and members of the community in order to gain assistance and support in this important endeavor. Such involvement can help create a sense of we-ness focused on rebuilding community values with the ultimate purpose of providing "an opportunity for deep human satisfaction, the kind found only when we are engaged with one another, and to strengthen the community as a moral infrastructure, the most important morality-enhancing factor other than individual conscience" (Etzioni, 1993, p. 142).

Suffice it to say that communitarianism provides yet another conceptual framework for creating an alternative vision for public schools. Communitarianism echoes the needs others have expressed in having our schools become a much more valuable resource as our society grapples with concerns about moral decay and the lack of citizen participation in the democratic process. The implication for school leaders is how to take these potentially valuable conceptual orientations and model their utility for the future well-being of both the individual and society.

AN APPLICATION OF DEMOCRATIC LEADERSHIP

Our discussion thus far speaks of the "what" of democratic leadership but not necessarily the "how." Heifetz and Sinder (1988) offer some sage advice for persons assigned to the task of providing leadership in the public arena. They suggest that

> the public official is faced with the challenge of managing the discovery, shaping, and rediscovery of each step in the problem-defining and -solving process over time. He [*sic*] must be able to lead the relevant community of interests in facing unwanted situations, investigating what can be changed and what cannot, discovering what it is willing to define as a problem, applying insights from other areas, and fashioning the life adjustments that will constitute the material of any solution. (p. 198)

To support problem solving in the public arena, communications becomes a key factor. Deetz (1992) describes the importance of communications for accomplishing mutual understanding that in turn is critical for successful political or democratic leadership. The effectiveness/ineffectiveness of communications become contextual with a concern for participation. Deetz writes that "from a participation perspective, communication difficulties arise from communication practices that preclude value debate and conflict, that substitute images and imaginary relations for self-presentation and truth claims, that arbitrarily limit access to communication channels and forums, and that then lead to decisions based on arbitrary authority relations" (p. 161).

Recognition of the unique demands and complexities that confront public leaders, particularly in a democratic environment, and the danger of substituting inauthentic communications for authentic communications forms a backdrop for examining the strategic management process (SMP).

Nutt and Backoff (1992) articulate a step-by-step approach for implementing a strategic planning process that is rooted in political theory and acknowledges the importance of participation by stakeholders. In the debate to decide on strategic directions for an organization, such as a school, the SMP provides a balance between full, open participation of all parties involved and representational, guided participation of a subset of persons.

The SMP was created to help public sector organizations meet rising demands for services and new directions in a pluralistic environment of competing values. Often public leaders become confused and overwhelmed by incessant and contradictory advice and expectations. Worse yet, however, the public and members of these organizations begin to express discouragement and feelings of alienation, which in part stems from a lack of clear direction or sense of accomplishment. The SMP attempts to integrate ongoing management or administration of an organization with long-range, strategic management. This involves a juggling act, finding a balance in a maelstrom of issues or issue tensions. As Nutt and Backoff (1992) write, "Strategy is used to focus action, create consistency or continuity, but most significantly, to give organizations a new or renewed sense of purpose" (p. 58).

Two major concepts that guide the SMP are *strategy* and *issue tensions.* Strategy is derived from the Greek *strategos,* a set of maneuvers carried out to overcome an enemy during combat. Military metaphors notwithstanding, athletes, business leaders, and political leaders share a common vision for strategy as they attempt to bring about a desired end or goal by using a number of very specific actions that seem logically linked to the desired outcome. Citing Andrews (1980), Nutt and Backoff adapt this notion to an organizational context by arguing that

> strategy is defined by decisions an organization makes that determine or reveal objectives, purpose, or goals; create the principal policies and plans for achieving its aims; define the range of businesses or services the organization is to pursue; identify the kind of economic and human organization it is or intends to be; and specify the nature of the economic and noneconomic contribution to be made to the organization's shareholders or trustees, employees, customers, and communities. (p. 57)

When we consider the vision of the principal at Valley View we can appreciate the potency of strategy in enabling the attainment of a long-range goal. She saw the need to mobilize the school board and members of the community to address the inadequacy of their school and to embark on a process made up of many small decisions that eventually led to building a new school. In a sense, a strategy can unleash and direct energy at resolving impeding tensions in order to bring some order to chaos. And, if guided by some democratic principles, the strategy can be extremely effective in providing an opportunity to learn about and implement universal values that are worthy of support and effort. In effect, a strategic planning process attempts to manage the dialectic between the old and the new by creating a synthesis upon which to build a future. The Valley View experience illustrated the potency of strategic thinking. Nutt and Backoff (1992) seem to have Valley View in mind when they observe that "decline is averted or reversed by strategic action that correctly interprets important signals" (p. 126).

The second important concept for strategic management is the notion of issues and tensions associated with these issues. According to Nutt and Backoff, "An *issue* is defined as a trend or event, arising inside or outside an organization, that can have an important influence on the organization's ability to reach its desired future" (p. 119). Issues often capture the attention of people within an organization and often generate considerable energy either to beat back certain views or to alleviate certain tensions. Issues become a tension in part because of the tangled web of political forces that tug at an organization and pull it in different directions at the same time. Issues are defined as tensions "between two developments that represent polar opposites or contradictions within the organization or between the organization and its environment" (p. 127).

Nutt and Backoff (1992) reinforce the discussion in chapter 7 on dialectical leadership. They agree with the premise that dealing with one opposing force while ignoring the other can result in negative spin-offs or lost opportunities; attempting to deal with both sides of the issue has greater potential for creating win-win strategies. Issues are not problems to be solved but paradoxes to be transcended. The proposal of expanding the Valley View school board to five members from three members during the heat of the school bond debate had the effect of integrating the opposing forces.

Nutt and Backoff (1992) describe six generic issue tensions that can be triggered by various organizational situations:

1. Meeting demands during change may trigger tension between *transition* and *productivity*
2. Determining who gets what during change may trigger tension between *equity* and *transition*
3. Fairness clashing with traditions may trigger tension between *equity* and *preservation*
4. Squeezing a stressed tradition-ridden system may trigger tension between *preservation* and *productivity*
5. Reconciling cost cutting with human commitments may trigger tensions between *equity* and *productivity*
6. Dealing with inertia during change may trigger tensions between *transition* and *preservation*

Seeking and understanding issue tensions are critical to effective strategic action. As we stated in our discussion of dialectical leadership, it is important to anticipate and identify the polar positions and work with them in a holistic manner. The alternative of ignoring or sweeping aside the opposing forces can result in a negation of the intervention or the creation of an opposite effect. The principal at Valley View was very prudent in her relationships with the varying factions surrounding the school bond vote, appearing to be neutral while clearly desiring a change in the situation facing the school and community. Most important, however, is that she remained open and willing to listen and communicated with these various factions so that when the struggle was over, there was an acceptance of the final outcome. This was in part accomplished by integrating various wishes for the new school.

The SMP involves six stages that are dynamically related. Figure 8.1 provides an overview of the SMP stages and related processes. What it does not show is the use of a strategic management group (SMG) that is responsible for guiding the SMP. More on this later. As can be observed in the figure, in addition to the six stages are three steps common to each of the stages. The early stages emphasize formulation of background and insights on the situation facing the organization and the latter stages stress implementation. A brief description of each stage follows.

FIGURE 8.1   Stages of the strategic management process

SOURCE: P. C. Nutt & R. W. Backoff, *Strategic Management of Public and Third Sector Organizations: A Handbook for Leaders,* 1992, Jossey-Bass, San Francisco, CA, p. 167. Reprinted with permission of Jossey-Bass Inc., Publishers.

	Steps		
	Search for:	Synthesis of:	Selection of:
Stage One: Historical Context 1. Trends and events 2. Directions 3. Ideals			
Stage Two: Situational Assessment 1. Strengths 2. Weaknesses 3. Opportunities 4. Threats			
Stage Three: Strategic Issues Tension Agenda			
Stage Four: Strategic Options 1. Action sets 2. Strategic themes			
Stage Five: Feasibility Assessment 1. Stakeholder analysis (internal/external) 2. Resource analysis			
Stage Six: Implementation 1. Resource management 2. Stakeholder management			

Stage One: Historical Context

This stage examines and surveys trends, events, directions, and ideals that characterize the pressures being directed toward an organization. The examination of trends may focus on a number of factors, such as demands, needs, resources, programs, and management practices of the organization. The trend facing Valley View was a general spiraling down of community support for the school and a school rapidly becoming a physical hazard and a relic of educational practices rooted in the past. Directions describe the organization's progress from the perspectives of "moving away from" and "moving toward." Valley View Elementary School was moving away from the self-contained classroom model of education to greater fluidity and use of specialists to support and supplement classroom instruction. Ideals create a balance between tensions and provide some future direction without demanding specific outcomes. Ideals can be articulated as best- and worst-case scenarios. The worst case for Valley View was a school that would be closed because of safety violations or being unable to meet state standards. The best case was to build a new school that was up-to-date and met the needs of both the children and the community.

Stage Two: Situational Assessment

Stage one helps in understanding an organization's history and future potential. Stage two examines the immediate situation facing an organization. A strategic management group (SMG), alluded to earlier, plays an important role in Stage two. This is a group of representatives from key stakeholder groups who have an interest in an organization's future directions. These persons can be representatives from inside groups (e.g., employees, mid-level supervisors, etc.) and external groups (e.g., policymakers, clients, funding sources, etc.). This group works in close cooperation with the chief executive or top manager of the organization. In an educational context, this would be the principal and/or school superintendent.

This group participates in a process of searching for, synthesizing, and selecting the major strengths, weaknesses, opportunities, and threats (SWOTs) facing the organization. The historical stage helps provide some of this information. Candidness by SMG members is critical to Stage two and its success in obtaining a realistic picture of new possible directions.

Stage Three: Strategic Issues Tension Agenda

Stages one and two set a context for raising the core issues that are in need of being managed by the organization. It is important to keep in mind that these issues may shift in a more volatile environment, thus Stage three needs to be revisited periodically. Issues need to be discussed from the perspective of why they are important and why are they worthy of attention. Issues are expressed as tensions of opposing polar views, with an eye toward managing and reconciling these opposite forces. The SMG and its deliberations uncover details of these issues, discuss their implications for strategic directions, and rank their importance. Janusian thinking (having the capacity to see in two directions simultaneously) is critical to the success of Stage three.

Valley View faced numerous issue tensions, not the least of which was the tension over spending more money for a new school. A great deal of Janusian thinking went into understanding this basic issue and finding alternative solutions. Lobbying the state legislature and inviting the governor to visit the community to celebrate the enactment of a new and higher state aid formula helped reduce the resistance to paying more taxes locally. In addition, effort was made to hear suggestions on how a new school could better serve the community, which led to a larger gymnasium and community library being incorporated in the school's design. An all-encompassing strategy was central to gaining sufficient support to pass the school bond vote.

Stage Four: Strategic Options

Stage four begins the shift from analysis to implementation. Using a strategy worksheet (see Figure 8.2), members of the SMG engage in a process of searching for, synthesizing, and selecting an action strategy that evolves out of an analysis of the issue tensions facing the organization. As Figure 8.2 makes clear, strategic actions build on strengths, overcome weaknesses, exploit opportunities, and block or blunt threats. In this case, the "strategy is made up of action ideas that have a common theme" (Nutt &

FIGURE 8.2 Strategy worksheet

SOURCE: P. C. Nutt & R. W. Backoff, *Strategic Management of Public and Third Sector Organizations: A Handbook for Leaders,* 1992, Jossey-Bass, San Francisco, CA, p. 438. Reprinted with permission of Jossey-Bass Inc., Publishers.

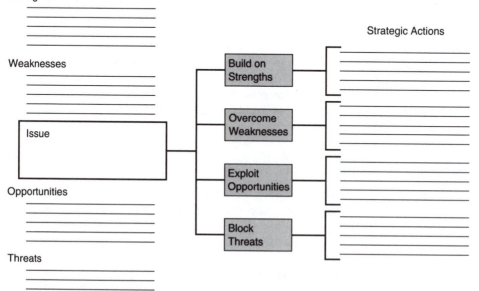

Backoff, 1992, p. 187). Typically the strategy becomes an incremental movement that balances opportunity with threat.

Stage Five: Feasibility Assessment

This stage focuses on who will be affected by the suggested strategic actions and how other persons could affect the proposals, if and when implemented. This activity is what Nutt and Backoff call a stakeholder analysis; as they explain it, "We focus on the people and organizations with political, financial, managerial, and professional interests or stakes in the strategy and try to anticipate how they might respond as the strategy is communicated and implemented" (p. 190).

A second part of the feasibility assessment is to focus not only on financial resources to implement the strategy but to consider political, legal, managerial, and professional resources. The goal is to identify key people and power centers that will require careful orchestration during implementation of strategic plans.

Stakeholders are classified along the dimensions of the stakeholder's importance to implementation and his or her position of support or opposition on the issue being addressed. The stakeholders are clustered into groupings of low-priority stakeholders (low importance and high support), advocate stakeholders (high importance and high support), problematic stakeholders (low importance and high opposition), and antagonistic stakeholders (high importance and high opposition). Different approaches will be needed for different stakeholders, ranging from active lobbying for support to ignoring or minimizing contacts. Nutt and Backoff (1992) believe that "everyone is a potential stakeholder in a public organization, which calls for careful assessments of a stakeholder's motives to block the strategy and his or her power to do so" (p. 195).

Stage Six: Implementation

Strategic implementation involves management of resources and stakeholders as articulated in Stage five. Here specific tactics are identified and implemented for the different categories of stakeholders suggested in the feasibility assessment of stakeholders. For example, the following tactics are suggested for the different types of stakeholders:

- *Antagonistic* stakeholders: Identify potential coalitions by determining which neutral actors in the problematic and low-priority categories are closely aligned or related to the antagonistic stakeholders.
- *Advocate* stakeholders: Provide information to reinforce advocates' beliefs.
- *Problematic* stakeholders: Prepare defensive tactics to be used if a coalition of problematic stakeholders emerges and takes a public position opposing the strategy.
- *Low-priority* stakeholders: Provide low-cost education for those near the boundary of important and unimportant stakeholders. (Nutt & Backoff, 1992, pp. 196-97)

The management of resource sources and stakeholders places greater emphasis on political tactics than on power tactics. It requires care and intelligence in dealing with persons who are in opposition or in support of an organization's desired strategic plans. All parties must be considered important and legitimate actors, and rules of democracy and politics become exceedingly important. Valley View exemplified political action within a democratic framework. The various maneuverings of both groups played to the large middle and uncommitted group. Eventually the pro-bond-issue folks prevailed but not without a struggle and a shift in tactics as their strategy unfolded. In any event, the end result did not split the community into polarized antagonistic groups. All parties had a shot at achieving their position and with the election of anti-bond-issue representatives to the school board came an opportunity to have a voice on future decisions concerning the new school.

CONCLUSION

Exploring leadership as a democratic process permits us to reexamine some fundamental assumptions about the role and function of education in a democratic society. Democracy as a metaphor surfaces many images that are often not viewed in a positive light. We can see confusion, inefficiency, misunderstanding, and even antagonism being reinforced and repeated. Often we seek the quick, easy answer and as a result defer to those in positions of authority. There appears to be a lack of appreciation for a governance system that provides for freedom, equal voice, and responsibility. Is this, in part, because of our educational system's failure to provide both knowledge *and* experience in democratic processes? Barber (1992) reminds us that

> public education is education for citizenship. In aristocratic nations, in elitist regimes, in technocratic societies, it may appear as a luxury. In such places, education is the private apprenticeship in the professions, the credentialing of elites, and perhaps the scholarly training of a few for lives of solitary intellect. But in democracies, education is the indispensable concomitant of citizenship. Where women and men would acquire the skills of freedom, it is a necessity. (p. 15)

We must ask ourselves to what degree our schools and the leaders of our schools are preparing citizens for a democratic society not just by word but also by deed. Can we continue to operate hierarchical and authority-centered institutions and still prepare persons for citizenship in a democratic society? These are questions that present and future educational leaders need to confront if in fact schools are to be truly effective. As important as higher math and reading scores are to a literate society, opportunities to practice, in a real sense, democratic behaviors need at least equal consideration.

In the absence of any official rules, schools can become narrowly engaged in and distracted by micropolitics. Micropolitics are not necessarily a bad thing except when they infringe upon the rights of others and resort to forms of subterfuge and intimidation. In organizations built on principles of democracy, rights and responsibilities are more clearly articulated and public. Politics are forced to operate within a moral or ethical framework, which acts as a cross-check against individual political maneuverings. Mechanisms or processes should exist for holding individual actions accountable regardless of position of authority and for seeking redress for inappropriate actions. For democratization of educational institutions to occur, we need leaders more grounded in democratic principles and who understand their role in providing for wider participation than is currently the case.

Schools are in a position to be a positive social force in rebuilding democratic values and a sense of community. The first step in this process is to sense the need and to see possible ways schools can play this role. Hopefully this chapter has provided some metaphors and concepts of workplace democracy and communitarianism that will encourage this line of thinking. In addition, the SMP outlined provides a process for moving into new strategic directions based on widespread participation in decision making. Giroux (1992) states this more forcefully: "The most important task facing educators is not about collecting data or managing competencies, but constructing a pedagogical and political vision which recognizes that the problems with American schools lie in the realm of values, ethics, and vision" (p. 16).

Although democratic processes are not without faults and limitations, they may be the best we have for addressing our problems and getting people involved in their solutions. We may need constitutional conventions in our schools and their communities to create wells of optimism that can be tapped and that will help renew a spirit that our forebears must have felt as they struggled in defining a democratic form of governance. They worked in a hostile world steeped in traditions of royalty and the divine rule of monarchies, and they had the audacity to believe that people were capable of ruling themselves regardless of birthrights or status. What they accomplished in Philadelphia was described as a miracle. Can new leaders be found to carry on their work in our organizations and communities?

DISCUSSION QUESTIONS

1. Do you believe current educational leaders tend to reinforce dependence rather than independence and greater responsibility in solving their organizational problems? Can you provide examples from your own workplace experiences to support your response to this question?

2. Do you agree that schools and classrooms should incorporate more democratic principles in their daily operations? Why or why not?

3. Do you agree that schools are being more greatly controlled by external forces and special interest groups who are more removed and more distant from local schools? What are the consequences of the erosion of local control?

4. How do micropolitics play out in your educational organization? What are its pluses and minuses? Do these politics help to create a positive or negative work environment? If negative, how could they be improved? If positive, what makes them so?

5. Does it make sense for educational organizations to follow the strategic management process? Why or why not?

SUGGESTED ACTIVITIES

1. Investigate workplace democracy further and report on its potential application to your educational organization. What are its strengths, weaknesses, opportunities, and threats?

2. Develop a proposal to democratize classrooms or courses from the elementary school level to graduate level. How would they be organized, what bill of rights should be developed, how would citizenship be defined, who would have a right to vote and on what issues, how would grievances or violations be handled, etc.?

3. Similar to suggestion 2, plan a "constitutional convention" for an elementary or secondary school. Consider the SMP as a process for pulling off such an effort.

4. Investigate the SMP from a participative democratic perspective. How could the SMP be improved to ensure an open, fully participative process?

5. Investigate communitarianism and its potential for addressing many of the moral issues facing schools and communities at the present time.

REFERENCES

Andrews, K. R. (1980). *The concept of corporate strategy.* Homewood, IL: Irwin.

Baldridge, V. J. (1971). *Power and conflict in the university.* New York: Wiley.

Ball, S. J. (1987). *The micro-politics of the school.* New York: Methuen.

Barber, B. (1984). *Strong democracy.* Berkeley, CA: University of California Press.

Barber, B. R. (1992). *An aristocracy of everyone.* New York: Ballantine.

Blase, J. (Ed.). (1991). *The politics of life in schools.* Newbury Park, CA: Corwin Press.

Clark, D. L., & Meloy, J. M. (1989). Renouncing bureaucracy: A democratic structure for leadership in schools. In T. Sergiovanni and J. Moore (Eds.), *Schooling for tomorrow: Directing reform to issues that count* (pp. 272-94). Boston: Allyn & Bacon.

Cozzens, S. E. (1993). Science as an open institution. In J. Murphy & D. Peck (Eds.), *Open institutions.* Westport, CT: Praeger.

Deetz, S. A. (1992). *Democracy in an age of corporate colonization.* Albany: State University of New York Press.

Etzioni, A. (1993). *The spirit of community.* New York: Crown.

Fischer, F. (1990). *Technocracy and the politics of expertise.* Newbury Park, CA: Sage.

Garson, G. D., & Smith, M. P. (1976). On public policy for self management: Toward a bill of rights for working people. In G. D. Garson & M. P. Smith (Eds.), *Organizational democracy* (pp. 115-35). Beverly Hills, CA: Sage.

Giroux, H. A. (1992). *Educational leadership and the crisis of democratic culture.* University Park, PA: University Council of Educational Administration.

Hargreaves, A. (1991). Contrived collegiality: The micropolitics of teacher collaboration. In J. Blase (Ed.), *The politics of life in schools* (pp. 46-72). Newbury Park, CA: Corwin Press.

Heifetz, R. A., & Sinder, R. M. (1988). Political leadership: Managing the public's problem solving. In R. B. Reich (Ed.), *The power of public ideas* (pp. 179-204). Cambridge, MA: Ballinger.

Keith, S., & Girling, R. H. (1991). *Education, management, and participation.* Boston: Allyn & Bacon.

Kirst, M. W. (1989). Who should control the schools? Reassessing current policies. In T. Sergiovanni and J. Moore (Eds.), *Schooling for tomorrow: Directing reform to issues that count* (pp. 66-88). Boston: Allyn & Bacon.

Mason, R. M. (1982). *Participatory and workplace democracy.* Carbondale: Southern Illinois University Press.

Mickunas, A. (1993). The public domain. In J. Murphy & D. Peck (Eds.), *Open institutions.* Westport, CT: Praeger.

Murphy, J. W., & Choi, J. M. (1993). Decentering social relations. In J. Murphy & D. Peck (Eds.), *Open institutions* (pp. 161-76). Westport, CT: Praeger.

Nutt, P. C., & Backoff, R. W. (1992). *Strategic management of public and third sector organizations.* San Francisco: Jossey-Bass.

Pateman, C. (1976). A contribution to the political theory of organizational democracy. In G. D. Garson & M. P. Smith (Eds.), *Organizational democracy* (pp. 9-30). Beverly Hills, CA: Sage.

Quicke, J. (1986). Personal and social education: A triangulated evaluation of an innovation. *Educational Review, 38*(3), 217-28.

Rudduck, J. (1991). *Innovation, involvement, and understanding.* Milton Keynes, England: Open University Press.

Shulman, L. S. (1989). Teaching alone, learning together: Needed agendas for the new reforms. In T. Sergiovanni and J. Moore (Eds.), *Schooling for tomorrow: Directing reform to issues that count* (pp. 166-87). Boston: Allyn & Bacon.

Smith, S. C., & Scott, J. J. (1990). *The collaborative school.* Eugene, OR: ERIC Clearinghouse on Educational Management.

Waltzer, M. P. (1983). *The spheres of justice.* New York: Basic Books.

Section 2 Summary

Choosing a particular leadership style is not the same as selecting clothes to wear to a social event, but this analogy does permit us to examine some dynamics that come into play when selecting a style of leadership. How we choose to adorn our bodies depends on many influences. We may simply follow a trend and go with whatever is most convenient or available at the time; if we want to blend in with the social dictates of an occasion, then it becomes a matter of judging what fits best—formal dinners and weekend camping retreats obviously call for entirely different outfits. On the other hand, if we want to make a statement and challenge past practices, there probably is no more visible way to do so than to dress differently. Finally, we cannot wear certain items if they are not accessible or we are not aware of them. Picking clothes can be a habit grown out of convenience or a challenge that requires considerable contemplation and expense.

Leadership styles and practices, like clothes, come in all shapes and sizes. Those of us who desire to be more effective in our leadership roles face a similar challenge of determining what will fit best. We may consider what fits well with our values, personality, and philosophy *and* what fits the sociopolitical context in which we wish to participate as a leader. Or we may say the heck with it, let the chips fall where they may, and do what comes naturally. This latter approach may work, but if it does not, we are back to square one.

Sergiovanni (1992) discusses the connections and interactions of the heart (values), the head (mindscapes), and the hand (decisions, actions, and behavior) in influencing our leadership style. He emphasizes that becoming a successful leader requires understanding our mindscapes, the mental pictures we have about how the world works and that help shape our respective realities. He further suggests that "not all management and leadership mindscapes are equal. Some fit the world of practice better than others. The better the fit, the more successful the practice will be" (p. 9).

In section 2, Leadership Perspectives, we reviewed a number of alternative views of leadership. Primarily we examined emerging needs of educational organizations and suggested leadership processes that would fit well with these trends. (See Figure S2.1 for an overview.) There is some agreement that our educational organizations will continue to face uncertainties and complexities that stem from an unstable postindustrial society in which old assumptions are having to give way to new ones. In this ever changing environment, we will need leaders who understand these underlying driving forces and have a vision of what educational organizations can become. We are asking leaders to wear clothing that fits all sizes and can be adjusted to fit all situations.

Therefore, the foregoing chapters addressed leadership not as an act but as a process in which the dynamics permit multiple levels of exchange and participation. It is through these interactions that necessary change becomes articulated by vision, charisma, trust, and empowerment. These ingredients provide a foundation for the tranformational leader.

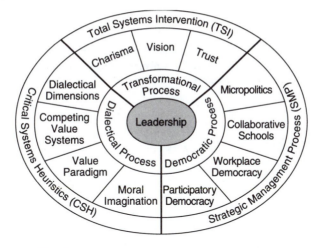

FIGURE S2.1 Leadership perspectives and major concepts

In the process of implementing or reacting to change, however, many difficult day-to-day and long-range choices must be made. A leadership process needs to be enriched with an understanding of and appreciation for opposing views, competing value systems, and their related paradoxes. A moral imagination that focuses on universal values through praxis and within a dialectical context offers a way of thinking through these paradoxes so that they do not become self-defeating. These are the ingredients of dialectical leadership.

To help take the onus off any one person and to provide a way of sorting through complex issues, a return to our democratic principles is in order. The time is right to take a serious look at the contradiction of living in a society based on democratic principles while working in an organizational environment based on hierarchy and top-down authority. Democracy in the workplace offers an opportunity for greater voice on issues that do not have simple, straightforward answers and that require greater understanding and commitment for their resolution. Thus, our wardrobe is rounded out with a greater appreciation of the promise of community within a democratic milieu, one that recognizes the importance of the individual while simultaneously providing for the needs of the community. These are the ingredients of democratic leadership.

Section 2 in its totality offers a wider array of mutually related concepts that should help in reflecting upon leadership processes at present and into the future. Keep in mind, however, Jones's (1989) observation that "The way in which we think about leadership is strongly influenced by our conceptions of social reality" (p. 7)—which brings us back to the challenge of selecting the clothes that best fit the occasion. Our choices are often limited by our capacity to imagine the alternatives and the willingness to take some risks. These are two perspectives essential for successful leaders of the future.

REFERENCES

Jones, B. D. (1989). Causation, constraint, and political leadership. In B. D. Jones (Ed.), *Leadership and politics* (pp. 3-16). Lawrence: University Press of Kansas.

Sergiovanni, T. J. (1992). *Moral leadership.* San Francisco: Jossey-Bass.

School Reform Perspectives

Our focus has been to develop an appreciation of the multiple perspectives that exist in describing and understanding organizations and leadership. In section 3, we will explore varying perspectives on school reform. Understanding efforts at school reform, particularly in the late 1980s and early 1990s, is of equal challenge to understanding the complexities of organizational behavior and its leadership. It does seem, however, that our discernments of education are potentially clouded with an additional layer. Many opinions abound concerning the ends and means of education. Much of what we believe about education and schooling influences our perception of what is "good" or "bad" in school reform. As Goens and Clover (1991) write,

> Perception is influenced by values, attitudes, experience, education, and environment. . . . Values act as a filter or screen for perceptions, which affect how people react to their world. Perceptions contain judgments, which are based on values. . . . Perception has the power to liberate or constrain thought. For individuals whose perception is based on blind faith, information to the contrary will not affect or alter thinking. Having a sense of wonder, however, opens minds to ideas and phenomena that are new and previously unexplored. (pp. 12-13)

For many, the American experience with school reform is itself filled with wonderment. The United States, given its size and diversity, may be unique in its frequency of school reforms. Some suggest that school reform is as American as apple pie. In our country, school reform is not a trivial pursuit: The history of American education up to the present time is replete with efforts at reform in response to the multiplicity of perceptions and values represented in its pluralistic environment (cf. Rippa, 1992).

Education in our country is often viewed as an explanation for perceived failings in the American way of life. For example, in 1957, the Soviet Union launched a satellite called *Sputnik* that for many symbolized the failings of our schools to teach, particularly science and mathematics. Ironically, in spite of people's perceptions of the failings of our schools, at the same time schools are seen as the cure to societal problems. As one wag suggested, in America we do not have revolutions and military coups, but rather we pass legislation that requires schools to address everything from driver education to drug and sex education.

The phenomenon of schools being viewed as central to correcting societal ills and thus facing continued calls for reforms can be attributed to several qualities special to American education. First, we do not have a large centralized education bureaucracy at the federal level that can direct educational reform nationally. The U.S. Constitution does not address the role and responsibility of the federal government in educational matters; these are assumed to be a state responsibility. In fact, it was not until the Carter administration that a cabinet-level position in education was created; the next president, Ronald Reagan, made part of his platform the elimination of the position and a reduction in the scope of the federal role in education. The ironies of politics, however, eventually altered his plans; we will discuss this later in our overview of school reform, but for now it is important to appreciate our unique governance structure. It is a structure filled with ambiguities and ensures a continued tension over who controls education between local school boards, state legislatures and departments of education, the federal government, and teacher organizations.

Second, because of the strong emphasis on local-level, lay control of schools, as exemplified by school boards, there is a tendency for schools to reflect local values and expectations. This is both good and bad news concerning school reform or responsiveness to societal needs. It is certainly more difficult to control thousands of school boards when it comes to implementing perceived needs for change. On the other hand, if local values reflect strong support for their schools then education in these schools has the potential to attain a higher level of quality. In any regard, much can happen on the way to school reform. State financial and technical support and local taxpayers' willingness to stretch their financial resources can be very critical to maintaining or achieving a high standard of educational performance. The unique quality of local control, albeit under constant challenge by outside influences, does produce over time some strange and unusual school reform results.

Third, our educational systems are challenged by the struggle to find a balance in the dialectic of meeting equally the needs of *all* students or focusing on the special needs of subgroups of students, for example, the financially disadvantaged or the gifted. Our schools are challenged legally and morally with concerns over educational opportunities; many state funding formulas are being litigated in state and federal courts to determine how well they are meeting the standards of adequacy and equity. Since wealth is not equally distributed across school district boundaries, some districts have greater capacity to fund their schools than others. State aid to education is theoretically designed to ensure that each school in the state can meet a minimum standard of education (adequacy) and that there is a comparable amount of funding behind each student across the state (equity). In practice it does not work out this way, and significant discrepancies among school districts' support of education can be observed, in turn perpetuating inequities across class, racial, and/or ethnic lines.

The net effect of these special features of American education (minimum federal control, greater emphasis on state and local control, and legal and moral concerns for equity) results in school reform becoming a very, very political process. Dow (1991), in his extensive study of curricular innovations (particularly *Man: A Course of Study*) in American schools in the late 1960s and early 1970s, concluded that "decisions about educational reform are driven more by political considerations, such as prevailing public mood, than they are by any systematic effort to improve instruction" (p. 5). Understanding the politics of school reform helps us see the effect of a pluralistic society creating a paradoxical environment in which there are simultaneous calls for change and stability. It also helps us see why school reform is difficult and often fails. As Sarason (1990) explains, "The problem is not what to do but how to think, how to take seriously the idea that there is a universe of alternative explanations for past failures of reform. Some wit—I think it was Mencken—said that for any problem there is a simple answer that is wrong" (p. xi).

Reframing reform and developing multiple insights concerning the implementation of educational programs are underlying themes in this book. Section 3 will provide the third leg of the stool as we try to understand past and present efforts at school reform. It begins with an overview of the history of school reform and introduces a school reform case, *Hope Springs Eternal*. Following this overview and case, chapters 9, 10, and 11 present three major contemporary strategies—school choice, school restructuring, and school-based management—for school reform. Section 3 closes with a summary of three school reform movements.

HISTORY OF SCHOOL REFORM

Early Times

The history of American education is a continuing saga of efforts to honor the past but also to break with tradition. In our early history, as a new nation, we attempted to transfer and copy European culture, but we also added a special touch reflective of our nascent democratic ideals. Our early education efforts were closely linked to religion and primarily served the children of the upper class. Men like Franklin, Washington, and Jefferson were visionaries who saw the importance of federal-level support for education and the role of education in strengthening a sense of nationalism. Washington's Farewell Address urged the advancement of education for the national welfare. Jefferson believed "the primary requisite of a free society was a continuous system of public education" (quoted in Rippa, 1992, p. 58). His efforts in Virginia resulted in proposals for tax-supported elementary schools and secondary schools that were to provide free education for gifted poor students. Unfortunately the new republic was not ready to embrace a tax-supported educational system until the early 1800s. Before the emergence of the common school movement in American education, secondary education was a privilege of select youth, usually males, and was provided by private schools and academies.

Devastating economic and health conditions in Europe, plus a perception that America was a land of opportunity, brought waves of immigrants in the mid-1800s. This resulted in concentrations of people in cities, most of whom lived in slums and poverty. Child labor was quite common and often under the most appalling conditions. Early labor leaders began to agitate for educational reform based on educational equality. Emerson's lectures and writings gave voice to the worthiness of individuals regardless of their social status. According to Rippa (1992), Emerson gave "new strength and conviction" to the notion of man as reformer and inspired "one of the greatest reform movements in American history" (p. 87). Reports of successful reforms of European education were being widely disseminated in the United States. The common school movement was beginning to take shape and was articulated by Horace Mann through articles he wrote in his biweekly *Common School Journal* from 1839 to 1852. Hundreds of educational societies and associations were formed to influence public opinion in favor of free schools.

The common school movement was not without controversy. Some critics saw this movement as not being prompted solely by humanitarian concerns, but rather by a desire to provide compliant and trained workers for our emerging industrialized society. The movement also raised other issues, including the need for the wealthy to pay for the education of workers' children. There was strong opposition to paying property taxes for school support, a concern expressed in the 1830s that still echoes in the 1990s. Other concerns raised included the problem of public schools competing with parochial schools and whether educated workers were even needed. Rippa (1992) writes that the movement for public school support faced two major obstacles: "the general belief that a 'free' education was only important for 'pauper' children of poor families, and the use of 'rate bills' that permitted the public schools to levy a special tax, often on a per diem basis, on those parents with children enrolled in the schools" (p. 104).

At the close of the Civil War, many states eliminated the rate bill through legislative action. By 1865, most of the states were firmly committed to three principles: (1) The primary responsibility for supporting education was the state's and not the family's; (2) the state had the right to raise monies through taxes to support educational expenses; and (3) the state should establish nonsectarian, publicly supported schools open to all children regardless of creed or financial status. According to Rippa (1992), "More than any other single factor, this idea of a public school open to *all* is the most distinctive feature of American education. It was a nineteenth-century ideal that has endured to the present time" (p. 110).

Concerns in early American education were not focused only on policy issues. According to Cuban (1990), attention was also focused on instructional and curricular practices. Cuban observed, "In America, over a century and a half ago, pedagogical reformers condemned teacher-centered instruction with its emphasis on a textbook from which students recited already-memorized information, and with teachers doing most of the talking to the entire group and asking rapid-fire questions" (p. 4). These pedagogical approaches triggered new theories about student learning. By the mid to late 1880s, new emphasis was being placed on having schooling connected to the real world of the child. Child-centered progressives in the late 1880s and early 1900s advocated for more active involvement of the learner. Innovative methods included small group instruction, activity projects, joint planning between teachers and students, and using new technologies such as films and radio.

In 1893, the so-called Committee of Ten, under the chairmanship of Harvard University President Charles Eliot, recommended a common curriculum for all students. The committee urged that all high schools teach four years of English and three years of history, science, mathematics, and a foreign language. According to Passow (1986), this was a watershed for reform in secondary education. It is also interesting that these early recommendations have been under continuous attack up to the present time; in many ways, however, secondary schools have demonstrated considerable resilience in resisting these attacks. For example, progressives attacked the notion of one best way for all children and argued for allowing children to take different courses according to their interests, capacities, and vocational futures; the comprehensive junior and senior high school evolved from this kind of thinking in the early 1900s. These new innovations sowed the seeds for subsequent criticisms and another wave of reform following the Second World War.

Post–World War II

In the 1950s, critics were aiming at the soft pedagogy and the curricula offered students in our public schools. The National Science Foundation, established in 1950, was responsible for major changes in science and math curricula. James Conant, also a Harvard University president, conducted a study of secondary schools in the mid-1950s and concluded that there was a need for more rigorous academic content for able, college-bound students. His recommendations triggered a wave of small secondary school closings and the creation of extensive school busing for transporting students to centralized, comprehensive junior-senior high schools. Specifically, according to Rosenfeld and Sher (1977), "In 1950, there were 83,718 school districts in America. By 1960, a mere ten years later, the number of school districts was *halved* to 40,500. And it was halved again during the following decade, so that by 1970 only 17,995 school districts remained" (p. 39). School consolidations resulted in school closings and schools boards' deferring much of their authority to trained professionals.

Further evidence that our schools were not challenging students came with the launching of the Russian satellite *Sputnik* in 1957. No single event had greater impact on public opinion or more strongly reinforced the conclusion that the American education system was failing in the race with the Soviet Union for world leadership. The National Defense Education Act was one of the most invasive efforts of the federal government in the improvement of education. This act resulted in massive funds being expended to upgrade the teaching of science, mathematics, foreign languages, and in the improvement of guidance and counseling services, particularly in secondary schools. Joining this effort at school improvement were the National Science Foundation and private foundations.

The 1960s were awash with innumerable curricular and organizational experiments, many of which left a faint imprint on the sandy beaches of school reform. There was a feeling by many (Goodlad, 1984; Passow, 1986; and Silberman, 1971) that the efforts of the late 1950s and throughout the 1960s had little lasting impact on changing the educational process or outcomes. Explanations included

- too much emphasis on content and not enough on how to teach the content
- misguided attempts to bypass classroom teachers in the design of "teacher-proof" curricula
- limited efforts at teacher in-service programs
- conflicts in instructional methods and curricula content that emerged in schools, communities, and academic circles
- the failure to link these ambitious changes to teacher preparatory and certification systems

The high hopes of the 1960s were demoralized in the 1970s. Toch (1991) states it rather strongly: "To be blunt, the 1970s left public education in a shambles" (p. 4). The 1970s are known for plummeting enrollments (46 million students in 1971 to 39 million students in 1982), property tax revolts (e.g., Proposition 13 in California in 1978 and Proposition 2½ in Massachusetts in 1980), divisive and protracted teacher strikes, the turning of the schools into a major battleground for civil rights movements (e.g., school desegregation), and widespread student protests, somewhat prompted by the criticisms of schools being overly bureaucratized and impersonal.

There was also evidence of decline in academic standards. A reduction in graduation requirements to one year in math and science, a drop in enrollments in foreign languages, and an increased enrollment in what was perceived as the less rigorous general course of study buttressed this claim. There were some efforts to address these emerging ills by emphasizing "basic competencies." Throughout the mid and late 1970s, school improvement efforts were directed at improving students' basic skills and implementing statewide testing programs to ensure acquisition of these skills. In spite of this focus on basic competencies, however, there was an emerging perception entering into the 1980s that the quality of American education was declining and in trouble.

Nation at Risk

As *Sputnik* was to mold public opinion concerning the needs in education in the late 1950s and early 1960s, President Reagan's National Commission on Excellence in Education report, *A Nation at Risk,* had a similar effect in 1983 and beyond. This report launched a spate of educational reform reports. According to Passow (1989), subsequent to the *At Risk* report, "well over 300 state-level task forces were working on some aspect of school reform, with governors, legislators and state education departments all vying for leadership" (p. 15). This report and others spawned the so-called excellence movement in education.

The excellence movement advocates voiced the cry that school reform was essential if the United States was to maintain its competitive edge in world markets and world leadership. The linkage of education to global economic competition motivated a cross section of American leaders from government and the private sector to reach a consensus on the need for school reform. With the business community's involvement came added pressure and support for the excellence movement; the participation of leading corporate CEOs helped overcome the resistance of fiscal conservatives to increase funding for schools.

Ironically presidential politics and Ronald Reagan's second run for the White House gave a boost to school reform that might not have been there if circumstances had been different. As mentioned earlier, Reagan's administration desired to play down the federal role in education and had rejected, according to Toch (1991), a 1981 request of then Secretary of Education Terrel Bell to appoint a national commission to study education. After being rebuffed, Secretary Bell commissioned his own department-level task force. Reagan and his aides attempted to misuse and squash the *At Risk* report until they recognized that it had struck a responsive chord in the body politic. From that point forward and into the presidential campaign, Reagan ran with the report and offered himself as a strong supporter of placing a higher priority on education at the federal level. His active pursuit of this issue gave greater recognition and attention to educational issues. Toch (1991) concluded that "the president's participation was such an important catalyst to the reform movement largely because it gained the movement tremendous media coverage" (p. 27).

By December of 1986, the issues commanding attention were more rigorous academic standards for students and more recognition and higher standards for teachers. To this end, 45 states and the District of Columbia increased high school diploma requirements, 34 states and D.C. set minimum requirements, 42 states increased math requirements, and 34 increased science requirements. Other reforms included lengthening the school year and school day (Pipho, 1986). These actions primarily represented a top-down, centralized effort at school reform.

Soon a sense began to emerge that these mandated efforts were having minimal effect on the performance of individual schools. This realization, according to Cuban (1990), led to an emphasis on decentralized decision making, which was supported by research suggesting that the school should be the unit of change and by corporate leaders pointing to the success of deferring decisions to the lowest level of the organization. Policymakers introduced school-site councils, school-based management, and the restructuring of schools; for example, in 1989, the city of Chicago placed each of its 595 schools under the management of 11-member school-site councils whose membership was made up of both parents and practitioners.

While the excellence movement was gaining force and widespread attention, there was a group of educators who became concerned about the lack of attention given to equity issues, particularly at the local school level. The equity issue was given prominence as part of the effective schools movement, which built on the original research of Brookover and Lezotte (1977) and Edmonds (1979). Their research and that of others countered the assumption of many that poor, African American children were not capable of learning and achieving as well as their white, middle-income counterparts. This movement has given hope to minority-dominated schools that they can, through forceful leadership and careful attention to the instructional process, make a difference in the achievement levels of all students, but particularly those of minority and low socioeconomic backgrounds.

Conclusion

The school reform movement continues to be a checkered cloth of attempts at changing schools. It is peppered with repetition, fade outs, and revisits to old solutions. Joyce (1986) believes this is the case because school reform is driven by false assumptions, such as

- Yesterday's good, solid schools provide the model for the future
- Schools can be improved by insisting on higher standards
- Schools can be improved without changing their operating structure
- The finger of blame can be easily and accurately pointed
- The innovations of the sixties and seventies made the schools worse
- Getting rid of the poor students will do the trick
- There is little research about how to improve education—our opinions are probably as good as the implications of the knowledge base (pp. 28-39)

In regard to this last myth, Joyce observes, "Many boards and central administrations discuss, without reference to the existing knowledge base, how to group children, how to reach the 'slower' or 'less-motivated' students, what curriculums to choose, and how to invest in technology; they seem to believe they can operate de novo" (p. 39). This de novo approach to school reform by local schools may help explain why reform seems to rise and fall with political causes and perceived failings of the public schools.

Cuban (1990) has a different explanation for what he calls the continuous waves of reform as demonstrated in our historical overview. He believes that too much faith is placed on the rational process of examining and solving school problems, particularly from a top-down perspective. Further, he argues that there is too much reliance on political explanations that suggest cycles of dominance or decline of different value systems over time. He believes that not enough attention has been given to the fact that schools are unique organizations that rely on tax support and operate under lay governance. Schools are made up of many constituent groups (e.g., parents, voters, volunteers, advocates, and critics) that they must satisfy for their survival. Schools, because of their dependence on support from their constituencies, must be responsive to perceived problems of these constituencies; for example, if youthful drug use is seen as a problem, schools will eventually design and implement drug education programs. Cuban argues:

The unique organizational characteristics of this taxpayer supported public bureaucracy [schools] governed by lay policymakers merge with the imperative to retain the loyalty of the system's constituencies. Both help to explain schools' obvious vulnerability to pressures for change from external groups. When value conflicts arise and external pressure accelerates, both get wedded to an organizational drive for retaining support of critical supporters; such conditions push school districts to try novel programs, join regional and national efforts to improve curriculum, and adopt innovative technologies so as to be viewed as worthy of continued endorsement. (p. 10)

Accommodating these various constituencies can create organizational inconsistencies and contradictions. For example, in order to maintain teacher support, it is necessary to uncouple classroom instruction from the control of policymakers and administrators; however, there is a simultaneous need to demonstrate to external groups, like parents and taxpayers, that school matters are under the control of appointed or elected leaders. Thus, bargains are struck that permit teachers a degree of classroom instructional autonomy with some constraints as to the degree to which they can act independently on curricular matters. These deals will ebb and flow depending on external perceptions of educational needs and problems and the professional expertise and commitment of teachers. This exchange process may help explain why school reforms recycle, albeit in slightly different forms.

CHAPTER HIGHLIGHTS

In section 3, we will examine three major contemporary school reform movements. Although there may be some overlap of the movements, for purposes of clarity and illumination we will explore them separately. For example, school-based management can be seen as a form of school restructuring; however, school restructuring comes in many forms, and focusing on it separately allows us to examine its multiple dimensions. By the same token, a separate and specific treatment of school-based management provides the opportunity to explore the unique characteristics of one of the more popular and major efforts at school restructuring.

We will begin section 3 with a chapter on school choice, chapter 9, in part because of its inherent controversy and contradictions but also because many of its advocates see school choice offering the best potential for breaking the mold of past educational practices. Others are less sanguine and see school choice as a potential death knell for public-supported efforts at attaining equal educational opportunities for *all* students regardless of socioeconomic status. Following that, in chapter 10 we will examine the multiple dimensions of the school restructuring movement of educational reform. Chapter 11, on school-based management, closes out our examination of contemporary school reform efforts and sets the stage for section 4, Perspectives on the Future. To help smooth the segue to section 4, a brief summary of the school reform strategies is presented at the end of section 3.

A brief overview of each chapter follows. As in the previous sections of this text, each of the chapters follows a comparable format. In exploring each school reform strategy, the chapters provide an introduction and background concerning the strategy, theories underlying it, models and approaches currently being implemented, arguments for and against, and a general conclusion.

Chapter 9: School Choice

Of the three school reform movements, school choice probably is the most controversial and has the best potential for departing significantly from established views of how public education should be provided in our country. Much of the push for school choice is based on marketplace values and the belief that the only way to force school reform is to give parents a greater voice in how schools operate by providing them the power to choose their children's schools. Critics are quick to point out the limitation of marketplace values being applied to the provision of educational services: Many fear that those who have the means (financial and political) will be winners in a school choice reform strategy, while others will be stuck in circumstances that do not permit much choice, if any at all. This chapter explores the various dimensions of this controversy, alternative approaches presently being tested or advocated, and the underlying philosophy of and research on efforts at school choice.

Chapter 10: School Restructuring

Many critics of schools believe that the solution to school improvement is large-scale restructuring. This notion and its language is normally associated with businesses or manufacturing firms attempting to work their way out of a fiscal crisis. The application to schools and school-related problems is a combination of good intentions and a shotgun approach to correcting school ills. School restructuring is a broad concept and means different things to different people. This chapter explores the definitional problem of school restructuring and discusses many examples, models, and approaches, for example, Copernican Plan, Coalition of Essential Schools, Paideia, Success for All, Comer, and charter schools. As with school choice, there are arguments in support and against school restructuring and these respective arguments are reviewed. The chapter concludes with a discussion of the dilemma that the school restructuring movement presents to responsible persons at the local level: finding the balance between preserving effective past practices and experimenting with promising future practices. The school restructuring chapter illuminates the dynamics of this dilemma and what should be the final arbiter in making critical choices.

Chapter 11: School-Based Management

School-based management is a very popular form of restructuring and warrants a special review. This chapter examines school-based management from a variety of perspectives and also illuminates some of the complications of implementing a school-based management strategy. Advocates of school-based management express a strong belief in the positive virtues of delegating control and decision making to persons closest to the action: teachers, administrators, and parents. However, if it were that simple, school-based management would have been implemented a long time ago and on a much larger scale than at present. This chapter explores these dynamics and examines in some detail underlying theories for school-based management, especially decentralization. Any effort to push down to the school level greater responsibility for determining the fate of the students poses the question of school governance. In the final analysis, however, school-based management will rise or fall on the willingness of persons at the local level to take on the challenges involved in improving educational opportunities for students. Chapter 11 discusses this and other issues and provides a thorough review of the dimensions of school-based management.

CASE: *HOPE SPRINGS ETERNAL*

To guide our understanding and appreciation of the implications of school reform strategies, we will explore a secondary school's restructuring efforts. This case provides a real-world example, although names have been changed to protect the identity of those involved, of how a typical school mediated numerous influences and maintained its commitment to change.

Introduction

As the title of this case implies, we will explore a secondary school that continues to be involved in a school reform effort. Country View Union Junior and Senior High School is an ordinary school that serves multiple communities with little fanfare or extraordinary support. It is a school, however, that warmed slowly to a vision of reform and embarked on this path with modest expectations. But maybe more importantly, members of the school, and to a lesser degree members of the community, had an unflinching belief that they could make a difference in the lives of their students. To do this, they saw the need to make a commitment to school reform and take it a day at a time in the vague hope that perhaps things would get better.

COUNTRY VIEW UNION JUNIOR AND SENIOR HIGH SCHOOL

Country View school sits in a wide expanse of open flat land near a main highway that supports a considerable amount of traffic between two major cities and a number of medium-sized towns along the way. When traveling on this road, one can easily observe the school building and its outdoor recreational and athletic fields. The building is a conventional two-story, rectangular design with a couple of transportable buildings off to one side. It is painted white with bright blue entranceways and doors. The driveway leading up to the front of the school is designed to accommodate typical large yellow school buses that are used to transport students from some distance. Beyond the school building and athletic fields is a thick forest made up of a mix of hardwoods and pines that provide a rich green backdrop. In the fall, however, much of the green changes to a beautiful blend of yellows and reds and draws many tourists to the area. Chances are the tourists, like many of the local residents, will hardly take notice of Country View school.

Part of the explanation for such little attention being given to Country View is its location and its role as a union or centralized junior and senior high school. As mentioned in our historical overview of school reform, during the late 1950s and early 1960s many small high schools were closed and their students transferred to larger, consolidated or union schools. A consequence of this movement was a number of communities across the country losing their small, community-based schools. Often consolidation was forced upon reluctant communities by state policymakers and top-down decision-making processes.

Country View was born during the school consolidation movement. It emerged out of the stress and controversies that normally accompany the closing of cherished local, small-town high schools. The choice of its new geographic location was at best a political compromise. In fact, the site location for Country View is exactly midway between two moderate-sized towns that have historically enjoyed strong rivalries, often resolved on the playing fields of their respective schools. Thus, in one sense, Country View was in the perfect location: halfway between these two towns and near the main highway to allow easy access by school buses; on the other hand, because of its location and the manner in which it came into existence, it is not strongly identified with any single community and suffers some benign neglect.

Country View school is part of a supervisory union overseen by a superintendent and staff whose responsibilities include administrative oversight of the Country View school and six elementary, K–6 schools. These elementary schools with enrollments ranging from 50 to 400 students, are located in neighboring communities. The superintendent is assisted by an associate superintendent for curriculum and professional development and a director for special education. The superintendent's duties include general supervision of the building principals and liaison with the respective schools and their school boards in the supervisory union. Country View has a 12-member school board that includes representatives from each of the feeder schools and the district at large.

It should be noted that state education law permits a form of school choice. Country View is designated by the elementary school boards in the supervisory union as the preferred school of attendance. However, each elementary school board may opt to allow parents to select a secondary school from among other public and private schools but not religiously affiliated schools. Distance, transportation costs, and higher tuition rates serve as some constraint on these choices. If parents request permission for their children to attend another secondary school they may receive tuition support equivalent to the tuition charged by Country View. Obviously, if tuition charges are higher at the school of choice, the parents will need to make up the difference; most likely they'll also have to provide their own transportation. At present, only a small percentage of parents have elected to send their children to another secondary school.

The economy of this supervisory union is tightly linked to the cities located to the north and south, which are an hour's drive from the Country View school. As a consequence, a vast majority of people in this area work and commute to medium-sized manufacturing firms in the region. There are a few remaining dairy farms in the area but the number is shrinking as a consequence of the federal dairy buy-out program. There is a sizable population, approximately 20 percent, of families that are at or below the poverty level, many of whom rely on welfare and part-time jobs in small businesses like auto repair shops. A recent survey identified nearly 1,500 adults within the attendance area of Country View school in need of basic literacy training.

The Country View school has over 60 faculty serving slightly over 700 students, grades 7-12. The organization and curricula of the school prior to its restructuring effort were traditional in nature. The administration of the school included a principal, an associate principal, and department chairs for English, mathematics, social studies, science, business education, foreign languages, industrial arts, home economics, music, and physical education. The departmental structure reflected a subject-driven curriculum which grouped students into three tracks: college bound, general, and vocational-technical. The principal had overall administrative responsibility for the school, and the associate principal was primarily responsible for the junior high grades 7 and 8 and student discipline for all grades.

School Reform: Year 1

Year 1 of the reform process began in the spring when the superintendent of schools initiated a community steering committee of business and school leaders who were interested in economic development and school restructuring. The establishment of this group was the beginning of a saga of school reform that has continued to the present. The community representatives began their conversations around the need to reestablish a sense of community and to begin a process of economic development for the area. The school leaders, including some of the Country View high school teachers, began conversations on how they might "reinvent" the high school. The superintendent and other school and community leaders believed that changes were needed at the high school, particularly for the non-college-bound students. Four subcommittees were established to study program outcomes, school/community relations, school and business integration, and the development of a learning center. These committees worked on separate reports during the spring semester and submitted their results at the end of the school year. An ad hoc committee of some department chairs and administrators met for a half day during the summer to study these reports. They identified 13 themes or strands in the reports and designed a school board and faculty questionnaire. To get the flavor of what this ad hoc committee had in mind, the following quote is taken from the introduction to the questionnaire:

> A number of meetings have been held with the faculty and with the local community asking what we can and should do to make our educa-

tional program the best that it can be. People were asked to think about what a better school would look like if they had the freedom to reinvent the school without the restrictions we commonly face. With each meeting, the ideas became better refined. Some issues took on more prominence while others descended in importance.

The 13 strands identified were as follows:

    I: Early and primary education (elementary)
   II: Middle schools concepts (elementary/secondary)
  III: Basic skills and remediation
  IV: Liberal arts core
   V: Differentiated student programs
  VI: Demonstrated mastery
 VII: Lifelong learning
VIII: Business/education linkages
  IX: Adult and parent learning
   X: Counseling
  XI: Integration with social services
 XII: Decision making by those affected
XIII: Learning for all

A brief description was provided for all strands and the respondents were asked to indicate to what degree each was worthy of "further time, energy, and money." The results of the survey suggested three areas of high need: middle school, early and primary education, and decision making by those affected. Strands III, IV, VI, X, and XIII were some distance from the top three and clustered into a middle-level priority grouping. The lowest ratings were assigned to strands of lifelong learning, integration with special services, and business/education linkages.

It is interesting to observe that levels below the high school received highest priority for reinvention and the business/education linkages received the lowest ranking; this had to be somewhat disheartening since the superintendent and some business leaders were interested in identifying some possible joint ventures. For example, in addition to the subcommittees and questionnaire activities, during the summer of the first year the superintendent investigated the possibility of creating a school-based enterprise. This concept, developed by J. Sher at North Carolina State University, nurtures a business venture in the school that eventually spins off into the community as a full-fledged business. The superintendent felt such a school-based enterprise would provide new opportunities for non-college-bound students, aid in the economic development of the area, and breathe some new life into the high school's curricula, particularly business education. Unfortunately the superintendent, after visiting some demonstration projects in North Carolina, concluded that such an effort would require phenomenal up-front investment of time and energy and he did not see anyone in the school system willing to provide this kind of leadership, including himself. In light of the survey results, this was probably an accurate perception.

The school year opened in the fall with a mix of optimism and pessimism. On the positive side, there was a feeling among many school and community leaders that their planning could move forward; this was somewhat boosted by the completion during the summer of a bandstand in one of the nearby towns, a result of a joint venture between the high school and the community. The bandstand served as a symbol of what could be done when the school and community cooperated. On the pessimistic side, some school crowding was being experienced at the high school and did not bode well for the future; also, upcoming teacher negotiations were being seen as a possible barrier to teacher support of the restructuring effort.

In the fall of Year 1, a planning group, made up of the superintendent, the high school principal, the associate superintendent, and a planning facilitator from a nearby university, met every Monday at 8:00 A.M. at the home of the high school principal. This group explored ideas that could guide the reinvention or restructuring of Country View Junior-Senior High School. Their first major task was to plan an all-day in-service meeting scheduled for October; other tasks included writing a grant for state funding to underwrite their restructuring interests and planning a community summit meeting on school-community cooperation.

The October in-service meeting kicked off a season of debate, consciousness raising, and micropolitics at Country View. The principal conducted the meeting assisted by the planning facilitator from the university. A spectrum of topics under the general theme of reinventing the school was discussed in small and large groups throughout the day; topics ranged from heterogeneous versus homogeneous grouping of students to cooperative learning and interdisciplinary teaching. At the end of the meeting, the facilitator congratulated them on a good day, "wished them luck with their new endeavor," and left. Suddenly the principal could sense an undercurrent of discomfort, until finally someone asked, "What is this new endeavor?" The principal answered somewhat obliquely that the reexamination of "what we do at Country View" was the new endeavor. That's when a line began to emerge between groups interested and not interested in any changes at the school.

While the faculty began to debate what and how changes should occur at Country View, the planning group continued to meet at the principal's home. They prepared a grant proposal to the state for restructuring funds to achieve three targets:

1. To impact student achievement gains, including a reduction in the dropout rate from 20 percent to 5 percent over two years and to increase the number who go on to higher education from 47 percent to 66 percent in three years. Various curricular and program changes were proposed, including revising the length of the school day and school year, adopting a mastery learning philosophy, and establishing a new student assessment program and alternative education program.

2. To pursue continuous, lifelong learning activities, including an adult literacy program, a community education center, community service corps, and training for pregnant teens and young parents.
3. To facilitate economic development through a joint council for economic education, joint planning between the towns, an education summit, and career exploration and preparation.

The grant did include some input from a guidance counselor who had some expertise and interest in the lifelong learning component of the grant; beyond that, however, there seemed to be minimal teacher input and involvement. A presentation was made to representatives at the state department of education.

Also during the fall, a group from the community met to discuss initiating a community-based strategic planning process in one of the major towns in the Country View area. The superintendent provided the initial leadership in setting up this meeting and attempted to provide some vision of how Country View could cooperate with this community. In attendance, besides the superintendent, were the associate superintendent, the local town manager (who had some experience with strategic planning in another community), a selectperson from the town's governing council, a local parish priest, some retired citizens, and members of the business community. A willingness emerged to plan a so-called summit at which a larger number of community and school leaders could discuss the desired future for this town and how resources, including the school, could support such a vision. The meeting took place during the spring, on a Saturday, with a modest turnout. Many ideas were explored but little tangible commitment or follow-through emerged from the meeting. It seemed that people were either too busy or did not or could not see the need for committing energy to any new ventures.

As activities of one sort or another were moving along in the fall, the teachers began to express some discontent about what was being planned and envisioned for the Country View school. After the grant proposal hearing, which was well received and approved by the state and resulted in an award of $10,000, there was a shared feeling that more teacher involvement was needed. During the spring semester, a steering committee was established at Country View that included teacher representatives chosen by the faculty to be chaired by the high school principal. Also, one of its members was designated to join the Monday morning meetings at the principal's home. This committee became more visible in the restructuring efforts and took responsibility in delineating issues, planning in-service meetings, and representing the faculty's perception of the needs of the school. They attempted to counter early impressions of a top-down planning process and espoused the values of inclusiveness (opening the process to all teachers, including the resisters) and empowerment in the identification of student needs, especially the low-track students.

It is interesting to note that at this early stage of their restructuring effort the faculty fell into three distinct groups. One group, including members of the steering committee, were very concerned about unmotivated students, at-risk students, and reports of parental abuse and neglect. Thus, this group saw that change was needed if these students were to be better served. Another group of teachers, who did not work with many problem students or generally did not have any problems with students, were less convinced of the need to make any changes. A third group of teachers may have had some challenges in working with these bored or troublesome students but because of other pressures, higher priorities, or a certain amount of indifference were not very motivated to take on any changes.

Year 1 closed with a bombshell of sorts when both the principal and associate principal announced their resignations in order to accept other positions. Many teachers felt betrayed or abandoned just as they began to take some risks in advocating and supporting the change process. The steering committee, however, stepped into the breach and requested a special meeting with the board. They, along with the departing administrators, persuaded the board to create a three-person management team and appoint two assistant principals from the faculty ranks. The lead principal was to be recruited from outside the school. However, this did not work out, and a third member of the management team came from the teaching ranks of Country View. Thus, what could have been a major setback ended on a positive note.

School Reform: Year 2
The steering committee was very effective in following through on their vision of teacher inclusiveness and empowerment in defining the needs and planning strategies for addressing these needs. The Monday morning group discontinued meeting and deferred to the steering committee. The initial and most visible successes of this group were arranging a summer one-week in-service institute at Country View sponsored by a nearby university and attended by 18 local faculty members. This summer institute provided a means of interacting with national, regional, and state experts and leaders involved with secondary school change of one sort or another. Also, the institute provided time for the faculty members to meet, hash out the issues, debate what they were hearing from different experts, and to plan. The steering committee had significant input into the design and content of the institute.

Year 2's fall opening of school included a report by those who attended the institute to the rest of the faculty of Country View. Enthusiasm and camaraderie were in evidence and swept the faculty up with feelings of inclusiveness. Morale reached an all-time high as the school year unfolded, boosted by the steering committee's leadership and sincerity in wanting all faculty involved in identifying the issues or questions concerning restructuring. The steering committee designed a network of committees to further study the needs or intervention options at Country View. Fifty-eight of the 62 faculty signed up to work on one or more committees; in addition, 18 students were chosen to meet biweekly with a steering committee member to explore their views on restructuring the school. In recognition of the centrality of the steering committee to the change process at the school, a report from the committee became a fixed agenda item at the monthly school board meeting and a board representative joined the committee.

As an outgrowth of the summer institute, the junior high moved to a middle school philosophy and detracked the seventh grade. They were no longer referred to as the junior high; they began to meet separately from the high school teachers and schedule their own in-service meetings during the school year of Year 2; they laid out plans for total detracking of students and the establishment of interdisciplinary teams of teachers. The committees established by the steering committee, with approval of the faculty, included in-service/training, adult ed/lifelong learning, action research/evaluation, interdisciplinary projects, scheduling teams, communications (media/outreach/PR and student forum), resources/archives, and vocational education. In-service meetings took on a significant role in cross-committee communications, emphasized team building, and focused on the planning of an interdisciplinary curriculum project in the spring. Also, considerable attention was given to heterogeneous grouping of students at the senior high school level.

In late spring of Year 2, the entire school engaged in a one-week interdisciplinary curriculum project that involved all the teachers and students of the school. It was a sizable undertaking and was inspired by a nearby secondary school, one with a smaller enrollment, that had gained recognition for conducting similar projects over a number of years. The planners of the idea saw it as a means of breaking down the typical barriers between curricular disciplines, student groups, and faculty. It was also seen as a way to generate both faculty and student interest in collaboration and an appreciation for multidisciplinary perspectives on a common topic or theme. The project received mixed reviews but most agreed it was worth the effort and did not diminish interest in interdisciplinary teaching.

Part of the state's effort at encouraging local initiatives in the restructuring of schools was the development of a fund from private and public sources to sponsor locally designed projects. In addition to grants, of which Country View was a recipient, the state board of education indicated their willingness to waive regulations in order to remove any perceived barriers to restructuring. Country View accepted this offer and requested a number of waivers. The request that proved most controversial, and was some embarrassment to the state, involved a waiver of licensure for the administrative triumvirate; it so happened that only one of the three teachers appointed as a team to replace the two principals was certified. In addition, it was the desire of these three teachers and the school faculty that they operate as a team of administrators rather than in the typical hierarchal approach with one person in charge. After much negotiation and public media coverage, a compromise was struck that required one person to be designated as head principal for the record and the other two teachers who were not certified received temporary licensure. This solution was not fully satisfactory to Country View but they felt they could live with it for the short term.

Year 2 closed on a positive note and a survey of the faculty provided the troika of administrators with an exceptionally high performance rating. The teachers were proud of having their colleagues in the primary leadership positions of the school. In addition, 22 teachers agreed to participate in the second in-service institute to work on interdisciplinary units, including art, history, and science; auto maintenance and technical math; science and technology; and romantic and classical music and literature.

School Reform: Year 3

Out of the second summer institute came a number of decisions and goals for Year 3, which started with much promise and a host of new changes. The goals identified included:

Goal One: Connections for excellence
- Expand interdisciplinary work/ninth grade teams

Goal Two: Community support and involvement
- Volunteer program—use of community volunteers in school programs
- School report card day—open house where community rates performance

Goal Three: Structure time and setting to focus on learning and uninterrupted instruction
- Scheduling changes

Goal Four: Encourage enthusiasm for lifelong learning
- Adult education at Country View open to community; library, computers, etc.

Decisions were made that Country View would join, with other schools in the state, in designing and experimenting with student portfolios in English and math for grades 8, 10, and 12. Plans were made to implement a process for creating an individual four-year educational plan with parent input and involvement. Advisory teacher teams were established to guide students' learning choices and to deal with affective behavior.

Schedule changes were made that included heterogeneous grouping of students through grade 10. Core classes of English, social studies, math, and science for grades 7/8, 9/10, and 11/12 were scheduled back-to-back to facilitate team planning of interdisciplinary instruction. Also, the schedule permitted a common teacher planning time and a full day a month for teacher and administrator in-service meetings. The school day was shortened by eliminating study halls but lengthening class periods to permit class time for homework. The schedule also called for an intersession between the fall and spring semesters, at which time thematic units would be taught in schoolwide mini courses across grade levels.

A local newspaper reported on Country View's progress in restructuring goals and indicated that in addition to the $10,000 grant from the state, the school had been successful in receiving seven additional grants to the total of $172,000. These grants covered the establishment of a writing center for students; curricular development, especially in integrating history, art, and technology and drama and living arts; and vocational rehabilitation. Country View was also successful in receiving state waivers of various regulations, including length of the school year, length of the school day, diploma requirements for industrial arts and living arts, and certification requirements for teachers involved in team teaching.

During Year 3 the steering committee experimented with student involvement by adding two student representatives. They also, along with the student council, organized the student body into small groups to discuss school problems on a biweekly basis. Items from these discussions were routed to the student council and the steering committee for further discussion and appropriate action.

An analysis was done on student performance. Overall student test scores had increased, the distance between high and low performers was not increasing, and the student performance curve moved higher with the lower end being smaller. Less time was lost in disciplinary problems and there were fewer and less serious problems. The school was even experiencing less vandalism. In addition, the school was able to establish a new learning lab in the cafeteria, which helped approximately 60 students each day with problems in any courses they were taking. This learning lab was staffed by student interns from a nearby university who were participating in a new field-based teacher training program.

Year 3 closed on a sweet note. Country View teachers and the school board settled the teachers' contract in record time. A collaborative negotiation strategy was followed, which included an emphasis on personal relations (negotiators got to know one another on a personal level) and clarification of available fiscal resources before determining how to divide the pie. The contract resulted in an average salary increase of 4.4 percent and extra pay for a master's degree. The board also agreed to provide subsidies for attending conferences, graduate school, and sabbatical leaves.

It is clear that in just over three years Country View had made significant progress in implementing a variety of changes, improving the school's climate, and improving its relationships with the school board and community. Many factors contributed to the progress made, but teacher involvement and commitment became central in moving the school restructuring process along. The school restructuring effort was infused with a spirit of believing in everyone's capacity to problem-solve and to build mutual respect. As one teacher expressed it, "Country View is nirvana for the eternally optimistic."

This case provides a context in which to further explore alternative strategies for school reform, including school choice, school restructuring, and school-based management. Country View, now a middle school and high school, provides a holistic view of a school reform effort championed by a variety of ordinary persons with an intuitive sense and desire to provide more opportunities for kids than had been provided. Although the process was not neat and orderly, it was based on rock solid values that were shared by many key individuals.

REFERENCES

Brookover, W. B., & Lezotte, L. W. (1977). *Changes in school characteristics coincident with changes in student achievement.* East Lansing: Institute for Research on Teaching, Michigan State University.

Cuban L. (1990). Reforming again, again, and again. *Educational Researcher, 19*(1), 3-13.

Dow, P. B. (1991). *Schoolhouse politics: Lessons from the Sputnik era.* Cambridge, MA: Harvard University Press.

Edmonds, R. R. (1979). Some schools work and more can. *Social Policy, 9,* 28-32.

Goens, G. A., & Clover, S. I. (1991). *Mastering school reform.* Boston: Allyn & Bacon.

Goodlad, J. I. (1984). *A place called school.* New York: McGraw-Hill.

Joyce, B. R. (1986). *Improving America's schools.* White Plains, NY: Longman.

Passow, A. H. (1986). Beyond the commission reports: Toward meaningful school improvement. In A. Lieberman (Ed.), *Rethinking school improvement.* New York: Teachers College Press.

Passow, A. H. (1989). Present and future directions in school reform. In T. J. Sergiovanni & J. H. Moore (Eds.), *Schooling for tomorrow.* Boston: Allyn & Bacon.

Pipho, C. (1986). States move closer to reality. *Phi Delta Kappan, 68,* 1-6.

Rippa, S. A. (1992). *Education in a free society.* White Plains, NY: Longman.

Rosenfeld, S. A, & Sher, J. P. (1977). The urbanization of rural schools. In J. P. Sher (Ed.), *Education in rural America: A reassessment of conventional wisdom.* Boulder, CO: Westview Press.

Sarason, S. B. (1990). *The predictable failure of educational reform.* San Francisco: Jossey-Bass.

Silberman, C. E. (1971). *Crisis in the classroom: The remaking of American education.* New York: Vintage Books.

Toch, T. (1991). *In the name of excellence.* New York: Oxford University Press.

chapter 9

School Choice

Making choices is part of living in a democratic society. We choose our elected leaders, we choose where we wish to live, we choose our employment, and we choose our friends and our significant others. And our choices do not end there. There is an array of daily situations in which we practice the art of choice, including when to get up, what to wear, what to eat, what to read, what radio or TV station to listen to, and more. Philosophers and economists have a great deal of interest in how we go about this process of choosing. Yet choice making is so endemic to our lives that we either take it for granted or just give it very little thought; we often run on automatic pilot and are unaware of choices made in the past or to be made in the future.

On the other hand, there are many persons who will argue that choice is more a myth than a reality. So often our choices are seriously constrained and other factors have greater influence over our choices than we do. In political elections we are often limited to two candidates who are more similar than different; new directions in health care are targeted at limiting our choice of health care providers; because lawyers are often prohibited from advertising, we must rely partly on word of mouth as a basis for selection. Choice of career or job in a period of high unemployment may become a choice of the lesser evil in order to survive economically. Choices are clearly limited by real circumstances, and the making of some choices is more or less a foregone conclusion or abstract exercise.

Schmookler (1993) discusses how a market economy, such as we have in the United States, plays a significant role in shaping our values and governing our choices. Part of living in a free society that is greatly influenced by a market system is the strong emphasis on choice. Often people do not realize, however, how their choices are being shaped and what trade-offs are necessary. Liberty allows persons to make choices even if they are unwise. Schmookler drives this point home: "Young parents who

217

choose careers and money over care of their young infant are simply making their own free choice. But in a deeper perspective, the minds and hearts that make such choices have been molded by a society that has itself been shaped by the forces of the market" (p. 12). Choices and consequences emerge from a complex array of personal desires, opportunities, and societal influences that often transcend our consciousness regarding choice.

The school choice movement, in the United States and other countries, such as the Netherlands, Canada, and Australia, is gaining some momentum as a significant strategy for school reform. Lieberman (1989) believes that "educational choice" is necessary because of the failure of local school boards to bring about school reform and outlines three factors that have contributed to this failure:

1. the decision-making structure of education, which has encumbered educational decisions with statutory provisions governing pupils, teachers, administrators, school board members, etc.; with how funds are raised and spent; and with an array of legal requirements
2. the special interests that are adversely affected by any school reform proposal and their activism in defeating uncoordinated efforts at educational reform
3. the short-range view of most political and educational leaders, where the appearance of reform seems more important than the substance of reform

Lieberman sees educational choice as the only way to increase competition between schools and minimize the influence of the three factors. He advocates privatization of education, in which the public functions in education would be delegated to the private sector. A transfer of responsibilities, in his judgment, would foster private schools that would compete with other private and public schools; then the weaker institutions would have to meet the competition or fade from the scene.

Lieberman's is one perspective on school choice that is a logical extension of both our desire to make choices and the value of competition in a market system. In this chapter, we will explore other perspectives, underlying theories, alternative approaches, and the pros and cons of varying strategies for school choice. We will conclude the chapter by reviewing related research on school choice and suggestions for initiating a school choice policy. The case *Hope Springs Eternal* will provide an opportunity to illustrate related concepts.

BACKGROUND

School choice provides an opportunity for more extensive change in school structures and processes. A recent report by the Office of Educational Research and Improvement (OERI) (1992) in the U.S. Department of Education stresses that school choice "is a means to a variety of ends; it is not *the* end" (p. 1). The report emphasizes that school choice can link to school restructuring and school-based management. In the context of school choice, the writers argue, a sense of ownership and commitment to school improvement becomes everyone's responsibility. Greater expectations should emerge for students, teachers, administrators, and parents to invest time and energy in facing school problems and making needed changes. As Country View's school staff became more conscious and reflective about their policies and practices, the circle of persons involved expanded. School choice at Country View took on a different meaning and made teachers, in particular, aware that they had choices at the school that were mostly being ignored.

The OERI report (1992) stresses two parts to the definition of public school choice: The first part defines the obvious dimension of the "right of students and parents to choose the public school they or their children attend"; the second stresses the way choice gives "teachers, administrators, parents and/or students the opportunity to create distinctive schools which recognize that there is no one best school for all children" (p. 1). The teachers at Country View began to appreciate that there was no one best way to meet the needs of their students and saw the need to explore alternative strategies.

The Carnegie Foundation for the Advancement of Teaching issued a report in 1992 which described different forms of school choice. Essentially they suggest three forms: districtwide, statewide, and private school choice. Districtwide choice permits parents and students to select from different schools within the same district. Statewide choice permits choice across school district boundaries. As the report details, 13 states currently permit interdistrict choices and another 21 are considering it. The third and most controversial approach is the private school choice, which calls for a voucher plan and permits parents to send their children to private schools at public expense. Some of its proponents call it the "G.I. Bill for Children."

But as the report points out, choice is even more complicated than the three forms suggested. Choice has come to mean providing a wide range of programs and school sites for gifted students, dropouts, and special interests of students. Choice in Minnesota, the first state (in 1987) to establish statewide choice, has also meant permitting high school students early entry into college.

Although it was not until 1987 that school choice became a contemporary strategy for school change, the notion of parents having choices for where and how their children are educated has been around for some time. In our overview of the history of school reform, we observed that parents frequently exercised their right of choice by having their children attend private schools. According to Coons and Sugarman (1978), "The intellectual roots of the current debate on educational choice can be traced from Thomas Paine and Adam Smith in the eighteenth century, through John Stuart Mill in the nineteenth century, to a variety of conservatives, liberals, and radicals in the twentieth century" (pp. 18-19). The right of parents to send their children to schools other than the public schools was confirmed in 1925 in a landmark case (*Pierce v. the Society of Sisters*) in which the U.S. Supreme Court struck down an Oregon law that attempted to require all children to attend public schools.

Friedman (1962) was an early advocate of a voucher system that would permit both wealthy and poor parents a means of school choice. His proposals languished until the late 1960s, when researchers like Christopher Jencks revitalized interest in a voucher system and earned the support of President Lyndon Johnson. In 1972, the federal government set up a voucher demonstration project in Alum Rock School District in San Jose, California. This experiment was short-lived when a Rand Corporation report in 1974 revealed that students who participated in the experiment fell academically behind those students who attended other Alum Rock schools. According to Bridge and Blackman (1978) and Rasmussen (1981), however, parents in the Alum Rock experiment were satisfied with the schools of their choice but at a much lower level than the non-voucher parents. Also, geographic proximity, rather than curriculum content, was the major determinant of parental choice.

It took the conservative agenda of the Reagan administration to breathe new life into the voucher concept; specifically, Secretary of Education William Bennett was successful in drawing public attention to the issue of parental choice. In 1985, the Reagan administration proposed that Chapter I of the Educational Consolidation and Improvement Act permit individual vouchers for disadvantaged children. Public opinion polls in 1983 and 1986 revealed that a majority of Americans supported a voucher system and parents' having the right to select their children's school. It is interesting to note, however, that while there was support to permit choice, only 25 percent of the parents surveyed would actually select a different school for their children (Gallup, 1986).

Johanek (1992) argues that since World War II, there have been critical changes in how we organize our daily lives, particularly the role of public and private forces. These trends include

- government increasing its role in the market and in "private" life
- individuals lessening their involvement in "public" realms
- private life being increasingly "marketized"

According to Johanek, our lives have become more privatized:

> Malls offer a paradigmatic example of private citizenship. Private institutions on private property existing primarily as centers for intensive shopping now serve many of the purposes of the old public squares. Community organizations hold concerts, many young and old socialize, and next-door neighbors finally meet each other in the mall. (p. 154)

He does point out, however, that malls are different from traditional public places in that they do not provide the same political rights of free speech or free assembly. Private security guards can enforce social order and exclude undesirable persons from the premises. Malls exist primarily for economic purposes, but serving "public" purposes as a secondary effect is desirable from a business point of view.

These interlocking and mutually reinforcing relationships further complicate the distinction between what is public and what is private and what policies are best suited for each arena. The slide toward greater choice and pursuit of self-interest serves the private sector well but raises some concerns for the public sector. According to the Carnegie Foundation report (1992), "Adopting the language of the marketplace, education is portrayed as a solitary act of consumerism" (p. 86). School choice is compared to the process of shopping around for a VCR or new automobile. Yet schools serve both a private benefit and a public good: We build schools not only to enhance the opportunities for the individual but to inculcate important societal values, including a vision of community. We will revisit this issue later, but for now we might conclude from our historical struggles that the foundation for school choice is confused with our identity as both public and private citizens in a democracy that guarantees certain individual rights and social protections.

THEORIES OF SCHOOL CHOICE

School choice theories are drawn from a variety of disciplines, including philosophy, economics, sociology, and political science. Various proponents use these theories and perspectives to help explain and justify policies of school choice. At the same time opponents seize upon related concepts to discredit their arguments. In this section, we will highlight some of these arguments as they are drawn from philosophy, economic theory, public choice theory, and decentralization theory.

Philosophical Views

Kane (1992) reviews philosophical foundations of choice. He argues that "the choices we make and the resulting schools we create are grounded in the assumptions and commitments we make concerning the foundations of the human spirit and intellect" (p. 47). In this context, the human spirit is concerned with our ultimate conceptions of ourselves, our world, and our moral responsibilities. Schools play a major role in shaping these conceptions, since the nature of the school and its community place more or less emphasis on certain values over other values. Thus, the question of choice carries with it less concern for *how* children are taught and more concern for *what* children are taught. Kane asks, "Who has the right, through the schools, to guide the emerging intellect and spirit of the individual?" (p. 50). Fundamentally, school choice calls for clarity concerning the respective rights and authorities of the individual and the state.

Our democratic system plays a dominant role in ensuring that all children receive an adequate education and that their rights to this education are protected. In other forms of government (e.g., communist, theocratic, and totalitarian), the state assumes a different posture on the degree to which educational choice is permitted. A fine balance must be found in a democratic society in regard to educational choice that ensures that the state plays both a protective role and an enabling role in the intellectual development of its citizenry. Any new education policy, such as school choice, must face the test of how well it ensures the development of both the citizen and the individual.

The notion of choice has a simplistic appeal and may be seen as a fast track to school reform. Kane (1992) warns, however, of striking a Faustian bargain in which we attempt to develop "intellectual capital" for certain economic and political needs and in doing so lose the soul of democracy.

Economic Theory

The notion of intellectual capital fits well with economic theory and its centrality to the school choice movement. School choice advocates often rely on economic or marketplace concepts and words to explain the virtues of school choice. Words such as *consumer, competition, efficiency, excellence, supply and demand,* and *product* are part of the economist's rhetoric.

Elmore (1988) discusses two dimensions of educational choice: The demand side explores the degree to which the consumer should play a central role in determining the nature of the educational product; in the supply side the suppliers are given a degree of autonomy and flexibility in responding to consumer demands. At present, consumers (i.e., parents and taxpayers) do not directly purchase their education system. Also, consumers and providers do not have autonomy in determining the nature of the school system; local boards and professional administrators operate within a framework of federal and state policies. In fact, as pointed out in the Country View case, even when the state exhibited some willingness to lighten up on regulations they found it difficult to support their words with deeds.

The introduction of economic theories and marketplace strategies into the public domain is problematic at best; on the other hand, the bureaucratic system that the state has created to fulfill its educational function is not without problems as well. As Kerchner and Boyd (1988) state, "The hidden hand of the market may prove unsteady in its grip; likewise, governments may not succeed when markets fail to turn private vices into public virtues" (p. 100). They argue that bureaucracies and markets are prone to different failures. Table 9.1 illustrates these failures vis-à-vis the four values of choice, excellence, equity, and efficiency.

As illustrated, each of these values can be compromised by less than ideal circumstances. Often the arguments for school choice are negative arguments, couched in the worse terms. Those favoring market strategies for school choice tend to highlight the worst-case scenarios of public control and public-run bureaucracies; those on the other side point out the worse features and limitations of market strategies. School choice presents us with a public policy dilemma of having to weigh the potential virtues of applying economic theory to public sector needs and services.

Wells and Crain (1992) offer a critique of economic rational choice theory; this assumes that when given tuition vouchers, families will act rationally, in a goal-oriented fashion, in the selection of the best school for their children. They suggest

TABLE 9.1 Market and bureaucratic failures to support four values

	Choice	**Excellence**	**Equity**	**Efficiency**
Market Failure	Too few providers	Undisciplined market	Discriminate by wealth	High transaction costs
Bureaucratic Failure	Inflexibility	Inconsistent or weak standards	Discriminate by political influence	Monopoly costs

SOURCE: W. L. Boyd & C. T. Kerchner, *The Politics of Excellence and Choice in Education,* 1988, The Falmer Press, New York, p. 100.

that such rationality is bounded or constrained by the "lack of market resources and their [families'] perceptions of where they fit into the social hierarchy" (p. 66). It may be more difficult, for example, for poor and minority families to choose schools that are dominated by wealthy and white students. Wells (1991) found this was the case because poor and minority families placed greater emphasis on the comfort and familiarity of their neighborhood school even though they believed that distant suburban schools were better. Bridge and Blackman (1978) observed a similar tendency of parents being inhibited in their gathering of information of school quality factors. Wells and Crain (1992) draw some interesting inferences and raise some tough questions about parent choice and school improvement:

> Indeed, one could argue that maximizing on the social clout of a given school is highly rational, especially for an upwardly mobile family. Similarly, one could argue that maximizing on the comfort, familiarity, and convenience of a same-race school is an equally rational choice for an isolated and alienated black family. But will choices based on such nonacademic factors lead to any real and meaningful educational improvement? Will these "rational choosers" place pressure on schools to provide better services to all children? (p. 70)

Research thus far on school choice suggests that parents and children consider the availability of transportation as the major factor in determining their choice of schools. Rationality, as suggested by economic theory, flounders a bit as a guide when applied to the complex and subjective world of everyday living and survival.

Public Choice Theory

On the other hand, Weeres (1988) creates an interesting argument by suggesting that municipalities and schools have been engaged in a form of market competition for some time. Drawing upon public choice theory, he argues that communities and schools have attempted to maximize their self-interest. It is evident that many communities that have the means have placed considerable emphasis on quality schools in order to be successful in attracting new businesses and manufacturing plants. Several states have engaged in considerable fanfare surrounding their efforts at school improvement. These efforts are reinforced by business leaders who argue that the choice to locate in certain places is based in part on the quality of education in the area. As Weeres points out, however, this form of competition has placed greater pressure on the centralization of educational decision making, particularly at the state level, which ironically runs counter to permitting more decentralization and responsiveness to parents at the local school level.

Decentralization Theory

Decentralization theory offers some support for the school choice movement. The Center for Policy Research in Education (CPRE) (1990) reports on decentralization as a means for improving schools: "The decentralization movement has also gained momentum from the argument that those who are ultimately responsible for the success of teaching and learning—teachers, students and parents—need to participate in key school-level decisions about instruction" (p. 1).

CPRE reports on research that found 25 states experimenting with different levels of decentralization in an attempt to find a balance between state-level and local-level interests. The research reveals four forms of differential treatment being applied to local school districts:

1. accreditation based on outcome measures
2. rewards for high-performing schools and sanctions for low-performing schools
3. technical assistance for low-performing schools
4. regulatory waivers to encourage innovation and flexibility

It is yet to be seen if these adaptations by the states will yield greater local control or just a more sophisticated form of state control and coercion. If the latter be the case, then parent choice and parents' influence on their school of choice will be greatly constrained.

The theories and philosophies that are being used to either defend or attack school choice offer interesting perspectives. As we move to more specific approaches or models for school choice, we will observe elements of these theories and philosophies in their respective designs.

SCHOOL CHOICE MODELS/APPROACHES

School choice models or approaches run the gamut from various forms of privatization to controlled choice. Historically, educational choices included Christian day schools, fundamentalist schools, parochial schools, private schools, and home schools. More recently, starting in the 1960s, we observed the proliferation of alternative schools, which grew in 1981 to an estimated level of 10,000 schools serving 3 million students (Raywid, 1984). In the 1970s, magnet schools embodied the next major movement to provide school choice in response to court-ordered desegregation; today, magnet schools of one form or other exist in nearly every major metropolitan area. In the 1980s, we witnessed further revisions in state policies that expanded beyond these earlier options and created a wider range of experiments with school choice. In this section, we examine some of these strategies and related research.

Voucher Plan

The earliest form of privatization of school choice was the voucher plan. Vouchers, according to Lieberman (1989), "are government payments to consumers or on behalf of consumers who may use the payment at any institution approved by the government for the purpose of the voucher" (p. 7). Often vouchers are pieces of paper inscribed with a monetary value; food stamps are an example. It is anticipated, however, that education vouchers would be in the form of credit to be claimed by a school.

Besides the Alum Rock experiment, the city of Milwaukee has tried the only actual application of a voucher plan. Under the Milwaukee plan, parents may send their children to private, nonsectarian schools in the city. Each participating school receives approximately $2,600 per student, which is the average amount of state aid paid by Wisconsin to the public schools. The school or the parent may provide transportation and either is reimbursed at the end of the school year. The program targets disadvantaged families whose incomes are below 1.75 times the poverty level ($22,000 for a family of three). Participation is limited to 1 percent of Milwaukee's public school population.

Thus far the Milwaukee plan calls for little oversight of the participating private schools, which must meet only one of the following standards:

- At least 70 percent of the voucher students must advance one grade level each year
- Average attendance must reach at least 90 percent
- At least 80 percent of all participating students must demonstrate significant academic progress
- At least 70 percent of the families of voucher students must meet the parental involvement criteria set by the private school

The Carnegie Foundation (1992) concluded in their review of the Milwaukee plan that it

> has failed to demonstrate that vouchers can, in and of themselves, spark school improvement. A few students have been enabled to leave the city's public schools, and they feel pleased with the decision they have made. But no evidence can be found that the participating students made significant academic advances or that either the public or private schools have been revitalized by the transfers. Further, Milwaukee simply does not have enough nonsectarian private schools willing or able to participate in the voucher plan to make much difference to the vast majority of children. (p. 73)

More time may be needed but early indicators suggest that the voucher plan has some limitations and is not necessarily living up to its expectations for bringing about school reform in any sizable way. No doubt the over 600 participating students and six nonsectarian schools that have become schools of choice are deriving some benefits from the Milwaukee voucher plan. As far as having significant impact on the Milwaukee school system, however, we will have to wait and see if more happens.

Charter Schools

Another form of privatization of government services is the contracting out of these services to private sources. In 1991, Minnesota passed legislation permitting the establishment of charter schools. These schools are state funded but operate with a minimum of state control, an arrangement that permits teachers and others the opportunity to create their own schools. Charter schools have three years to meet their stated objectives, including achievement goals, or risk losing their charters.

Districtwide Choice

Generally, districtwide choice permits parents and their children to select schools within the school district's boundaries. The choice, however, is not absolute. Typically, parents list several school choices; final placement is limited by available space and desegregation requirements, and there are usually some controls to prevent creating elitist schools limited to only the gifted, motivated, and well-behaved students.

According to the Carnegie Foundation report (1992), there are only three very successful examples of districtwide choice: East Harlem in New York City; Cambridge, Massachusetts; and Montclair, New Jersey. In the opinion of Carnegie, these three systems are sufficiently different from other forms of districtwide choice to make them notable. First, they have essentially eliminated the neighborhood school concept by requiring parents to be more active decision makers concerning school choice. Second, they have placed a stronger emphasis on cooperation and school improvement throughout the entire system. Third, their respective school choice policies grew out of a long, painstaking, grassroots process.

After carefully examining these three systems and assessing their strengths and limitations, the Carnegie Foundation report concluded that even though these systems have not solved all their problems, they seemed to have lit an innovative spark: "Because of choice there is a strong desire in these districts to continue innovating, to offer more and better options, and above all, to distribute opportunities fairly to all children" (p. 46). The report attributes much of this success to a willingness to work together in shaping a school choice policy that attempts to address concerns for school reform.

Statewide Choice

Statewide choice provides parents and their children an opportunity to choose schools across school district lines. As with districtwide choice, however, there are limitations: Space constraints and the need to maintain desirable levels of racial balance are most prevalent.

Despite its growing popularity with state legislatures and the strong endorsement of the National Governors' Association, statewide choice has been weakly supported by parents. For example, only four-tenths of 1 percent of the Arkansas student population attend schools outside of their school district; on the high end, Minnesota reports about 1.8 percent student involvement. Other states typically range from 0.9 percent to 1.2 percent.

Besides space constraints and desegregation requirements, the Carnegie Foundation reports that parents' satisfaction with their neighborhood school is the most likely reason for limited participation. Further, the report judges that current policies have not resulted in creating sufficiently distinct choices; that most states have not provided sufficient transportation assistance to make other school choices realistic; and that states have not provided sufficient and consistent information or verified its accuracy, making it most difficult for parents to make an informed decision.

Even though the student involvement in statewide choice has been limited, the impact of these choices on smaller and/or poorer school districts has been dramatic in some cases. This can be attributed to the practice of having state funds follow the student; in Iowa, California, and Utah, even a portion of local funds follows students to their new schools. For all these reasons, the Carnegie Foundation concluded "that responsible and effective statewide school choice does not exist in America today" (p. 62).

Controlled Choice

Another form of school choice is controlled choice, usually a euphemism for deseg-regation. Under a controlled choice program, parents are permitted to choose their children's public school as long as their choice does not alter the racial balance of the receiving school. According to Kolb and Rose (1990), controlled choice is guided by three assumptions:

1. More students are likely to achieve at a higher level when schools provide a variety of learning methods, structures and subjects to match student needs
2. The best school system is one in which a diverse population is integrated in all the schools
3. More effective education occurs when students, parents and school staff work together to decide what kind of education the community's schools should offer (p. 38)

According to Young and Clinchy (1992), Cambridge, Massachusetts, successfully implemented a controlled choice intradistrict plan as part of their desegregation effort begun two years earlier. Under this plan, families may choose among the districts' 13 K-8 schools, each of which offers alternative programs ranging from language immersion to whole language with many different varieties in between. Parents submit their preferences to a parent information center, which is responsible for the final placement of students. Criteria used in making these assignments include

- racial balance, by which no school may enroll more than 55 percent minority or majority students
- distance from school, with closer students given preference
- school assignment of siblings (students with a sibling in the school have preference)

According to Young and Clinchy (1992), the Cambridge controlled choice program has been successful (improved achievement test scores support this claim) in part because schools are not allowed to set selective criteria for admission. Schools are selected on the basis of interests and all programs are open to students. Parents, however, do have to provide their own transportation. Young and Clinchy believe that the "'controlled choice model,' appears to hold the most promise for promoting accountability, equity, and diversity" (p. 31).

Controlled choice programs offer a balance between individual freedom and social conformity. Admittedly, choice is circumscribed by the number, variety, and quality of schools available, but there are some genuine choices, and the public's interest in providing racial and socioeconomic diversity, as part of the educational process, is protected.

Home Schooling

Lieberman (1989) sees home schooling as a way for public schools to shed some of their load. Generally, home schooling "refers to any effort to meet compulsory education statutes by instruction in the family residence " (p. 274). Home schooling often has to walk a tightrope in satisfying state compulsory attendance laws and curriculum requirements. Home schooling opportunities usually grow out of parents' and children's personal concerns. In some cases, parents may feel the school is unable to provide the kind of individual attention and support that they can in the comfort of their home; other parents are trying to avoid an uncomfortable situation where they either disapprove of the educational program of the school or feel that their child is at some risk in attending the school.

Lieberman summarizes four educational arguments for home schooling:

1. The family is the most important educative influence on children
2. Children educated in school tend to succumb to peer pressures which are outside the control of the teacher
3. The family is most important to the social and emotional development of children
4. Home schooling fosters constructive social development (p. 285)

It is difficult to pin down the magnitude of home schooling, except to note that all states permit some type of home instruction. However, only 23 of them have laws that govern home schooling; 18 allow home schools if the process for approval is followed; 17 require standardized testing; and 3 states require that the home school teacher be certified (Sherrer, 1991). Lieberman estimates that 200,000 families and 500,000 children were involved in home schooling in 1987. Sherrer cites the number of home-schoolers in New England alone increasing from 371 in April, 1989, to 627 in February, 1991.

It is equally difficult to establish the success of home schooling. Frost and Morris's (1988) research illustrates the problem. They report four sources of test data on home-schoolers' performance; however, they question the results of three studies because of the reliance on parent-administered exams. In the one study that had better controls, home-schoolers were found to outperform their in-school counterparts in all areas except math. Other research (Moore, 1979; Fox, 1987; Ray, 1987) generally supports the claim that home-schoolers score about the national average on academic achievement tests. In spite of the often heard complaints of educators, home-schoolers do not appear to suffer in obtaining an education and may even be better adjusted socially and emotionally, particularly in having high self-esteem.

School choice comes in many forms and will no doubt continue to expand and contract with the winds of educational change. The research results are often mixed and not totally reliable in answering questions of the effectiveness of these alternative approaches. But as we know, decisions about educational issues often are not resolved by research findings but through political debates and power. In the next section, we shall delineate the arguments put forth by various interest groups for or against school choice.

PROS AND CONS OF SCHOOL CHOICE

As can be expected, any tampering with the status quo will get a response from persons most threatened by the change and those who see the greatest possible benefits. School choice is no exception, and the battle lines have been drawn and redrawn depending on the latest adaptation or proposal. Probably the most controversial aspects of school choice surface when various approaches begin to cross the hazy lines between church and state and public and private domains. As we review the pro and con positions, their arguments will link to these controversial areas.

Arguments for School Choice

Proponents of school choice form a strange amalgam of liberals, conservatives, religious leaders, civil rights activists, economists, and politicians. This group of strange bedfellows seems to share one thing in common: They believe schools, as currently organized, do not address the concerns and needs of American society, and that only through parent activism, in the form of school choice, can schools be forced to change.

Their concerns are that public schools have become too large and bureaucratized and thus unresponsive to the needs of students. Teachers are seen as being less concerned with the needs of children and more interested in the "perquisites of their profession" (Lee & Sexton, 1988, p. 79). Chubb and Moe (1990) argue: "When it comes to educational decision making, particularly at the state and local levels where effective authority resides, the most powerful political groups by far are those with vested interests in the current institutional system" (p. 12). As a consequence, Lee and Sexton argue, "public schools are becoming increasingly top heavy with administrators, cost per student in the public schools has been rising, and there has been a dramatic drop in the SAT scores over the last 20 years, most pronounced among students who attend public schools" (p. 80). Dekis (1987) expresses the concern of conservative Christians with the "breakdown of discipline, a lack of emphasis on basic skills, and a neglect of moral values and religion" (p. 52) in the public schools.

Parents are often outside the loop on important decisions concerning their child's education and cannot compete with the entrenched power structure of educational professionals. Parents seem to have little to say about "which schools their children will attend, which teachers will teach them, what content they will study, when and how they will study it, what values will be emphasized and enforced, which educational goals will be paramount and which goals will receive short shrift" (Raywid, 1987, p. 767).

It is through parent choice that this power imbalance can be righted. Allowing choice, proponents argue, will empower families and give them greater legitimacy for participating in important decisions concerning the education of their children. This may be particularly true of traditionally disenfranchised groups such as the poor and minorities. It is through school choice that there can be a reallocation of power. Finn (1989) expresses it quite well: "Choice augurs a rearrangement of power and authority relationships in American education, and the farther reaching and more comprehensive the choice policy, the more total the reallocation of power" (p. 32). A way to turn this power relationship into a more positive force is with school choice. Elmore (1988) sees experimenting with choice as "a way of engaging creative energy of parents and educators in the solution of serious educational problems, independent of whether choice by itself is a good or effective thing to do" (p. 94).

The Carnegie Foundation report (1992) cites three arguments most frequently used to support school choice:

1. Choice is a key ingredient of school improvement
2. Choice will give disadvantaged families educational opportunities now only available to the affluent
3. Choice is a fundamental right rooted in the American experience

Young and Clinchy (1992) would add accountability to this list of arguments: "Choice promotes accountability because a public school no longer has a captive clientele that can be taken for granted" (p. 12). In other words, when parents unhappy with their school situation are free to explore other options, schools are forced to compete for students; any dramatic dip in enrollment sends a clear message to the school that something has to change.

A well-designed choice program, such as the controlled choice program of Cambridge, Massachusetts, can address major issues facing school systems, particularly in urban areas. The issues of equity and diversity can be better resolved in a situation where general guidelines of school choice address these problems directly. Forced busing and other mandated programs without school choice have had serious repercussions and created a backlash from the people for whom these policies were designed. Controlled choice, with the express purpose of ensuring both equity and diversity goals, has real potential to alleviate the negative effects of racial segregation and inequitable distribution of school funds.

The advocates of school choice have been persuasive in recognizing the ills and deficiencies of American schools and drawing upon our democratic ideals and marketplace theories to propose a strategy to improve schools. It is difficult to argue against choice when it is such a part of our culture. On the other hand, as we will discover from those who do not favor a school choice option, much can go astray on the way to implementing choice plans. In spite of some serious concerns about relying on school choice for solving our educational problems, choice advocates, like Chubb and Moe (1990), are not very shy in their claims for school choice:

> Without being too literal about it, we think reformers would do well to entertain the notion that choice *is* a panacea. This is our way of saying that choice is not like the other reforms and should not be combined with them as part of a reformist strategy for improving America's schools. Choice is a self-contained reform strategy with its own rationale and justification. It has the capacity *all by itself* to bring about the kind of transformation that, for years, reformers have been seeking to engineer in myriad of ways. . . . The whole point of a thoroughgoing system of choice is to free the schools from disabling constraints by sweeping away the old institutions and replacing them with new ones. (p. 217)

Arguments against School Choice

It is easier to find faults in proposed changes than to thoroughly test them over time; this is no less true for those who oppose school choice strategies. On the other hand, critics have serious and legitimate concerns about the rush to implement new school choice policies. The counterarguments run the gamut from suggesting that too little is known about the impact of school choice to suggesting that too much is expected of choice in solving the complex problems facing our schools. It is not surprising that much of the opposition to school choice comes from the educational establishment.

Shanker (1992), the former president of the American Federation of Teachers (AFT), has expressed grave doubts about school choice. For him, education is not a product to be purchased from a vendor, but rather it is a public good and in a democracy is part of the community's responsibility to prepare future citizens. He has indicated some willingness to support school choice among public schools only, which is also the policy position of the National Education Association (NEA). The National PTA expresses some concerns that not all students' needs, especially low-income and minority students, will be well served by school choice policies. The National School Boards Association and American Association of School Administrators express skepticism about the potential of school choice and, as with the AFT and NEA, strongly oppose public funds for private schools.

Rinehart and Lee (1991) discuss 12 common criticisms of privatization and choice:

1. Private schools may not give proper attention to socially important topics such as AIDS education, nutrition, or careers
2. Privatization will cause some schools to become resegregated
3. A system of private schools would be unfair to the poor and disadvantaged

4. Many parents would not or could not make appropriate educational choices for their children
5. Educational standards would surely fall under a privatized system
6. Privatization would dehumanize the schools. Students would be viewed only as dollar signs
7. Choice plans may be workable for cities and other densely populated areas, but they will never work in rural areas where students have to commute long distances
8. Transportation would be a problem for many students and thus place a limit on their freedom of choice
9. Many students and teachers could be hurt by the transition to a new system of privatized schools
10. Some students are so disruptive or problematical that no school would admit them. What would happen to these students?
11. Fraudulent and dishonest school owners and teachers would take advantage of students and parents
12. Why go through all this trouble since a privatized school system is no cure-all? (pp. 142–58)

Pearson (1993) is skeptical about business roundtables and chief executive officers of large corporations being in favor of school choice, since business operates to make a profit and school taxes cut into these profits. Many states are facing significant budget problems at the same time there are cries to improve our schools. As Pearson observes, "Education reform and improvement has traditionally meant more tax dollars—until choice. Choice provides the perfect marriage of convenience for business and politics. Now you can have reform at no additional cost" (p. 18). Choice in this context provides the opportunity to create the illusion of significant educational change while not having to provide large sums of additional tax monies.

After careful study of choice programs in Holland, Canada, and Australia, Brown (1992) concluded: "Choice will not result in market incentives to improve education. Choice will not improve educational opportunities for the poor. Choice will promote traditional schools, not innovative ones. Choice will not alter the influence of professional educators or increase the influence of parents in the schooling process. Private schools will become de facto public schools" (p. 184). In Brown's research, parents, students, and teachers continue to prefer traditional schools over innovative ones. The best way to ensure improvement of schools, according to Brown, is through fiscal parity. He is fearful that choice programs will produce a dual school system of rich and poor schools, similar to the situation in Australia.

The opponents of school choice do not paint a rosy picture when it comes to anticipating the results of choice. They strongly feel it is a misguided effort that is distracting the public from more serious forms of school reform. It gives the impression of being an easy way of improving schools while overlooking the need for additional resources and hard work. School choice does not win high marks from the educational profession, with the possible exception of choice among public schools only. Even under a controlled choice framework, however, there is skepticism that school choice is a disguise for reducing taxes. More information and research are needed to check out the promises of the proponents and to answer the questions of the opponents.

CONCLUSION

School choice comes in many forms, and thus far we have had only a limited amount of experience with this innovation. Those who favor expanding school choice are true believers and strong advocates; on the other side, we can see the risks involved and understand the calls for caution. Possibly, if a choice plan is done correctly, it stands a chance to increase the educational opportunities for students and their families. Nathan (1987) suggests 10 features to be included in a desirable choice plan:

1. a specific list of skills and knowledge expectations
2. transportation for low-income children
3. student assignment procedures that advance desegregation, which means that unlimited choice will be unlikely
4. parent information and counseling
5. interdistrict transfers
6. fiscal protection for small districts
7. equalized funding across districts
8. planning, training, and professional development funds available to teachers
9. a survey of parent preferences and system assessment
10. continuing oversight so the system does not experience unexpected results (p. 750)

These qualifications make sense in light of the criticisms leveled at school choice proposals. In tight, and possibly even in good fiscal times, however, it is difficult to see states and local communities providing the resources to support Nathan's features. School choice would no longer appear to be the bargain that some of its advocates suggest; to others, it would be seen as taking needed resources away from mainstream educational concerns.

Young (1992) provides a planning process derived from studying school systems that successfully implemented a controlled choice program. He suggests four distinct phases:

- Phase I: Mechanisms for Initial Planning
  - Build a constituency
  - Create a citywide parent/professional/community council
  - Conduct parent/professional surveys
- Phase II: Development of a "Controlled" Choice Plan
  - Develop a student assignment policy
  - Design a "controlled" choice plan

- Create a parent information system
- Phase III: Planning Individual Alternatives or Magnets
    - Establish individual school planning teams
    - Develop an individual school plan
- Phase IV: Implementation
    - Inform the community
    - Assign staff and students to alternatives or magnets
      (pp. 108–22)

This planning process should provide an opportunity to speak to the many features Nathan suggests are needed for an effective school choice program. Young does caution that the above planning process and actual implementation take time and commitment to the concepts of accountability, equity, and diversity. Young adds further a key point: "Choice without a variety of high-quality and diverse options to choose from is a pseudo-innovation that produces little significant change" (p. 124). With quality choices, school choice has the potential of making a big difference in the lives of American students. This is particularly true when school choice takes on the tone and orientation that the teachers have ascribed to it at Country View Junior and Senior High School. These committed professionals are not waiting for external policymakers to define solutions for them. Their experience suggests that choice may be more in the mind of the chooser than in some externally perceived or mandated reality.

DISCUSSION QUESTIONS

1. If you were asked to give a presentation at an upcoming parent meeting on school choice, what points would you emphasize and what position would you advocate?
2. As an educational professional, do you support the criticisms of school choice? Why? Would you support "controlled" school choice? Why or why not?
3. Are there alternative forms of school choice not presently being advocated that you believe are more feasible than current models or approaches?
4. What stance do you believe educational leaders should take on the issue of school choice?

SUGGESTED ACTIVITIES

1. Set up a debate between two groups, one pro-school-choice and the other anti-choice. Each group should conduct additional research on the topic and then argue its position to a neutral panel of laypersons.
2. Conduct a survey in your school district of parents, teachers, and students concerning their opinions on school choice and under what conditions, if any, the idea would be acceptable to them.
3. Contact persons in any neighboring school system who are experimenting with a school choice program and ascertain their opinions on the effectiveness of their plans.

4. Write to or contact legislative leaders concerning their opinions and understanding of school choice.

REFERENCES

Bridge, R. G., & Blackman, J. (1978). *A study of alternatives in American education, Vol. IV: Family choice in schooling.* Santa Monica, CA: The Rand Corporation.

Brown, F. (1992). The Dutch experience with school choice: Implications for American education. In P. W. Cookson, Jr. (Ed.), *The choice controversy* (pp. 171-89). Newbury Park, CA: Corwin.

The Carnegie Foundation for the Advancement of Teaching. (1992). *School choice.* Princeton, NJ: author.

Center for Policy Research in Education. (May, 1990). *Decentralization and policy design.* New Brunswick, NJ: author.

Chubb, J. E., & Moe, T. M. (1990). *Politics, markets, and America's schools.* Washington, D.C.: The Brookings Institution.

Coons, J. E., & Sugarman, S. (1978). *Education by choice: The case for family control.* Berkeley: University of California Press.

Dekis, J. H. (May, 1987). Should government help kids attend public school? *Christianity, 31,* 52-53.

Elmore, R. F. (1988). Choice in public education. In W. L. Boyd & C. T. Kerchner (Eds.), *The politics of excellence and choice in education* (pp. 79-98). New York: Falmer.

Finn, C. E. (November, 1989). The choice backlash. *National Review, 41,* 30-32.

Fox, L. P. (1987). Home school curricula: Constitutional issues. *Dissertation Abstracts International, 48/05,* (University Microfilms No. DA8719157).

Friedman, M. (1962). *Capitalism and freedom.* Chicago: University of Chicago Press.

Frost, E. A., & Morris, R. C. (1988). Does home school work? Some insights for academic success. *Contemporary Education, 59,*(4) 223-27.

Gallup, A. M. (1986). The 18th annual Gallup Poll of the public's attitude toward the public schools. *Phi Delta Kappan, 68*(1), 56.

Johanek, M. (1992). Private citizenship and school choice. In P. W. Cookson Jr. (Ed.), *The choice controversy* (pp. 146-70). Newbury Park, CA: Corwin.

Kane, J. (1992). Choice: The fundamentals revisited. In P. W. Cookson Jr. (Ed.), *The choice controversy* (pp. 46-54). Newbury Park, CA: Corwin.

Kerchner, C. T., & Boyd, W. L. (1988). What doesn't work: An analysis of market and bureaucratic failure in schooling. In W. L. Boyd & C. T. Kerchner (Eds.), *The politics of excellence and choice in education* (pp. 99-116). New York: Falmer.

Kolb, F. A., & Rose, R. (December, 1990/January, 1991). Controlled choice in Fall River, Massachusetts. *Educational Leadership, 48*(4), 38.

Lee, D. R., & Sexton, R. L. (September, 1988). The public school lobby vs. educational vouchers. *USA Today, 117,* 79-81.

Lieberman, M. (1989). *Privatization and educational choice.* New York: St. Martin's Press.

Moore, R. (1979). *America's greatest educational system.* (ERIC Document Reproduction Service No. ED 192 873).

Nathan, J. (1987). Results and future prospects of state efforts to increase choice among schools. *Phi Delta Kappan, 68,* 746-52.

Office of Educational Research and Improvement. (August, 1992). *Getting started: How choice can renew your public schools.* Washington, D.C.: U.S. Department of Education.

Pearson, J. (1993). *Myths of educational choice.* Westport, CT: Praeger.

Rasmussen, R. (1981). *A study of alternatives in American education, Vol. III: Teachers' responses to alternatives.* Santa Monica, CA: The Rand Corporation.

Ray, B. D. (1987). On case studies of four families engaged in home education. *Home School Researcher, 3*(3), 5-10.

Raywid, M. A. (April, 1984). Synthesis of research on schools of choice. *Educational Leadership, 41*(7), 70-78.

Raywid, M. A. (June, 1987). Public choice, yes, vouchers, no! *Phi Delta Kappan, 68,* 762-69.

Rinehart, J. R., & Lee, J. F. (1991). *American education and the dynamics of choice.* New York: Praeger.

Schmookler, A. B. (1993). *The illusion of choice.* Albany: State University of New York Press.

Shanker, A. (July, 1992). Bush's new voucher program: G.I. bull. *The New Republic, 207*(30), 23.

Sherrer, M. K. (May, 1991). *Home schooling in rural New England: An alternative educational choice.* Unpublished doctoral dissertation, University of Vermont.

Weeres, J. G. (1988). Economic choice and the dissolution of community. In W. L. Boyd & C. T. Kerchner (Eds.), *The politics of excellence and choice in education* (pp. 117-30). New York: Falmer.

Wells, A. S. (1991). *The sociology of school choice: A study of black students' participation in a voluntary transfer plan.* Unpublished doctoral dissertation, Teachers College, Columbia University.

Wells, A. S., & Crain, R. L. (1992). Do parents choose school quality or school status? A sociological theory of free market education. In P. W. Cookson Jr. (Ed.), *The choice controversy* (pp. 65-82). Newbury Park, CA: Corwin.

Young, T. W., & Clinchy, E. (1992). *Choice in public education.* New York: Teachers College, Columbia University.

chapter **10**

School Restructuring

Restructuring is a word in vogue, not only in educational circles, but also in the business arena. As major corporations face huge losses or bankruptcy, their solution to these financial problems is often a restructuring of their operations. It is no wonder, given the influence of business on the public sector, that restructuring would be seen as a solution to educational problems. As many political and educational leaders are discovering, however, that which can be easily ordered by a chief executive officer of a large corporation or Chapter 11 federal bankruptcy judge is very different from what a local school board president or school superintendent can demand at the local school level. A result of these organizational differences has been a restructuring effort in education that has taken on many shapes with varying degrees of success. Because of these complexities and other influences, school restructuring has come to mean different things to different people. As Kirst puts it, "Restructuring is a word that means everything and nothing simultaneously. . . . It is in the eyes of beholder" (cited in Reavis and Griffith, 1992, p. 2).

Murphy (1991) reinforces the value of multiple perspectives in understanding school restructuring:

> Looking in multiple directions, or using multiple frames, to understand the phenomenon of restructuring of schools enhances the portrait we are able to paint. At one level, the use of multiple perspectives helps guarantee that all the parts are included in the picture. At a second level, it ensures that subtle differences and contrasts are faithfully captured. Finally, it helps make explicit the tensions and rough edges likely to be overlooked when only one or two perspectives are employed. (p. x)

Restructuring not only needs to be understood from varying perspectives, but as a metaphor, it provides an opportunity to perceive the operations of educational systems in yet another light. According to Moorman and Egermeier (1992), restructuring as a concept provides a framework in which people can engage in a dialogue over what seem to be intractable and deeply troubling problems: "It [restructuring] provides the basis for reframing problematic situations so that effective social action can be taken" (p. 21). They compare the present restructuring movement in education with Cohen, March, and Olsen's (1972) notion of the organizational "garbage can," in which poorly structured problems, solutions, and choice situations are in search of one another.

Country View High School epitomized this condition as the faculty and administration cast about for an understanding of their problems *and* emerging educational innovations. Their in-service meetings involved lengthy discussions on the needs of the school ranging from dealing with at-risk students to increasing adult literacy and of new educational strategies ranging from mastery learning to heterogeneous grouping. Their experience illustrates the power of introducing the concept of restructuring into the lexicon of the school staff. Moorman and Egermeier (1992) express it well: "The restructuring metaphor has stirred up the 'garbage can,' bringing to light problems and solutions that have been buried or strewn about the edges" (p. 25).

As a consequence of stirring up the "garbage can," restructuring has taken on many different meanings and definitions. Tye (1992) defines restructuring as "programs designed to foster decentralized decision making and site-based management" (p. 10). O'Neil (1990) greatly expands this definition by citing the National Governors' Association's (Elmore, 1988) framework:

- *curriculum and instruction* modifications
- *authority and decision making* decentralization
- *new staff roles* created to encourage greater collaboration
- *accountability systems* linking rewards and incentives to student performance (p. 6)

In Reavis and Griffith's (1992) view there is a national consensus emerging on the "seven elements of restructuring":

1. site-based decision making
2. a shift to a market-drive orientation
3. an increase in and shift in the focus of technology use
4. a shift in instructional emphasis linked to new understandings of human cognition
5. a shift in curriculum with more emphasis on students constructing their own meaning
6. a shift to hierarchies within teaching
7. a change in accountability toward more performance-oriented/real life assessments of students (p. 2)

Reavis and Griffith argue that the restructuring effort in the United States is no small matter and cite a 1989 survey of the Council of Chief School Officers, which reported 30 states having implemented one or more of these aspects of restructuring.

Murphy (1991) takes a systems view of restructuring: "Restructuring generally encompasses systemic changes in one or more of the following: work roles and organizational milieu; organizational and governance structures, including connections among the school and its larger environment; and core technology" (p. 15). He believes systemic changes get at the relationships between state officials, usually employed in state departments of education, school districts' superintendent and staff, and local school principals and teachers. Each of these relationships is significantly altered in a restructuring effort with greater decision-making authority delegated to classroom teachers. To many persons, restructuring involves turning the hierarchical organizational chart upside down and placing the teacher at the top, the commissioner of education at the bottom, and the school superintendent and principal in between. According to Murphy, restructuring places greater emphasis on teachers as leaders; principals, superintendents, and state officials as facilitators; and students as workers.

In Moorman and Egermeier's (1992) view, restructuring is a process to determine the best way of improving educational performance. They conclude: "Restructuring is thus an effort to crystallize from disparate parts of knowledge and belief an alternative conceptualization of what education can and should be and how we can achieve a new vision" (p. 16). Or as Lewis (1989) suggests, "Perhaps restructuring can best be described as renewal" (p. iv).

For our purposes, this chapter on school restructuring will focus on systemic alterations that develop new arrangements, roles, and relationships. Although some writers include both school choice and site-based management as part of the restructuring movement, these components are explored separately. As we observed in chapter 9, school choice can produce little substantive change in how schools are organized and/or operated. On the other hand, school-site or site-based management is a major manifestation of restructuring and will be given special treatment in the next chapter.

This chapter initially will explore some background to show how restructuring as a school reform strategy became a major effort of the 1990s. Following this, we will review various theories of school restructuring, including common sense theory, open systems theory, quality of work life theory, and some aspects of political and economic theory. With these concepts as backdrops, more specific models or approaches to school restructuring are presented, followed by an examination of the pros and cons of restructuring. We will then draw some general conclusions at the end of the chapter. Throughout and where appropriate, we will revisit our case, *Hope Springs Eternal,* to illustrate aspects of school restructuring.

BACKGROUND

It is important to appreciate the origins of the calls for school restructuring. School restructuring in many ways grew out of the perceived problems with educational bureaucracies and failures of previous efforts at school reform. As we learned earlier, school bureaucracies have come to be known as organizations that emphasize division of labor; hierarchical levels of authority; actions based on written policies, rules, and regulations; an impersonal environment; and career orientation. These traits may have been appropriate when our schools were characterized more by homogeneity of students and adults and had a consensus of purpose. Reavis and Griffith (1992) write:

> Students must be sufficiently uniform to be "batch processed," or they must be pliable enough so they can be shaped for batch processing. In a similar vein, teachers must either be uniform or must be pliable enough that they can be batch processed. As long as these assumptions hold, the bureaucratic organization can be both efficient and effective. However, students are becoming increasingly diverse through immigration, changing social mores, and access to external technological resources such as computers and television. Similarly, teachers are no longer the compliant, lower-middle-class females that for decades filled the ranks of teaching. (p. 4)

Reavis and Griffith describe how in many ways the bureaucratic form of school organizations created major problems with which present educational leaders must cope. For example, a tightly structured curriculum precludes teacher discretion in meeting the needs of students; emphasis on student control that stresses orderliness and routine defeats the goal of creating an independent thinker. Also, bureaucracies have a way of becoming self-serving, which places greater emphasis on procedures and precedent than on creativity and entrepreneurship. Further, bureaucratic schools, particularly secondary schools, have become highly segmented, which makes it very difficult to accommodate any educational innovations.

Lewis (1989) explores a number of reasons why there is greater emphasis at present on radical, bottom-up change as opposed to incremental improvements:

- *business/industry demand for survival*—Large corporations see their survival and competitive edge closely linked to radical school reform. Future and present workers must have the ability to self-regulate and self-direct their work, have conflict resolution skills, and be capable of higher-order thinking. Also, because of the declining labor pool, we cannot afford high levels of school dropouts.

- *military increase in requirements*—Once viewed as the employer of last resort, the military is now declining as a viable option for high school dropouts. The U.S. Army recruits exclusively high school graduates because of the increased use of technology in the military.

- *women still being held back*—Underachievement and lack of recognition of women's potential can result in a serious depletion of needed talent in the future.

- *avoidance of a social disaster*—Good educational programs can avoid the establishment of a two-tier society, dividing the well-educated and affluent from the less-educated and poor.

- *need for building anew and rebuilding*—There is a growing need to provide more care and educational opportunities for the very young (birth to age five); to establish dropout prevention programs, particularly at the middle school or junior high levels; and to serve needy families with integrated educational and social services.
- *engagement and bonding issues*—A growing concern is the lack of motivation of present-day youth in engaging learning opportunities. In addition, there appears to be less interest in bonding to one's community and in taking civic responsibility. There is growing evidence that youth are more engaged in unskilled employment than taking part in voluntary community service.
- *a new valuing of teaching*—Greater recognition has been given recently to the central role of teachers in motivating and teaching students important skills and understanding. Efforts at including teachers in school reform initiatives have shown that teacher involvement is essential to successful school change.

According to Murphy (1991), the fundamental conclusion from a number of analyses of educational systems and the need for school restructuring was that "schools were characterized by intellectual softness, a lack of expectations and standards, inadequate leadership, a dysfunctional organizational structure, conditions of employment inconsistent with professional work, and the absence of any meaningful accountability . . . the basic infrastructure was found to be in need of serious repair" (p. viii).

In spite of these strong arguments for reexamining and redesigning the organizational nature of schools, there are forces against school restructuring. Lewis (1989) suggests a number of "pulls" against basic restructuring: short-range views, overriding impatience, settling for minimums, competing demands, taking the easy route, ambiguous goals, and the lack of incentives.

In any event, the conditions outlined above raise strong arguments for school restructuring. Reavis and Griffith (1992) define characteristics of restructured school systems that build on a central tenet of teamwork:

- a flatter organization
- management functioning as coordinators and facilitators
- decisions made by groups and at the lowest level
- greater diversity among schools
- a broader set of indices for student performance
- teachers assuming greater responsibility for total school reform
- collaborative relationships between teachers and administrators
- student learning as the primary focus for school decisions
- strenuous efforts at eliminating organizational elements that do not promote greater integration of educational programs

School restructuring is more than modifying a few courses or hiring aides or another specialist to support classroom teachers; this background review suggests it is a deeper and more significant departure from past practices. School restructuring calls for a basic reshaping of a school's mission, a reorganization to meet this new mission, new assumptions about how teachers relate to each other and to administrators, grouping students differently for instruction and having them play a new role in the learning process, and more focus on integrating and evaluating the curriculum. In one way or another, Country View manifested many of these dimensions as they addressed and altered their way of operating to meet the demands associated with their restructuring goals.

THEORIES OF SCHOOL RESTRUCTURING

Much of the school restructuring literature suffers from a lack of theory to guide the various approaches. Certainly the persons at Country View did not operate from any overarching theory; they took a very pragmatic view of their problems and tried to match them with various existing educational innovations. Country View revisited its school mission, designated a middle school concept, initiated heterogeneous grouping of ninth graders, and encouraged team teaching, to name a few examples. Newmann (1993) refers to this as an implied theory "grounded largely on the assumption that new organizational structures will increase either the commitment or the competence of teachers and students" (p. 4). This approach to school restructuring is extensive and forms a basis for what Newmann refers to as a common sense theory. Other theories include an amalgam of economic and political theory often identified as decentralization, open systems theory, and quality of work life theory.

Common Sense Theory

Common sense theory supports inferences about the connections between organizational structure and student outcomes. Newmann (1993) defines the possibilities: "New organizational structures will presumably either increase the commitment (motivation) of adults to teach and students to learn or they will increase the competence (technical capacity) of adults to offer a better learning environment" (p. 5). These twin outcomes of commitment and competence are essential to successful school restructuring efforts. For Newmann, these twin perspectives are dependent on four themes:

- Theme 1: *Depth of understanding and authentic learning*—Greater emphasis is placed on student learning that goes beyond the traditional orientation of the transmission and reproduction of rote knowledge. The desire is to move beyond the "basics" and apply knowledge to more complex and real-life problems.
- Theme 2: *Success for all students*—Greater emphasis is placed on teaching all students, especially those from culturally diverse backgrounds and with histories of school failure.

- Theme 3: *New roles for teachers*—Greater emphasis is placed on conducting a complete analysis of what new roles are needed and reinforcement for and education in the roles that new structures require.
- Theme 4: *Schools as caring communities*—Greater emphasis is placed on not only the qualities of the individuals but also the qualities desired for the school as an organization.

These four themes can be supported by what Newmann calls the building blocks of a common sense theory of educational restructuring: high standards for both teachers' and students' performance, high incentives/high stakes for persons to commit the energy to these high standards, local empowerment for teachers and parents, and collaborative organization to achieve collective goals.

Common sense theory offers a framework for explaining the purposes and problems of school restructuring. It is rooted in the common practices of schools addressing core issues with dramatic and often radical solutions. It stands on the faith that a process of restructuring will contribute to the twin goals of competence and commitment of teachers and students—an ambitious agenda that will no doubt create significant tensions between persons with traditional and those with progressive views of education.

Decentralization Theory

As Murphy (1991) points out, decentralization theory is buttressed by political and economic arguments. Decentralization builds on the proposition that the closer the governance process is to the people affected, the more responsive it is to their demands and interests. Murphy observes: "Interwoven in this grassroots notion of responsiveness are issues of democracy, constituent influence and control over organizational decisions, ownership of public institutions, trust, and organizational accountability" (p. 1). Decentralization potentially allows for greater participation in governance, facilitates the change process, and prevents outside power centers from controlling an organization.

Proponents of decentralization argue that it provides a theoretical orientation for guiding school restructuring efforts. Advocates of school-based management, for example, see decentralization theory as a central argument in delegating greater autonomy and control to teachers at the local school level. From a political perspective, teachers would be more responsive to their "clients" and in turn would receive more support. With greater authority and responsibility often comes greater accountability. Instead of implementing someone else's plan, teachers become responsible for defining their own plans and implementation processes. They no longer can defer to outside authorities to defend their practices but must assume more responsibility for their actions. Parents and students can get closer to the center of action and have some influence on the decisions being rendered on their behalf. The delegation of authority to the local school should result in greater responsiveness to student and family needs and theoretically improve the educational process.

From an economic perspective, decentralization encourages greater competition and cost effectiveness. With the delegation of authority, school staffs are forced to address not only curricular and instructional issues but also budgetary issues. An awareness of the limitation of funds and how best to allocate these monies becomes the responsibility of persons who, under a more centralized system, would not normally have to address this issue directly. Reality sets in when resources to meet the rising demands and expectations of teachers and parents are limited: Choices become more critical, forcing schools to balance pressing needs and limited funds. Under decentralized conditions, it becomes increasingly clear that meeting the needs of students requires not only parent and community moral support but also financial support. There is even some evidence decentralization can save up to 2 or 3 percent of a school district's budget (Carnoy & MacDonell, 1990).

In chapter 11, we will explore decentralization theory and its various applications in more depth. Here, it is sufficient to say that decentralization can potentially establish new and significantly different relationships between teachers at the local school level and their supervisors at the district and state levels. The implications of these new relationships for school reform are yet unknown, but decentralization theory is stimulating many interesting applications for new forms of school governance.

Open Systems Theory

In chapter 5, we examined systems thinking as a metaphor for organizations. Open systems theory provides a framework for the restructuring of schools (cf. Chrispeels, 1992). It recognizes that schools are complex social organizations made up of numerous internal and external processes and relationships. Under this theory, schools are seen as having multiple internal subsystems and being embedded within multiple external suprasystems. As with multiple boxes contained within one another, the school is located in the middle of this hierarchy (see Figure 10.1). As we move away from the school we see layers or boxes that include the immediate school community, the school district and larger community, and the state and federal governments. There is a constant flow of energy and information back and forth between these layers of suprasystems often expressed as inputs, outputs, and feedback. As a metaphor, the nested boxes help us visualize the boundaries between the various suprasystems but also demonstrates their closeness to and influence upon the whole system. Other elements of open systems theory are the presence of purposes or goals and transformative or throughput processes.

The implications of open systems theory for school restructuring are numerous. First, it highlights the complexities of school restructuring and the ripple effect upon adjoining systems of any changes that may occur at the local school level. Schools obviously do not operate in a vacuum and thus are seriously constrained by systems in their environment. These interlocking relationships offer a second implication for school restructuring and partially explain why dramatic changes are so difficult to implement. Over time, as a school interacts with its environment, it establishes a certain homeostasis. This balance in external relationships allows the school, as a system, to

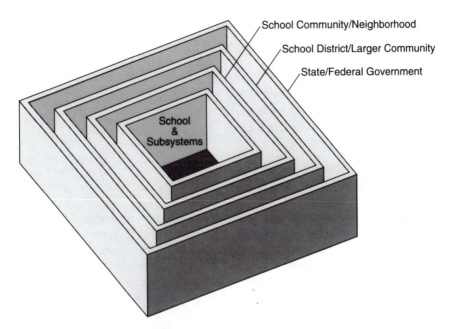

School Community/Neighborhood
School District/Larger Community
State/Federal Government

School & Subsystems

FIGURE 10.1   Systems within systems

operate without excessive tensions. However, as soon as any changes of the magnitude of school restructuring are introduced into the open system, the environmental systems will react. It is more often the case than not that these external systems will attempt to maintain the status quo. The experience of Country View illustrates this phenomenon well. When they attempted to deviate from the traditional form of a certified principal in charge of the school to a troika of teacher-leaders, they ran into resistance: They were informed that this arrangement was not possible because of state licensure regulations. Obviously, the state department of education had a different view of Country View's troika plan for school leadership and was not as flexible as the school had hoped. Open systems theory reminds us that school restructuring plans face a test beyond the system's boundaries that may preempt the best of intentions.

Quality of Work Life

Schools, as organizations, provide working conditions on a continuum from healthy to unhealthy. Teachers often work under conditions of high stress with threats to personal safety and long hours with minimal breaks. These conditions along with low salaries and a lack of public support have led to a demoralization of the teaching profession. Several school improvement efforts have attempted to address this problem by increasing the professionalization of teachers. Most school restructuring models or approaches alter appreciably the working conditions of teachers.

According to Louis (1992), the quality of work life (QWL) indicators include seven criteria consistent with educational reform efforts:

- respect for adults
- participation in decision making
- frequent and stimulating professional interaction
- frequent, accurate feedback, leading to a higher sense of efficacy
- use of skills and knowledge
- resources to carry out the job
- goal congruence

Louis (1992) reports on eight case studies of schools attempting to determine what QWL indicators are most compelling for teachers. The findings went beyond the initial QWL indicators and surfaced other important dimensions, including the importance of being treated with respect. Louis reports: "Where teachers are treated with respect—and in turn, treat students with respect—the teacher's quality of work life is high *even where there is little other evidence of significant restructuring*" (p. 148; original emphasis). Other dimensions included having the opportunity to use existing skills and learn new ones, having the opportunity to work in collaboration with other teachers, receiving feedback outside the context of collaboration, and having resources, particularly time, to participate in staff development and collaborative work efforts. A surprising finding of the study was the "lack of significance attributed to *empowering teachers* through formal participation in decision making" (p. 150). It seemed that teachers valued broad informal influence more than formal opportunities to participate in specific decisions.

The QWL theory forces an examination of underlying assumptions of a restructuring effort that might not be normally pursued. Given that a major emphasis of school restructuring is greater teacher involvement, QWL indicators provide a cross-check for determining whether this involvement results in the improvement of the working conditions of teachers.

Summary

These theories contribute in unique ways to the implications of school restructuring. No one theory provides the guidance needed to plan restructuring activities, but taken together, they offer valuable insights. Common sense theory alerts us to the importance of addressing commitment and competence throughout the restructuring process. Decentralization theory reveals the political and economic assumptions associated with placing greater responsibility and accountability at the lowest possible level in an organization. Open systems theory makes it apparent that schools operate in a complex web of interlocking, interdependent relationships and thus must recognize the implications of any proposed restructuring changes for other closely linked systems. And finally, restructuring efforts have significant implications for teacher behavior and relationships, and the quality of work life theory alerts us to factors affecting teachers' working conditions. These theories help establish a backdrop for exploring alternative models and approaches to school restructuring.

SCHOOL RESTRUCTURING MODELS/APPROACHES

School restructuring has taken many forms and schools are using many different approaches. These multiple and varied models and approaches are difficult to isolate or to limit to a few examples. As can be expected, schools use a variety of strategies to guide their restructuring efforts, ranging from selecting a known or specific model to a more inductive process guided by some general goals or principles. Interestingly, even in cases of schools attempting to follow a more prescribed and established school restructuring model (e.g., Paideia or the Essential Schools), variability in adapting this model to local conditions seems unlimited. More on this later. In this section, we will examine in detail the various models/approaches being advocated. We will initiate our discussion with some general models or dimensions and then look more closely at other specific models. Along the way we will spice our review with related research on the implementation or impact of these models.

General Models or Dimensions

Elmore (1990) presents three general dimensions for school restructuring with underlying assumptions, emphasizing that the three dimensions should include (1) a focus on methods of teaching and learning, (2) changes in the preparation and work environment of teachers, and (3) a shift in the traditional power relations between the school and its clientele. Conley (1993) expands on Elmore's general dimensions by sorting 12 dimensions into the categories of central variables, enabling variables, and supporting variables. Figure 10.2 portrays these broad categories, their respective variables, and the relationships between them.

As seen in Figure 10.2, Conley covers Elmore's three dimensions and builds outward from learner outcomes to school governance and teacher leadership. According to Conley, the central variables are the "raison d'etre of public education" (p. 107). Changes in what teachers teach, how they teach, and how these are evaluated are fundamental to the educational process and require more than incremental changes. Often school restructuring does not get to the core technology of a school but tinkers with variables more distant from those that have a direct impact on student learning outcomes.

Conley's theory is that the central variables are dependent on the enabling variables of the learning environment—the information processing technology; school-community relations, particularly the involvement of parents; and time or the alteration of the school's schedule. In turn, the enabling variables are dependent on supporting variables of governance, which address forms of decentralization of decision making; teacher leadership or professionalization; personnel structures, which close the gap between teachers and support staff; and working relationships, which stress greater collaboration.

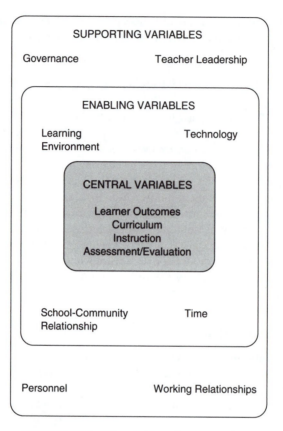

FIGURE 10.2 Dimensions of restructuring

SOURCE: D. T. Conley, *Roadmap to Restructuring,* 1993, ERIC Clearinghouse on Educational Management, Eugene, OR, p. 106. Reprinted with permission of ERIC Clearinghouse on Educational Management.

Conley's conceptual model of 12 dimensions of school restructuring provides a holistic picture of major variables and their interrelationships. True restructuring is linked to changes to student outcomes, but it is not possible to affect these changes without simultaneously addressing a number of key and supporting variables. Conversely, focusing only on the trimmings—such as school governance, time schedules, and teacher leadership—does not automatically ensure changes in learning outcomes. The core technology of the classroom must receive direct attention in order to ensure that there will be some impact on students' learning.

Philosophical/Research-Based Models

Philosophical/research-based models or approaches to school restructuring, according to Stringfield (1993), "offer the greatest challenge to traditional schooling and affect at least two of the following three core areas: the decision-making structure of the school, instructional methods, and the content of the core curriculum" (p. 4-3). In this category of school reform, Stringfield includes the Coalition for Essential Schools (Sizer, 1992), Paideia schools (Adler, 1982), Comer School Development program (Comer, 1992), and Success for All program (Madden, Slavin, Karweit, Dolan, & Wasik, 1991). Table 10.1, which draws on the work of Stringfield and his colleagues, summarizes the major features of these school restructuring approaches.

The Copernican Plan

Carroll (1989) offers an approach to restructuring secondary schools that is simple but significant. Using Copernicus as his role model and inspiration for defying strongly held viewpoints, Carroll challenges what we might consider sacrosanct in the scheduling of subjects in secondary schools. According to Carroll, "The Copernican Plan is predicated on the assumption that if the schedule for students and teachers is completely reoriented to provide conditions that will accommodate better instructional practice, many practices identified with more effective instruction can be implemented" (p. 25).

The traditional high school schedule allocates approximately 50 minutes for six to nine classes each day for 180 days. In the Copernican Plan, students are enrolled in one four-hour class each day for a period of 30 days or enrolled in two two-hour classes for a trimester of 60 days. These macroclasses, as Carroll calls them, free up additional time that can be allocated for other purposes such as seminars that integrate knowledge across traditional disciplines. Figure 10.3 illustrates how a schedule would operate and allows for combining different macroclass schedules.

A schedule change as dramatic as the Copernican Plan does not automatically ensure that teachers will change their instructional styles. On the other hand, teaching within four- or two-hour time blocks makes the overreliance on lecture methods more difficult and prompts efforts by teachers to use student-engaging methods of instruction. Carroll argues that the macroscheduling of courses helps facilitate quality instruction, including more opportunity for individualization of instruction. The normal schedule means teachers on average teach 125 students in five classes each day for a full school year; the Copernican Plan reduces this load by at least 20 percent by scheduling six classes per year per teacher. Large time blocks and fewer teachers in contact with students in the course of a school day reduce problems of scheduling special events or having time to follow up on homework assignments.

The Copernican Plan also proposes granting five diplomas: academic honors diploma, academic diploma, occupational honors diploma, standard diploma, and completion diploma. Each diploma establishes a minimum number of credits for graduation and students can elect which diploma they wish to earn. Students in the Copernican Plan receive credit for mastery of course objectives rather than the traditional letter grade.

These features of the Copernican Plan provide an opportunity to reexamine traditional assumptions and practices of instruction in secondary schools. As Copernicus challenged the conventional wisdom that the earth was the center of the solar system, Carroll, in his plan, is challenging long-held views of instructional schedules and grading practices in traditional high schools.

TABLE 10.1   Major instructional and noninstructional features of four school restructuring models

Coalition of Essential Schools	Paideia	Comer	Success for All
Instruction			

• Tone of trust and shared values/high expectations of students
 • Interdisciplinary curriculum and team teaching
 • Small class size and frequent student-teacher interaction
 • In-depth coverage of "essential" questions and more time on fewer subjects
 • Student as an active and cooperative learner
 • Teacher as instructor, counselor, and manager
 • Community of learners
 • Assessment through demonstration
	• Use of three methods of instruction/ outcomes:
	   1. Socratic
	   2. Didactic
	   3. Coaching
	 • Based on "Great Books of the Western World"
	 • Equality of opportunity to learn
	 • Shared inquiry among students and teacher
		• Acceptance of whole child through attention to individual differences and the social/affective development of the child
		 • Parent involvement in the classroom and home support for academic activities
		 • Classroom support services
		 • Collaboration of staff in classroom instruction
		 • Improved academic performance
		 • Positive social relationships among students
			• Ninety-minute reading groups, with homogeneous grouping by ability: 15 to 20 students in each group.
			 • One-on-one reading tutorials for 20 minutes
			 • Cooperative learning
			 • Use of certified reading teachers as reading tutors
			 • Shared format of instruction across groups
			 • Progression from STaR to big books, to oral/written composition to Peabody Language Development Kits to Beginning Reading to district basal reader
			 • Reading assessment of all students changed every 8 weeks to tutoring and reading groups
			 • No grade retention

Noninstruction			
• Staff development in at least one professional development activity per year • Staff commitment of their own time • Parent involvement	n/a	• Positive and supportive school climate • Staff and parent development on Comer strategies • Establishing and involving community links	• Staff development • Program facilitator • Parent involvement

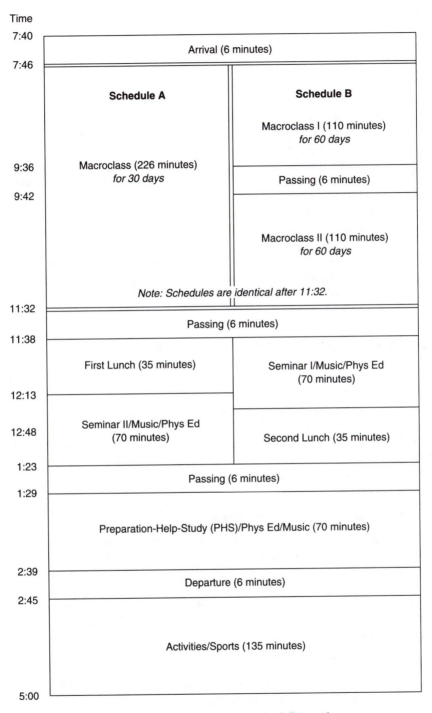

Time

7:40	Arrival (6 minutes)	
7:46	**Schedule A**	**Schedule B**
		Macroclass I (110 minutes) *for 60 days*
9:36	Macroclass (226 minutes) *for 30 days*	Passing (6 minutes)
9:42		
		Macroclass II (110 minutes) *for 60 days*
	Note: Schedules are identical after 11:32.	
11:32	Passing (6 minutes)	
11:38	First Lunch (35 minutes)	Seminar I/Music/Phys Ed (70 minutes)
12:13		
12:48	Seminar II/Music/Phys Ed (70 minutes)	Second Lunch (35 minutes)
1:23	Passing (6 minutes)	
1:29	Preparation-Help-Study (PHS)/Phys Ed/Music (70 minutes)	
2:39	Departure (6 minutes)	
2:45	Activities/Sports (135 minutes)	
5:00		

FIGURE 10.3   Copernican Plan student scheduling options

SOURCE: Reprinted with permission of The Regional Laboratory for Educational Improvement of the Northeast and Islands from *The Copernican Plan: Restructuring the American High School* by Joseph M. Carroll. Copyright 1989.

Charter Schools

The charter school, as a reform strategy, was briefly addressed as an option for increasing school choice. Not surprisingly, charter schools can also serve as a vehicle for school restructuring. As Budde (1988) explains, charters are written agreements that have a historical precedent going back as far as 1215, when King John signed an agreement with his barons that came to be known as the Magna Carta or great charter. In an educational context, a charter can become an agreement, for example, between a school district's central office and a local school; the form and content of this charter would depend on negotiations between the school district and local school representatives. Presumably these charters would be guided by some new vision of a reformed or restructured school, but again, like the Copernican Plan or any other school restructuring strategy, this is not guaranteed.

Thus, as a model of school restructuring, the charter plan permits a school district to enter into a process of encouraging and supporting local school restructuring. School district personnel would need to have clear expectations for restructuring, possibly building on Conley's (1993) 12 dimensions, before they agreed to the "charter."

PROS AND CONS OF SCHOOL RESTRUCTURING

As with any effort to begin anew, school restructuring has generated its share of arguments for and against such dramatic changes. Given the depth and radical nature of some of the school restructuring proposals, normal power structures and proponents of the status quo have expressed serious concerns. At the same time, there are those who feel that the incremental change model has produced little change of any significance and only through dramatic school restructuring will there be an increase in learning opportunities for *all* children. An examination of these arguments is next.

Arguments for School Restructuring

Proponents of school restructuring have little difficulty conjuring up arguments for their position. They can point to dropout rates, crime, drugs, and violence in schools; the demoralization of teachers; declining SAT scores; and teenage pregnancy. These conditions, particularly in urban areas, call out for significant changes in how schools are structured and operated. Hess (1991) reviews some of these conditions in the Chicago school system, which led to experimenting with a new governance system. The Chicago School Reform Act made new provisions for the allocation of resources; the first required a cap on administrative costs that would force the downsizing of the district's central office and, as a result, free up nearly $40 million to be redistributed to local schools. Thus, one strong argument for school restructuring is cost savings and redistribution of financial resources, particularly in large urban school districts.

The Chicago School Reform Act further stipulated the creation of local school councils with three major responsibilities: to adopt a school improvement plan, to adopt a budget to support the plan, and to hire a new principal or rehire the existing principal for a four-year performance-based contract. Using the Chicago case as an example, proponents argue that learning conditions for students are not likely to improve without greater voice by laypersons at the local school working closely with members of the professional staff, including teachers and principals.

According to Lane and Epps (1992), one of the major side effects of the school restructuring movement has been a greater emphasis on outcomes. Two outcomes have received special notice: the acquisition of higher-order thinking skills and the academic success of *all* children. This renewed awareness is important to creating new opportunities and challenging old practices. As Lane and Epps explain, "At the simplest, operational level, the message of restructuring is that organizations must have some fairly explicit and meaningful sense of mission or goals in order to perform well. At the school level, precisely what mission is selected is less important than that there be one that guides what the school does in a way its participants believe is special" (p. 37). This argument recognizes the importance of a school's being viewed as an organization first and not as a collection of independent classrooms. Second, as a consequence of being an organization, its members should develop a consciousness that they are capable, through joint and coordinated efforts, of achieving desired outcomes.

Lane and Epps (1992) argue further that the restructuring movement in education has enriched our assumptions about the nature of reality, knowledge, and human behavior. The merging of positivism with interpretive and constructivist assumptions has yielded a new set of "guiding tenets for education":

- Schools and the educational system can best be understood as a combination of rationality and indeterminacy
- Schools as organizations exist in part as pregiven, independent of the individuals contained within, and in part as an organized stream of experience shaped by implicit agreements, negotiated and confirmed by its members over time
- Members of school organizations are more productive and fulfilled when they act within organizational frameworks that are both deterministic and voluntaristic
- Interactions within schools are guided by a combination of bureaucratic and participatory democratic processes

Essentially these authors argue that only through a fundamental challenge of what people perceive as the "real school" can a paradigm shift occur. It is the school restructuring movement that can potentially blend the opposing positions of the old and new ways of thinking about the educational process.

Finally, Astuto and Clark (1992) argue that through restructuring, schools can become learning communities. Such communities of teachers and students should be based on beliefs about freedom in the workplace:

- Schools are organized as teaching and learning work units with authority and power vested in the professional staff

- Diffused responsibility directs everyone's attention to the effectiveness of the whole
- Educational improvement is achieved by responsiveness and responsibility to individual students' growth and development

Teacher empowerment and leadership can take on greater importance and recognition as part of a restructuring effort. Without the restructuring of responsibilities and accountability, old power sources and hierarchically dependent relationships will remain in force. It is only through fundamental change or restructuring that these old ways of doing business will change.

Arguments against School Restructuring

The arguments against restructuring come in many shades. A major argument is concerned with the meaning often attached to the word itself. The notion of restructuring seems to place a great deal of stress on the *structure* of schools and less on the purposes or content of schools. In other words, considerable faith is needed in what restructuring can produce. As we observed in our review of theories and models of school restructuring, no organizational design can ensure that improvement of learner outcomes will necessarily follow.

Further, as Newmann (1993) argues, "Conceiving an agenda of powerful content for a single teacher for a single class is much easier than actually cultivating [teachers'] commitments and competencies" (p. 6). Research findings (Cusick, 1983; Pauly, 1991; Powell, Farrar, & Cohen, 1985) have demonstrated the difficulty in getting agreement and coordinated effort between classes and teachers within schools. Restructuring is no easy task, and the difficulty of teachers finding time within their very tight schedules further exacerbates this problem.

Tye (1992) argues that even if initial success is obtained through a restructuring effort, seldom are these newly learned behaviors institutionalized. People are to fit into new expectations the best they can and often receive little or superficial in-service training to help cement and reinforce any new behaviors. Tye suggests that "before restructuring can be successful, it becomes important to identify behaviors that must change" (p. 10).

Tye also points out that restructuring a school is more than realigning certain of its parts. Restructuring as a movement is itself a political change strategy: It is an attempt to create a new order and to place power in the hands of persons—teachers and parents—who heretofore have not had much power. It is an attempt to reallocate resources and provide more educational opportunities for students of low-income and minority backgrounds. Persons who have the power at present and who are benefiting from present school structures and policies are not likely to roll over and play dead. A great deal of haggling and long negotiations will be needed to work out a peaceful transfer of power.

Another problem with school restructuring is that there is no consensus on a definition of what it means. Kirst (cited in O'Neil, 1990) "predicts the 'restructuring' movement may soon starve, victim of a lack of agreement on goals, policy options to support it, and clear ways to measure its impact" (p. 10).

Murphy (1991) summarizes a number of concerns and implementation issues that he sees with school restructuring:

- lack of attention to the core technology
- lack of connection between restructuring efforts and student outcomes
- potential disequalizing effects
- funding concerns
- noncritical adoption of business ideology
- troubling contradictions

No doubt because of many of these problems, there is, as Hess (1991) points out, little evidence of improvement in student achievement. Even in cases where successful restructuring seems to have taken place, there appears to be little significant change in student performance. This does not necessarily suggest that restructuring efforts should be abandoned, but it certainly raises a red flag and calls for careful monitoring of the process to ensure a tighter linkage to classroom instruction and changes in student behaviors. It also points out, particularly at the secondary level, the importance of including the major stakeholders in the educational process—the students. At present, there is little evidence of students playing a significant role in addressing their needs and expectations. They are often viewed as passive participants willing to abide by whatever teachers and parents offer them. This may be more or less true with primary-school-age students but is less so with older students. Student cooperation or lack of it can make or break the best-laid plans of educators.

Louis (1992) claims the problem with restructuring is its focus on structure, giving less attention to human values and relationships. As she explains, "restructuring must nurture and reflect broader changes in values and human relationships in schools. When teachers and students believe that they are working in a caring and stimulating environment, school-specific structural changes can evolve to fit specific needs and preferences of the school" (p. 154).

CONCLUSION

The restructuring of schools highlights, according to Newmann (1993), the dilemma of how much should be retained from the past and how much should be new and different. As he describes, the restructuring of schools challenges "us to design organizations that stimulate thoughtful use of the strengths in both traditional and progressive visions" (p. 11). Schools today, and in the future, will continue to face a diversity of students and families with a variety of cultural backgrounds and home environments. Newmann argues that these conditions will necessitate a greater degree of differentiation in curricular offerings, while at the same time we must attempt to define a common experience for all students.

Tye (1992) offers some advice on how schools might handle this dilemma and ensure that they in fact get better. He suggests the following steps:

- a reaffirmation of the importance and universality of public education
- developing curricula at the school site
- changing our management behaviors and challenging assumptions of hierarchy, accountability, and interchangeable parts
- developing a focus

Tye is a strong advocate of decentralization of decision making and the need to focus school reform at the school site. (The implications of this point of view will be addressed in chapter 11.) When we examined leadership as a democratic process, as in chapter 8, we began to appreciate the importance of the school in nurturing and furthering democratic principles. Tye reinforces this ideal and sees school restructuring as a means of obtaining greater autonomy for the local schools and in turn reactivating the interests of teachers, students, and parents.

These fundamental changes that school restructuralists advocate are not quick fixes to the educational problems of this country. School restructuring cannot be accomplished over a summer break but requires thoughtful and committed effort over a long haul, at a minimum of three to five years. Country View's experience illustrates how long it takes to make changes that are acceptable and that stick. School restructuring is not for the faint of heart or the ambivalent leader. It offers some promise but no guarantees that schools will get better even after considerable and dedicated effort.

DISCUSSION QUESTIONS

1. Considering the multiple dimensions to school restructuring, what do you believe is the essence of this movement?
2. Do you believe the school restructuring movement has potential in making significant changes in our schools? Why or why not?
3. What do you see as the major barriers against successful school restructuring? How might these be overcome?
4. Do you feel incremental change over time has greater potential for effective school change than school restructuring does? Why or why not?
5. As a professional educator, what is your stance regarding school restructuring?

SUGGESTED ACTIVITIES

1. Review the alternative models for school restructuring presented in this chapter and reported in other sources. Develop a paper or oral presentation on which of these models you believe has the greatest potential for improving schools in general or a particular school specifically.

2. Much has been said about the promise of school restructuring in improving student achievement and performance in general. Conduct a review of recent research and determine the degree to which these promises have been fulfilled.

3. Conduct a class discussion on what should be the purposes or goals of school restructuring. Identify and explore the various dilemmas facing school restructuring, such as centralization and decentralization, traditional and progressive educational practices, diversity and standardization, differentiation and commonality, and equity and special interests.

4. Visit and report on a school involved in a restructuring effort. How closely does this school approximate or address Conley's 12 dimensions of school restructuring?

5. Conduct more research on the quality of work life (QWL) concept and explore its relevance to school restructuring.

REFERENCES

Adler, M. J. (1982). *The Paideia proposal.* New York: Macmillan.

Astuto, T. A., & Clark, D. L. (1992). Challenging the limits of school restructuring and reform. In A. Lieberman (Ed.), *The changing contexts of teaching.* Chicago: The National Society for the Study of Education.

Budde, R. (1988). *Education by charter: Restructuring school districts.* Andover, MA: The Regional Laboratory for Educational Improvement.

Carnoy, M., & MacDonell, J. (1990). School district restructuring in Santa Fe, New Mexico. *Educational Policy, 4*(1), 49–64.

Carroll, J. M. (1989). *The Copernican plan.* Andover, MA: The Regional Laboratory for Educational Improvement of the Northeast and Islands.

Chrispeels, J. H. (1992). *Purposeful restructuring: Creating a culture for learning and achievement in elementary schools.* Washington, D.C.: Falmer.

Cohen, M. D., March, J. G., & Olsen, J. P. (1972). A garbage can model of organizational choice. *Administrative Science Quarterly, 17,* 1–25.

Comer, J. (1992). *A brief history and summary of the school development program.* New Haven, CT: Unpublished manuscript.

Conley, D. T. (1993). *Roadmap to restructuring.* Eugene: ERIC Clearinghouse on Educational Management, University of Oregon.

Cusick, P. A. (1983). *The egalitarian ideal and the American high school: Studies of three schools.* New York: Longman.

Elmore, R. F. (1988). *Early experience in restructuring schools: Voices from the field.* Washington, D.C.: National Governors' Association.

Elmore, R. F. (1990). *Restructuring schools.* San Francisco: Jossey-Bass Publishers.

Hess, G. A. (1991). *School restructuring, Chicago style.* Newbury Park, CA: Corwin Press.

Lane, J. J., & Epps, E. G. (1992). Introduction and overview. In J. J. Lane & E. G. Epps (Eds.), *Restructuring the schools: Problems and prospects* (pp. ix–xvi). Berkeley, CA: McCutchan.

Lewis, A. (1989). *Restructuring American schools.* Arlington, VA: American Association of School Administrators.

Louis, K. S. (1992). Restructuring and the problem of teachers' work. In A. Lieberman (Ed.), *The changing contexts of teaching.* Chicago: The National Society for the Study of Education.

Madden, N. A., Slavin, R. E., Karweit, N. L., Dolan, L., & Wasik, B. A. (April, 1991). Success for all. *Phi Delta Kappan, 72*(8), 593–99.

Moorman, H., & Egermeier, J. (1992). Educational restructuring: Generative metaphor and new vision. In J. J. Lane & E. G. Epps (Eds.), *Restructuring the schools: Problems and prospects.* Berkeley, CA: McCutchan.

Murphy, J. (1991). *Restructuring schools.* New York: Teachers College Press.

Newmann, F. M. (March, 1993). Beyond common sense in educational restructuring: The issues of content and linkage. *Educational Researcher, 22*(2), 4-13, 22.

O'Neil, J. (April, 1990). Piecing together the restructuring puzzle. *Educational Leadership, 47*(7), 4-10.

Pauly, P. (1991). *The classroom crucible: What really works, what doesn't, and why.* New York: Basic Books.

Powell, A. G., Farrar, E., & Cohen, D. K. (1985). *The shopping mall high school: Winners and losers in the educational marketplace.* Boston: Houghton Mifflin.

Reavis, C., & Griffith, H. (1992). *Restructuring of schools: Theory and practice.* Lancaster, PA: Technomic Publishing Co.

Sizer, T. R. (1992). *Horace's school.* Boston: Houghton Mifflin.

Stringfield, S. (1993). *Urban and suburban/rural special strategies for educating disadvantaged children, second year report.* Baltimore: Johns Hopkins University Press.

Tye, K. A. (September, 1992). Restructuring our schools, beyond the rhetoric. *Phi Delta Kappan, 74*(1), 8-14.

chapter 11

School-Based Management

School-based management (SBM), also known as school-site or site-based management, is a third strategy for school reform receiving enormous attention and experimentation in schools across the United States and Canada and in European countries. SBM links well to the school restructuring movement reviewed in chapter 10 and somewhat tangentially to school choice as reviewed in chapter 9. As Bechtol and Sorenson (1993) observe, "School-based management in the restructured school means bringing the responsibility for decisions as close as possible to the problem. It means creating ownership for those responsible for carrying out decisions by involving them directly in the decision-making process and by trusting their abilities and judgments" (p. 36).

SBM provides greater voice for teachers, principals, and in many cases parents in policy areas of budget, personnel, curricula, strategic planning, and school change. On the other hand, school choice, according to Herman and Herman (1993), "is a more profound change; it is a sharply etched and immediately-felt restructuring innovation . . . making true customers out of parents . . ." (p. 232–33). Though SBM may not be as dramatic as school choice strategies, it does involve local persons, primarily teachers, principals, and parents, in a process of incremental change at the school site.

Like most innovations in education, SBM has many different definitions. Herman and Herman (1993), in their review of multiple definitions, identified three common elements:

- the shift/exchange and balance of decision-making authority with regard to autonomy and accountability
- the consensus that those closest to, most impacted by, or primarily responsible for any decision implementation should be the decision makers

- the empowerment and involvement of principals, teachers and other staff, and community in school decision making

These elements are often manifested at the school site in the form of teams or advisory councils. These groups, which are cross-representational in nature, have responsibility for general oversight and policy directions of the school, which often necessitates a transfer of power and responsibility from a school district board of education and its central office to a local school council. The local school council may become a quasi-board of education but will tend to operate in a more informal manner with less legal and bureaucratic requirements and include representatives not typically found on most boards of education (e.g., teachers, students, support staff).

SBM links to school reform by placing greater responsibility and accountability on the professional judgments of teachers and principals with the support and advice of parents and students. Majkowski and Fleming (1988) link SBM to school improvement by suggesting that

> The improving school is one in which the learning outcomes for students are updated continually to reflect new needs, where instructional strategies and techniques accommodate different rates, styles and abilities, and where decisions about management of all the school's resources (including those in the community) are guided by the requirements of the teaching-learning process (p. 10).

The focus on the teaching-learning process is central in the thinking of many experts on SBM. However, as we explore more details of its various designs and applications, we will discover that SBM can lapse into policy and macrolevel governance issues and into debates that are far removed from the classroom. As one wag put it, "It is often difficult to remember when fighting alligators that the original purpose was to drain the swamp."

In the subsequent sections of this chapter, we will explore the background of the SBM movement, review some theories that undergird SBM, look at specific models or approaches, and highlight the arguments for and against it. Also, where appropriate, we will report on the research and link some of the concepts associated with SBM to the Country View Junior-Senior High School restructuring effort that included many of the elements of SBM. Finally, at the end of the chapter, we will explore some general conclusions to be drawn from the SBM movement.

BACKGROUND

The present move to SBM is a reversal of the school consolidation movement in the United States that was initiated in the late 1800s and peaked in the 1950s and 1960s. The industrialization of the United States contributed to the migration of people from the countryside to the cities and resulted in the closing of many small, rural schools and the consolidation of the remaining smaller schools into larger ones. Centralization was a prevailing educational policy and inefficient, small, and often somewhat informally operated schools were out. As is often the case with educational change, past policies and practices reemerge and have currency under new conditions. Such is the case today, with a renewed interest in reducing large school systems and large schools to smaller, more manageable units.

Earlier attempts at SBM were encouraged by the Fleischman Commission of 1971 in New York and the Governor's Citizen Committee on Education in Florida in 1973. Each of these advocated decentralization or establishment of school-centered organizations. Florida, California, Ohio, Massachusetts, and Minnesota experimented with various forms of state-level policies to establish greater local autonomy and accountability. The educational reforms of the 1980s focused extensively on SBM initiatives.

Much of the appeal of SBM, particularly to policymakers, was its notable success in increasing productivity in U.S. businesses. Research (Peters & Waterman, 1982; and Bennis and Nanus, 1985) and anecdotal reports were praising the success of employee involvement, high levels of participation, use of a team approach, decentralization of decision making, and the downsizing of corporate headquarters. Peters and Waterman's (1982) study of the best-run companies in the United States gave impetus to greater employee involvement and responsibility in solving business problems and promoting new ventures. The lessons learned from business practices are continuing to be explored into the 1990s and are providing impetus and legitimacy for the SBM movement.

In addition to the management practices of the business world, a number of school reform reports, most notably *A Nation at Risk,* have documented the sorry state of American schools. These conditions have stimulated a number of studies, more reports, and legislative actions for correcting the problems of American education. Many experts and political leaders have concluded that if our educational system is to be improved, it must be done at the local school level. According to Herman and Herman (1993), there are five major reasons for the current emphasis on school-based interventions:

1. Current research on effective schools and teaching indicates that the best way to ensure improvement in schools is to focus change efforts at the building level
2. Current research on the principalship indicates that the "key" instructional leader in a school district is the building principal
3. Business and industry want schools to improve so that the schools' products (students) are more productive workers, which, in turn, will make American business and industry more competitive with foreign nations'
4. The number of adult illiterates and the huge student dropout rate, especially in large cities and in minority populations, alarm practically everyone; this leads to an undereducated, dependent populace and an expensive drain on the finances at the national, state, and local levels
5. Organizations like the Commission of the States, governors' organizations, and federal and state legislatures are being made aware of the political necessity to support school improvement efforts by the lobbyists for business,

industrial, and educational groups; they are reacting politically to this pressure by mandating or pressuring in other ways for restructuring our schools

These conditions have combined to give greater strength and support to SBM as a major school reform strategy. As Weiler (1993) points out, however, this movement toward greater decentralization presents the states with an interesting paradox. It is evident from the state's perspective that the transfer of greater authority and responsibility to the local school site is potentially a good strategy for conflict management and increasing local problem solving; on the other hand, the state has some legitimate concerns and a need to maintain control in order to ensure equity and adherence to acceptable standards and practices. How these seemingly contradictory positions are worked out is crucial to the ultimate success of SBM initiatives.

The Country View case illustrates this dilemma. The state made a general statement of its desire to waive regulations in order for local schools to take more initiative in solving local problems but faced some difficulties when asked to waive licensure requirements for Country View's troika of school administrators. Country View school officials felt the request was in keeping with the spirit of the state's proclamation, only to learn that there were hidden limits to this open invitation for state waivers. Clearly the state is not a single, united organization tightly coupled and of one mind. The state education department is a public bureaucracy whose existence is highly dependent on its oversight function and the enforcement of rules and regulations. The rhetoric of upper-level educational bureaucrats and political leaders fell on the deaf ears of lower-level bureaucrats whose expertise and status link to ensuring school-level compliance with state regulations, including professional licensure of school principals.

In addition to state-level controls, another layer of controls exists in most school districts, further complicating the problems of implementing the ideals associated with SBM. Brown (1990) reports a number of problems typically experienced by building principals when dealing with the central office of their school districts; complaints range from getting permission to buy equipment, such as an office copier, computers, furniture, and so forth, to the selection of school personnel. The issue of how resources are allocated to different schools in a district and the freedom to make building-level choices in using these shared resources get to the heart of who is in charge. As Brown observes, "The difficulty appears to be that the persons *responsible* for the education of students have *little authority* to control educational resources, while persons *not responsible* for students have *authority* to control resources for the schools" (p. 6). Often because of this lack of authority, principals have to resort to devious budgetary tactics or spend a lot of time lobbying central office administrators.

As sensible as SBM appears to be in answering the perceived needs for school reform, it is not without its problems and may not produce the nirvana that many persons seek. The jury is still out, but it may help us appreciate the potential of SBM to examine some underlying theories that guide those who are responsible for conceptualizing and implementing SBM.

THEORIES OF SCHOOL-BASED MANAGEMENT

Many of the practices of SBM are drawn from combinations of ideas grouped under the generic theory of decentralization. Other theories that relate closely to the notion of decentralization and deserve some special recognition include management theory, democratic theory, and organization theory, particularly the perspective offered by professional bureaucratic theory.

Decentralization Theory

In chapter 10 on school restructuring, we briefly discussed decentralization theory and its influence on school restructuring, particularly SBM. It is interesting to note that decentralization can be traced back many centuries and, according to Kochen and Deutsch (1980), occurred when one-man empires collapsed. The Roman Empire's longevity was in part attributed to its decentralized system, which gave greater autonomy and authority to regional governors and generals. The great land mass of the empire and difficulty with communications from Rome to outlying areas may have made decentralization inevitable.

It is also important to understand why there is a tendency of organizations to centralize authority and decision making. Organizations, by their nature, are concerned with order and ensuring the accomplishment of certain tasks. On the other hand, accomplishing tasks may require some degree of disorder. As we know from experience, schools are not the most orderly places as teachers and students engage in a variety of teaching/learning activities. However, when the choice is order or creative individual pursuits, order tends to win out.

Those who serve at the apex of an organization assume greater responsibility for the long-term health of the organization. They tend to hold views that question the degree to which persons at lower levels are able to understand these strategic issues or are competent to deal with them. As a consequence, according to Mintzberg (1979), organizations retain more power at the top of the organization than may be necessary. Brown (1990) concludes that "the need for order and the tolerance of relative disorder appear to influence the degrees of centralization/decentralization which may be observed in organizations. Crisis, the larger picture, competency, and trust each may influence the willingness of the apex to share decision making authority" (p. 33).

Since persons at the upper level of organizations have certain powers often ascribed to them by law and precedent, decentralization in an organization may need to be a negotiated redistribution of power and authority to make decisions. Even in the states where SBM has been seen as a viable school reform strategy, implementers have had to face the problem of redistributing authority from boards of education and superintendents to principals and/or school councils. Often there is sufficient ambiguity in the legislation to require further negotiations at the local level.

During such negotiations, the function and nature of decentralization can get lost in the discussion. Decentralization, according to Brown (1990), should be seen not for its inherent value but rather as an instrument for achieving certain desirable objectives or outcomes. Brown suggests further that decentralization should be seen "as *the extent to which authority to make decisions is distributed among the roles in an organization*" (p. 225).

According to Mintzberg (1979), this authority can be redistributed along two main dimensions in an organization: vertical and horizontal. The vertical dimension involves moving authority up and down the hierarchy of the organization. In educational organizations, this would involve school boards and superintendents sharing with or giving up certain authority to school principals and school councils. Personnel selection and budget control may be two areas of compromise. The horizontal axis refers to the extent to which authority for decision making is delegated sideways. Again, typically in educational organizations central office staff members assume or are delegated authority for decisions, including, for example, school expenditures or personnel assignments. Under most SBM plans horizontal authority is affected and in most cases decentralized to the school principal.

Brown (1990) found, however, that the transfer of authority for decision making in school districts advocating SBM approaches is not that straightforward. Using Mintzberg's theory of selective/parallel decision making, Brown observed in some SBM arrangements that the central office delegated some decisions while retaining authority over others; he found that central offices often retained authority over matters of payroll, collective negotiations, and general district policy. Parallel decision making involves the same decisions being made in different places, thus requiring greater coordination. Curricular development, for example, may be carried on both at the school-building level and at the central office level, which necessitates some clarification regarding who should take responsibility for what.

The Country View case illustrates the negotiated nature of decentralization as they coped with the resignation of their two principals and the belief that teachers needed a greater voice in the restructuring of the junior-senior high school. As a consequence, the teachers proposed to the board the appointment of teachers from within the school as principals and the creation of a steering committee made up mostly of teachers who would be charged with the responsibility of shepherding the school's restructuring process. The board of education indicated a willingness to appoint two assistant principals from within but preferred to recruit the principal from without. This was the plan until the recruitment process failed to find a viable outside candidate; then the board bowed to the wishes of the teachers and appointed three teachers to the building administrative roles formerly held by the resigning principals.

In large school districts with several school buildings, decentralization poses other problems, the biggest of which is the question of the degree to which schools should be treated equally and share in district resources. A common sense approach would suggest that each school should be as comparable as possible. However, this does not always work out to everyone's satisfaction and leaves school districts groping for a fair and equitable policy. An example of this struggle and dilemma is revealed in the distribution of personal computers. Some school districts have a districtwide standard that requires so many computers per student in each school. On the surface this appears fair; unfortunately, such a policy can preclude a school from determining its own needs and priorities, which may mean more or fewer computers per student. Parents who observe a discrepancy between schools may call "foul" if other schools have more computers than theirs.

Obviously the issue is larger than which schools get more or fewer computers. The issue is one of equitable distribution of fiscal resources and who determines how districtwide resources should be distributed. Too much local school discretion or decentralization can lead to enormous differences in educational opportunities between schools. Decentralization can create the politics of smoke and mirrors, resulting in rewarding some schools while other less aggressive and politically weak schools get what is left over.

Brown (1991) defines three beliefs essential to effective decentralization; at the same time, he offers his perspective on the dilemma of equity and local school autonomy.

1. "Some variability is good." Brown argues that not all schools need the same kind of coffee maker, copying machine, and instructional equipment, nor do they need the same staffing arrangements and use of paraprofessionals and support staff. Schools vary so much in the needs of their students, skills and competence of staff, and parent expectations that to force conformity on equipment and staffing may result in wasted and unused resources.

2. "Schools often know best." Unfortunately in districts where decisions are highly centralized, these decisions often miss the mark concerning the needs of local schools. Centralized decisions of staff development and curriculum development can result in teachers finding themselves dragged to workshops to work on a math guide or attend in-service on new math instructional techniques when they already have this expertise or their students have greater needs in other content areas, such as reading. Teachers often wonder what drives districtwide meetings and are suspicious that the meetings are more symbolic in nature and serve other purposes besides trying to improve classroom instruction. SBM provides an opportunity for teachers to act on the needs of students in their school that often do not fit with districtwide aspirations for more uniformity in curricula and teaching methods. Brown would argue that teachers in their respective schools are in the best position to judge the needs of their students and should have an opportunity to demonstrate their ability to meet these needs.

3. "Schools are usually trustworthy." Brown discusses a school board's observation that the teachers in their district would not avail themselves of staff development unless prompted by a special allocation of $100,000. Much to their surprise, when they established SBM each of the schools planned for greater staff development on their own than the board had expected. The point is that local school teachers and principals share certain professional commitments and attempt to act prudently with taxpayers' money. Essentially, these professionals attempted to put their students' interests first. Decentralization does not necessarily lead to abuse of the public trust.

These key beliefs are essential, according to Brown, if decentralization is to work. He feels these beliefs "must always be kept in mind and accepted. Otherwise, forget it; decentralization should not proceed" (p. 15). The process of decentralizing a school system does force some examination of certain assumptions and attitudes toward teachers and principals who will have these new responsibilities.

Bimber (1993) writes that decentralization can take two forms, the first being administrative decentralization, in which authority is shifted downward within the structure of the school system. Essentially those responsibilities held by the superintendent and central office staff are now taken over by the principals and teachers. The second form is political decentralization, which involves a shift of authority to a governing body such as a local school board or citizen council. Some SBM strategies call for a combination of these two forms and provide more authority to both the principal and teachers and to a citizen council. The 1989 Chicago and 1969 New York decentralization efforts included both forms. Each school district must decide for itself, unless mandated by state law, which of these forms or some combination of the two will best fit its system. No doubt trust and perceived competence of potential participants in a decentralization effort will play a role in making this decision.

It comes down to three basic arguments for decentralization, according to Weiler (1993): the redistribution argument, the efficiency argument, and the cultures-of-learning argument. The redistribution argument speaks to the sharing of power. The efficiency argument stresses greater cost effectiveness through the more efficient deployment and management of resources. The cultures-of-learning argument emphasizes the decentralization of educational content or recognition of subcultures and the inclusion of their values in the educational process. Endemic to these arguments is the dilemma of control and legitimacy with which centralized and decentralized authorities must contend. Persons who function at the apex tend to emphasize power but often at the cost of legitimacy, which is eroded by their lack of closeness to the persons they desire to control. On the other hand, those at the bottom of the hierarchy may have greater legitimacy by proximity to the situation but have difficulty attaining control beyond their small and intimate circle. This dilemma goes to the heart of school reform: Those desiring some control over the school reform agenda on a national, state, or regional level, particularly with a concern for equity and equal educational opportunities, must contend with local preferences and needs. Policymakers need to walk a fine line and experiment in finding ways to balance the forces of control and legitimacy.

Management Theory

Drawing heavily on management science for theory and practice, SBM uses a managerial approach to optimize decision making and quality control. To appreciate different perspectives on managerial options or approaches, we will explore three orientations: Likert management styles, participative decision making, and quality management.

Likert Management Styles. Early in this text, we alluded to Likert's (1967) work on managerial styles and levels of participation in decision making. He developed a four-system schema for describing discrete conditions observed in organizations of varying types, including schools. The system one type of organization is characterized as punitive and very authoritarian; system two is paternalistic and authoritarian; system three organizations use a more consultative approach; system four situations engage in widespread decision making, greater vertical and horizontal communication flow, friendly relations between superiors and subordinates, motivation based on participation, greater trust, and shared control. The system four organization type provides a theoretical model for widespread participation and decision making within an SBM context.

The level of involvement in a system four organization is congruent with Bonan's (1991) report of Kirst's philosophy of school-level decision making. First, the principal is seen as the site manager who controls school resources and is responsible for the success of the school. Second, under the philosophy of lay control, parents are seen as consumers having a major stake in the school's performance. Third, schoolsite policy making involves teachers and enhances their self-concept and professional image. And fourth, the philosophy of parity suggests that no one group has complete control of a school. All groups—teachers, administrators, parents, staff, and students at the high school level—"deserve a place at the table, and the best arguments should prevail" (p. 23).

Participative Decision Making. Lindelow, Coursen, Mazzarella, Heynderickz, and Smith (1989) find that participative decision making (PDM) is essential to the successful operation of SBM. As they point out, considerable research on schools demonstrates the growing frustration of teachers; feeling left out of the decision-making loops, teachers are calling for a greater voice in their jobs and profession and feel they should be consulted in decisions affecting students. PDM is congruent with democratic principles, which we discussed in chapter 8, and should lead to decisions that get implemented. In addition, there is strong evidence that PDM can improve the morale and climate of a school.

Some successful approaches to PDM in an SBM environment include teacher leadership teams (which we observed at Country View and will expand upon later in this chapter), school improvement teams (also employed at Country View), and quality circles. The focus for each of these approaches may vary slightly, but each approach provides a process for teachers to play a significant role in identifying needs or problems, generating alternative strategies, and implementing promising interventions. The key is to recognize the legitimacy of various members playing a significant role in enhancing the quality of life at their school.

It should also be recognized that regardless of participatory strategy, a cost in terms of time and energy is required to implement PDM successfully. Quite often teachers and others have not had much experience in participatory decision making and may need the help of staff development programs and outside consultants. A planning facilitator from a nearby university played a significant role at Country View, aiding them in dealing with the complications of a PDM process.

Quality Management. Another significant management theory that is having extraordinary impact on private sector management, and now to some degree on educational administration, is total quality management (TQM). TQM has been pioneered by several management experts (Shewhart, 1931; Juran, 1979; and Feigenbaum, 1951) but most notably and recently by Deming (1986). Quality management emphasizes continuous improvement, client satisfaction, and doing it right the first time and every time. Deming identifies 14 characteristics of quality management, most of which are intended for private sector organizations; 8 of these actions, however, have implications for educational organizations:

1. create constancy of purpose
2. adopt a new philosophy
3. institute training on the job
4. institute leadership
5. drive out fear
6. break down barriers between departments
7. institute a vigorous program of education and self-improvement
8. put everyone to work to accomplish the transformation

Kaufman and Zahn (1993) stress the relevance of quality management for education and six critical factors (Figure 11.1) for continuous improvement of educational quality. They also discuss QM+, which they define as the concern of quality management with, in addition to other quality indicators, "the success and well-being of tomorrow's child in tomorrow's world" (p. 6). These critical factors provide SBM with a theoretical grounding that places emphasis on providing quality educational opportunities for students and parents and on building a team approach.

FIGURE 11.1   The six critical success factors for QM

SOURCE: R. Kaufman & D. Zahn, *Quality Management Plus,* 1993, Corwin Press, Newbury Park, CA, p. 25. Reprinted by permission of Corwin Press, Inc.

Critical Success Factor 1:
Be willing to move out of today's comfort zones and use new and wider boundaries for thinking, planning, doing, and evaluating.

Critical Success Factor 2:
Use and link all three levels of results (mega, macro, and micro) for defining and delivering quality.

Critical Success Factor 3:
Everyone demonstrates a passion for quality: Everything everyone does, constantly and consistently, is directed toward improving the quality of what is used, done, and delivered.

Critical Success Factor 4:
Everyone—learners, teachers, administrators, parents, employers, neighbors—is on the same team. Quality is what everyone is after, and everyone will make a unique and collective contribution to achieve it.

Critical Success Factor 5:
All decisions are made on the basis of solid, objective, relevant performance data.

Critical Success Factor 6:
Building a cooperative team—whose members learn from each other and put the purposes of the QM+ effort above comfort and continuously improve—is the key for moving from quality intention to realization.

Democratic Theory

As suggested with PDM and a flashback to chapter 8 on democratic leadership, SBM can benefit from democratic principles and notions of empowerment. Snauwaert (1993) expresses concern that centralization overlooks the value of human development and, in fact, impedes it by denying people the opportunity to participate in school governance and learning from such experiences. Snauwaert also sees a correspondence between democratic practices and the educational process: A democratic environment is conducive to supporting teaching "as a fluid, complex, and creative act" (p. 33). From this perspective, democratic governance, which is possible within an SBM system, has the potential of a double payoff: helping teachers grow professionally and enhancing the quality of the educational process.

Bailey (1991) advocates a connection between SBM and empowerment which, in a democratic environment, is a desired outcome. One perspective is to see empowerment as a fundamental shift of authority, which means gaining a major role in shaping public policy and being held accountable to the public. Another perspective is to view empowerment less dramatically and more as professionalization, where teachers act like, and are respected as, professionals. To enable teacher empowerment to grow, Bailey would shift the primary responsibility for the following functions from school district offices to school sites:

- preparation of budgets
- curriculum development
- hiring and firing
- tenure assessment
- merit pay provisions
- implementation of career ladder provisions
- textbook selection
- discipline codes
- teacher assignments
- student evaluation systems

Empowerment of teachers as professionals is critical to attracting and keeping the best and brightest. Assuming responsibility for the above functions within a climate of mutual respect, the tone of which is often set by the school superintendent, is critical to making empowerment a reality within the context of SBM.

Professional Bureaucratic Theory

As we discussed earlier in this text, most school systems operate as a bureaucracy with centralized and hierarchical authority relationships, division of labor, and a strong emphasis on compliance with rules and regulations. Even to the unsophisticated eye and certainly to those of us who have worked in such environments, it is obvious that bureaucracies by their nature are not very supportive of efforts to decentralize and to establish SBM systems. Abbott (1969), Anderson (1968), and Rogers (1968) speak to how school organizations designed on bureaucratic principles can greatly impede school change and innovation.

Mintzberg (1979) sees organizations with a discerning eye and has identified five different forms of bureaucracies and configurations of organization: the machine bureaucracy, the divisional form, the professional bureaucracy, the simple structure, and the adhocracy. Given school organizations' legacy as bureaucratic structures, the professional bureaucracy may offer a realistic model for SBM.

The professional bureaucracy gives greater autonomy to staff and is appropriate for dealing with relatively stable conditions in which tasks are relatively complicated. Universities, hospitals, and as we move toward SBM, schools match these characteristics. Typically the structure of a professional bureaucracy is flat, authority is decentralized, and standardization and integration are achieved through professional training and established professional norms. The Mountain View School District case in section 1 is an example of a professional bureaucracy and demonstrates the impact of greater autonomy and professional forbearance. The superintendent of Mountain View may not have fully appreciated the basic nature of her organization as a professional bureaucracy and thus ran into considerable resistance as she attempted to consolidate and centralize her power.

The MVSD case illustrates the potential conflict that can emerge between the organizational elements of a bureaucratic structure and the performance of highly qualified and competent professionals. Where compatibility and balance exist between these polar extremes we would expect the organization to operate smoothly. Country View seems to exemplify this compatibility in which the board of education, the school district's superintendent, and school principals and teaching staff are negotiating their respective rights and responsibilities. On the other hand, when bureaucratic rules and standardization become perceived as impediments to the effective performance of professional duties, stress and disorder are introduced into the organization. SBM permits a negotiated order between these two extremes and encourages a sense of professionalism to operate within a professional bureaucracy.

SCHOOL-BASED MANAGEMENT MODELS/APPROACHES

SBM models and approaches are as varied as schools and school districts. Hannaway (1993) illustrates this diversity by describing two districts, District A and District B. In District A, the superintendent of schools had two major objectives to guide the establishment of SBM, the first being the desire to have school-level persons "buy into" district policies and the second being the encouragement of "entrepreneurship." These objectives resulted in balancing centralized and decentralized controls; budget and personnel decisions, for example, were decentralized but curriculum decisions remained centralized. District B followed a more laissez-faire approach, with confidence in teachers to make the right decisions. More details on these respective school district approaches follow.

District A Approach

Each principal had a lump sum of money that was discretionary and was to be used to cover any school costs except salaries and major capital expenses. Only 10 percent of the school's budget was actually discretionary, but the principals and teachers felt this was a sufficient amount to identify priorities and address important local school needs. There were additional monies available from a districtwide special grants program and PTA fund-raising efforts.

The principals in District A had considerable say over personnel matters, including staff recruitment and hiring and how monies were distributed for different positions at the school. Each school received personnel staffing units—an algorithm for determining the number of full-time-equivalent persons to be assigned to each school—and different types of personnel cost different units (e.g., the cost for an aide differed from the cost for a teacher).

At the district level curriculum decisions were made by committees of teachers and chaired by principals since there were no district-level curriculum specialists. Even though curriculum decisions were centralized, the process was highly participatory. All courses at the high school were approved by a district committee made up of one teacher for each subject area. The district also had articulation committees made up of representatives from the different levels of schooling (elementary, middle, and high school), who examined the curricula for coherence and integration across these levels.

Staff development remained the responsibility of both the schools and the district. A district-level committee oversaw and made plans for districtwide staff development programs and meetings. At the same time, individual schools carried on their own staff development activities.

According to District A's superintendent, the district followed a loose-tight approach to their decentralization approach: Each school had autonomy and discretion in specified areas and at the same time the district stressed coherence and quality control across the educational programs in the district.

District B Approach

In District B, the school superintendent expressed considerable faith and confidence in teachers to make decisions in the best interest of students. As a result the teachers had responsibility for curricular decisions and, with parent involvement, the selection of principals. In fact one school, like Country View, chose not to rehire their principal, instead creating a teacher committee to manage the school.

District B received financial assistance from a national foundation that supported the district's education reform effort. The district formed an education reform group whose objective was to redesign education by focusing school-level attention on student learning, with strong emphasis on keeping the decision-making authority at the classroom and school levels.

Decisions were facilitated at the school level by a school improvement program (SIP) committee with at least one teacher representative for every ten teachers.

Teacher-initiated proposals were reviewed by the SIP and then submitted to a district-level SIP executive committee made up of teacher representatives from each school-site SIP. Proposals were reviewed but not approved by building principals. District-SIP-approved proposals were forwarded to the school superintendent and then to the executive director of the foundation for funding. Any restructuring proposals had to go to the school board; proposals that did not require funding were handled within the school.

Since decentralization and SBM were relatively new and experimental for the district, the superintendent had intentionally held off any formal evaluations of school improvement proposals. The goal was to encourage teachers to be creative in a risk-free climate and not squelch ideas in their early stages.

Both school districts had very lean central offices and each stressed the importance of support and service to the schools and their teachers. Administrators in District A spent considerable time together and used the district's goals and mission statements as frames of reference. In District B, the principals spent less time working as teams and more time working with teachers in their individual buildings; they also received less guidance and support from the school district office.

These approaches demonstrate the subtle differences an SBM approach can have in any given school district. SBM administrative arrangements and policies are most likely to be characteristic of the administrative style or philosophy of the particular school superintendent as supported by the school board. These two examples illustrate the difference in how much authority each school can have in a school district made of many schools and the degree to which decisions need to be coordinated at a central level.

Democratic Governance Approach

Districts A and B illustrate the variability of teacher involvement, authority, and school versus district control. Glickman (1993), on the other hand, advocates an approach to SBM that is guided by the development of a covenant and entails a charter for school decision making that in turn activates the covenant. As we discussed in chapter 8 and explored in other places, a school's primary raison d'être should be developing citizenship and an understanding of democracy. Glickman expresses it more forcibly:

> What difference does it make if we graduate 100 percent of our students, or if SAT scores rise twenty points, or if our students beat other countries in achievement in science when they have not learned how to identify, analyze, and solve the problems that face their immediate and larger communities? Our country would be better served by schools that produce caring, intelligent, and wise citizens who willingly engage in the work of a democracy than by schools that produce graduates who do well on isolated subgoals. (p. 9)

Thus, Glickman uses the notion of covenant to capture a "sacred" obligation to learning principles derived from a vision of citizenship and democracy. The covenant should be (1) derived from all persons affected, (2) derived through a democratic process, (3) focused on teaching and learning that is school specific, and (4) a guide for future decisions about school priorities. Principles of learning that might be developed through this process and included in a school's covenant are:

1. Learning should be an active process that demands full student participation in pedagogically valid work. Students need to make choices, accept responsibility, and become self-directed.
2. Learning should be both an individual and a cooperative venture, where students need to work at their own pace and performance levels and also have opportunities to work with other students on solving problems.
3. Learning should be goal-oriented and connected to the real world, so that students understand the applications of what they learn in school to their outside lives and communities.
4. Learning should be personalized, to allow students, together with their teachers, to set learning goals that are realistic but challenging, attainable, and pertinent to their future aspirations.
5. Learning should be documentable, diagnostic, and reflective, providing continuous feedback to students and parents, to encourage students and train them in self-evaluation. Assessment should be used as a tool to develop further teaching and learning strategies.
6. Learning should take place in a comfortable and attractive physical environment and in an atmosphere of support and respect, where students' own life experiences are affirmed and valued and where mistakes are analyzed constructively as a natural step in the acquisition of knowledge and understanding. (C. D. Glickman, *Renewing America's Schools: A Guide for School-Based Action,* 1993, Jossey-Bass, San Francisco, CA, p. 25. Reprinted with permission of Jossey-Bass Inc., Publishers.)

Glickman sees the covenant as only one part of a three-part framework that also includes a charter and a critical-study process. The charter provides an understanding of how decisions are to be made, using three guiding rules of governance:

1. Everyone can be involved in decision making
2. No one *has* to be involved
3. Once decisions are made, everyone supports the implementation

Stress is placed on identifying what can be achieved and not on what cannot be controlled. Also, local school decision making should be targeted toward core and comprehensive types of decisions. Each school faces a range of decisions that include, starting at the least significant level, (1) zero-impact decisions of lunchroom supervision or bus duties, (2) minimal-impact decisions of textbook adoption or in-service activities, (3) core-impact decisions of curriculum or instructional programs, and (4) comprehensive-impact decisions of school budget or hiring of personnel. Obviously, core and comprehensive decisions are most worthy of attention and will have the greatest influence on whether the principles of a school's covenant are to be achieved.

Glickman defines four ground rules for the establishment of school governance groups:

1. All major groups should be represented, with access always open to others
2. Regular classroom teachers should be in the majority
3. The school principal should be a "standing" (automatically included) member
4. The group as a whole should fairly represent the gender, ethnic, and socio-economic populations of the entire school community

Governance systems take many forms and usually involve some balance between representational and direct participation. A school charter may establish a hybrid model that includes a school council of elected members or volunteers who establish priorities and initiate task forces of representatives from various school and community groups. These task forces are charged to study certain issues and report to the school council. The school council can either make decisions based on these reports or return to the body at large for a final vote.

The third part of the democratic governance approach framework, according to Glickman (1993), is the critical-study process. This process is directed at determining the degree to which the school is being successful in meeting the learning needs of its students. The major method for determining success is a form of self-study or action research based on questions created from within the school. As Glickman states, "Information must infuse the school, so that critical thinking, generating, consuming, and action become the norms of the organization" (p. 51).

The democratic governance approach, as articulated by Glickman, provides a rather detailed blueprint for establishing an SBM system based on democratic principles and the importance of focusing on the needs of students to function in a democratic society. This approach differs significantly from the previous examples of Districts A and B in very important ways. Glickman's stress on citizenship and democracy and their infusion in the school's governance and self-study are critical conceptual and philosophical differences. These values may or may not emerge in District A or B, but under Glickman's approach they are central to establishing an SBM effort.

Contract Approach

In chapters 9 and 10, we discussed the notion of charter schools, which operate under some general policy and agreement with the state or with a district central office. These charters spell out general expectations and performance outcomes and tend not to be written in strict contract language concerning specific goals and associated costs. The contract approach suggested by Bimber (1993) and tested under Great Britain's 1988 Education Reform Act stresses greater accountability to the goals of a contract. The contract sets a level of performance mutually agreed upon by a central authority and local authority but does not prescribe the means by which these goals are to be accomplished. The contract leaves to the local authority discretion concerning how it will organize itself, whom it will employ, and what methods it will use.

The local unit is to be judged periodically on how well it is achieving the conditions of the contract. Some parameters of the central authority will prevail, particularly those of equity and fairness.

Contracts reduce the emphasis on rule-based controls of centralized authority. Local units are not judged by their adherence to rules and regulations but rather how well they meet the performance goals outlined in the contract. This approach is more significant than just establishing advisory councils or local decision-making committees: Local schools have major discretion over their structure and operations and are much more accountable for results as specified in the contract.

According to Bimber (1993), the contract relationship may take the form of the arrangement between district offices and "grant-maintained" schools in Great Britain. Under this arrangement, local schools may opt out of their district's control and acquire a grant-maintained status. This in effect is a contract freeing the school of district administrative control. The school receives an increase in funding equivalent to its share of administrative costs associated with the school district's administration and agrees to meet centrally determined educational goals, but it is free to carry out these goals in its own way.

School Performance Indicators

Clearly, the effectiveness of any charter or contract depends, in part, on the specificity of desired outcomes written into the agreement. A recent movement by states at the policy level is to employ this principle for funding schools. In other words, states will reward schools based on performance. According to Richard and Shujaa's (1990) research, "13 states are formulating or have already established school incentive plans" (p. 116).

Those who favor a policy of school incentive plans argue that (1) schools are loosely coupled, complex organizations in need of external performance incentives; (2) school incentives overcome obstacles to cooperation often created by individual pursuits, and (3) school incentive plans encourage a shift of authority to the local school that should result in educational improvement.

The incentive plans come in two forms: "fixed" and "competitive" performance standards. Under fixed conditions schools compete against predefined standards; under competitive conditions schools compete with each other. All schools should be eligible for an award under the fixed conditions, whereas only a certain percentage of schools would be eligible under competitive conditions. Presently the state of New Jersey is exploring a fixed approach where schools would receive financial rewards, for example, for reducing the number of children needing compensatory education. South Carolina uses a competitive approach, rewarding the top 25 percent of its schools based on annual achievement-gain scores; the schools compete with similar schools and are grouped in five categories of socioeconomic status.

Indiana uses a combination approach in a two-tier system. In the first tier are schools that meet state improvement standards and share $4 million on a weighted per-pupil basis. The schools in the second tier are rank-ordered based on their size of gain; $6 million is distributed on the basis of rank or size of gain. Performance is measured in a variety of ways but usually includes some test of student achievement plus other measures such as dropout rates, daily average attendance rates, and number of students taking and scoring well on advanced placement examinations. Some states, such as Missouri and California, are willing to include more subjective measures like grades; parental attitudes; student, principal, and self-evaluations of teachers' classroom management skills; quantity and quality of student writing; number and type of books read; and participation in a fine arts program. In most cases, it is the school's overall or aggregated performance as opposed to individual students' gains that determines the school's eligibility for a financial reward.

Richard and Shujaa (1990) concluded from their study of incentive plans that success is dependent on some combination of technical, political, and economic conditions: "The plan must have a high degree of perceived fairness and face validity. It must also have broad political support from education associations, government, and the community. Finally, the plan must be relatively immune from state economic growth cycles. Ironically, it is during times of economic constraints on state budgets that incentive plans could be most useful as policy instruments of symbolic value" (p. 139).

In effect, school performance indicators recognize the special and unique qualities of individual schools and provide incentives that are real for SBM. SBM becomes less of an abstract exercise within a state policy framework when it provides financial (and no doubt symbolic) rewards for specific and measurable outcomes. Whether the state and local agenda are the same is debatable, and state requirements may preclude local initiatives. When that happens, SBM may become the handmaiden of the state and lose the power to energize local school and community leaders in meeting locally perceived needs.

PROS AND CONS OF SCHOOL-BASED MANAGEMENT

With any school reform proposal come varying opinions of its value and possible threat. SBM is no exception, even though it seems on the surface to make sense and is in keeping with American traditions of democracy and local involvement in determining the fate of children and the community.

Arguments for School-Based Management

The arguments for SBM evolve around two well-established propositions, according to David (1989):

1. The school is the primary decision-making unit
2. Change requires involvement and ownership

For historical, cultural, and political reasons, each school, if given the opportunity, will make different decisions concerning its organization and operation. SBM allows the flower of uniqueness to bloom in a school and permits identification of local problems, needs, and strategies for addressing these conditions. Local schools seem to have greater flexibility, and potentially more creativity, in solving their problems than larger, more centralized units. Knowledge of resources, including teacher competence, exists at the local level and can be integrated into the decision-making process. As mentioned several times in this chapter, some degree of local autonomy in decision making is consistent with the political freedom that we enjoy in our society.

Brown (1990) reports on several studies suggesting that SBM can be financially efficient and effective. It can result in savings as local teachers and administrators exercise prudence in spending only monies that are needed rather than budgeted amounts set by the central office. Also, it has been found that local schools with some discretion to allocate resources can be more effective in achieving equality of educational opportunity.

SBM provides an opportunity for teachers in particular to expand their professionalism in attaining desired educational goals. According to Bimber (1993), "central authority still monitors performance but does not prescribe methods and procedures" (p. 31). Teachers in their classrooms have an opportunity to draw upon their experience and training in working with students and making the idealized goals of education a reality. Energizing teachers to this important task can be one of the major contributions of SBM.

According to Levine and Eubanks (1992), SBM is congruent with research on school change. First, SBM recognizes that change cannot be mandated from outside but must be developed from within on a school-by-school basis. Second, the empowerment of teachers, administrators, and others at the local level acknowledges that fundamental and lasting change takes at least two to three years to initiate. Third, research shows that increases in student achievement are dependent on teachers taking an active role in making decisions about instruction and related matters. Also, research on effective schools demonstrates the importance of building site coordination and planning under the strong leadership of the principal. These research findings provide strong support and impetus for the SBM movement.

Reyes (1990), upon reviewing the arguments and research that advocate greater teacher involvement under decentralized conditions, identifies a new conceptualization of "high-level participation (HLP) schools." These schools provide an opportunity to rethink the structure and roles of teachers. Specifically, HLP schools provide opportunities to:

1. create a flat organization with high levels of teacher participation
2. redesign teacher relationships and emphasize team teaching, job enrichment, and self-managing teams
3. demand greater involvement of administration in using innovative management practices that can contribute to greater organizational effectiveness and quality of work life
4. increase teacher commitment to the school, its activities, and the well-being of its students
5. provide cross-training and learning opportunities for teachers, including school finance, budgets, taxation, and state regulations
6. facilitate communications and produce more persons in a school system who are knowledgeable and informed decision makers

SBM provides a new context for teachers, administrators, parents, students, and other local school persons to become engaged in the operation of their school. It permits the school to operate in such a manner that students and adults solve their own problems and can create a wholesome environment. The learning from such opportunities is limitless and ensures the growth and development of all persons. According to Hannaway (1993), the beneficial effects of decentralization "may be due more to control, motivation, and learning effects associated with the professional interactions produced by the management arrangements than to efficiency effects typically presumed to flow from the increased discretion that accompanies decentralization to knowledgeable actors" (p. 151). SBM advocates see new opportunities that had been precluded under hierarchical, bureaucratic, and centralized systems.

Arguments against School-Based Management

In spite of the idealism and underlying philosophy associated with SBM, its implementation is fraught with serious problems. Levine and Eubanks (1992) identify six major obstacles in carrying out the promise of SBM:

1. inadequate time, training, and technical assistance
2. difficulties in stimulating consideration and acceptance of inconvenient changes
3. unresolved issues involving administrative leadership and enhanced power among other participants
4. constraints on teacher participation in decision making
5. reluctance of administrators at all levels to give up traditional prerogatives
6. restrictions imposed by school board, state, and federal regulations and by contracts with teacher organizations

The path to maximizing the opportunities that advocates suggest SBM can create is paved with significant obstacles. The teachers and administrators at Valley View overcame some of these quite handily while others continue to challenge them. In-service training and use of outside consultants helped overcome their knowledge gaps. Having a university nearby that saw as part of its mission technical assistance and support certainly helped in this regard. Turnover of the principals helped minimize any unresolved issues between the teachers and school administration. Also, having principals appointed from the ranks of the teachers increased teacher optimism and trust. Teacher participation in decision making is evolving and is generally supported by the superintendent and school board.

At Country View there are still difficulties in accepting inconvenient changes and minimizing constraints on teacher decision making, though progress was made in gaining teacher support for establishing teacher teams, integrating curricula, and implementing schoolwide theme units. The constraint of time continues to be a challenge for which the teachers have not found any easy answers except to do a lot of planning and staff development during summer in-service institutes. And, as we observed, state regulations pose some challenge in pursuing certain innovative ideas for the school.

Bailey (1991) highlights some other potential problems with SBM. First, change takes time, and given the frenetic life of teachers, there is not much time to spare for taking on school governance issues. Just keeping up with normal teaching responsibilities and exploring new curricular and instructional opportunities does not leave much time and energy for wrestling with schoolwide problems. Second, SBM can raise unrealistic expectations for what can or should be accomplished through an SBM effort, particularly when many of the problems facing schools are embedded in the community and outside the control of an eager and optimistic group of teachers, parents, and administrators. Third, there is an aura of uncertainty surrounding schools and how they should or could become more effective. This ambiguity does not make school-level decision making a very easy task. Unfortunately there are no quick and easy answers to many of the problems facing schools today, and to expect SBM to quickly transform a school into a wholesome and effective operation is unreasonable. Schools need all the help they can get, which means going beyond the boundaries of the school and drawing upon the resources and expertise in the school district, the state, and beyond. Simply turning over the responsibility for decision making to eager teachers does not automatically endow these nascent decision makers with the wisdom and creativity needed to solve some pretty knotty problems. On the hand, the reason these problems still exist is that others do not have any easy answers either.

SBM has limits and may not be the solution for needed school changes across all districts or schools. According to Brown (1990), because of the variability between school districts—particularly along the lines of leadership, level of support, size of district, and local expertise—a blanket emphasis on SBM by a state may be unwise. Besides the limitations of different schools to manage an SBM system, there are times when it is unwise to decentralize. Brown (1991) identifies the following circumstances in which it would be unwise to entertain decentralization and SBM:

- when other major initiatives are under way
- when the district is experiencing severe retrenchment
- when the district is quite small
- when there are major disagreements in principle

As mentioned earlier, in discussing school reform by school choice or restructuring, the bottom line has to be whether the innovation results in improved instruction and increased student learning. SBM, like the other interventions, does not necessarily pass this litmus test either. It clearly offers some promise, but diligence is needed to ensure that students have increased opportunities and derive some tangible benefits. Without these assurances or targeted efforts, SBM may be, as we said before, nothing more than smoke and mirrors that give the impression that something important is being done when little or no evidence can be found to support these claims.

Then again, as Elmore (1993) suggests, the politics of school reform do not necessarily play to the needs of instructional improvement or student achievement. Rather it is a question of control, and SBM strategies clearly threaten established power relationships. Elmore states, "Debates about centralization and decentralization in

American education, then, are mainly debates about *who* should have access to and influence over decisions, not about *what* the content and practice of teaching and learning should be or *how* to change those things" (p. 40).

One risk of initiating an SBM effort in a school system is its potential to slip into political debates over power and control and lose sight of the original purpose: to improve educational opportunities for students.

CONCLUSION

It seems that SBM, possibly more than school choice or school restructuring, presses school reformers on some big questions. For Hannaway and Carnoy (1993), "the promise of decentralization must be couched in a much larger debate: What do Americans want their educational system to be, and how much time, energy, and money are they willing to devote to it?" (p. 235).

Clearly, managing a school at the local level is far more demanding than deferring to a centralized authority that assumes a lion's share of responsibility for the operation. There has to be a willingness to put in the extra time and effort needed to address the myriad issues and needs that school-based leaders cannot avoid. SBM is not for the faint of heart or for those who are ambivalent about getting involved in making major decisions about kids and programs.

We also need to keep in mind that SBM is not a monolithic concept resulting in schools operating in similar ways. The permutations resulting from the application of SBM strategies are unlimited, constrained only by the creativity and value preferences of those involved. The options available under SBM to a school district and local school decision makers are without end.

SBM does present some dilemmas to policymakers at the federal and state levels. It is clear that SBM grants greater voice and authority to local school leaders to determine educational priorities and opportunities for students. State and federal departments of education recognize that teachers, administrators, and parents are in a much better position to determine needs and to be motivated to meet these needs than those further removed. Yet, policymakers have to be watchful that local decisions do not seriously impede or counteract major policy concerns of the state or federal government. There are many examples of this tension, but one that puts it in perspective is the issue of mainstreaming children with physical, mental, or emotional disabilities. Many teachers think children with disabilities are better served by special teachers in separate classrooms. We have to wonder whether the progress to date in integrating students with major disabilities would be as far along as it is if we had a strong SBM system in place.

SBM offers many new opportunities for local people to get involved in the education of their students. But it also raises some concerns about the degree to which local decisions should be autonomous and the degree to which they are closely monitored and guided by state and federal policy concerns. We have to be sure that less politically influential groups, like the handicapped and low income, do not suffer at the hands of a more powerful and self-centered, active elite.

A major study by Rand (Hill & Bonan, 1991) came to five major conclusions about SBM:

1. Though site-based management focuses on individual schools, it is in fact a reform of the entire school system
2. Site-based management will lead to real changes at the school level only if it is a school system's basic reform strategy, not just one among several reforms
3. Site-managed schools are likely to evolve over time and to develop distinctive characters, goals, and operating styles
4. A system of distinctive site-managed schools requires a rethinking of accountability
5. The ultimate accountability mechanism for a system of distinctive site-managed schools is parental choice

These conclusions capture the multiple dimensions and ramifications of school-based management. SBM does appear to have considerable potential for addressing many of the problems facing schools today. On the other hand, it offers no guarantee that these problems will in fact be addressed and may only result in passing the buck to the local level, where resources may be slim and where motivation to get entangled in the web of school improvement may be low. In spite of these concerns, Brown (1991) believes, based on his research of SBM efforts, "that the educators and others who believe that districts and schools can somehow be made better are encouraged to explore further the ideas surrounding decentralization" (p. 266). He may be right.

DISCUSSION QUESTIONS

1. What features of SBM do you find promising and what features do you find unpromising? Why?
2. We have discussed democratic principles at many points in this and other chapters. How do you feel about linking Glickman's ideas to SBM? What problems would you anticipate? How might these be overcome?
3. If your school and/or school district were considering SBM, what form do you suspect it would take? What forces or factors would shape a particular SBM approach at your school?
4. Time and expertise seem to be major constraints to an SBM effort. How could these be overcome? Is it worth it? Why or why not?
5. How does SBM compare with school choice and school restructuring? How do they overlap or where are there distinct differences?

SUGGESTED ACTIVITIES

1. Decentralization has many advocates at this time. On the other hand, there are many who see more centralization as a way of saving money and being able to dictate school changes. These differing opinions provide grist for a good debate on the merits and demerits of de-

centralization. Establish debate teams or roundtable discussions on this issue after class members have had an opportunity to further research the pros and cons of decentralization.

2. Conduct some applied research by surveying or interviewing teachers on their interests in setting up and participating in an SBM system.

3. Assume for the moment that you have been assigned to a task force to explore alternative strategies for school reform. Drawing on the three chapters in section 3, what ideas would you favor and advocate? Develop a position paper or oral presentation on which method of reform would make sense for your school to explore.

4. Some teachers would rather spend their time and energy figuring out the best ways to teach their students and have little or no interest in getting involved in schoolwide issues or concerns. How do you feel about this issue? What suggestions do you have for addressing this issue and finding some compromise or accommodation?

5. Many critics of school reform feel that it could become all smoke and mirrors and enmesh people in debates that have little to do with the central mission of a school, that is, teaching students. What is your position on this issue? In your opinion, how can school reform both improve the learning of *all* students and improve the overall climate of the school? Develop a school-site plan that would make this a reality.

REFERENCES

Abbott, M. (1969). Hierarchical impediments to innovation in educational organizations. In F. Carver & T. Sergiovanni (Eds.), *Organizations and human behavior: Focus on schools* (pp. 42–50). New York: McGraw-Hill.

Anderson, J. G. (1968). *Bureaucracy in education.* Baltimore: Johns Hopkins University Press.

Bailey, W. J. (1991). *School-site management applied.* Lancaster, PA: Technomic Publishing Co.

Bechtol, W. M., & Sorenson, J. S. (1993). *Restructuring schooling for individual students.* Boston: Allyn & Bacon.

Bennis, W., & Nanus, B. (1985). *Leaders: The strategies for taking charge.* New York: Harper & Row.

Bimber, B. (1993). *School decentralization.* Santa Monica, CA: Rand.

Bonan, J. J. (1991). *Decentralization and accountability in education.* Santa Monica, CA: Rand.

Brown, D. J. (1990). *Decentralization and school-based management.* New York: Falmer.

Brown, D. J. (1991). *Decentralization.* Newbury Park, CA: Corwin Press.

David, J. (1989). Synthesis of research on school-based management. *Educational Leadership, 46*(8), 45–53.

Deming, W. E. (1986). *Out of the crisis.* Cambridge, MA: MIT, Center for Advanced Engineering Technology.

Elmore, R. F. (1993). School decentralization: Who gains? Who loses? In J. Hannaway & M. Carnoy (Eds.), *Decentralization and school improvement* (pp. 33–54). San Francisco: Jossey-Bass.

Feigenbaum, A. V. (1951). *Quality control principles, practice, and administration.* New York: McGraw-Hill.

Glickman, C. D. (1993). *Renewing America's schools.* San Francisco: Jossey-Bass.

Hannaway, J. (1993). Decentralization in two school districts: Challenging the standard paradigm. In J. Hannaway & M. Carnoy (Eds.), *Decentralization and school improvement* (pp. 232–42). San Francisco: Jossey-Bass.

Hannaway, J., & Carnoy, M. (1993). Epilogue: Reframing the debate. In J. Hannaway & M. Carnoy (Eds.), *Decentralization and school improvement* (pp. 232–36). San Francisco: Jossey-Bass.

Herman, J. J., & Herman, J. L. (1993). *School-based management: Current thinking and practice.* Springfield, IL: Charles C. Thomas.

Hill, P. T., & Bonan, J. (1991). *Decentralization and accountability in public education.* Santa Monica, CA: Rand.

Juran, J. (1979). *Quality control handbook* (3rd ed.). New York: McGraw-Hill.

Kaufman, R., & Zahn, D. (1993). *Quality management plus.* Newbury Park, CA: Corwin Press.

Kochen, M., & Deutsch, K. W. (1980). *Decentralization: Sketches toward a rational theory.* Cambridge, MA: Oelgeschlager, Gunn & Hain.

Levine, D. U., & Eubanks, E. E. (1992). Site-based management: Engine for reform or pipedream? Problems, prospects, pitfalls, and prerequisites for success. In J. J. Lane & E. G. Epps (Eds.), *Restructuring the schools: Problems and prospects* (pp. 61–82). Berkeley, CA: McCutchan.

Likert, R. (1967). *The human organization.* New York: McGraw-Hill.

Lindelow, J., Coursen, D., Mazzarella, J. A., Heynderickz, J. J., & Smith, S. C. (1989). Participative decision making. In S. C. Smith & P. K. Piele (Eds.), *School leadership: Handbook for excellence* (2nd ed., pp. 152–67). Eugene, OR: ERIC Clearinghouse on Educational Management.

Majkowski, C., & Fleming, D. (1988). *School-site management: Concepts and approaches.* (ERIC Document Reproduction Service No. ED 307 660).

Mintzberg, H. (1979). *The structuring of organizations.* Englewood, Cliffs, NJ: Prentice-Hall.

Peters, T. J., & Waterman, R. H. (1982). *In search of excellence: Lessons from America's best-run companies.* New York: Warner.

Reyes, P. (1990). Linking commitment, performance, and productivity. In P. Reyes (Ed.), *Teachers and their workplace.* Newbury Park, CA: Sage.

Richard, C. E., & Shujaa, M. (1990). School performance incentives. In P. Reyes (Ed.), *Teachers and their workplace* (pp. 115–40). Newbury Park, CA: Sage.

Rogers, D. (1968). *110 Livingston Street.* New York: Random House.

Shewhart, W. A. (1931). *Economic control of quality of manufactured product.* New York: Van Nostrand.

Snauwaert, D. T. (1993). *Democracy, education, and governance.* Albany: State University of New York Press.

Weiler, H. N. (1993). Control versus legitimation: The politics of ambivalence. In J. Hannaway & M. Carnoy (Eds.), *Decentralization and school improvement.* San Francisco: Jossey-Bass.

Section 3 Summary

Deciding on a school reform strategy can be compared to deciding to marry or start a family: the processing of choices, options to consider, values dilemmas, and persons to be involved all come in to play. School reform is no less complicated and places on people some difficult choices—though often they are not guided by any greater consciousness than they employ when choosing where to go on vacation. As in choosing vacations, schools continue to pursue their activities as they have done in the past. It is not uncommon for persons to simply do what they did last year, be it visiting parents or the same cottage on the lake or staying at home and getting caught up on necessary maintenance projects—all of these are continued because of comfort with practices that made sense at one time in the past. And so it can be with school reform. Schools continue doing basically what they have done in the past because it seems to make sense, it may be working, and/or it may be the lesser of many evils.

There are other parallels between school reform and choice of vacation trips. Doing the same old thing come vacation time can have its deleterious effects; routines and past practices can leave us unsatisfied, feeling we're in a rut, wishing for conditions that may force some change or consideration of new options. When such an awareness occurs, we may be beset with many factors to consider or we may be tempted to throw caution to the winds, to embark on a change for no other reason than for change's sake. Certainly responsible advocates of school reform would deny that efforts at reform are based on a blind faith that change is of itself, regardless of its content, a positive thing. Given the difficulty, however, of documenting "progress" or the impact of even a deliberate, thoughtful change process, we have to wonder what does underlie change advocates' call for school reform. We are often left wondering why some persons are willing to devote innumerable hours in meetings, discussions, workshops, whatever, for what seems to be little or no gain on the perceived problems that provided the initial momentum. On the other hand, we could ask why people seek the safety and comfort of the status quo and seem to have lost the feelings or drive associated with new ventures. The answers to these questions may get at the heart of what does or does not drive persons to consider new options in their lifestyle, either as an educator or as a vacationer.

In section 3, we explored three major foci and their many permutations for school reform. To choose or not to choose among these options is a major question (see Figure S3.1 for an outline of these options). There is little doubt that school reform options press persons at all levels of the educational enterprise to grapple with some fundamental questions. Unfortunately, so much of the time many of these persons are not fully informed of their choices and find themselves swept up in a momentum not of their choosing, as may be the case when we find ourselves embarking on a trip that some enthusiastic friend or travel agent convinced us to take, because, in part, we did not take the time to examine what we really wanted to do with our discretionary time. As one expert on planning forewarns, "Plan or be planned for."

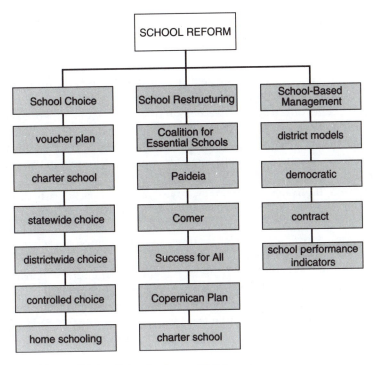

Figure S3.1   School reform options

Our survey of school reform options included a detailed examination of school choice, school restructuring, and school-based management. Although we examined each separately, we have to recognize what they share in common:

- They raise basic value questions about authority, right of choice, empowerment, and the purposes of education
- There are equally strong arguments for and against each reform strategy
- Each suffers from the same potential defect: It may not result in improving educational opportunities for students
- The implementation of school reform is totally enmeshed in politics and political systems
- At present, most school reform efforts provide little or no opportunity for the voices of students to be heard and assume students to be passive partners in the school reform process

Finally, it is interesting to speculate on the degree to which persons embarking on school reform are guided by democratic ideals and an interest in local needs. Our review of the research on school change reveals the importance of focusing on the school as an individual and unique organization and the importance of supporting change efforts directed at this level. This often means giving greater autonomy and responsibility for determining the change agenda to those at the building level. Although this makes sense for a variety of reasons, we also have to be concerned with how fairly *all* children will be treated when resources are in short supply and the stakes are perceived as high. The big challenge is whether local reformers will practice the best of our democratic ideals and support open, free, and equal access to educational benefits or retreat to more benign treatment of certain groups and pursue selfish motivations. Regardless of the school reform strategy embarked on, change or status quo advocates alike will eventually have to reflect on this challenge.

Country View's school restructuring effort was firmly rooted in the philosophy of equal educational opportunity for all students, and many at the school and in the community were motivated by their concern for students, particularly those who seem to suffer neglect and, in some cases, abuse. Clearly their job is incomplete and ongoing. Their challenge thus far has been to maintain a sense of balance and adapt to feedback from a variety of sources, as they attempt to figure out what will work best for the interests of all. There is little doubt that, as they move forward with de-tracking of students and emphasizing more integrated and interdisciplinary teaching, they will be exposed to both positive and negative feedback from students and parents. The balancing act that is necessary in school reform can be exemplified by these kinds of conditions that so often force unpopular or difficult decisions. It is no wonder some have compared school reform to changing a tire on an automobile racing down a highway.

We need to understand that school reform choices, like vacation choices, are often decided on the run. If we wait until we have everyone in agreement or willing to buy into certain desired outcomes, we most likely will miss the plane and end up staying at home, wondering why we lacked the spirit to get our act together sooner.

In section 4, we will reframe school reform from the various metaphors of organization and leadership. This will provide more opportunity to appreciate both the complexity and richness that alternative perspectives can provide us when dealing with ideas as ambiguous as school reform.

Perspectives on the Future

This text has provided us with a rich inventory of concepts concerning organizations, leadership, and school reform. These theories bring us, more or less, up to date on ideas that provide perspective on educational organizations. But knowledge knows no boundaries and is not about to reach a plateau; our lives continue to be enriched by new ways of thinking about and understanding the human experience. We cannot bring down the final curtain without pointing the way toward new knowledge, including emerging theories and global trends. Thus, in this final section, we add a fourth leg to our stool and present a futures perspective.

Part of this futures perspective is to engage in the artistry of reframing school reform. We know the push for school reform will not subside, and yet it seems that schools are being forced to accept externally driven solutions to their problems with little or no opportunity to reflect on the proposals. The challenge to schools is to gain time to appreciate fully their own organizational reality and experience it long enough to see the potential in making changes. But time is a luxury many schools do not have when faced with outside pressures to change.

A way to begin is to reframe the touted reforms in light of some metaphors that offer an opportunity to discover their meanings and implications. In this final section, we explore a reframing approach using a number of metaphors of organizations, leadership, and school reform. These are primarily illustrative and provide one way, of many, for reflecting on the implications of the three main strategies of school reform explored in this text: school choice, school restructuring, and school-based management.

With these thoughts as a backdrop, an overview of the chapters follows.

CHAPTER HIGHLIGHTS

Chapter 12: Linking Reframing to School Reform Strategies

This chapter demonstrates a particular reframing approach and explores various insights surfaced by the exercise. Each of the reform movements is examined but in different ways; for example, school choice is examined from the perspective of culture and dialectical leadership, school restructuring is reframed with the metaphors of theater and transformation, and school-based management gets scrutinized through the lenses of politics and democratic leadership. These multiple views represent only a subset of possible angles from which school reform might be gauged. The chapter closes with some conclusions suggested by the reframing exercise.

Chapter 13: Trends and Implications

The closing chapter for this text unveils some global trends and emerging theories that further challenge our understanding about organizations, leadership, and school reform. Specifically, an exploration of economic, social, and demographic trends reveals some potential relevance to educational systems in the immediate and long-range future. If some of these trends continue, they will offer schools both opportunities and challenges worthy of further contemplation. In addition to these trends, three promising theories are explored for their potential for thinking about organizations and leadership. The theories include chaos, organizational cycles, and feminism. Each offers a unique perspective on new knowledge and how it may help, either as a metaphor or lens, for reflecting on school organizations and change in the future.

The chapter closes with the vision of artistry in linking theories of organization and leadership to school reform. Using quilt making as a metaphor suggests the value of visualizing concepts in order to reinforce them; the designs rendered will be unique to the quilt maker's creativity, unless he or she chooses to work in teams and combine respective visions into one large display. This final chapter encourages the artistry of creative reflection and synthesis required of present-day and future leaders of school organizations.

chapter 12

Linking Reframing to School Reform Strategies

The mere mention of school reform provokes different images in people's minds. If you happen to be a policymaker sitting on an education committee in the state legislature, your image may be of schools in bad shape, bloated school district bureaucracies, and students not reaching their potential. If you are a parent, you may have the image of teachers being overpaid and insensitive to the needs of your child. From a classroom teacher's perspective, you see uninformed people meddling in matters of which they have little or no understanding. School reform has come to mean different things to different people, positive and negative, and these mental images often influence attitudes and behavior toward the educational enterprise.

A classroom teacher, for example, may feel parents are indifferent to what their child is learning at school. This image of the parent by a teacher may prompt him or her to complain of parents' lack of concern and to preach that parents should get more involved. An alternative image might include parents being overburdened with child care and economic survival, prompting a more sympathetic response by a teacher and an expression of encouragement. As Eliza reminded Professor Higgins in *My Fair Lady:* When he treated her like a flower girl, she acted like a flower girl, but when he treated her like a lady, she acted like a lady. We get what we expect and these expectations are driven in part by our mental images.

As suggested throughout this text, mental images play an important role in determining our behavior. Senge (1990), for example, discusses mental models and their influence in understanding and explaining our social world. As he observes, "new insights fail to get put into practice because they conflict with deeply held internal images of how the world works, images that limit us to familiar ways of thinking and acting" (p. 174). He argues further that mental models are powerful in affecting what we do because "they affect what we *see*" (p. 175).

It appears that no one is free from this influence, neither noted scientists nor children playing on school playgrounds. Kuhn (1970) points out how scientists become trapped in their particular paradigms, and classroom teachers can tell many stories of children's imaginations keeping them from trying something new, whether on the playground or in the classroom.

Fortunately, this is a condition that can be corrected, though it requires some will and conscious effort. Morgan (1986, 1993) advocates a process of imaginization through the use of metaphors; Bolman and Deal (1991) suggest reframing through the use of lenses. Sergiovanni (1992) emphasizes the importance of examining mindscapes and how they shape our realities. Most importantly, however, each of us has to come to the realization that we have the power to break with old thoughts by purposefully experimenting with other mental images. These authors and others support the value of reframing our thoughts in order to discover new perspectives that may liberate us from the constraints suggested by Plato's allegory of the cave, as portrayed in the *Republic*.

The relevance of reframing to understanding school reform or school leadership should be self-evident. Yet, there is some mystery about where our schools and other educational organizations are going and what role leaders should play in this movement. Some critics have voiced the concern that we are presently suffering from a crisis of perception. That is, we are unable to imagine new and creative ways and thus find ourselves bogged down with old ideas and ways of doing things. We continue to apply the machine metaphor and view organizations as rigid, hierarchical, authority-driven institutions. We continue to see change as a rational process or a threat to our well-being. Now, more than ever before, there is a need to engage in new ways of thinking about educational problems and ways in which schools can make needed and desired improvements.

On the other hand, how we disengage from our shopworn images and typical responses to school leadership and reform is less clear. To make reframing more explicit, the metaphor of an eye examination offers some possibilities. Figure 12.1 shows typical equipment used by an optometrist to determine whether a client needs corrective lenses. There is the traditional wall chart with letters decreasing in size. Here we have substituted in big letters and smaller letters various strategies linked to school reform. This is to suggest that as we get closer to specific ways of implementing school reform, we still face the challenge of observing smaller details.

Some distance from the wall chart is a piece of equipment with which the examiner can rotate different lenses; these lenses are of different focal lengths and can be adjusted until we can clearly see the set of letters. Imagine for the moment that we can insert lenses taken from a box labeled "organization" or "leadership metaphors" into this piece of equipment; each lens represents the various organizational and leadership metaphors discussed in earlier chapters. The number of combinations of lenses is vast, as is our ability to combine metaphors and related concepts. We can put two different organization metaphors side by side, or we can focus on one organization metaphor but incorporate different concepts associated with it. We can begin to see the various permutations of lenses (or metaphors and related concepts) that we can insert to help us perceive a different image on the wall chart.

Obviously the process of switching metaphors is not as mechanical as using expensive eye examination equipment. The process of reframing is more fluid and de-

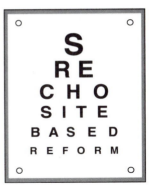

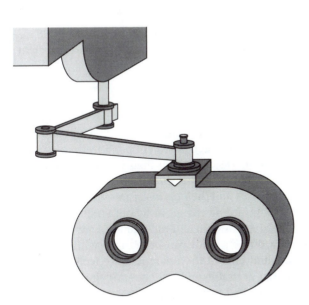

FIGURE 12.1 Eye chart and lens-changing machine

pendent on our ability to think consciously of different metaphors and related concepts while engaged in a wide assortment of daily activities. As with any skill, the first few attempts are awkward and seem impossible to accomplish, but the longer we practice it, the more comfortable and intuitive our use of the skill becomes.

To help us identify different metaphors and theories of school reform, the summary chapters of each section of this text highlight concepts associated with each of our metaphors (see Figures S1.1, S2.1, and S3.1 and the suggested questions in the Section 1 Summary). The lenses for examining school reform can be intuitively or deliberately selected. The important thing is to develop a comfort level with experimentation or adopt a playful approach (Bolman & Deal, 1991) in the use of different metaphors.

In this chapter, we will explore combinations of metaphors and demonstrate various insights they elicit for explaining certain dynamics or complexities of school reform. Our intent is to explore and contrast various metaphors and related concepts with an eye toward seeing new images associated with the three main strategies for school reform (school choice, school restructuring, and school-based management).

REFRAMING SCHOOL REFORM

Given the vast number of lenses at our disposal, we cannot explore all the combinations available to us. As the optometrist does not use all of the lenses at his or her disposal, we too will be selective. For purposes of demonstrating the power of reframing, we will explore only the following combinations:

- culture and dialectic metaphors for examining school choice
- theater and transformation metaphors for examining school restructuring
- political and democratic metaphors for examining school-based management

Reframing School Choice

As we know, school choice can take many different forms. In chapter 9 we explored the voucher plan, charter schools, statewide choice, districtwide choice, controlled choice, and home schooling. Each of these approaches, except possibly home schooling, implies students having to travel some distance from their home and neighborhood or community school. We have all witnessed the effects of redistricting school boundaries or the closing of schools. Parents and their children are often very vociferous about these changes and argue strongly for no change in school assignment. These encounters should serve to remind us that children and their families are not objects on a chessboard; the transfer from a home school can be fraught with emotional trauma. We need to appreciate that children and their parents have feelings and expectations that make such a move either desirable or threatening. Seeing school organizations as cultures and seeing leadership as a dialectical process, we may appreciate some of the forces pushing and pulling at parents and at the advocates of school choice.

Organizations as Cultures.   When we view a school as a culture, we have to appreciate how that culture came into existence and how it has been sustained over time. Teachers, administrators, support staff, parents and students—all, in one way or another, influence a school's culture and subcultures. Culture in organizations suggests some kind of social glue that connects and holds together different parts of the organization. Public opinion polls reveal that most parents feel their child's school is doing a good job; there is no doubt that the culture of their child's school contributes to this positive feeling. This suggests, in part, that those who desire to send their child to another school may in fact be persons who feel disconnected from their neighborhood or community school. The school's culture and/or its subcultures may not be sufficiently inclusive to provide the kind of "meaning" that people seek from their organizational affiliation. The school may not have the core values or expectations that the parents seek for themselves and their children. As a consequence, there is a feeling that a new and different school may have more to offer in spite of its unknown qualities. The lens labeled "culture" reveals an image of parents grappling with a decision of school choice that may not be as rational as economists suggest. In fact, according to Langer (1989), people are blinded to a wider range of choices because of cognitive commitment, defined as a rigidly held belief, or mindset, that shuts out alternative views of a situation. Culture can be one factor of many that reinforces or influences this mindset.

Organizations as culture remind us of our emotional side and the importance of having a sense of identification and meaning often derived from social groups. Successful schools and their cultures recognize the importance both of cherishing the individuality of its members and inspiring community. In schools where students and parents feel a close attachment, there is less desire to change schools. On the other hand, where parents and their children do not feel this connection, or worse, feel alienated by the school's culture, then the choice of another school is desirable.

The lens of culture should remind us that the forces to stay with a school may be greater than the pulls to consider another school, regardless of the promise associated with the new school. The prospect of school choice prompts an image of present-day immigrants being forced to escape desperate situations or motivated to change by the promises of a better life. There are no guarantees that the new opportunity will be any better than present circumstances, but parents and their offspring are vulnerable to overstated promises and the endless search for a better life. If school choice were widely implemented, it might have the side effect of creating alienated parents and children, particularly if the schools of choice do not come up to expectations. Schools with inclusive cultures may provide the glue, a sense of being connected that many people in our society seek; thus, the chance to choose another school would be neither desired nor welcome.

Dialectical Leadership.   Thinking of school choice from a leader's perspective helps us appreciate the value of the metaphor (or lens) of leadership as a dialectical process. Making school choice an active policy in a school district or state creates a situation that could be described as dialectical in nature. It also creates a condition in which leaders have to deal with value conflicts and value choices.

When we examine school choice from the point of view of culture, we can appreciate the importance of stability and sense of belonging that a culture can provide. When we examine school choice from the perspective of a dialectic, we have to recognize the effects of pluralism and uncertainty. School choice, as a school reform strategy, has a stated goal of destabilizing the status quo and forcing change. Change often carries with it the necessity of making choices among options of equal value. Change also introduces moral and ethical dilemmas and the possibility of some people being winners and others being losers. Change conditions heighten the awareness of ambiguity and subjectivity in making choices that may benefit from a moral framework to guide decision makers. Change, by its very nature, creates a dialectical condition resulting in paradoxes, dilemmas, and dualisms.

Advocates of school choice may be getting more than they bargain for. The destabilization of the status quo in school organizations brought on by school choice places additional pressure on school leaders to confront the dialectical process. Leaders, whether in sending or receiving schools, need to recognize the ambiguities and dilemmas that people are coping with and the imperative to ground these choices in some fundamental principles. Under a school choice policy, parents and their children have to grapple with the choice to stay or to leave their present school. This presents the parents with many unknowns, including the dilemma of short-term versus long-term benefits of their choices. It also presents school leaders with parents who are experiencing the contradictions of control and dependency, conflict and compromise, and hostility and compassion.

The use of a dialectical lens also raises the question of who benefits from a policy of school choice. A revisit to Flood and Jackson's (1991) 12 critically heuristic boundary questions helps in conducting a critical analysis of school choice. Those questions include Who ought to be the beneficiary? What ought to be the purpose? What ought to be the measure of success? Who ought to be the decision taker? and What are the worldviews of the involved or affected? These questions attempt to elicit the hidden value choices and determine who benefits most from a proposal like school choice. Unfortunately, there is some evidence that low-income and minority groups benefit least and middle- and upper-income and majority groups benefit most.

The dialectical perspective raises even more fundamental questions about the forces promoting the change and whether these conditions could be addressed in more preventative ways. That is, would it not be wise for building- and district-level educational leaders to develop a philosophy of inclusion and to reach out to those groups of parents and students who feel disenfranchised from the present system? Can these leaders develop a system of governance in their districts and in their schools that empowers and gives voice to *all* stakeholders? What could be learned, for example, by rotating school choice through the lens of leadership as a democratic process? As we explored in chapter 7, leadership viewed through the dialectical lens suggests that leadership is art, science, *and* philosophy. This seems to be even more true under conditions of school choice.

Reframing School Restructuring

Like school choice, school restructuring also comes in a number of different forms. we reviewed the models of the Coalition of Essential Schools, Paideia, Comer, Success for All, Copernican Plan, and the charter school. All of these, in one way or another, attempt to establish new relationships between teachers and students and focus attention on the instructional and learning process. Much of the school restructuring research suggests that in spite of good intentions, there is little evidence of positive effect on the learning outcomes of students. Yet in spite of this apparent lack of success in impacting student learning, the call for school restructuring continues, and well-intentioned teachers and administrators in schools across the country continue to devote considerable time and effort to "restructure" their schools.

These conditions provide a challenging context for reframing school restructuring through the metaphors of organizations as theater and leadership as a transformational process.

Organizations as Theater.   Theater, as a lens, provides an opportunity to see a restructuring effort from a different perspective. First, there is the obvious activity of restructuring being played out on the stage called school. As any wise theater patron knows, however, that which can be observed directly or seems most obvious is not the full story. Often it is the subplots or subtexts being played out backstage and offstage that provide real insight into what's going on and why. Theater attempts to convey a number of messages, often in very subtle ways, using drama, comedy, symbols, and props that often confuse and amuse us. The theater metaphor provides an opportunity to look beyond the obvious—the stated restructuring plan—and see other motivations, desires, and relationships.

Theater consciousness prevents us from being taken in and helps us appreciate that there is an actor behind a character, a playwright behind a script, a director behind a performance, and a reality behind the appearance. It is our task to focus the lens more carefully and determine what is going on with a school restructuring process. As mentioned earlier, there are any number of models and strategies (or scripts) for restructuring a school. The theater metaphor prompts questions about why and how a particular script is chosen. If theater is to survive, it must be worthy of support from audiences, actors, scriptwriters, and directors. This is no less true of getting school restructuring underway. It needs the support of many persons, and the particular approach (or script) chosen will be reflective of the aspirations of the many persons needed to make a restructuring effort (or play) possible.

For example, if a school is considering joining the Coalition for Essential Schools (CES), it is clear that Sizer (1984) is the scriptwriter; he has written the script that is to be followed by participating schools. In order to put this play (CES) on, however, we need to find a stage (or school), a director (principal), actors (teachers), auxiliary players (students), and audience (parents, taxpayers, board of education). As we know, much can happen before an opening show and the eventual performance of the play. Scripts get rewritten, actors are selected or deselected, directors resign, and so forth, which help us appreciate the human dimensions and complexities in getting the "act" together. So it seems to be with trying to implement school restructuring plans; unfortunately, school changes are performed in real time, with little or no opportunity for even a dress rehearsal.

The theater metaphor helps us appreciate the complexities of implementing new programs and how difficult it is to maintain fidelity to a particular script or a school change strategy. We need to appreciate the actor behind the character. The teacher who is being asked to behave differently is often ill prepared for his or her new role and may not even be the right person for the part. Yet schools often have little or no choice as to who the actors are and must work with those available (restructuring strategy), provide rehearsals (in-service meetings/workshops) while the play is being performed (implemented), and operate with whatever feedback is available from a director (principal or curriculum supervisor) or fellow actors (teachers). And of course, there are the critics who express their reviews in many forms (e.g., newspaper articles, letters to the editor, complaints to the board of education).

Theater reminds us that acting is a process of discovery and finding a fit. Actors try to keep a balance between role making and role taking behavior: a balance of self and role. This is no less true of teachers being called upon to assume new roles and behaviors. A wise director understands this tension and offers direction that enables the actor to achieve a balance. Actors are encouraged to stand back from their enactment of a role and reflect on this tension. Also, we in the audience are prompted to stand apart from the interactions on the stage and discover deeper meaning from asking the question: Why are we doing this thing anyway?

To add more complexity to implementing school restructuring efforts, theater reminds us that most plays are made up of protagonists and antagonists and their respective heroes and villains; in school parlance, we refer to antagonists as "resisters." Also, in most serious play situations, like school restructuring, there is an effort to control the plot; in melodrama, however, the plot controls the characters. School re-formers can start out attempting to control the "plot" of school change only to find themselves being controlled by the "plot" with tragic or farcical consequences.

Theater also helps us appreciate the importance of appearances. Space, scenery, and props are important and convey subtle messages of their own. Their congruence and linkage to the plot and subtext of the play are important; incongruity can be confusing and distract persons from understanding the underlying themes of the play. This is also true of schools. In order to earn the support of the public (audience), certain appearances need to be maintained. Schools have come to be known by the subjects they teach, age-graded instruction, and the physical appearance of a school building. School reform scripts that deviate too far from these standard symbols run some risk of gaining little or no support from important patrons. We have seen past efforts that have failed (e.g., nongraded schools, multi-age classrooms, open education, schools without interior walls), partly because they have deviated from stock appearances.

Theater and school restructuring share much in common. We are reminded of our foibles and limitations as human beings over control of our lives and events that affect us. We are also shown our need to seek meaning and greater understanding of what it takes to be human. Theater and school restructuring present us with many experiences and opportunities by which we may grasp, at least for a moment, insight about more fundamental (why?) questions of life.

Transformational Leadership.   Leadership as a transformational process links well to school restructuring. As a metaphor, it reminds us of the qualities of leadership that have potential for enabling a successful school restructuring effort. It reminds us of leadership's significant role in developing a vision for the future, articulating congruent strategies, aligning people with the desired change, motivating and inspiring people, and advocating change. Leaders involved in school restructuring have the enormous task of keeping people focused on why restructuring is needed and on the potential payoff. This may seem obvious; however, considerable research suggests that restructuring efforts lose their way and often do not have the impact on student learning that was part of the original vision.

Also, leadership as a transformational process brings to our attention the importance of the balance between the what and the how. It is not enough to have a vision (what) without ways of achieving that vision (how). Several writers and educational researchers discovered that leadership *and* management are crucial to successful change. Leadership focuses on strengthening a school culture; fostering staff development; engaging in frequent conversations about cultural norms, values, and beliefs; sharing power; and using symbols. Management functions also need addressing; these often include planning and budgeting, organization and staffing, control and problem solving, and producing a degree of predictability. How a particular school and its leaders attain this balance between leadership and management is unique to that school. It is important that persons in the organization develop an appreciation for both functions and nurture their use (cf. Fullan, 1993).

Other concepts associated with transformational leadership are noteworthy when considering school restructuring; these include empowerment and trust. Empowerment comes about as a result of involvement but also through a sense of accomplishment, through engagement in verbal interactions that help persuade and develop some emotional arousal, and through observing change in others. These processes can help members of a school feel stronger and less powerless.

The other side of the empowerment coin is trust: trust in leaders who can balance the what and how, but also trust in oneself to be able to meet the unpredictable challenges that come with school restructuring. Teachers in particular must sense that, as a group of professionals, they have the wherewithal to cope with new problems that often accompany change and to see these problems not as threats but as incentives. Creating this mindscape within a professional staff is essential to opening up honest communications and permits learning from mistakes. Successful change at the student level is dependent on being able to see what does *and* what does not seem to be working. Trust in oneself and colleagues makes it possible to be forthright about what is happening during a restructuring effort and permits exploring potentially corrective options.

Transformational leadership responds to the call for higher levels of morality and motivation. These notions are no less important to members of a school community embarked on a restructuring effort. We are challenged to see beyond viewing a new intervention as a "thing" to be put in place, but rather as a process committed to serving the needs of all students. With such an image, school restructuring has a better chance to fulfill its promise and to avoid the pitfalls of political debates shaped primarily by concerns based on self-interests.

Reframing School-Based Management

The various theories and processes of school-based management offer an excellent opportunity to examine the subtle implications of politics and democratic principles in school organizations. SBM is strongly anchored in the theory of decentralization and the granting of greater power to persons at the lowest possible level of an organization's hierarchy. Such a shift in power threatens the status quo and previously established power centers that attempt to influence educational policies and practices, including how schools are structured, what is taught, and how it is taught.

Organizations as Politics. When we view school-based management through the lens of organizations as politics, we can see its inherent political dynamics. SBM is based on the assumption that students will be better served if those closest to home have the power to make decisions that affect their well-being. When considered in the abstract, this perception makes sense and is a worthy goal. If we consider, however, the current structure of most school systems with their more centralized policy- and decision-making authority, then we can see that the transfer of power to the school site may not come easily. We are asking those persons who have authority and major responsibilites (i.e., superintendents, central office consultants, school boards) to transfer this authority to building principals, teachers,and local advisory committees. We have to ask, Why would they agree to that?

This is not to suggest that we do not have benevolent upper-level administrators and policymakers who have altruistic tendencies an genuinely believe that students can be better served by giving more responsibility to persons at the building level. But we have to recognize that many persons who have achieved a certain status and recognition, acquired considerable influence, have valuable skills and knowledge, and are strongly motivated to serve students and teachers from a centralized position are not likely to walk away from their responsibilities or to change their behaviors overnight. The transfer of power, from a political perspective, is not usually accomplished without some stress and conflict. Seeing organizations as politics helps us understand these underlying tensions and offers ways of analyzing these dynamics and finding strategies to minimize their negative impact.

As was discussed in chapter 3, politics, in even the most healthy organizations, is inevitable. Many persons may wish either to deny this fact or refuse to play any role in its furtherance. Moving to SBM makes politics even more inevitable. SBM requires that power be shared, as may not have been the case before, and that new relationships be established in order to achieve the ideals for which SBM is being promulgated. Disagreements and debates can be expected over decision-making authority, status appointments, resource allocations, and the selection of alternative means and ends— all of which necessitates having persons equipped with skills and knowledge about sources of power, coalition building, bargaining, and conflict management.

To be successful as a school reform strategy, SBM requires politician-managers who can anticipate points of disagreement and prevent issues from polarizing or immobilizing people within a school. Such persons need to be able to identify the partisan groups, read developing situations, analyze the special interests, respect power sources, and anticipate who, what, and why. A wise politician-manager knows when to avoid, dominate, accommodate, compromise, and/or collaborate. The important thing is to develop a comfort with the politics that will emerge in the implementation of SBM and be conscious of the choices of action when confronted with resistance, conflict, or outright rebellion.

Politics at any time can get messy, but politics during change can also create many ethical dilemmas. Those in leadership positions can anticipate having to make very difficult choices between maintaining long-term collegial relationships and pushing for needed changes in spite of the resistance or discomfort these may create. Persons with authority and/or power can expect to face situations that challenge their ethical bearings. This may get to the heart of failed school reform strategies. Leaders at the building level, who are dependent on mutually supportive relationships, may not be prepared for difficult choices and may not have developed an ethical framework to guide them. The golden rule of doing unto others as you wish them to do unto you may be a starting point, but it is equally valuable to remember that school change should be dedicated to increasing the quality of education for students.

Success in creating new opportunities for students requires confronting those individuals who have other interests or priorities. Seeing schools as politics requires greater consciousness of the ramifications of trying to implement SBM and the importance of political skills. Politician-managers, sensing what is right for kids, have a much better chance of successfully implementing an SBM strategy. One way of ensuring this vision's implementation is to consider leadership as a democratic process.

Leadership as a Democratic Process.   Examining SBM through the lens of leadership as a democratic process opens up some interesting possibilities. Right off we have to acknowledge that no one person, such as a principal, can implement any model of SBM without the support and commitment of other members of the organization. On the other hand, we also must recognize that the micropolitics of implementing SBM is inevitable: There are bound to be members in any school who feel that the current organization and operation of the school fit them just fine and see little need to experiment with SBM approaches; and, of course, at the same time there will be members who feel dissatisfied with the status quo and wish for a greater voice in determining new policies and practices. This typical situation calls out for leadership that can find an acceptable way through the various and often conflicting value systems that any proposal for change stirs up. Leadership as a democratic process offers a plausible approach to reconciling differences and provides an image of leadership often missing in school organizations.

One of the realities that promoters of SBM face is a vacuum in rules or governance structure in which new proposals can be carefully discussed. Often schools rely on past practices in introducing ideas for change, which leans heavily on administrators attempting to mobilize teachers to consider potential changes. Cross-representational committees or task forces form and deliberate, eventually providing a report to the faculty, administration, and the board. There are a number of limitations to this approach that inhibit full participation and/or produce a gap between a task force and others. One of the main constraints of the traditional committee deliberations is the absence of a governance structure guided by written rules and procedures. Thus, committees and task forces, as noble as they may be, operate in a governance vacuum. The absence of a set of by-laws that makes clear to everyone concerned how studies by committees will be processed and decided upon at best results in confusion and at worst in chaos. A high level of ambiguity concerning governance can be a breeding ground for micropolitical behavior that can easily get out of control and derail the best of intentions.

Unclear procedures for adopting new innovations, such as SBM, can make schools vulnerable to outside forces, including federal and state agencies, the courts, interest groups, professional reformers, and interstate organizations. Schools are often placed in a reactive mode because of the lack of any clear rules, norms, guideposts, or approved forums for deliberating over proposals regardless of source; then they become pawns on a chessboard of the macropolitical world and are used for the furtherance of the political agenda of national leaders.

Another side effect of unclear governance procedures is the alienation that teachers, principals, parents, and students can feel when they are called on to implement changes that they have had little or no voice in designing or accepting. One of the major ironies of educational institutions in a democratic society is their capacity to behave in autocratic ways with little or no opportunity for members to influence their structure and operations. We may wonder about the subtle message being served up to young people who see teachers struggling to be heard and they themselves with few or superficial opportunities to express their views on any proposed educational innovations. It seems to be the case of, Do as we say but not as we do; that is, in the stated curricula of a school, we offer content that stresses the importance of democratic principles, while in the unstated curricula, we emphasize compliance and acceptance of decisions by authority figures.

This is not to suggest that schools and their school systems do not have policies and procedures that guide officials in revising or creating new policies. A closer examination of these policies, however, may reveal an imbalance toward central authority and little or no clarification on how schools can take on greater autonomy for determining their own policies and procedures. Teachers have made inroads in school districts through negotiations in matters of salary, fringe benefits, and other related personnel policies, but their influence in matters of budget, curricula, and school programs is less clear. Students and parents have had even less clarity or opportunity to express their views on school matters that affect them. At the building level, in particular, teachers, parents, and students are vulnerable to shifts in the degree to which their participation is or is not desired, merely by a change, for example, in principals. Present-day policies and laws provide principals and superintendents with discretion concerning input by other members of the school community. Unfortunately, this authority makes others feel they have limited opportunity to influence how a school functions. There may be a feeling that carefully considered ideas can be summarily discharged based solely on the wishes of a principal or superintendent. Until there is a willingness of persons advocating SBM to examine and clarify the underlying governance structure of a school and school system, persons cannot feel that their right to participate has any real relevance or guarantee.

Leadership as a democratic process recognizes that *all* persons matter and is committed to ways of ensuring that their voices are heard in the deliberations necessary to make an organization successful. Leadership as a democratic process in schools recognizes the importance of preparing future citizens for our society in an environment that provides direct experience in democracy. Such leadership helps to create a "workers' bill of rights," which states up front the value of the individual and his or her autonomy within a democratic environment—an environment that gives people the right to express their needs and seek group understanding and in which ideas are based on the most persuasive arguments and not on formal authority.

SBM approaches, guided by democratic processes and rules of an open, inclusive environment, can create or reinforce the paradox of balancing individual and group rights. As we have observed in our readings thus far, there is a tension between recognizing individual rights and the rights of others. The push for using democratic principles in establishing an SBM plan may need to be balanced with concerns for building a sense of community. Communitarianism emphasizes the responsibility of the individual toward one's friends and neightbors. In a school context, communitarianism emphasizes the role of the school in creating bonds among various factions within and outside of the school.

The lens of leadership as a democratic process helps us appreciate that SBM should be more than tinkering with the details of participatory methods: It must be focused on fundamental changes of the governance structure. The creation of a "constitutional framework" can give persons associated with a school an understanding of how their voice can be expressed and how individual rights can be balanced with collective rights. It is important, however, that the creation of such a framework be done by those who will be affected by it. One way to create this framework is by having a constitutional convention in which representatives of various stakeholder groups meet to hammer out the respective roles and processes for governing a school. SBM that is led by democratic leaders, builds upon democratic principles, and has a constitutional framework can create an environment with potential for long-term support of democratic ideals and that provides a sense of purpose for those associated with the school.

In this context, the task of leadership is to lead the community to face all situations, to investigate what can and should be changed and what cannot. A democratic decision-making process does not mean that authority figures, unilaterally or in consultation with others, would not make the same decision as the group. Rather, democratic decision making goes to the heart of our existence and purpose for living. It is through our participation in problems (or messes, as some people like to describe them) and problem management that we grow and learn to appreciate our own abilities and the needs of others. To be sheltered from all of this by benevolent decision makers is to be denied the opportunity to discover our capacity to contribute to the quality of our lives and to that of others.

CONCLUSION

In this chapter, we explored the value of reframing school reform with the metaphors of organization and leadership developed in sections 1 and 2 of this text. Clearly we limited this exercise to a selected set of metaphors; for example, we did not explore any of the school reforms from the metaphor of organizations as brains, nor did we test to the full extent the various combinations of metaphors available to us. Also, we did not apply one metaphor or set of metaphors consistently across the school reform options. Therefore, we do not know what additional perceptions would have surfaced given a different mix or a different approach to reframing. However, even with a small subset of metaphors we did elicit some insights that may have escaped our notice had we not attempted this reframing exercise.

If, before this reframing experience, we wondered why school reform is so difficult to attain, this question should have been answered to some degree. The advocates of quick-fix or top-down imposition of change need to go back to the drawing board. Schools are not machines that require replacement parts or fine tuning: They are human enterprises with all the promises and frailties that go with that. We cannot minimize the exercise of free will and its impact on organizations like schools. Schools are such an interesting mix of hopes and broken dreams that to expect an orderly movement toward change, no matter how desirable, is naive.

On the other hand, this does not mean that there is no hope for our schools to correct their mistakes and to create a better place for their members. In fact, if nothing else, the reframing exercise opens up a wider range of ways of seeing school organizations and their leadership that may not have been possible with more conventional ways of thinking about schools. The diversity of values and expectations that exist within a school and its community can be seen not as threatening but as an asset. Reframing with metaphors of the kind illustrated in this text should put leaders at ease and permit more thoroughly contemplated approaches to managing school problems. For good or ill, smooth sailing and bad weather go hand in hand. To expect one without the other is like hoping that life will be free of stress or conflict.

Does this mean that we should give up hope of a better way and a better day? Obviously not. We are challenged, maybe destined, however, to cope endlessly with finding the balance between order and disorder. And no doubt when we think we have figured it out, we will be reminded of our inability to master the elements. It is our quest to overcome our limitations and to reshape the world. We go to great expense in mastering the problems of space travel in the hope that we will unlock some of the mysteries of life; we go to similar expense in changing schools in the hope that we will create a better life for ourselves and our youthful charges. As with space travel, we experience flawless flights and disastrous setbacks, but we do not give up the quest. Metaphors explored in this text remind us of both our limitations and potential. We should know by now that we are not going to arrive at a final destination but are part of an endless venture that we hope will make some positive difference in the lives of all of us.

The metaphors and their related concepts explored thus far offer an interesting array of ways to view our school organizations and the leadership therein. We should recognize, however, that our inventory of potential metaphors is unlimited and will continue to grow. In the final chapter, we will explore some promising metaphors on the horizon that offer fresh possibilities for understanding the complex process of school leadership and school reform.

DISCUSSION QUESTIONS

1. What views are most interesting and/or perplexing as a consequence of the reframing exercise in this chapter?
2. What possible courses of action do you see flowing from this reframing exercise?
3. In your opinion, does the reframing exercise illustrated in this chapter offer any perspective on problems facing your educational organization?
4. What conclusions do you come to after examining the ideas in this chapter? Does reframing with metaphors as lenses offer some promise to coping with daily challenges *and* long-term needs for change in educational organizations? What are its strengths and limitations?
5. Can you conceive of other ways to reframe problems besides the approach illustrated in this chapter?

SUGGESTED ACTIVITIES

1. Take any metaphor or a combination of metaphors and reframe a change effort in your educational organization. What ideas surface? What strategies are suggested? How might you "act" differently based on your reframing analysis?

2. The brain metaphor for organizations was not explored in this chapter. Using a selected subset of concepts from chapter 5, conduct a similar reframing exercise of the three school reform strategies explored in section 3.

3. Use a different mix of organizational and leadership metaphors and apply them to the three school reforms. Contrast the results of this mix with those in this chapter and/or contrast your insight with others.

REFERENCES

Bolman, L. G., & Deal, T. E. (1991). *Reframing organizations.* San Francisco: Jossey-Bass.

Flood, R. L., & Jackson, M. C. (1991). *Creative problem solving.* New York: Wiley.

Fullan, M. (1993). *Change forces.* New York: Falmer.

Kuhn, T. S. (1970). *The structure of scientific revolutions.* Chicago: University of Chicago Press.

Langer, E. (1989). *Mindfulness.* Boston: Addison-Wesley.

Morgan, G. (1986). *Images of organization.* Beverly Hills: Sage.

Morgan, G. (1993). *Imaginization: The art of creative management.* Newbury Park, CA: Sage.

Senge, P. (1990). *The fifth discipline.* New York: Doubleday.

Sergiovanni, T. J. (1992). *Moral leadership.* San Francisco: Jossey-Bass.

Sizer, T. R. (1984). *Horace's compromise.* Boston: Houghton Mifflin.

chapter 13

Trends and Implications

In the movie *Mindwalk* (which is based on Capra's [1983] *The Turning Point*), one of the principal characters expresses concern that the present-day crisis facing humankind is a crisis of perception, the ways in which we perceive our social world. She laments that many of today's leaders and ordinary citizens are unable to break with the paradigm developed by Descartes and others, with its strong emphasis on people functioning in mechanical and predictable ways. As a physicist, she stresses the importance of systems thinking and seeing the human experience as holistic and interdependent. Life is a consequence of a long evolutionary process, and our capacity to understand the complexity of the human experience is dependent on internal influences (i.e., our worldview) and external influences (i.e., the worldviews of others).

Historians stress that unless we are good students of history, we are destined to repeat the mistakes of the past. Futurists, on the other hand, express the importance of studying trends and looking forward in time, particularly if we wish to be proactive rather than reactive to trends in progress. Systems thinking includes a mix of past, present, and future thinking and places us inside the system as a participant rather than outside, looking in as an observer. This shift in perception is important if we are to appreciate that we are both the problem and the solution. The more we are able to understand our inner thinking and its influence on how we perceive and behave, the greater is the likelihood that we will appreciate our human qualities, including our ability to exercise free will.

Persons are prompted to act in certain ways for a variety of reasons often not fully understood or appreciated. The richer our repertoire of insights in understanding what seems to be the unpredictable behavior of ourselves and others, the more likely we are to respond in more effective ways. This text, hopefully, with its rich overview of past and present theories of organizations, leadership, and school reform, provides a base for generating alternative views and insights. However, our task is not complete without attempting to anticipate what new challenges face us in education and what additional theories we may be able to draw on to face them. This chapter will look ahead and attempt to anticipate the future and its implications for the reframing and reforming of our experiences in educational organizations.

First, we will examine some global trends that are facing our society and that will have some bearing on the future of our schools. Following this examination, we will explore some demographic trends in the United States and their implications for schools in the future. This analysis will open the door to examining other emerging theories that offer some potential for reforming schools for the third millennium: chaos theory, organizational cycles, and feminist theory. This exploration of a futuristic perspective or frame will permit us to stress the importance of hearing new voices, often the voices of minorities and of women, and appreciating their views of organization and leadership. Finally, we will conclude our use of different metaphors with a quilt maker's rendition of important humanistic *and* systems perspectives. This will help us see the artistry involved in creating learning systems in which new forms of organization and leadership will be needed to effectively change schools to meet the challenges facing them in the third millennium.

GLOBAL TRENDS AND THE THIRD MILLENNIUM

In but a short period of time, on January 1, 2000, we will enter the third millennium. For some this will mean little but perhaps how to survive another New Year's party. For others, however, the image of embarking on a third millennium will give pause for reflection and projection. It is an opportunity to ask, Where have we been? and Where are we going? or Where would we like to go? In many ways, the discussion in this book partly answers the first question and foreshadows answers to the second and third. As Cooley (1993) states, "In a strictly literal sense, what we will experience at midnight on December 31, 1999, will be not the passage from one millennium to another but merely the ordinary transition from one second of time to the next. Unlike ordinary new years, however, the occasion will offer us an unprecedented chance to evaluate our progress and enjoy a sense of renewal" (p. 126).

This significant shift in time lubricates the natural tendency we have, according to Slaughter (1993), to give full range to the human mind over time past, present, and future. We feel an interconnectedness with all things past and future. Cooley (1993) suggests that two hundred years is our space in time. We look back over the past hundred years to contemplate our roots in the lives and cultures of our parents and their parents; we look forward to the next hundred years "with our children and theirs to the world which is growing organically, day by day, from our present reality" (p. 117). We also need to appreciate that those born in 1995 will be entering college in 2013. This awareness helps us appreciate a sense of time, its continuum, and the importance of recapturing a sense of future. Day-to-day events are not isolated or devoid of meaning; the days aggregate and accumulate over time and can preset future options or directions.

When we think of the future we typically think of breakthroughs in technology—robots, space stations, biotechnology, and the like. But according to Naisbitt and Aburdene (1990), "The most exciting breakthroughs of the 21st century will occur not because of technology but because of an expanding concept of *what it means to be human*" (p. 16; emphasis added).

Naisbitt and Aburdene believe we are entering a renaissance in the arts and spirituality. As our technology grows more dramatic and powerful, we will at the same time need to take into account the unique qualities of the individual. This renewed interest in spirituality no doubt will be expressed in many forms, part of which we explored within the concept of communitarianism, but we need to appreciate that spirituality can offer a framework within which answers to global environmental and social issues can be guided. The true nature of who we are and who we wish to become surfaces in our behavior and in the day-to-day choices we make in our lives. As Naisbitt and Aburdene put it, "Apocalypse or Golden Age. The choice is ours. As we approach the beginning of the 3d millennium, the way we address that question will define what it means to be human" (p. 17).

When it comes to judging the potential of the future, for some the glass is half full and for others it is half empty. Templeton (1993) believes we live in "a period of unprecedented discovery and opportunity, a blossoming time for mankind [*sic*]" (p. 2). He sees significant changes emerging politically, economically, culturally, and spiritually during the third millennium. Let's explore some of these potential changes.

Megatrends

In their book *Megatrends 2000,* Naisbitt and Aburdene (1990) report on ten overarching trends for the year 2000:

1. the booming global economy of the 1990s
2. a renaissance in the arts
3. the emergence of free-market socialism
4. global lifestyles and cultural nationalism
5. the privatization of the welfare state
6. the rise of the Pacific Rim
7. the decade of women in leadership
8. the age of biology
9. the religious revival of the new millennium
10. the triumph of the individual

We can anticipate that each of these trends will have varying degrees of influence on educational organizations and their leadership. Clearly the trend of women in leadership roles speaks directly to schools and the potential impact of the feminist perspective upon them. The increased number of women in principalships and superintendencies supports the significance of this trend.

The triumph of the individual certainly warrants greater attention in schools and to the special meaning of being human, particularly as a child evolves into adulthood. Ironically, in some ways it has been the technological breakthroughs of computers, computer networks, compact laser disks, videos, cellular phones, and fax machines that have democratized information and empowered the individual. Many would argue that we are just beginning to see the potential implications of this technology and the degree to which future generations will have greater control over their learning and access to information.

The availability of this new technology does not come without problems and challenges. The challenge for future generations, according to Slaughter (1993), is to assert dominance over technical development. Essentially his concern is that human development needs to accelerate to the greatest extent possible in order to ensure this technology is used to the betterment of humankind. Slaughter writes, "If base human motives such as greed, fear, arrogance etc. continue to be linked with powerful technologies, it is not hard to see the future as a continuing disaster" (p. 124). Or, as Kennedy (1993) observes, this new technology may result in future generations "picking up the value system of a shallow entertainment industry rather than the moral standards, discipline, and intellectual curiosity that equip a person to learn" (p. 308). He goes further to challenge as being far too unrealistic the assumption that schools can remedy this potential cultural crisis.

There is individuality, and there is community. In Naisbitt and Aburdene's (1990) opinion, individuals are not condemned to face the world alone: "Individuals seek community" (p. 300). Slaughter (1993) defines the need to set aside previous generations' contradictory values and establish new communal values of stewardship, selfless love, and obligations to future generations.

The trends of a renaissance in the arts and the age of biology certainly have implications for curricula and instruction in our schools. Again it is not a question of whether we should expose young learners to either the arts *or* science; the importance of these trends requires us to expose young persons to *both*. Both disciplines offer a greater understanding of our human qualities and our potential to discover and appreciate the meanings of life.

In fact, Harman (1993) expects that sciences and what he calls the metaphysics (i.e., philosophy) will come together early in the twenty-first century and "will be judged by future historians to be as consequential as was the scientific revolution of the 17th century" (p. 139). The emerging and restructuring of science will emphasize more participatory methodologies that encourage learning that can be garnered by " 'becoming one with' that which is being studied" (p. 142). Also the new science will favor "more holistic and organismic models in the biological and human sciences" and emphasize "subjective experiences as a valid 'window' through which to explore certain aspects of reality" (p. 142). He hastens to add that what he refers to as "extended" science is not a return to dogma and superstitions but rather an openness to alternative theories and explanations balanced by healthy skepticism and consensual validation of findings.

The megatrends discussed thus far suggest a utopian era is before us. Certainly Naisbitt and Aburdene (1990) are zealous in wanting to combat the voices of naysayers and critics of current trends. Maybe Ogilvy (1993) provides the right balance when he observes,

Despite the wonders of modern science there never seems to be enough: enough love, enough attention, enough respect, enough dignity. So we make

too much of the things we know how to make: war, toxic wastes, bad television. Perhaps there is a better way to organize our lives and our relationships, one that does not pit the demands of work against the delights of love.
Perhaps there is a way to reconstruct our world. But in doing so we cannot
base our reconstruction on the firm foundations of science. Nor will we be
able to depend on transcendent norms as a measure of the better, instead,
from what we have at hand: our existing legal system, our existing health
care system, our existing educational system, our existing families. So the job
is not altogether utopian. (p. 149)

Ogilvy advocates neither what he refers to as world-weary pessimism nor bubble-
headed optimism. He suggests an emergent paradigm approaching the "semiotic
turn," a broad shift in the sciences away from "positivism that would reduce symbols
to a physicalistic explanation of signification" to a system that "sees the semiotic realm
as an autonomous and irreducible domain for the interpretation of meanings, not the
measurement of facts" (p. 130).

Kennedy (1993) offers a sobering analysis of future trends. He observes that there
is a surge in the earth's population and rising demographic imbalances between rich
and poor nations. The present world population is at 5 billion and expected to increase to 10 billion by the middle of the next century, with most of the growth occurring in the poorest regions of the world. A second trend is the impact of technology
in making redundant traditional jobs, replacing them with new systems of production
and by doing so changing systems that have existed for over two centuries. A third
trend is the global financial and communications revolution making the gap between
poorer and richer nations more apparent. In sum, Kennedy suggests, "If my analysis is
roughly correct, the forces for change facing the world could be so far-reaching, complex, and interactive that they call for nothing less than the reeducation of humankind" (p. 339). This observation provides another perspective on school or
educational reform that is far more significant than anything we have discussed so far.

The transformation of our society and of course its social institutions, such as
schools, has already taken place, according to Drucker (1993). In his description of a
postcapitalist society, we have become a society of organizations:

Certain it is that in politics we have already shifted from the four hundred
years of the sovereign nation-state to a pluralism in which the nation-state
will be one rather than the only unit of political integration. It will be one
component—though still a key component—in what I will call the "post-
capitalist polity," a system in which transnational, regional, nation-state, and
local, even tribal, structures compete and co-exist. (p. 4)

As a result of these shifts and other factors, information and knowledge will become the lifeblood of the future well-being of our society and others. We are shifting
from expressing capital as land and labor to expressing it as information and knowledge. People in a postcapitalist society will be identified as knowledge workers and
service workers. A new synthesis will need to be created between the "intellectuals"

who are most concerned with words and ideas and "managers" who are most concerned with people and work. The educational challenge for the future will be transcending this dichotomy. Knowledge, which at one time was considered a private good, now has become a public good.

It is clear, according to Drucker (1993), that knowledge has and will continue to play a central role in the social and economic development of the world. Drucker identifies an additional area of influence of knowledge that he calls the "management revolution." This revolution has taken less than 50 years, from 1945 to 1990. Today's definition of a manager has become "one who is responsible for the application and performance of knowledge" (p. 44). We, as educational managers, carry an even heavier burden in not only applying new knowledge to the management of educational institutions but also playing a role in expanding and transmitting our knowledge about knowledge. Future knowledge needs to prove itself in action. According to Drucker, "What we now mean as knowledge is information effective in action, information focused on results" (p. 46). Maybe this is a good time for us to revisit John Dewey and his notions of experiential learning through the application of knowledge.

With these global trends or megatrends as a backdrop, let's shift our attention to demographic trends in the United States and their implications for schools.

DEMOGRAPHIC TRENDS IN THE UNITED STATES

Kennedy (1993) reports that the U.S. population in 1991 was 240 million and the projection is 301 million in 2025. In that population increase is the prospect of more elderly persons than children by 2030: In 1960 there were 16.6 million elderly (65+) and in 1990 31 million; there will be 52 million in 2020 and 65.5 million in 2030. Further, by 2050 whites will be a minority.

Hodgkinson (1992) reviewed the 1990 census data for implications for our society and schools for the period of 1990 to 2010. He found that over the decade of the 1980s, the United States increased its population by 22.1 million people, reaching a total of 248.7 million in 1990. As was forecast, our ethnic and racial mix has changed. While the total population grew by nearly 10 percent, that of whites grew by only 6 percent; the number of blacks increased by 13.2 percent; of Native Americans, Eskimos, or Aleuts by 37.9 percent; of Asians or Pacific Islanders by 107.8 percent; and of Hispanics grew by 53 percent. Ninety percent of the growth occurred in the South and West with California, Texas, and Florida accounting for half of the nation's growth. The states that are growing tend to be states with a high percentage of minorities, especially minority youth.

The fastest growing group during the decade of the eighties was prisoners, up 139 percent, from 466,371 in 1980 to 1,115,111 in 1990. According to Hodgkinson (1992), our country has the highest percentage of prisoners of any nation in the world. Black males make up 6 percent of our population but represent 47 percent of the prison population. As of fiscal year 1991, we spent on average $22,500 a year per prisoner, a costly investment when we consider that 73 percent of all prisoners released are back in jail within three years. More alarming, possibly to educators, is the fact that 82 percent of the prisoners are high school dropouts.

We have also observed a shift in the makeup of the American household. The classical two-parent, two-child family represents only 6 percent of all households in America. Total households increased by 15.5 percent over the decade of the eighties with single female parents (+21.2 percent), single male parents (+87.2 percent), singles living alone (+25.7 percent), and singles living with nonrelatives (+45 percent) representing the top gainers. Married couples with children decreased by 1.7 percent.

Hodgkinson (1992, p. 4) identifies other changes:

- 82 percent of all children (under 18) now have working mothers
- women who are single parents are raising 13.7 million children with a median family income of $10,982. Forecasters predict that 60 percent of today's children will live with a single parent at some time before they reach age 18
- over 1 million young mothers (age 20–24) could not work in 1986 because of the lack of quality or affordable child care
- in 1990, 13 percent of all children were regularly hungry, 25 percent were born to unmarried parents, and over 20 percent of all children under age 18 were poor
- in 1988, 57 percent of the nation's families and individuals could not qualify to buy a median-priced home

Projections of the U.S. population for birth to age 17 from 1990 to 2010 suggest a modest increase overall (267.7 million or +7.1 percent) in 2000 and 282.2 million (+5.3 percent) in 2010. We can anticipate a further decline in the number of whites

FIGURE 13.1   Percentage of eighth graders in low and high socio-economic groups who are proficient in advanced mathematics, by race and ethnicity, 1988

SOURCE: National Center for Education Statistics, *National Education Longitudinal Study of 1988, A Profile of the American Eighth Grader,* 1990. As in H. L. Hodgkinson, *A Demographic Look at Tomorrow,* 1992, Institute for Educational Leadership, Washington, D.C., p. 8. Reprinted with permission of Institute for Educational Leadership.

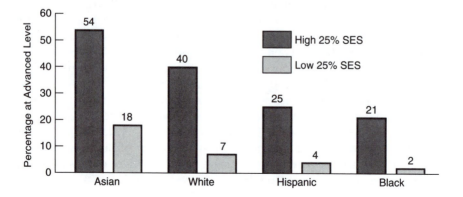

(−3.8 million) as compared to modest increases in the number of Hispanics (+2.6 million) and blacks (+1.2 million).

There appears to be a high correlation between social class and academic performance (see Figure 13.1). As Hodgkinson (1992) expresses it, "Show me a *minority child raised in a suburb and whose parents are college graduates,* and I will show you a child whose educational performance is roughly the same as that of a white child raised in a suburb by parents who are college graduates. . . . Much of what looks like race is really class" (p. 7).

IMPLICATIONS OF TRENDS FOR EDUCATION

As Figure 13.1 suggests, most lower-performing students are members of the lowest socioeconomic status (SES) group. Also, unfortunately, there is a high correlation between SES and minority status. These conditions will continue to present a challenge to schools in the future. Because of these relationships, according to Hodgkinson (1992), "America's best schools (and students) are located in the suburbs of our 40 largest metropolitan areas; the worst schools are located in the inner cities of the same metro areas plus some rural areas" (p. 9).

In Hodgkinson's view, it is time to take on the issue of wealth and class in the equity debate. Several states (e.g., Kentucky, Texas, Virginia) are confronting the inequities among school districts of spending for education. The disparities between poor inner cities and rural areas and their wealthy suburban counterparts have long been established; it now appears that the courts are holding state legislatures accountable for finding a more equitable educational funding formula. Given the rise in crime and costs of incarceration of criminals, it is in the interest of middle- and upper-income taxpayers to support better schools for inner-city and rural children. As mentioned earlier, more than 80 percent of America's one million prisoners are high school dropouts. As Achilles (1993) observes, "American prisons were full of non-readers; in North Carolina (1989) it cost nearly $30,000 per inmate per year in prison but less than $3,500 per pupil per year for education" (p. 26).

Hodgkinson (1992) expresses concern that our country is moving swiftly to a two-part society made up of the "information-rich" and the "information-poor." These groupings also distinguish the educational opportunities of poor children and their parents from higher-income children and parents. Educational technology and opportunities continue to expand for children living in suburban and wealthier school systems; this is not the case for most inner-city and rural students.

The problems of poverty and providing adequate educational, health, and social services will no doubt become a major issue for the late 1990s and early in the next millennium. Continued collaborations between and among social and educational service institutions will need to be a high priority. Greater prevention of educational, social, and medical problems needs to replace the higher costs of expensive and ineffective cures. We can no longer afford to write off a third of our youth. With a shrinking youth population available to our future labor force, every child is needed to build a healthy and robust society as we move to the third millennium.

IMPLICATIONS OF TRENDS FOR SCHOOL REFORM

The promising outlook suggested by megatrends is somewhat weighted down by demographics of the past decade and the trends implied by these statistics. While there is much promise for the information-rich portion of our society, the opportunities for the information-poor appear far less promising. What role, if any, schools will play in bridging this gap is an open question. An examination of policies and practices that limit access by virtue of a student's economic, social, ethnic, racial, and gender background is needed. To state it more positively, we need to consider what new policies and practices are needed to enhance the learning opportunities of *all* children (rich and poor), their parents, and their communities in the future.

We must recognize that the perception that our schools are in deep trouble is fraught with contradictory evidence and conclusions. We have the *At Risk* report of 1983 and all the subsequent reports on one side indicating the failure of American schools; on the other side, we have the Sandia report of 1992 (Carson, Huelskamp, & Woodall, 1993), plus articles (Berliner, 1993; Bracey, 1991; Huelskamp, 1993) that challenge the critics of American education. As Fullan and Miles (1992) observe, "Educational reform is as much a political as an educational process, and it has both negative and positive aspects" (p. 746).

These contradictions and symbolic gestures at school reform in part explain why schools that need to change do not. Unfortunately we cannot often tell the difference between those schools that are doing well with their students and those that are not, except, of course, in extreme cases. It is difficult to take gross measures of dropout rates, test scores, and teenage pregnancies and infer their implications for school change; given the numbers, what should be changed? Even individual measures of performance, such as standardized tests, raise questions of appropriateness of the items, a match to the taught curriculum of a school, and extenuating individual circumstances that interfere with a student's performance. Need for change is often in the eyes of the beholder; these perceptions can spark change or increase resistance to change. A fluid exchange of perceptions and ideas can more firmly establish both the strengths and weaknesses of a school and act as a baseline for comparing progress over time.

When teachers, administrators, and parents are mobilized, we do have better insights as to how successful change efforts might be conducted. Fullan and Miles (1992) and Fullan (1993) offer some basic themes or lessons derived from the literature on effective change. Fullan (1993) offers eight basic lessons:

1. You can't mandate what matters
2. Change is a journey, not a blueprint
3. Problems are our friends
4. Vision and strategic planning come later
5. Individualism and collectivism must have equal power
6. Neither centralization nor decentralization works
7. Connection with the wider environment is critical for success
8. Every person is a change agent (pp. 21–22)

As Fullan and Miles (1992) state, "Being knowledgeable about the change process may be both the best defense and the best offense we have in achieving substantial educational reform" (p. 752). Clearly this knowledge is vital, but it may not be the complete answer. To organize and lead schools to new heights of effectiveness, those persons who have a stake in their future will need to examine their frames or reference points and open them up for review and public exchange. With this exchange may emerge new insights and motivation to change. To further help in stimulating different ways of thinking about school organizations and leadership in the future, let's examine some emerging theories.

EMERGENT THEORIES FOR REFRAMING SCHOOL REFORM

In earlier chapters of this text, we explored many theories currently in vogue and helpful in examining school organizations and leadership. We also briefly alluded to additional theories that are worthy of further discussion even though their content and implications are still under development. Specifically we shall revisit and explore in more depth chaos theory, theory of organizational cycles or evolution, and feminist theory.

Chaos Theory

Given the level of uncertainty surrounding schools and the kind of leadership that is needed to help schools adapt to emerging environmental changes, chaos theory offers a different frame with which to consider these ambiguities. The everyday use of the word *chaos* suggests a condition out of control and on the verge of collapse. This image does not necessarily match the conditions of most schools in the United States, although those who are called on to supervise lunchroom and playground activities may concur with this interpretation. In our exploration of chaos theory and its applications, we shall examine its origins, contemporary definitions, concepts that may have some relevance to schools, and its value as a metaphor.

Origins of Chaos Theory.   The acceptance of chaos theory as worthy of scientific investigation has been slow and controversial. In some ways, it is a theory that nearly fell in the cracks between a clash of paradigms. On the one hand, those who favor the positivistic traditions and value of reductionism in the quest for nonequivocal, predictable findings consider the pursuit of chaos theory frivolous. Those who favor interpretism and its notions of holism and the unpredictable qualities of natural phenomena are intrigued by chaos theory but may be uncomfortable with its heavy reliance on mathematical reasoning and its application to social systems. There has been, however, an increased level of interest in chaos theory as a science for predicting the unpredictable, a contradiction, of course, but one that is capturing the imagination of many scientists at the present time.

Briggs and Peat (1989) trace the roots of chaos theory to ancient Chinese and Egyptian philosophies, which believed that "the forces of chaos and order were part of an uneasy tension, a harmony of sorts. They thought of chaos as something immense and creative" (p. 19). The establishment of yin and yang, the female and male principles, suggests a balance or harmonious relationship: Too much of either can result in chaos. It appears, however, that the introduction of science (reductionist science in particular, according to Briggs and Peat) distracted thinkers from the tension between order and disorder and focused primarily on a search for the predictable. According to Briggs and Peat, reductionism took a rather simple view of chaos:

> Chaos was merely complexity so great that in practice scientists couldn't track it, but they were sure that in principle they might one day be able to do so. When that day came there would be no chaos, so to speak, only Newton's laws. It was a spellbinding idea. (p. 22)

In some ways it was a fantasy that denied unpredictability rather than embrace it and explore its unique qualities. We have moved from this position of denial to observe some interesting patterns in so-called unpredictable disorder.

It was during the 1970s, according to Gleick (1987), that scientists, including mathematicians, physicists, biologists, and chemists, began to explore the dimensions of disorder. A decade later, chaos became shorthand for describing these multidisciplinary interests, and it became a hot topic. A new lexicon emerged with such terms as *fractals* and *bifurcations, intermittencies* and *periodicities, folded-towel diffeomorphisms,* and *smooth noodle maps.* According to Gleick, "To some physicists chaos is a science of process rather than state, of becoming rather than being" (p. 5). Briggs and Peat (1989) reinforce this when they argue that order, chaos, change, and wholeness are all woven together. These notions relate well to the complexities of school reform and the orientation needed by organizations and their leaders.

Kellert (1993) offers some support for the relevance of chaos theory to social systems. He suggests, "As a qualitative study, chaos theory investigates a system by asking about the general character of its long-term behavior, rather than seeking to arrive at numerical predictions about its exact future state" (p. 4). We will explore organizational cycles shortly, but at this juncture it is pertinent to emphasize that when it comes to school reform, there is some value in understanding what circumstances seem to lead to school change as opposed to seeking methods to ensure a specific end state. The study of complex and unpredictable behavior in dynamic systems is at the heart of chaos theory. As a metaphor for school reform, chaos theory encourages us to explore seemingly aberrant behavior and appreciate its contribution to the overall evolution of a school as a social system.

Definitions and Concepts of Chaos Theory.   As mentioned earlier and with any new intellectual venture, chaos theory has its own unique lexicon which is needed to explain new concepts. An example of this new language is Kellert's (1993) definition of chaos theory as "the qualitative study of unstable aperiodic behavior in deterministic nonlinear dynamical systems" (p. 5). This definition supports the explanation provided for the crash of a DC-9 airplane at the Denver airport. The investigators at the crash site concluded that "the culprit is the few grains of ice that passengers reported seeing on their plane's wings after the final deicing. These small seeds built up a turbulence powerful enough to bring the giant jet down" (Briggs & Peat, 1989, p. 13).

Scientists, using chaos theory as a paradigm, are developing new insights about what appear to be random and unrelated events. From waves in the ocean to stock market crashes to severe storms and floods in the Midwest, each catastrophe is seen as a convergence of a number of random events with an overall general pattern that merges into a dramatic occurrence. It is considered the science of "orderly disorder."

The DC-9 crash illustrates a number of concepts typically associated with chaos theory: the butterfly effect, turbulence and complexity, dissipative structures, random shocks, strange attractors, recursive symmetries, and feedback mechanisms. Griffiths, Hart, and Blair (1991) also explore these concepts through their application of chaos theory to a school district problem situation. In their analysis of this case, the butterfly effect was illustrated by a "small stimulus (the flap of the butterfly's wings in the industrial Northeast) leading to large effects (e.g., population and enrollment growth and tax base development)" in school systems (p. 445). Turbulence, in this case, consisted of the charges of incompetence and ensuing conflict that stemmed from the decision to locate a high school on top of the municipal well. When carefully examined, seemingly small, unimportant, and random events can reveal deeply embedded patterns; the ice droplets on the DC-9 wings and school district nonlinear events illustrate this phenomenon.

Lorenz, a mathematician and meteorologist, discovered this phenomenon by accident. Instead of starting at the beginning of a computer program for tracking and predicting weather patterns, he began in the middle and punched in numbers that were rounded off to the nearest thousandth rather than the six digits typically used (i.e., .506 instead of .506127). The result was a weather pattern that diverged from the normal, predetermined pattern. In fact, the divergence increased over time until there was no resemblance to the original pattern. From a very small variance came a significant and dramatic alteration to the pattern expected. An example within a school context is how standardized test scores appear very comparable at the end of first grade, but by sixth grade, for the same group of students, demonstrate greater variability. Figure 13.2 illustrates the Lorenz pattern.

Other graphs that display this phenomenon take on interesting patterns. For example, the Lorenz attractor (see Figure 13.3), takes on the appearance of an owl's mask or butterfly's wings and reflects the impact of changing the value of one of three variables. The extension of this image is a common explanation of the butterfly effect in which the flapping of butterfly wings in one region of the world links to violent storms in another region.

Turbulence, according to Kellert (1993), "remains an unsolved problem for classical physics; there is still no adequate theoretical account of the whorls and eddies that appear in waterfalls, whirlpools, and wakes" (p. 7). Like a stream, schools can appear to be flowing along smoothly as they strive to help children to grow and learn. But this tranquility is easily broken and turbulence is introduced into the system: Critics demand more emphasis on academics, parents want more homework, or teachers feel they are not respected; something inevitably comes along to disturb the status quo

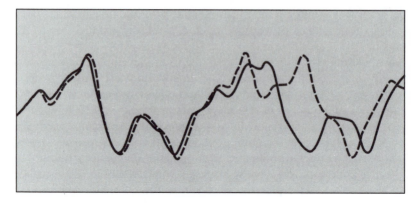

FIGURE 13.2 The Lorenz pattern

SOURCE: J. Gleick, *Chaos*, 1987, Viking Press, Bergenfield, NJ, p. 17.

and disrupts the equilibrium of the school. Chaos theory prepares us to anticipate these disturbances and the inevitable turbulence that will follow.

Interestingly, these initial disturbances may create a bifurcation in which the original pattern branches and creates more patterns of a similar nature. In a school context, it is not unusual for the conflict between two individuals to be replicated subsequently between other individuals in the same class or on the playground. As the flow of agitation and conflict continues, further bifurcating of these struggles may follow.

The notion of dissipative structures was suggested by the Nobel prizewinning physical chemist Prigogine (Prigogine & Stengers, 1984); he observed that phenomena that appear confusing and chaotic up close, appear at a more distant level to be orderly. It is not unusual to observe a number of school districts suffering the impact of voters' rejection of their school budgets and creating a chaotic condition. When viewed, however, from a higher level and over time we can see a pattern of school budget rejections, eventual passage, and state legislatures confronting school aid issues in order to provide local property tax relief. At the macrolevel, matters appear much more orderly than at the microlevel.

Another concept associated with chaos theory is "strange attractors." Attractors are a point in a system's cycle to which the system is attracted. There are fixed-point attractors that are predictable (e.g., a pendulum swing) and strange attractors which, according to Camel (1993), exhibit unpredictable and bizarre motions; in this case, "strange" is a reference to the geometry of the attractor. The dynamics of strange attractors are such that the patterns observed never repeat themselves but are iterative approximations of the initial pattern. For example, as mentioned earlier, the Lorenz attractor takes on the appearance of butterfly wings; it produces a pattern that is not capable of being predicted over time, yet after numerous iterations takes on an overall and consistent pattern. Schools engaging in reform desire to get it right, but one reform strategy piles atop another and makes predicting a final outcome impossible. Reform efforts take on the pattern of waves, as discussed in the introduction to section 3 (Cuban, 1990); they tend to repeat themselves but are not exactly the same as the previous wave.

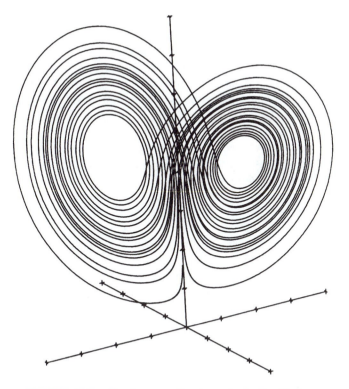

FIGURE 13.3   The Lorenz attractor or butterfly effect

SOURCE: J. Gleick, *Chaos,* 1987, Viking Press, Bergenfield, NJ, p. 28.

Another concept of chaos theory, dubbed "fractals," is reflective of a new realization among scientists, according to Briggs and Peat (1989), "that randomness is
interleaved with order, that simplicity enfolds complexity, complexity harbors simplicity, and that order and chaos can be repeated at smaller and smaller scales" (p. 43).
The measurement of this phenomenon quantitatively has led to the development of
fractal geometry (Mandelbrot, 1983), and according to Griffiths, Hart, and Blair (1991),
it has already found its way into the curriculum of some secondary schools.

Chaos Theory as a Metaphor.   Chaos theory may have more importance to us as
a metaphor than as a science. It challenges traditional assumptions about order and
predictability and helps us appreciate the randomness and disorder often associated
with educational organizations. Kellert (1993) believes that chaos theory "invites us
to revise our notions of scientific understanding" (p. 78) and suggests that we need to
see science as holistic, decentered, or dialogic. We could argue that there is a need to
see schools in the same light. Chaos theory offers a way to understand the origins of
unpredictability in simple natural systems and challenges any assumptions we may
have about predictability in complex social systems.

Science as an art is more appreciated since the advent of chaos theory than before.
Conditions of disorder and unpredictability do not easily respond to fixed protocols

and predefined intervention strategies. These conditions require greater ingenuity and creativity that allow the observer to explore new avenues of thought. Again, we are faced with the paradox and discomfort of having to shift our thinking from things we know to things we do not know or understand. Chaos theory suggests the need to be willing to shed shopworn assumptions about how things should operate and begin a process of carefully experimenting with new assumptions. Acceptance of feedback on our new "theories" will help determine how well our new assumptions are blending with or impacting the system we are attempting to influence.

The development of chaos theory provides us with some additional insights about systems' behavior. As mentioned earlier, chaos theory helps us to understand rhythms and cycles of behavior over time. A more holistic view taken in a longer time frame helps us appreciate the cycles of change in systems like schools. We can begin to appreciate that what seems disorderly in the short term and up close can be seen as more orderly in the long term and from some distance. In other words, schools are both disorderly and orderly and chaos theory helps us understand these seemingly contradictory states that can evolve over time.

Kellert (1993) pointed out the 50-year delay in the willingness to seriously consider chaos theory as offering another angle on the development of new scientific paradigms. Kuhn (1970) describes the difficulty of scientists committed to a particular paradigm to shift and explore alternative frameworks; we explored this issue in chapter 1. Kellert, however, offers an additional explanation that may have some implications for future efforts at school change. He argues that one of the strongest metaphors for science has been the image of the universe as a machine and the role of the researcher to discover its inner workings. As he states, "The mechanistic view of the world served as a legitimating ideology for the project of dominating nature, while at the same time functioning to secure a hierarchical social order" (p. 156). This allegiance to dominance and hierarchy seems to fit well with how males view the world. On the other hand, the feminist perspective is less hierarchical and may offer a new way to think about school organizations and the leadership thereof. More on this later.

Chaos theory appears to have left its mark. Davies (1993) suggests that "even accepting a strictly deterministic account of nature, the future states of the Universe are in some sense 'open.' Some people have seized on this openness to argue for the reality of human free will" (p. 221). Maybe we can be hopeful that the exercise of free will within a school context will protect schools from being treated like machines and promote seeing them as organic systems evolving to a new state. Schools are like the fractals of snowflakes: From a distance they look the same but upon closer examination their uniqueness becomes evident. It is this uniqueness that chaos theory helps us to appreciate.

Organizational Cycles

Chaos theory illuminates patterns or cycles of behavior over time. Certainly our historical reviews of organizational theory, leadership theory, and school reform illuminate the phenomenon of evolutionary change over an extended time. The longer view provides a more comprehensive picture of human events and enables us to better appreciate current conditions that evolved from past policies and practices. However, schools often view their present-day efforts at school reform as ahistorical, assuming that past efforts have little or no bearing on present efforts. To help us appreciate the cyclical nature of organizations, we will examine yet another metaphor for school reform: organizational cycles or evolution.

Our inclination to view organizations as static with little or no history may be a reflection of our culture's strong emphasis on the practical. The ability to shed what some might perceive as the shackles of the past can be seen as both a blessing and a liability. On the positive side, we have, in a sense, the opportunity to create a new beginning each day. This view allowed our country to grow and prosper with the creativity and ingenuity that come with fresh starts. On the other hand, we discover in strange ways how much of what we do each day is repetitive and an extension of what we did yesterday. This paradoxical behavior creates the tensions that eventually break log jams of resistance to change and permits a greater flow of new ideas. The metaphor of organizational cycles or evolution helps us examine the phenomenon of change over time. Kimberly (1980) writes,

> By forcing theorists [that's us] to think through carefully where the metaphors are appropriate and inappropriate, their use can lead to the raising of important new questions and perhaps to the recasting of old ones. This should not be construed as a request to reinvent the wheel. Rather it is a challenge that at worst may represent a form of intellectual pragmatism but that viewed more positively represents an effort to freshen and reanimate organizational theory and research. (p. 10)

Thinking of organizations as evolving through cycles of behavior over time (versus as static systems) has been largely ignored by academics and researchers. Kimberly (1980) offers five reasons why this is the case:

1. Most studies of organizations tend to be snapshots, done at a particular point in time, which ignore past experiences
2. Organizational studies are dependent on individuals who share their experiences in the organization for a very limited time
3. Most organizational studies are rooted in the methodologies that dominate the disciplines of psychology and sociology, which tend to be positivistic in nature. Hence, the limitations of verifiability and reproductivity of historical and case study methodologies are viewed negatively
4. The sponsorship of organizational research is often concerned with improvement in performance, which generally constrains the kinds of questions pursued and the time frame for the study
5. Most academicians who conduct organizational research must produce results in a relatively short span of time, which precludes conducting more long-term studies that would illuminate cyclical changes

We should not, however, permit these constraints to inhibit our curiosity about how organizations change over time and in what ways they repeat patterns of the past.

Much of the underlying theory or perspective on organizational cycles grows out of the biological cycle of birth, growth, and death. The direct application of biology to organizational development has both strengths and weaknesses. It defines organizations as open systems able to exchange energy with their environments; thus, as parts of the system wear down and lose exceptionally talented people, we would expect the organization to replace these individuals. Yet, it does not always work out this way. On the positive side, the metaphor of cycles shows that organizations, like most living entities, go through distinctive stages of development; thus, they are limited in their ability to sustain high performance levels indefinitely, particularly in light of environmental changes.

Recognizing that organizations go through periods of growth and decline is important, but at the same time we need to recognize that there is nothing predetermined about this. That is why the metaphor of organizational cycles challenges us to study organizations over time.

Organizational Birth.   Organizational birth is one chapter in an organization's biography. In the private sector, organizations often owe their beginning to entrepreneurs or founders who had the drive, ingenuity, and ability to garner resources and followers. We often assume that schools were there from the beginning and we have little or no knowledge of how they were founded. Their beginnings, in most cases, grew out of more pragmatic needs of providing educational opportunities to an increasing population of children and young adults. But these assumptions about the origins of schools overlook the persons who played an important role in their establishment and in setting their course for the future. These beginnings of an organization, according to Miles (1980), "can have an important influence on both the quality and duration of its life" (p. 442).

Tucker, Singh, and Meinhard (1990) explore the implications of Stinchcombe's (1965) "imprinting" hypothesis, in which "he argues that organizations construct their social systems with the social resources available at the time of their founding and they tend to retain the characteristics they acquired of their founding over the course of their life spans" (p. 183). These authors present three reasons why founding characteristics persist over time:

1. Founding characteristics may be more efficient for a given purpose and therefore have a competitive edge over other ideas
2. Founding characteristics may be preserved because organizations are insulated from environmental pressures by vested interests, advocates of tradition, and legitimate and strong ideological forces
3. The organization may not have to face competitive forces

Certainly the last point resonates for school organizations and can explain, in part, why advocates of school reform are pressing for greater school choice by parents and children. Tucker, Singh, and Meinhard conclude from their research that the institutionalization of an organization results in a taken-for-granted character, making it more resistant to change: "We found in this research that whether or not organizational change occurs is influenced, in part, by founding conditions. This suggests that organizational imprinting is another source of inertia in populations of organizations, and that incorporating it into future studies will help extend understanding of conditions under which inertia occurs" (p. 197).

In some ways, school restructuring is an attempt to create a new beginning that may overcome a school's inertia toward change. Unfortunately the advocates of school restructuring, who are seeking a fresh beginning, must cope with the imprinting experiences of the past. The birthing experiences of an organization may not be as benign as our naïveté suggests.

Organizational Growth.   Organizational growth is another biographical chapter and has many dimensions to it. Growth in profit-making organizations is measurable and explicit, often measured in the volume of sales or profit and in size (number of employees or locations). For nonprofits, such as schools, growth is more ambiguous; it may include size (number of students and staff), number of program and curricular offerings, and status or prestige. Growth denotes a process that reflects change from a beginning state—e.g., being small, having limited responsibilities, and being relatively unrecognized—to gaining significance in each of these factors.

Organizational growth links to organizational learning. In earlier chapters we explored this concept and the degree to which it is targeted at individuals or the group, whether it is more or less reflective (double-looped learning), and the degree to which it is enactive or proactive. Miles and Randolph (1980) distinguish between organizational learning that is driven by enactment processes, which provide learning from doing, and proactive processes, which involve strategic planning. In their opinion, organizational transformation and learning need to be sustained by "a continuum of learning approach mixes anchored by the nature of the organizational setting at the time of creation" (p. 79).

Miles and Randolph (1980) suggest three primary conditions for organizational learning: (1) reasonable stress induced by negative feedback, (2) catalytic leadership, and (3) organizational slack, which permits reflection and problem solving. The first two conditions are in plentiful supply in most school organizations, although some would debate the degree to which schools are blessed with catalytic leadership. The third condition, however, is much more problematic and is the greatest cause for concern by administrators and teachers. The lack of time and a feeling of sensory overload are the most common complaints of teachers, who are expected to provide classroom instruction while at the same time make organizational and instructional changes.

Where organizational learning is not effective, organizations can experience the limits of growth, often followed by collapse. Senge (1990) explores private, for-profit organizations that experience rapid growth that soon spins out of control and eventually results in failure. Peoples Airline is an example of rapid growth followed by collapse. They offered cut-rate fares; the resulting enormous volume and expansion affected the quality of service, borderline chaos ensued, and ultimately the airline could not sustain itself. The collapse we see in public sector organizations is more subtle and insidious. Schools teeter between excessive demands and rising expectations as a result of being seen as the solution to endless societal problems (e.g., poverty, domestic abuse, drug abuse, violence, boredom). We witness schools that fail to educate and, worse, become uncontrollable environments in which teachers' and students' personal safety is fragile at best. Schools are asked to serve as surrogate parents and to provide meals, guidance, discipline, and protection that normally the family would provide. Soon schools get overextended, order breaks down, and people lose confidence in the ability of schools to fulfill their original obligations of educating our youth. Schools are beginning to experience decline much like businesses that are too successful and collapse from overload.

Organizational learning is not an automatic cure, but according to Senge (1991) and others, it offers an opportunity for organizations to anticipate their problems and prevent them from totally disrupting the organization. We will return to this notion at the close of this chapter and discuss how organizational learning might serve as a bridge to the future.

Organizational Decline.   Organizational decline is difficult to witness and is often obfuscated or denied, in part because of our inability to face failure. According to Whetten (1980), at the personal and professional levels, our society is imbued with the growth paradigm; this makes it difficult to acknowledge decline, resulting in various forms of rationalization and denial. The slow economic growth of the nineties has had an extraordinary effect on public and private organizations. We are witnessing massive layoffs, closing of businesses, reduction and elimination of government services, and schools and colleges experiencing retrenchment because of declining enrollments and budget shortfalls. Yet, each day the public is fed promising economic indicators that suggest things are beginning to turn around and economic recovery is within our grasp. Maybe we need to think more about what decline denotes and how to live within our means.

Decline in an organization, according to Whetten (1980), has two principal meanings. The first denotes "a cutback in the size of an organization's work force, profits, budget, clients, and so forth" (p. 345). The second describes "the general climate, or orientation, of an organization" (p. 346) and speaks to stagnation that can occur in more mature organizations, which is often precipitated by the loss of a competitive edge, excessive bureaucratization, and complacency. The patterns of decline can vary from organization to organization, with some experiencing it rather dramatically in a short span of time and others experiencing it more subtly and almost imperceptibly over a much longer duration. The latter form of decline is often compared to a frog in water being brought to a boil. Unfortunately for the frog, as the water moves closer to the boiling point, its body adjusts to the increasing temperature and so it does not realize in sufficient time its fate.

Sources of decline for organizations in the public sector, according to Levine (1978), include organizational atrophy (allowing units or services to decline by neglect); political vulnerability (organizations' goals and programs being whipsawed by unresolved public policy debates); problem depletion (circumstances altered by changing social needs); and environmental entropy (unresolved conflicts leading to disorder). Clearly schools are, to varying degrees, experiencing aspects of each of these sources. Because of present and anticipated dramatic demographic shifts and changing lifestyles, schools operating on old assumptions and with an aging faculty find themselves lacking the muscle to meet these new challenges. Their political vulnerability is on the increase; more and more state legislatures are attempting to micromanage schools through macrolevel policies and regulations. Many schools find themselves unable or unwilling to face these new problems. Finally, schools are facing the consequence of economic, environmental, and social forms of entropy (cf. Rifkin, 1989). No wonder decline resonates with the extreme conditions being observed in poor urban and rural areas. The challenge to declining organizations is how to turn around these conditions and experience some aspect of renewal, as was observed in Valley View and Country View schools. Clearly denial and defensiveness will not cut it. A more proactive and enactive approach, guided by principles of organizational learning, may set the conditions necessary for avoiding a high level of disorder and for experiencing rebirth.

Organizational Cycles and Dilemma. Tichy (1980) argues that organizations have three interrelated problem cycles. The first is the technical design problem; here organizations have to face the problem of providing social and technical resources to ensure productive outcomes. The second is the political allocation problem, which grows out of the problem of allocating power and resources. The third is the ideological and cultural mix problem, which is concerned with what values need to be held by people in order to ensure a normative glue to hold the organization together.

As displayed in Figure 13.4, the cycles overlap and interact with each other over time. The peaks denote a high need for adjustment and the valleys suggest a smooth, nonproblematic time for that cycle. The diagram also indicates that the level of stress and need for problem solving are high when the cycles peak, indicating uncertainty and the need for attention and resolution.

FIGURE 13.4   Three interrelated organizational cycles

SOURCE: N. M. Tichy, "Problem Cycles in Organizations and the Management of Change." In J. R. Kimberly, et al. (Eds.), *The Organizational Life Cycle: Issues in the Creation, Transformation, and Decline of Organizations,* Jossey-Bass, San Francisco, CA, p. 166. Reprinted with permission of Jossey-Bass Inc., Publishers.

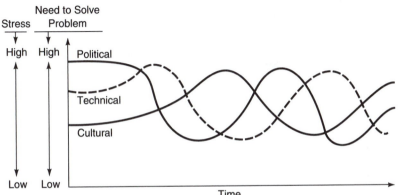

Tichy (1980) goes on to state that these cycles "trigger one another in a dialectical process; that is, a peak in one cycle will eventually trigger a peak in one or both of the other cycles" (p. 169). Regardless of what events cause a cycle to peak, leaders or a core group of the organization experience a sense of uncertainty, the results of which are stress and the need to do something. Triggers include:

1. environmental changes (e.g., unpredictability and complexity)
2. technological changes (e.g., new services and new methodologies)
3. shifts in agreement among organization members over goals of the organization (e.g., splits in the ranks over future directions)
4. splits in agreement over the means of getting the work done in the organization (e.g., differences on how to best structure the organization)
5. changes in people (e.g., bringing in new administrators or bringing in women or minorities in a white-male-dominated organization)

Each of these triggers is apropos school organizations and can help illuminate the change process that is endemic to schools. Tichy says, "The management of change consists of predicting, channeling, guiding, and altering the three cycles. These adjustments, which can be seen as forces that carry the organization through time, are cyclical in nature. . . . Successful change must rely on the ability to predict cycles and to channel and guide them" (p. 173-74).

Tichy's thinking puts the so-called waves of school reform in a more positive light and suggests that change is inevitable. We might think more about the management of these cycles and overall change rather than criticize schools for not being able to get it right with their first efforts at change.

A final observation from this review of organizational cycles is an overall dilemma facing leaders in organizations: If there is some degree of determinism of problem cycles and future organizational behavior is predetermined by experiences during the founding of the organization, what role should we expect of organizational leaders? We have been imbued with the notion that leaders should *solve* problems; maybe, as Ackoff (1974) suggests, we should be more realistic about what leaders can do and at best expect them to *manage* organizational "messes" successfully—particularly since, as organizational cycles seem to suggest, yesterday's solutions are today's problems and much of what upsets the equilibrium of the organization is environmentally caused and outside the control of any individual.

If organizational cycles do not provide sufficient reason for rethinking the nature of leadership and school reform, possibly a feminist perspective will offer further encouragement.

Feminist Theory

Education has always attracted large numbers of women interested in teaching and working with young people in the schools of America. Yet, as Shakeshaft (1987) observes, in proportion to their numbers, women have been underrepresented in formal positions of leadership (e.g., principal and superintendent). For example, in

1984–1985, women represented 83.5 percent of the elementary teachers but only 16.9 percent of the elementary school principals, and 50.1 percent of secondary school teachers but only 3.5 percent of secondary school principals and 3 percent of district superintendents. These numbers, however, tell only part of the story. Missing from our consciousness for a long period of time has been a clearer understanding of the implications of a female perspective in organizations such as schools. With the emergence of feminist theory in the last 20 years, we are beginning to develop greater insight about the effects of organizations that operate primarily from a patriarchal orientation.

Very recently, for example, research has been undertaken on the effects of schooling on girls. Sadker and Sadker's (1994) research over the past decade shows that boys get more individual attention than girls, resulting in a gap in academic achievement. On tests given to college-bound high school students, although women score slightly higher (2 to 4 points on a scale of 200 to 800 points) than men, on average, in German, English composition, and literature, men score much higher (57 to 24 points) on physics, European history, chemistry, advanced math, general math, biology, Latin, and American history. From their research, the Sadkers conclude that there are different expectations for the sexes; this was most clearly symbolized by the chalkboard headings of "Brilliant Boys" and "Good Girls" observed in one classroom.

For 20 years, feminists have been expressing their views on what it means to be a woman in a man's world. Schools typically reflect the greater society and its value systems; this is no less true in the case of gender. As Ferguson (1984) says, "The traditional experiences of women in our society shed light on bureaucracy in two ways—by revealing persistent patterns of dominance and subordination in bureaucracy that parallel power relations between men and women, and by suggesting a different way of conceiving of the individual and the collective that reflects the caretaking and nurturant experiences embedded in women's role" (p. x). These thoughts lend new meaning to the song "Why Can't a Woman Be Like a Man?" from the movie *My Fair Lady.* Burrell and Hearn (1989) observe further "that gender has either been ignored, treated implicitly as male, considered an organizational 'variable,' reduced to relative stereotypes, or been analyzed in a blatantly sexist way" (p. 10). Our task is to strip away the prejudice often expressed toward feminist theory and listen to the voices of both men and women who have examined gender and sexuality in organizations.

To suggest that there is one feminist theory would be misleading at best (cf. Shanley & Patemen, 1991; or Donovan, 1992). Feminism, as with any intellectual and political movement, is very diverse in nature. At best we can capture some of its highlights and appreciate its potential in redefining our ways of knowing organizations in the present and the future. Clearly feminist theory challenges our assumptions about male dominance and its influence in defining organizations and women's role therein.

According to Bem (1993), there have been three dominant beliefs about men and women throughout the history of Western culture: (1) that men and women are fundamentally different psychologically and sexually, (2) that men are inherently the dominant and superior sex, and (3) that these male and female differences and male dominance are natural. This naturalness was seen as part of God's grand plan and reinforced through religious teachings and practices.

It was not until the middle of the nineteenth century that the women's rights movement began to challenge America's dualism of constitutional equality and denial of political rights to women. The first wave of the feminist movement focused on women's basic political rights and revealed the discrepancy between political ideology and treatment of women in our society. It was not until the 1960s that "the second wave of feminist advocacy raised social consciousness still further by exposing—and naming—the 'sexism' in all policies and practices that explicitly discriminate on the basis of sex" (Bem, 1993, p. 1). This second wave exposed us to discriminating practices that resulted in women being paid less than men for the same work and fewer women in professional schools and roles.

Bem (1993) describes these underlying assumptions about male and female differences as "lenses of gender," and states: "Not only do these lenses shape how people perceive, conceive, and discuss social reality, but because they are embedded in social institutions, they also shape the more material things—like unequal pay and inadequate day care—that constitute social reality itself" (p. 2). She goes on to define these lenses and their effect on social reality. The first is the lens of androcentrism or male-centeredness. The effect of androcentrism is that the male experience is seen as the standard or norm and treated as human, whereas the female experience is treated as a deviation from the norm and as "other" behavior. The second lens is gender polarization, which extends and superimposes male-female differences onto nearly every social aspect of our lives. These differences dictate modes of dress, social roles, and ways of expressing emotion and experiencing sexual desire. The third lens is biological essentialism, which legitimizes the previous two lenses by treating them as natural and inevitable consequences of the intrinsic biological natures of men and women.

These lenses firmly establish male power as embedded in our social institutions and channels females and males into different and unequal roles. Also, these lenses result in our internalizing these assumptions about male power, resulting in its institutionalization throughout society.

Ferguson (1993) states that feminist theory "entails both problematizing and embracing subjectness" (p. 15). She describes the feminist struggle for equity within existing structures and related theories by centering on women's experiences and efforts to deconstruct the gender subject altogether. She along with other contemporary feminists wish to emphasize "persons-in-relations" rather than autonomous selves and argue that more attention should be devoted to needs rather than defending rights. The struggle for women, according to Ferguson, is recognizing the value of discovering and sharing what is uniquely feminine and at the same time recognizing that women establish connections to others in a variety of contexts that may have significant influence in defining what is feminine.

The problem becomes whether it is possible, therefore, for women to establish sisterhood and still pay "more attention to the differences among women—particularly those of race, class, ethnic background, and sexuality" (Donovan, 1992, p. 187). Bem (1993) claims this problem is at the center of the third wave of the feminist movement. The question for her and her colleagues is whether women can forge a political interest group that can be served by any single program of social change. Her concern is that there are such inherent differences among women "that there can be little or no common cause among them and hence no possibility of a common feminist solution to their female inequality" (p. 182).

In spite of these differences, feminists, including sympathetic and supportive males, see the need to interject the feminist framework into the social world in such a way that political realities can be examined with a critical and reflective eye. This is no less true in attempting to understand the questions of power and rationality in society and in its social institutions. Ferguson (1984) describes the need for a "feminist discourse" that "can provide a way of thinking and acting that is neither an extension of bureaucratic forms nor a mirror image of them, but rather a genuinely *radical* voice in opposition" (p. 29). Hearn and Parkin (1987) refer to this "discourse" as a feminist critique that questions the very structure and hierarchy of organizations. According to them, the critique of hierarchy and advocacy for the small group as a fundamental organizing unit for organization is a basic element of feminist theory and practice.

Calas and Smircich (1992), as an example of the feminist critique, raise the concern that women have been denied any presence in organizational theory and that the male standard has been a basis of this denial. They ask the question: "How is organization theorizing (male) gendered, and with what consequence?" (p. 230). They advocate the need to engage in three activities: revising the record, reflecting on the revising, and rewriting gender relations.

Revising the Record. Revising the record involves addressing issues such as women's absence as knowledge producers and the potential effect of this absence on the choice of problems to research, the methodology chosen, and the interpretation of the results. These revising efforts focus on the following (Calas & Smircich, 1992, p. 235):

1. completing/correcting the record (e.g., attempting to account for women's absence and exclusion and adding women's contributions and experiences)
2. assessing gender bias in current knowledge (e.g., retracing history to assess the consequences of the underrepresentation of women; retracing patterns of questioning in multiple streams of research and assessing whose viewpoints are solicited and whose are absent; and assessing the extent to which the concepts used are male gendered)
3. making the "new" organizational theorizing (e.g., making the narratives of organizational theorizing more diverse; exploring topics of more concern to women; and rethinking the ground for judging what is true, good, and beautiful in organizational theorizing)

Reflecting on the Revising. Reflecting on the revising within feminist epistemology involves moving back and forth between "saying" and "doing," "a reflexivity that constantly assesses the relationship between 'knowledge' and 'the ways of doing knowledge'" (Calas & Smircich, 1992, p. 240). This assessment evaluates knowledge as it reproduces or changes existing gender relations and patriarchal models. Feminist reflexivity implies questioning the gendered nature of traditional epistemologies and institutional arrangements and whose interests have been served by traditional knowledge.

Rewriting Gender Relations. Rewriting gender relations involves an exploration of the intersections between feminism(s) and postmodernism. Feminism shares postmodernist critiques since they are consistent with feminist concerns about masculine logic embedded in the notions of "objectivity" and "reason." Feminist theory is seen "as a possible correction for the androcentrism and political naivety of postmodernism" (Calas & Smircich, 1992, p. 241).

Hearn and Parkin's (1987) revisit to the human relations era and related research, such as the Mayo studies (Mayo, 1960), illustrates some of the complications associated with this movement from a feminist perspective. For example, they reinterpret the Hawthorne experiments and the so-called Hawthorne effect; from a feminist perspective, the importance of informal relations emerged from a female nurse's involvement with male workers and how she dealt with their personal and emotional lives. She became a social nexus for the workers and, in fact, became an important source of what was going on in the lives of these workers for the researchers and managers. As Hearn and Parkin state, "the nurse was what the three male 'sub-groups' had in common; men were communicating by way of a woman" (p. 23).

The first stage of the Hawthorne experiment involved six women workers in the relay assembly test room. As we recall, this experiment brought to light the need for a better understanding of the human qualities of workers and the power of informal relations. The researchers were puzzled by the increase in production levels in spite of the 15 interventions taken by management (e.g., changes in the payment system, rest periods, arrangements for lunch, and changes in lighting). The understanding of the development of a compact social group and its contribution to productivity slowly evolved from this original study. According to Hearn and Parkin, these insights had a two-edged sword to their application: The human relations movement did open management's eyes to the importance of understanding the worker from a humanistic perspective, but this perspective was male. The upside was a more sympathetic and responsive management; the downside was that the workers were becoming better known to management and therefore vulnerable to being patronized and manipulated. Hearn and Parkin observe, "Indeed 'Human Relations' may be a metaphor for the 'authoritative' male investigation of the 'awkward' female, a little like the Victorian treatment of female 'hysteria,' or the medicalisation of gynecological problems" (p. 25).

Feminist theory enables a fresh look at the implications of organizational research and practices, particularly their effects on understanding the role and treatment of women in organizations. Due to the dominance of the male point of view, it has been assumed that androcentrism told the whole story and analyses about organizations were neutered or, at worst, women's needs were treated as a problem. Feminist theory attempts to see the downside and the flipside of the male view and advocates for more recognition of the female perspective and its contribution to organizational life.

Feminist theorists and researchers are raising a number of concerns about male dominance in organizations and its effects on the quality of work life. We will view next some results of their efforts.

Gender and Organizations.   Not only have women not been given credit for their contribution to major research findings, but according to Mills (1989), male domination comes in many other forms and has restricted women's participation in organizations. Some examples of male domination in organizations come in the form of male ownership and control, positions of status and authority, cultural values, and hegemony.

The consequence of these forms of male influence and control, according to Mills, is to "restrict the entry of women to the labor force, to filter women into a narrow range of occupations and to channel them into low pay/low status work, and overall reinforce notions of female inferiority" (p. 35). Women find themselves concentrated in jobs such as nursing and child care that reinforce the notion of women as "domestic" or in jobs that stress physical "attractiveness," further reinforcing male notions of female sexuality.

An additional consequence of male dominance is sexual harassment. Media reports continue to jar us concerning the degree to which women are subjected to sexual overtones ranging from displays of nude calendars to pinching and touching to threats and promises for sexual favors. Such treatment further diminishes our views of women and their potential value to organizations. What is appropriate behavior toward women from a legal perspective is still being clarified through litigation. Laws and court settlements, however, cannot rewrite the code of behavior that for so long has placed women in a position of being viewed as prey for satisfying male sexual drives and need for control and manipulation.

Sexual harassment is but one mode for defining gender relations and is an obviously negative perspective. Gender relations are complicated by a number of factors and are not easily isolated to a desired code of behavior. Even distinguishing the differences between gender and sex is not easily done. Gender, according to Acker (1992), is socially constructed, whereas sex is biologically given. She defines *gender* as "patterned, socially produced, distinctions between female and male, feminine and masculine" (p. 250). Gender is not something inherent, rather it grows out of our daily experiences and relationships in our work and in other settings. It is a socially constructed phenomenon subject to the ideological constraints that set limits on the behavior of both men and women under particular conditions at particular times. The consequence of these social constructions and deconstructions is the establishment of gender processes that define gender relations. As Scott (1988) suggests, gender is a pervasive symbol of power often resulting in various forms of exploitation and control.

Gender can also point out differences in attitude and behavior of persons in administrative positions. According to Shakeshaft (1987), men and women who are assigned similar responsibilities often approach their work differently. Her review of research on men and women administrators suggests that "there are some differences in the ways they spend their time, in their day-to-day interactions, in the priorities that guide their actions, in the perceptions of them by others, and in the satisfaction they derive from their work. These differences combine to create a work environment that is different for women than for men" (p. 170).

Studies, according to Shakeshaft, specifically suggest among other things that women conduct more unscheduled meetings, monitor less, take fewer trips away from the building, observe teachers more, engage in more cooperative planning, and favor more people-oriented projects. Other studies (Alderton & Jurma, 1980; Kanter, 1977; Mickey, 1984; and Williams & Willower, 1983) suggest that women in leadership positions often face conditions that contribute to their discomfort or withdrawal, particularly if they are in a minority. These studies further our understanding of the differences between the success of the principal of Valley View Elementary School and the lack of success of the superintendent of Mountain View School District.

The increase of women in leadership roles in organizations, according to Calas and Smircich (1992), has resulted in the creation of new organizational literature labeled the "women in management" literature; new female entrants have brought gender into management, whereas, in the past, management literature was neutered. But, according to Calas and Smircich, "gender *has* been present all along, even ignored or repressed" (p. 229). Now we are much more conscious of the implications of gender (male or female) both in the present and the past and can begin to appreciate the role gender plays in how persons perceive relationships in organizations in general.

The interplay of gender relations raises many questions and suggests the need to examine the effects of sexuality in organizations. According to Hearn and Parkin (1992), however, "most mainstream organizational theory either ignores the issue of sexuality or uses crude formulations thereof" (p. 60). One theory of sexuality proffered by Zetterberg (1966) has implications for organizations. Referred to as "the secret ranking," its basic premise is that status and power are acquired in part from physical attraction between individuals, although this is rarely explicitly acknowledged. Sexuality in organizations creates a paradox for individuals, particularly where there is physical attractiveness and the emergence of romantic relationships that are deemed inappropriate. This becomes even more complicated in unequal power relations such as student-teacher, secretary-boss, staff-supervisor, or in the hiring of staff. In these kinds of relationships, dependence and sexuality can become intimately combined in thought and in some cases action.

Burrell and Hearn (1989) point out that sexuality goes beyond sexual liaisons and relations: "Sexuality is a diverse and diffuse process: it is not a 'thing' brought into organizations, there to be organized" (p. 13). Rather the definition of sexuality needs to be broadened in two ways: It should be seen as an ordinary and frequent public process and it should be seen as one aspect of an all-pervasive "politics of the body." Thus, according to Burrell and Hearn, "sexuality includes a range of practices from feelings to flirtations to sexual acts, accomplished willingly, unwillingly or forcibly by those involved" (p. 13). How these relationships evolve and reproduce themselves over time and their impact on organizational functioning need more careful examination, particularly in educational settings. We have just begun to appreciate the treatment of female students by their male peers, let alone examined the impact of other combinations of gender relations among students, teachers, administrators, and support staff. Given the imbalance of power relations and vulnerability of youthful inexperience and naïveté, schools as organizations are fertile grounds for examining the many dimensions of sexuality.

Hearn and Parkin (1987) outline a way to examine sexuality in organizations and "bring to the surface" a part of men's unconscious world. They suggest that organizational sexuality can be observed through the dimensions of

- movement and proximity between people
- the expression of feelings and emotions
- ideology and consciousness concerning the construction of organizational reality
- language and imagery that often appear man-made and directed at defining ideal female images

To fully appreciate the functioning of schools and their effect on students, a missing ingredient has been the examination of the impact of sexuality. Sexuality and gender offer a new lens through which we might more thoroughly examine some of the behavior of students and teachers. It is possible that this area of interest has been kept in the closet too long and needs a fuller exposure if in fact we are to attain our ideals of developing mature and responsible adults.

A FINAL THOUGHT OR TWO

Throughout this chapter and the text as a whole, we have examined a number of theories and concepts that provide ways to understand educational organizations and the leadership therein. The artistry of pulling together these various ideas into a useful whole is like the creation of a quilt from many different and colorful pieces of cloth. The quilt maker (Otto, 1991) is faced with many choices of how the various pieces of cloth will be arranged and sewn together to result in an attractive covering or wall hanging. Some quilts are abstract and impressionistic, evidence of great opportunity for their creators to experiment; we are taken by their overall appearance before we can recognize how their parts contribute to an engaging first impression. Other quilts, however, are less abstract and are designed to represent elements of a story, describe historical events, or portray familiar symbols of life, love, or other emotional experiences of living within a family, a church, or a university. Their design and final creation are closely linked to the quilt maker's perceptual abilities. It is interesting, also, that many quilts are not the product of a single individual but come out of the combined efforts of several persons. Artistry does not have to be a lonely act but can grow out of a communal effort where ideas are shared and built on.

As we draw to a close, we are challenged to make our own quilts to capture those ideas worthy of providing a legacy and long-term image that can guide our efforts in making educational organizations noble and worthy places. We have a rich inventory of ideas to use, and though it would be easy to abandon them and copy someone else's pattern, as the future quilt makers of educational organizations we are challenged to pick what we feel offers promise and arrange it in such a way that we and our audiences can appreciate the final "product."

For one old quilt maker, the pieces of cloth that hold some attraction are the ideas related to

- organizational learning or learning organizations linked to systems thinking (see chapters 5 and 6) and organizational cycles (chapter 13)
- communitarianism (see chapter 8) linked to moral and ethical principles (see chapter 7)
- democratization (see chapters 8 and 11)
- gender equity or equal opportunity (see chapter 13)
- quality of work life linked to concepts of wellness (see chapter 8)
- theater and humor (see chapter 4)

When stitched together, these concepts provide a foundation for portraying what organizations can become and what leaders can believe in. One old quilt maker's quilt may not win any special awards but it can begin a dialogue with other quilt makers that in turn will help us all appreciate the beauty inherent in the lives of those who try to provide educational opportunities for others. The old quilt maker's may not be the ultimate design, but it may make some sense to others upon more reflection and discussion. And in the final analysis, if all else fails, one's quilt can be easily turned into a blanket and used to shelter one from the cold winds of cynicism and self-centeredness.

May your quilt bring color and beauty to your life and to others'.

DISCUSSION QUESTIONS

1. Of the various demographic and socioeconomic trends in progress, which do you believe are significant and should be paid more heed?
2. Given the conclusions you draw from these trends, what do they imply for school organizations, leadership, and reform?
3. Treating the theories of chaos, organizational cycles, and feminism as metaphors and/or lenses, what important messages or images do they offer for schools of tomorrow?
4. What of feminist theory makes sense in light of your experiences in educational institutions? How could a balance be found between patriarchal and matriarchal thinking in educational institutions?
5. What new research should be considered when we look through the lens of gender or sexuality?

SUGGESTED ACTIVITIES

1. Expand upon the review of future trends in this chapter and investigate contemporary literature and reports for additional trends not explored here. Report on their implications for school reform.

2. Some persons may have difficulty accepting some of the assumptions of feminist theory and gender studies. Conduct a reality check in your organization on the degree to which gender is an issue and the effects of androcentrism. Locate a trusted female colleague or two and have an in-depth discussion of their experiences and treatment as women in their educational organization.

3. Become a conceptual quilt maker. What major concepts, theories, and/or metaphors in this text made an "impression" and are worth holding onto as you grapple with issues and problems in your organization? How would you array these concepts into a quilt pattern? Could you make a drawing that represents your pattern?

4. Now that you have read this chapter and the text as a whole, write a letter to a close friend and tell this person what you believe are the current issues facing school reform and what you think should be done about these issues.

5. And finally, write to me (Dr. Robert V. Carlson, College of Education and Social Services, Waterman Building, Burlington, VT 05405 or use my e-mail address of RVCarlso@moose. uvm.edu) your thoughts about theories of organization and leadership and their implications for school reform. I would appreciate hearing from you.

6. I am interested in collecting other case studies of schools and school systems that have been engaged in a reform process over time. I invite you to investigate such a case, write it up, and share it with others, including myself. As I look to update this text, your case may provide a much appreciated example of the human dynamics involved in reforming present-day educational organizations.

REFERENCES

Achilles, C. M. (1993). A curmudgeon's view. In J. R. Hoyle & D. M. Estes (Eds.), *XICPEA: In a new voice* (pp. 24–34). Lancaster, PA: Technomic.

Acker, J. (1992). Gendering organization theory. In A. J. Mills & P. Tancred (Eds.), *Gendering organizational analysis.* Newbury Park, CA: Sage.

Ackoff, R. L. (1974). Beyond problem solving. *General Systems, XIX,* 237–39.

Alderton, S. M., & Jurma, W. E. (1980). Genderless/gender-related task leader communication and group satisfaction: A test of two hypotheses. *Southern Speech Communication Journal,* 46(1), 48–60.

Bem, S. L. (1993). *The lenses of gender.* New Haven, CT: Yale University Press.

Berliner, D. C. (1993). Mythology and the American system of education. *Phi Delta Kappan,* 74(8), 632–40.

Bracey, G. W. (1991). Why can't they be like we were? *Phi Delta Kappan,* 73(2), 104–17.

Briggs, J., & Peat, F. D. (1989). *Turbulent mirror.* New York: Harper & Row.

Burrell, G., & Hearn, J. (1989). The sexuality of organization. In J. Hearn, D. L. Sheppard, P. Tancred-Sheriff, & G. Burrell (Eds.), *The sexuality of organization* (pp. 1–28). Newbury Park, CA: Sage.

Calas, M. B., & Smircich, L. (1992). Re-writing gender into organizational theorizing: Directions from feminist perspectives. In M. Reed & M. Hughes (Eds.), *Rethinking organization* (pp. 229–53). Newbury Park, CA: Sage.

Camel, A. B. (1993). *Applied chaos theory.* New York: Academic Press.

Capra, F. (1983). *The turning point: Science, society, and the rising culture.* New York: Bantam.

Carson, C. C., Huelskamp, R. M., & Woodall, T. D. (1993). Perspectives on education in America. *The Journal of Educational Research,* 86(5), 261–310.

Cooley, D. A. (1993). Health and medicine. In J. M. Templeton (Ed.), *Looking forward* (pp. 107-28). New York: HarperCollins.

Cuban, L. (1990). Reforming again, again, and again. *Educational Researcher, 19*(1), 3-13.

Davies, P. (1993). Is the Universe a machine? In N. Hall (Ed.), *Exploring chaos: A guide to the new science of disorder* (pp. 213-21). New York: Norton.

Donovan, J. (1992). *Feminist theory.* New York: Frederick Ungar.

Drucker, P. F. (1993). *Post-capitalist society.* New York: HarperCollins.

Ferguson, K. E. (1984). *The feminist case against bureaucracy.* Philadelphia: Temple University Press.

Ferguson, K. E. (1993). *The man question.* Berkeley: University of California Press.

Fullan, M. (1993). *Change forces.* New York: Falmer.

Fullan, M. G., & Miles, M. M. (1992). Getting reform right: What works and what doesn't. *Phi Delta Kappan, 73*(10), 744-52.

Gleick, J. (1987). *Chaos.* New York: Viking.

Griffiths, D. E., Hart, A. W., & Blair, B. G. (1991). Still another approach to administration: Chaos theory. *Educational Administration Quarterly, 27*(3), 430-51.

Harman, W. (1993). The second scientific revolution. In S. M. Moorcroft (Ed.), *Visions for the 21st century* (pp. 139-46). Westport, CT: Praeger.

Hearn, J., & Parkin, W. (1987). *"Sex" at "work": The power and paradox of organization sexuality.* New York: St. Martin's Press.

Hearn, J., & Parkin, W. (1992). Gender and organizations: A selective review and a critique of a neglected area. In A. J. Mills & P. Tancred (Eds.), *Gendering organizational analysis* (pp. 46-66). Newbury Park, CA: Sage.

Hodgkinson, H. L. (June, 1992). *A demographic look at tomorrow.* Washington, D.C.: Institute for Educational Leadership.

Huelskamp, R. M. (1993). Perspectives on education in America. *Phi Delta Kappan, 74*(9), 718-20.

Kanter, R. M. (1977). *Men and women of the corporation.* New York: Basic Books.

Kellert, S. H. (1993). *In the wake of chaos.* Chicago: University of Chicago Press.

Kennedy, P. (1993). *Preparing for the twenty-first century.* New York: Random House.

Kimberly, J. R. (1980). The life cycle analogy and the study of organizations: Introduction. In J. R. Kimberly, R. H. Miles, & Associates (Eds.), *The organizational life cycle* (pp. 1-18). San Francisco: Jossey-Bass.

Kuhn, T. (1970). *The structure of scientific revolutions.* Chicago: University of Chicago Press.

Mandelbrot, B. (1983). *Fractal geometry of nature.* New York: Freeman.

Levine, C. H. (July-August, 1978). Organizational decline and cutback management. *Public Administration Review,* 316-25.

Mayo, E. (1960). *The social problems of an industrial civilization.* New York: Viking.

Mickey, B. H. (1984). You can go home again, but it's not easy. *Journal of the National Association for Women Deans, Administrators, Counselors, 47*(3), 3-7.

Miles, R. H. (1980). Findings and implications of organizational life cycle research: A commencement. In J. R. Kimberly, R. H. Miles, & Associates (Eds.), *The organizational life cycle* (pp. 430-50). San Francisco: Jossey-Bass.

Miles, R. H., & Randolph, W. A. (1980). Influence of organizational learning styles on early development. In J. R. Kimberly, R. H. Miles, & Associates (Eds.), *The organizational life cycle* (pp. 44-82). San Francisco: Jossey-Bass.

Mills, A. J. (1989). Gender, sexuality and organization theory. In J. Hearn, D. L. Sheppard, P. Tancred-Sheriff, & G. Burrell (Eds.), *The sexuality of organization* (pp. 29–44). Newbury Park, CA: Sage.

Naisbitt, J., & Aburdene, P. (1990). *Megatrends 2000.* New York: William Morrow.

Ogilvy, J. (1993). Earth might be fair. In S. M. Moorcroft (Ed.), *Visions for the 21st century.* Westport, CT: Praeger.

Otto, W. (1991). *How to make an American quilt.* New York: Ballantine Books.

Prigogine, I., & Stengers, I. (1984). *Order out of chaos.* New York: Bantam.

Rifkin, J. (1989). *Entropy into the greenhouse world.* New York: Viking Penguin.

Sadker, M., & Sadker, D. (1994). *Failing at fairness: How American schools cheat girls.* New York: Scribner's.

Scott, K. Y. (1988). Deconstructuring equality vs. difference: Or, the uses of post-structurist theory for feminism. *Feminist Studies, 14,* 33–50.

Senge, P. M. (1990). *Fifth discipline.* New York: Doubleday.

Shakeshaft, C. (1987). *Women in educational administration.* Newbury Park, CA: Sage.

Shanley, M. L., & Patemen, C. (1991). *Feminist interpretations and political theory.* University Park: Pennsylvania State University Press.

Slaughter, R. (1993). The promise of the 21st century. In S. M. Moorcroft (Ed.), *Visions for the 21st century* (pp. 117–30). Westport, CT: Praeger.

Stinchcombe, A. L. (1965). Social structure and organizations. In J. G. March (Ed.), *Handbook of organizations* (pp. 142–93). Chicago: University of Chicago Press.

Templeton, J. M. (1993). Introduction. In J. M. Templeton (Ed.), *Looking forward* (pp. 1–16). New York: HarperCollins.

Tichy, N. M. (1980). Problem cycles in organizations and the management of change. In J. R. Kimberly, R. H. Miles, & Associates (Eds.), *The organizational life cycle* (pp. 164–83). San Francisco: Jossey-Bass.

Tucker, D. J., Singh, J. V., Meinhard, A. G. (1990). Founding characteristics, imprinting, and organizational change. In J. V. Singh (Ed.), *Organizational evolution* (pp. 182–200). Newbury Park, CA: Sage.

Whetten, D. A. (1980). Sources, responses, and effects of organizational decline. In J. R. Kimberly, R. H. Miles, & Associates (Eds.), *The organizational life cycle* (pp. 342–74). San Francisco: Jossey-Bass.

Williams, R. H., & Willower, D. J. (1983, April) Female school superintendents' perceptions of their work. Paper presented at the annual meeting of the American Educational Research Association, Montreal, Canada.

Zetterberg, H. L. (1966). The secret ranking. *Journal of Marriage and the Family, 28,* 134–42.

Index